History and the New Left

Critical Perspectives on the Past

A series edited by Susan Porter Benson,
Stephen Brier, and Roy Rosenzweig

History
AND THE
New Left

MADISON, WISCONSIN,
1950–1970

Edited by Paul Buhle

Temple University Press
Philadelphia

Temple University Press, Philadelphia 19122
Copyright © 1990 by Temple University, except Chapter
7 copyright Richard Schickel, Chapter 9 copyright Saul
Landau, Chapter 27 copyright Saundra Grace, and Chap-
ter 28 copyright William A. Williams. All rights re-
served.
Published 1990
Printed in the United States of America

Library of Congress Cataloging-in-Publication Data

History and the new left.

1. Madison (Wis.)—Intellectual life. 2. Radicalism—Wisconsin—Madison—History—20th century.
3. Radicalism—United States—History—20th century.
4. Historiography—Wisconsin—Madison. 5. Historiography—United States. 6. United States—
Historiography. 7. University of Wisconsin. Madison.
8. Madison (Wis.)—Politics and government. I. Buhle,
Paul, 1944–
F589.M15H57 1990   977.5'83043   89-5132
ISBN 0-87722-653-9

*Dedicated to the memory of
Harvey Goldberg, Herbert G. Gutman,
and Warren Susman; also that of
Hans Gerth, Eleanor Hakim,
and Robert Starobin.*

Contents

Acknowledgments   ix

PAUL BUHLE   Madison: An Introduction   1

PART ONE: COLD WAR DAYS

1   WARREN SUSMAN   The Smoking Room School of History   43
2   HERBERT G. GUTMAN   Learning About History   47
3   WILLIAM PRESTON   WASP and Dissenter   50
4   GEORGE RAWICK   I Dissent   54
5   JEFFRY KAPLOW   Parentheses: 1952–1956   58
6   NINA SERRANO   A Madison Bohemian   67
7   RICHARD SCHICKEL   A Journalist Among Historians   85

PART TWO: FROM OLD LEFT TO NEW

8   BERTELL OLLMAN   From Liberal, to Social Democrat, to
        Marxist: My Political Itinerary Through Madison in
        the Late 1950s   101
9   SAUL LANDAU   From the Labor Youth League to the Cuban
        Revolution   107
10   JAMES WEINSTEIN   *Studies on the Left*   113
11   JAMES B. GILBERT   The Intellectuals and the First New Left
        118
12   LEE BAXANDALL   New York Meets Oshkosh   127
13   ROZ BAXANDALL   Another Madison Bohemian   134
14   HARRIET TANZMAN   Civil Rights and History   141
15   ELIZABETH EWEN   A Way of Seeing   148

PART THREE: CONFLICT AND CONSCIOUSNESS

16   EVAN STARK   In Exile   166
17   STUART EWEN   The Intellectual New Left   178
18   MALCOLM SYLVERS   Memories from the Periphery   183
19   PETER WILEY   Radicalized History   190
20   MARI JO BUHLE   Madison and Women's History   197

21 PAUL RICHARDS   A Madison Communist   205

22 MICHAEL MEEROPOL AND GERALD MARKOWITZ   Neighborhood
        Politics   210

23 PAUL BUHLE   *Radical America* and Me   216

24 GEORGE MOSSE   New Left Intellectuals/New Left Politics
        233

PART FOUR: OUR TEACHERS

25 RON MCCREA AND DAVE WAGNER   Harvey Goldberg   241

26 PAUL BREINES   The Mosse Milieu   246

27 ELEANOR HAKIM   The Tragedy of Hans Gerth   252

28 WILLIAM A. WILLIAMS   My Life in Madison   264

Appendix 1: WARREN SUSMAN   The Historian's Task   275

Appendix 2: LEE BAXANDALL, MARSHALL BRICKMAN, DANNY
        KALB   The Boy Scouts in Cuba   285

Name Index   291

Acknowledgments

This book has a peculiar evolution. Work on it began, in the middle 1970s, with Lee Baxandall gathering essays and documents from a wide variety of sources on Madison radicalism, mostly from the 1960s to the (then) present day. Of the material first gathered, only the commentaries by Paul Buhle, William Appleman Williams, and George Mosse remain in this volume. Dave Wagner, and then Paul Buhle, assumed charge of the project. In the process, the focus shifted very largely to historians and to a scattering of allied intellectuals. The problems of persuading various scholars to write about themselves and their past shifted the *modus operandi* to the interview. The contributions of Herbert Gutman, Warren Susman, William Preston, Saul Landau, Lee Baxandall, Nina Serrano, Elizabeth and Stuart Ewen, Rosalyn Baxandall, and Paul Richards grew directly or indirectly out of interviews conducted with them by Paul Buhle from 1980 to 1988.

I wish, then, to acknowledge Lee Baxandall's initiative and his help, in a variety of ways, along the path to the book's completion. Thanks are also due to those senior figures whose encouragement restored my flagging energies: William A. Williams and George Mosse, foremost, also the late Warren Susman and Herbert Gutman. Harvey Goldberg, in one of the last messages from his deathbed, also offered his high hopes for the project. Ron Grele made many useful suggestions. Tom Bates, whose book on the Army Math Research Center bombing will appear after this one, read my introduction carefully and made many useful suggestions. The editors of the Temple University Press history series—Susan Porter Benson, Steve Brier, and Roy Rosenzweig—have seen me through the final stages of the project with acuity, kindness, and patience. Press editors Janet Francendese and Terri Kettering have been patient and long-suffering in their work on the manuscript.

For all of us involved, former Madisonians especially but also those engaged with the various historial legacies, *History and the New Left: Madison, Wisconsin, 1950–1970* has tugged at personal memories of friends, teachers, and comrades now gone. The process has been painful at times because we miss the absent ones, named in the dedication, and will not cease missing them. Perhaps we who remain have been drawn more closely together, however. Without the collective spirit generated, I would have found this volume impossible to finish.

History and the New Left

Madison: An Introduction

PAUL BUHLE

Madison, Wisconsin, has long been known as a dynamic cultural center between the coasts, an Athens or at least a verdant intellectual oasis of the Midwest. Like Theodor Adorno's cultural critic, its sages have always seemed to have one foot inside their immediate milieu, one foot outside.[1] Since the latter decades of the nineteenth century, Madison scholars have intermittently explored the implications of America's frontier mentality by contrasting European civilization with our own. Meantime, the city's political progressives have developed their own practical critique through decades of recurrent resistance to monopoly and its extension, empire. Madison's most distinctive contribution to American life has been the fusion of various traditions—Old Northwest democracy with modern social–intellectual currents, grassroots political action with cultivated historical insight. Home of the "Wisconsin Idea" of the 1910s supplying intellectuals to the statehouse, Madison has in more recent decades offered the "Wisconsin school" of radical scholarship.

This book explores a crucial period in Madison's intellectual life, at a crossroads of history and culture. In particular, it considers Madison's status as a laboratory for the uses of history, the remaking of the historian, and the rebirth of American radicalism. It does not seek to explain why Madison shares, with so many other places, institutionalized and often hegemonic conservatism; it does not claim to present a picture of *most* Madison historians; and it does not deal

---

1. Theodor Adorno, "Cultural Criticism and Society," in *Prisms*, trans. Samuel and Shierry Weber (London, 1967), 23–24.

with Madison's variety of radicals, activists, and intellectuals outside a few key fields. Instead, it examines, through individual lives, the ways in which many young people from different backgrounds and several disciplines found in Madison new directions in their quest for America. Finally, it traces the perspective from which older intellectuals looked on—and how all the contributors now look back on—the same convergences.

Why focus on history? That is a key question for the book. But it is also a question that should be asked of social thought at large, particularly radical thought, from the later 1960s to the middle 1980s. Paul Berman has called social history the benchmark of the 1960s, much as the novel was for the "bohemian" 1910s and literary criticism was for the "Red Decade" 1930s. In each circumstance, social movements of the era provided a theater in which the symbols and symptoms of confidence, defeat, and pessimism or guarded optimism could be dramatized. The experience launched young intellectuals on a course for the remainder of their lives. For earlier generations discovering subjectivity and introspection, literature served in one way or another. For the searchers after what Hank Williams, Sr., called the "Lost Highway" of America, the choices not taken, history offered a way to reorganize and repose all the critical questions.[2]

The situation of the avant-garde college intellectual in the 1950s, whether professor or student, was unprecedented in several important ways. He or she possessed middle-class credentials in a consumer society that had rendered archaic, even among most radicals, the traditional Marxist expectations of an ultimate proletarian triumph. Often, the radical intellectual shared personally in the sharp upward mobility of once predominantly lower-class groups. But individual success did not necessarily banish radical idealism.

Here and there, intellectual dissenters from an earlier era offered crucial guidance and personal examples to new generations. Refugee scholars from Europe, plunged through exile into the dialectics of detachment, held court among fascinated students. Youthful refugees from the Old Left added their bit to the ambience. Together, these constituencies created a cadre of bright, disaffected American intellectuals eager to learn and to put ideas into practice. For the New Left and its successors, this cadre would prove invaluable.

This sounds too simple, and the essays that follow point up many contradictions. Yet already by the early 1950s, conditions existed in Madison for these three strains to coalesce. Dissenters would come together differently in San Francisco, from the Beat Generation and labor tradition; in New York City, from the New School and the East Village; and in at least half a dozen other American locations. But in Madison, hard questions often forbidden elsewhere in McCarthyite Middle America could be asked and given radical answers in an American vein. Here, the

2. Paul Berman, "The World of the Radical Historian," *Village Voice*, March 18, 1981. See also Jesse Lemisch, *On Active Service in War and Peace: Politics and Ideology in the American Historical Profession* (Toronto, 1975), 66–94, on the scholarly mainstream and the struggle for radical alternatives.

Leviathan state—merger of welfare and institutionalized warfare mechanisms into an apparently impregnable system endorsed in its essentials by a consensus stretching from modern liberalism to modern conservatism—found its historical–scholarly nemesis.

Madison's thinkers touched a chord. "We must name the system," said Paul Potter, president of Students for a Democratic Society (SDS), in a 1965 address to what was then the largest peace demonstration in the nation's history.[3] He did not mean capitalism or even imperialism in the old Marxist jargon, but something closer to the term historian William Appleman Williams had popularized in Madison, "Corporate Liberalism." The two words passed overnight into the national vocabulary: they formed an especially suitable description for a Democratic Party leadership that steered an almost reluctant military establishment toward a land war in Asia. The phrase seemed to explain the hitherto unexplainable; it responded to a need for understanding that was instinctually felt by tens of thousands of dissenters who were unable to place themselves on any standard political map. It also launched a larger field of inquiry about the true sources and manipulations of social institutions purportedly established for the public welfare.

The power of Williams's critique rested on an old tradition of American resistance to the state's imperial demands. But it also grew out of a critique of U.S. society and culture put forth by a circle of intellectuals associated with the Frankfurt School, including Williams's own teacher, Madisonian Hans Gerth. The Frankfurt circle's best-known member, Herbert Marcuse, amplified and popularized a sensibility associated with the international New Left. To this central idea, Madison intellectuals could add grounding in American life. The rejection of material abundance as the end goal for society, in combination with the criticism of the Cold War state, made American radical thought more important worldwide than it had ever been previously, and its scholarly participants a lasting intellectual force.

By the early 1970s, a "school" of foreign-policy historians who took their cue from Williams and from Vietnam had written a virtual library of fresh studies. By the mid-1970s and the end of the U.S. occupation of Vietnam, once-despised views reverberated through the halls of Congress. Echoes of this "Vietnam Syndrome" could be heard clearly in widespread opposition to U.S. intervention in Central America. In 1980, Williams's position papers circulated at the Democratic Party convention. During Jesse Jackson's presidential campaign, Williams's watchwords reappeared in mainstream foreign-policy dialogue. If the nation had not learned enough by then, it would no doubt have ample opportunities in misadventures to come.

Related Madison scholarship in the 1950s and 1960s exercised a broader if less consolidated influence on radical history. In the late 1960s and early 1970s, studies inspired by Williams gave way to analyses of black and working-class culture that captured the imagination of young historians nation-wide. Herbert Gut-

3. Quoted in Kirkpatrick Sale, *SDS* (New York, 1973), 188.

man, a Madison graduate, led the way. Madison Europeanists, chronicling close readings of intellectual and political life, took upon themselves the dark side, that is, the roots of Nazism—a subject more than pertinent to the U.S. racial strife of the time—but they also revived forgotten utopias. Women's history also took root. By the late 1980s, the extended study of popular and commercial culture yielded, among veterans of Madison, a radical critique of the historical method itself.[4]

Nor were such influences merely scholarly. To cite only a few exceptional individuals from separate Madison eras: Marshall Brickman, Woody Allen's collaborator on *Annie Hall*—arguably the cultural signature of the 1970s—had begun his public artistry with the Madison Left's anti-war skits of the 1950s; Lowell Bergman, destined to become the hardest-hitting producer of television's *Sixty Minutes,* had received his intellectual training from Madison historians in the middle 1960s; and Michael Mann, who as executive producer of *Miami Vice* may be credited with a monumental influence on 1980s culture via postmodern television styles, came of age politically in the Madison anti-Vietnam War movement.

These scholarly and popular areas of thought and cultural practice would certainly constitute sufficient grounds for claims to collective accomplishment. But perhaps Madison's subtler role, precisely at the juncture between scholarship and activity, has been the most important. Many contributors to this book vigorously discuss the meanings of the connection. The image of the citizen–scholar tends to dominate the early era, although by no means entirely; the image of the scholar–activist plays the same role in the later period, again with broad exceptions. The differences between the two images are more than anything generational. But the similarities grow with closer attention.

What made Madison unusual? To quote Paul Berman on the sometimes lamentable anti-intellectualism of the 1960s,

> One must remember that the atmosphere in the New Left during the bad old days was not very congenial to intellectual work. All political movements look down on such work—there's no time for study, you should be at the barricades—and the New Left looked downer than most. Somehow intellect got identified with war, napalm, and reaction, and to be against all evil things was to be against book-cracking, too.

4. A list of the outstanding Madison-trained scholars and their non-foreign-policy works would include Daniel Czitrom, *Media and the American Mind, from Morse to McLuhan* (Chapel Hill, 1982); Stuart and Elizabeth Ewen, *Channels of Desire: Mass Images and the Shaping of American Consciousness* (New York, 1982); Herbert G. Gutman, *Work, Culture and Society in Industrializing America* (New York, 1976); George Lipsitz, *Class and Culture in Cold War America: "A Rainbow at Midnight"* (South Hadley, Mass., 1982); Warren Susman, *Culture as History: The Transformation of American Society in the Twentieth Century* (New York, 1984).

The better-known foreign-policy works inspired by Williams are summarized and described in Bradford Perkins, "'The Tragedy of American Diplomacy' Twenty-Five Years After," *Reviews in American History* 12 (1984), reprinted in Lloyd C. Gardner, ed., *Redefining the Past: Essays in Diplomatic History in Honor of William Appleman Williams* (Corvallis, Ore., 1986).

"Abolish brains" was practically a slogan, though no one put it that way. Even left-wing brains came under suspicion.

But not in Madison. Berman calls a locally produced radical history journal, *Radical America,*

> an oasis for the New Left. Fountains played and trees bloomed. . . . For here was a magazine that at least in the areas of history and politics upheld the idea of serious thought and hard brain work. Every new issue testified that scholarly vocations could be found outside the academy. It stood for intellectual independence and radicalism, it translated the inarticulate concepts of the day into categories for analysis, it sent its most interested readers marching along paths of their own.[5]

Berman concludes on a personal note. A Columbia student militant in that splendid year, 1968, he found intellectual sustenance in the bimonthly packets from Madison—not prepackaged answers but encouragement to thought. "Many of the people who grew up with *Radical America* remember that as its best achievement."[6] So does the magazine's founder and editor–publisher, this writer, who also grew up in the process. Of course, *Radical America* succeeded only to a very small extent in extricating the militant scholar from the dilemmas of the American intellectual, so aptly described by F. O. Matthiessen:

> Our so-called educated class knows so little of the country and the people of which it is nominally part. This lack of roots helps to explain the usual selfish indifference of our university men to political or social responsibility. . . . Inordinate cleavage between fact and theory has caused us to go to every extreme, has been the reason why . . . the idealistic strain of our thought has often been so tenuous, so without bearing on the tough materialism of our daily practice.[7]

Not even the best efforts could break decisively through the barriers described here. Our protagonists could not possibly escape, in the wake of the system's recuperation after 1970, becoming spiritual exiles again. Yet at the best moments Madison helped them achieve something different. And that difference remained important as much for what they did *not* become as for what they did become. The great majority of them never ceased to be democrats who believed in the capacity of

5. Paul Berman, "Spirit of '67: Radical Americanism and How It Grew," *Village Voice Literary Supplement,* September 1983.

6. Ibid.

7. F. O. Matthiessen, *American Renaissance: Art and Expression in the Age of Emerson and Whitman* (New York, 1941), 475.

ordinary Americans to transform their society radically, through what Williams called history's "way of learning."

New York Intellectuals/Madison Intellectuals

The lineage of the literary avant-garde, at least until 1960, has generally been drawn to resemble the famous *New Yorker* cartoon caricaturing a Manhattanite's view of America. Beyond Tenth Avenue stretches the remainder of the continent, Ohio to Nebraska collapsed into an interstice beyond which lies California. In Daniel Aaron's *Writers on the Left* (1961), intellectual–cultural activity west of the Hudson, north of Croton, and south of Brooklyn seemed likewise exotic. Most subsequent treatments to date have failed to broaden the focus. "New York intellectuals," originally centered in the *Partisan Review* of the 1930s and 1940s and going on to the highest individual and collective prestige, have been credited not only with an overwhelming impact on their generation but also with an enduring influence on the aesthetics of post-1930s, post-Marxist successors.[8]

The dense if turbulent cohesion, as much as the individual brilliance of the inhabitants—whose parameters reach from Irving Howe in the near-Center Left to Irving Kristol and Gertrude Himmelfarb on the distant Right—unquestionably facilitated their considerable reputation. So did their strategic location. But the impact of the New York intellectuals, however exaggerated, suggests the possibility that other groups, in other centers, may also have been influential in fields of radical avant-garde activity less focused on cultural criticism. Before midcentury, such centers generally depended on short-duration waves of literary activity (e.g., the Chicago Renaissance) or institutions (e.g., *The Appeal to Reason* in Girard, Kansas). New York, publishing center and intellectual meeting ground for Europe and the United States, outlasted the alternatives.

New York's centrality as political, cultural, and publishing locus of the intelligentsia diminished considerably after the 1950s. The geographic dispersion of intellectual energies during the expansion of vast college systems pretty well obliterated the possibility of one "center" and posed the prospect of a multiple succession to intellectual leadership. Madison's burst of energy in the 1950s, like the very different one in San Francisco, arguably foreshadowed events.

From a more political perspective, the New York intellectuals offered only one, not especially representative model, of thought and action. They came of age against the cultural hegemony of a Communist party that was considerably less important or even noticed west of the Hudson (or east of Hollywood). They set their course with a stage-by-stage rejection of Marxist politics and a simultaneous vindication of the artistic and critical avant-garde. Different milieus, radical from a variety of Marxist and non-Marxist perspectives and distant from the coasts, expe-

8. Daniel Aaron, *Writers on the Left* (New York, 1961). The best source is Alan M. Wald, *The New York Intellectuals: The Rise and Decline of the Anti-Stalinist Left from the 1930s to the 1980s* (Chapel Hill, 1987).

rienced similar disillusionment with Russia and the prospective proletarian revolution, but on different grounds and with different conclusions.

Abundant mapping of the New York intellectuals' course—a sort of scholarly cottage industry—has explained their acceptance of post–World War II warfare-welfare capitalism as their antidote to Stalinism, and indeed their solution to all the major noncultural criticisms Marxism once posed. They found themselves, as a group, generally complacent about midcentury America. But not about its political critics. They regularly lambasted remnants of the Old Left, yielding no respect to such figures as civil rights champions with Left commitments. A leading New York intellectual, Lionel Trilling, was aptly described by one scholar as the literary equivalent to the Madisonians' *bête noir*, the Cold War historian–ideologue Arthur Schlesinger, Jr. Banishing American radicalism from its historical context of poverty and class or ethnic or racial exploitation to the realm of wickedly mistaken ideas, Trilling and Schlesinger epitomized the extraordinary self-satisfaction of the era.[9]

In a decade or so, they would confront the rise of a noncommunist, antiwar, and antistate New Left with the same repugnance and even a few of the same invectives that they had hurled at the old communists. (Quite understandably, Schlesinger would brand Williams a scholarly failure and a threat to political clarity.) Most of all, they saw their hard-earned status threatened. Steeped in high culture and neo-Freudianism, the New York intellectuals generally despised the musical tastes and the feminism of the new generation as much as they did campus demonstrations against the war in Vietnam. For the most rightward—often the most influential as well—the campus Children's Crusade seemed (at the time and even more so in retrospect) to have corrupted intellectual standards and moral values, posing a barbaric threat against which neoconservatism (or an arch Cold War, market-oriented neoliberalism) subsequently provided much-needed civility.[10]

Madison intellectuals, with all their internal variety, were another species. Their experience was not predominantly one of deradicalization. Having imbibed little of Marxism, 1930s-style, they had little to reject. More a succession of inter-

9. The pairing of Arthur Schlesinger, Jr., and Lionel Trilling is made neatly in Mark Shechner, *After the Revolution: Studies in the Contemporary Jewish American Imagination* (Bloomington, 1987), 74. See also Lemisch, *On Active Service in War and Peace,* for a similar analysis.

10. See the final chapter of Wald, *New York Intellectuals.* These voices have been joined, in their journey from Left to Center and Right, by three Madison intellectuals of roughly New Left vintage. Their voices are heard so often and so loudly in the pages of the *Wall Street Journal, Partisan Review,* the *New York Review of Books,* and *The New Republic* that they require no representation in this volume. They include a former Mosse student turned intelligence "op" and prominent go-between in secret Iran-Contra arms deals; a second former Mosse student, prominent public supporter of the U.S. military build-up in Europe and in recent years an academic employee of the military; and finally, a former Williams student and Madison "Red" now turned hysterical critic of the New Left. Two of their personal memoirs touch upon Madison days. See the largely neoconservative volume edited by John H. Bunzel, *Political Passages* (Glencoe, Ill., 1988).

linked milieus and journals than a single peer group, they shared the New Yorkers' belief in the centrality of cultural issues. But they responded very differently to the issues at hand.

In the Madison of our contributors, for instance, gentile meets Jew and Jew meets gentile, or Europe (in another light) meets America, on very un-New York political and cultural grounds. In Madison, among the young radical intellectuals self-depicted here, the yearning of individuals from each group for the reality of the other (perhaps it is the Other) has a poignancy extending from the Holocaust to the New Left and thematically from the Frankfurt School to baseball. Unlike the New York intellectuals' milieu, high culture did not dominate here, nor did Israel's growing dependence on the global strategies of the West produce a binding support for Cold War internationalism. One could argue, albeit against considerable evidence to the contrary, that Jews here became less Jewish; if so, their gentile comrades and lovers became *more* Jewish in the spirit of otherwise near-vanished secular *Yiddishkayt* embracing both radical politics and radical culture. Radical Madison was a *goyishe* city with a Jewish heart of passionate intellectual–political commitment.

Or, to take another theme absent from the New York intellectuals' agenda: the arcadian element of Madison experience, a factor with powerful resonance in our era of environmental endangerment. Madison's scenic beauty reflected, as its lakes do the sky on a perfect day, the possibilities of a life better than the all-too-American themes of acquisitiveness, civic boosterism, violence, and escape. The New York intellectuals complained about these things, sometimes eloquently, but *for themselves* above all, and on behalf of a quasi-European urban culture. Radical Madisonians, often eastern urbanites in temporary exile, tended to have a fundamentally different experience. By the late 1960s, as this book draws to a close, local environmental degradation had begun to reveal itself vividly, in overbuilding, traffic congestion, and premature eutrophication of the lakes that Longfellow had embraced ("O four jeweled diadems!"). One hesitantly projects the contemporary sense of impending catastrophe backward in time. And yet the loss of Arcadia has been a major theme in U.S. radicalism since at least the mid nineteenth century. Some of us have felt that loss as the worst defeat of all. The narratives in this book can be viewed as the dawning awareness that a better society means a quality of cooperative life in complementary relation with physical surroundings. Toward the end of the book, a desperation shows.

Such generalizations do not apply to the entire book. *History and the New Left* is a collective expression, particularized by many contrasting voices. Its structure reflects three distinctly different eras of intellectual coming-of-age. During the first, roughly 1950 to 1956, outward-bound members of the Old Left and others found, in the academic safe haven of Madison, a means and a reason to rewrite U.S. history from the inside out. They also found a political calling—a civil liberties response to McCarthyism—natural to their scholarly calling. In the second era, roughly 1957 to 1965, a collective move away from the Old Left made possible precocious intellectual institutions of the proto New Left and what might be called countercultural barricades against the threats to existence posed by the Cold War. During the final period of our study, from 1965 to 1970, the beginnings of intellectual activism became a widening stream, for a few years a rushing current of energy. Even at such a moment—or perhaps *especially* at that moment—Madison traditions returned in fresh and unanticipated forms.

Madison History

The sources of Madison's uniqueness surely begin with the city's name. James Madison, the author of *The Federalist No. 10,* perhaps the most concise articulation of America's constitutional precepts, has been depicted by William A. Williams as the architect of compromise between justice and empire. Madison's friend Thomas Jefferson sought to postpone the dilemma of the republic by positing everlasting expansion, a re-creation of the small political unit *ad infinitum.* Madison faced the issue squarely. He moved to embody within the Constitution an older sense of social restraint he called the "feudal system of republics," a planned westward expansion that would guarantee both economic advance and the "common motive."[11]

Madison the city might be described as a product of democratic expansionary policy. Its reputation among the native Winnebagoes as a site of beauty and plentiful game augured something splendid. Settlement by whites in the mid nineteenth century brought literary confirmation of its picturesque qualities and inspired a population growth from 9,000 at the turn of the century to nearly 400,000 metropolitan residents today. The land-grant University of Wisconsin was located just a mile from the state capital building in 1848. In that year, across the ocean, peasants and workers rose up in rebellion, and two young intellectuals fashioned *The Communist Manifesto.* Closer to home, in Seneca Falls, New York, an audacious group of women declared their right to full citizenship. Over the long term, the coincidence of events would take on special meaning for the Madison campus.

Almost from its inception, the college earned a reputation for liberalism. The school's founding document freed it from sectarian control, and its aims (if not yet practice) offered an open admissions policy to virtually any Wisconsin resident for any class taught on campus. Such liberal beginnings prepared the school for the regime of John Bascom, president from 1874 to 1887 and a true originator of the "Wisconsin Idea": a democratic, public institution serving the public interest. Bascom wove political engagement into his plans for a broad university curriculum. If farmers were to receive training for scientific agriculture, he argued, land should be distributed in democratic freeholds so as to make practice possible. If students were to be trained for citizenship, they should be protected from corrupting influences.

11. William Appleman Williams, *The Contours of American History* (Cleveland, 1961), 149, and Chaps. 4 and 5.

In this spirit, Bascom joined a Prohibitionist crusade that earned him the enmity of state political bosses tied to the "liquor ring." His Sunday talks provided life-long inspiration for many students, including Robert M. LaFollette.[12]

Bascom's ethical philosophy predicated later Wisconsin progressive–radical thought. Shocked by the contemporary division of wealth, he insisted in his bac-calaureate address of 1876 that church and state cease groveling before power and take up the standard of the general welfare. "Society must be converted, as dis-tinctly and fully converted as the individual," he argued, or else no moral conver-sion of the individual could succeed.[13] The university would become "permanently great," he said on another occasion, to the degree "in which it understands the conditions of the prosperity and peace of the people and helps to provide them." The school's ultimate significance would rest on the degree "in which it enters into the revelation of truth, the law of righteousness, and the love of man, all gathered up and held firm in the constitution of the human soul and the counsel of God concerning it."[14] A lesser man might have uttered these phrases as empty pieties. In Bascom the Emersonian, inner truth spoke its own language, if necessary, against the profane world. Indeed, Bascom's support of woman suffrage and the Knights of Labor increased his unpopularity among the university regents, who held the power of appointments in the university, and forced his resignation. The moral man had paid the price.[15]

He left behind not only a tradition of moral integrity but also two specific works of national importance. At the university, the study he had encouraged of American social development evolved into a scientific–economic methodology of note. Meanwhile, near the campus, spurred by LaFollette and others who sought to reintroduce integrity and openness in government, the Progressive movement took shape. New standards of academic freedom and university involvement in public affairs grew up almost as a marriage of these two developments. LaFollette's "Wisconsin Idea"—honest and progressive government of the people in place of patronage and corruption, and public interest instead of "selfish interests"—expressed an ardent if perhaps naive belief in American citizenship reborn.[16]

12. It is perhaps important to add that Bascom, in his struggles with the regents, maintained the widest popularity among the students. Merle Curti and Vernon Carstensen, *The University of Wisconsin, A History, 1848–1925* (Madison, 1949),1:246–274, 288–289. This recognized classic treats controversial questions with caution, but captures the basic democratic commitment and the recurrent tensions with precision and feeling. Without the Curti–Carstensen effort, the present work would have assumed a very different shape.

13. Quoted in ibid., 287.

14. Quoted in ibid.

15. Ibid., 288–292.

16. David P. Thelen, *The New Citizenship: Origins of Progressivism in Wisconsin, 1885–1900* (Columbia, Mo., 1972), 249.

The historian William F. Allen provided the mediating influence for the intellectual methodology. Perhaps the earliest "oral historian" in the nation (he became justly famous for his copying and annotation of Afro-American songs during Radical Reconstruction), he guided history scholarship for twenty years after his 1867 university appointment. Utterly opposed to existing styles of teaching "facts" and commanding rote recitation, Allen abandoned textbook memorization and even lectures in order that students could concentrate on original historical documents. This "epoch-making modification" in social science (as G. Stanley Hall called it) encouraged one gifted history student at the university to recast the entire vision of the American past.[17]

That student, Frederick Jackson Turner, elaborated on Allen's transhistoric vision of a frontier mentality extending from the Germanic provinces of the Roman Empire to the Old Northwest of colonial America, a mentality that breathed democratic life into decadent European civilization. Turner updated Toqueville's study of basic American characteristics and posed in the starkest terms the problems confronting U.S. society at the close of its continental empire. Turner's stress on American themes and scientific methods weaned the infant history profession from its myopic Yankee patricianism and indifference to the crude material life of ordinary inhabitants. Through Turner, Madison made a permanent mark on the writing of American history.[18]

A corollary development made systematic labor history possible for the first time. The labor economics scholar John R. Commons and his protégés arranged for a monumental collection of labor (and radical) documents at the State Historical Society of Wisconsin, which Turner had successfully promoted as a prime collector of raw American data. From the accumulated materials came the group's multivolume, pathbreaking *Documentary History of American Industrial Society,* guided by the philosophical notion that American labor had a unique stake in the culture and that government owed labor a measure of social regulation.[19]

Meanwhile, the university concept of untrammeled discussion that Bascom had established was put to the test. In 1892, a few years after the noted labor

17. Quoted by David B. Frankenburger, "William Francis Allen," in *Monographs and Essays by William F. Allen* (Boston, 1890), 14.

18. "Turner's Autobiographic Letter to Constance Lindsay Skinner," in O. Lawrence Burnett, Jr., ed., *Wisconsin Witness to Frederick Jackson Turner* (Madison, 1968), 64–65, indicates his debt to Allen. Burnett notes in the Introduction that Turner's abandonment of Wisconsin (where he felt the History Department had slighted him and the regents had undermined faculty autonomy) made the Wisconsin State Historical Society and its *Wisconsin Magazine of History* all the more determined to preach Turner's doctrine, which they did, through documents and exegesis, for decades. One of these essays, "Frederick Jackson Turner, Historian," by Avery O. Craven, well sums up Turner's reputation. See Burnett, *Wisconsin Witness,* 100–117.

19. For a recent comment on the shaping influence of the "Commons School," see David Brody, "The Old Labor History and the New," *Labor History* 20 (1979).

economist Richard T. Ely had been lured to Madison from Johns Hopkins, a contentious regent asserted that Ely advocated unionism and class strife. The "moral justification for attacks upon life and liberty based upon a theory which comes from colleges, libraries and lecture-rooms . . . is supported by the teaching and practice of the University of Wisconsin," he charged. This denunciation could have been simply reprinted every generation hence, saving conservative legislators and business-minded regents the effort of rewording their polemics. A *cause célèbre*, tried in the national press and then by the regents, Ely emerged victorious because of his prominence, and because a rightward drift had detached him from his youthful Fabian socialism. (Indeed, he admitted that if he were guilty of the charges, he *should* be dismissed.)[20] The regents, divided over the proper course to take, nevertheless chose this opportunity (however doubtful in the light of Bascom's treatment at their hands) to articulate Madison's credo:

> We cannot for a moment believe that knowledge has reached its final goal, or that the present condition of society is perfect. We therefore welcome from our teachers such discussions as shall suggest the means and prepare the way by which knowledge may be extended, present evils . . . removed and others prevented. . . . Whatever may be the limitations which trammel inquiry elsewhere we believe the great state University of Wisconsin should ever encourage that continual and fearless sifting and winnowing by which truth can be found.[21]

One need not take such phrases at face value. But they have a considerable symbolic content nevertheless. The democratic confidence of such sentiments offered, perhaps, a reprise of America's earlier revolutionary ideals, passed down the generations to the Midwest where republican optimism had not been quite exhausted.

Politically, the seeds for a distinctive Wisconsin politics had sprouted on the campus when young LaFollette organized unaffiliated students against the compact fraternity crowd. In his first run for public office, LaFollette found enthusiastic cadre in the university community. His supporters would soon epitomize Wisconsin's differentiation between public interests and selfish interests, drawing him ever closer to radical reform.

LaFollette's later gubernatorial tenure involved intellectuals more closely in political reform than they had been since the constitutional era or would be again until the New Deal. Agents and advisers in the regulation of railroads and the

20. Quoted in Curti and Carstensen, *University of Wisconsin,* 1:509; see also 1:508–527 on the controversy around Ely generally.

21. Ibid., 525. A later *Daily Cardinal* essay, "'Is There No Way?' The Wisconsin Story," October 25, 1952, noted that the plaque inscribed with the "sifting and winnowing" motto was refused by the university regents when first presented in 1910 and accepted only in 1915.

creation of direct primaries, architects and administrators of labor legislation, public sanitation, forest preservation, civil service reform, the state's intellectuals became LaFollette's political brain trust. As if to pinpoint the university origins for this development, LaFollette's autobiography recalls Bascom, in the last year of his life, visiting the governor with a final bit of advice. "You will doubtless make mistakes of judgment as governor," the old man warned, "but never mind the political mistakes so long as you make no ethical mistakes."[22] That would be the watchword of LaFollette's crusades and the pride of the intellectuals' contributions.

Wisconsin Democracy/American Democracy

These accomplishments took place in a less than happy context for American democratic prospects. The pan-African historian C. L. R. James wrote in 1950 that the world sums up American civilization in two men, George Washington and Henry Ford, the symbols respectively of democratic individualism and mass production.[23] The greatest American minds were baffled by the problem of reconciling the republican past of small-property democracy with the mass-society future of great propertyless millions. Turner reflected dolefully,

> The question is imperative, then. What ideals persist from this democratic experience of the West; and have they acquired sufficient momentum to sustain themselves under conditions so radically unlike those in the days of their origin? . . . Under the forms of American democracy is there in reality evolving such a concentration of economic and social power in the hands of a comparatively few men as may make political democracy an appearance rather than a reality? The free lands are gone. The material forces that gave vitality to Western democracy are passing away.[24]

Turner wondered if democracy might be salvaged by the power of public education to conserve and refurbish democratic ideals.

The university answered the need for action in reactive and limited fashion, addressing symptoms more than causes. Again, Richard Ely's retreat into a mild liberalism did much to ensure his public vindication. Conservative faculty members, openly opposed to unions and indifferent to the plight of the poor, were, of course, never required to pass a similar moderation test. The university and the local press always liked to have it both ways. During the Ely controversy, Wiscon-

22. *LaFollette's Autobiography: A Personal Narrative of Political Experiences* (Madison, 1911), 28.

23. C. L. R. James, "Notes on American Civilization" (ca. 1950), 1. Unpublished manuscript in possession of the writer.

24. Quoted in Richard Hofstadter, *The Progressive Historians* (New York, 1968), 83; see also Craven, "Frederick Jackson Turner, Historian." And see *Selected Essays of Frederick Jackson Turner: Frontier and Section* (Engelwood Cliffs, N.J., 1961).

sin newspapers called for an investigation of dangerous influences on the young; they then spun around to pronounce the regents' report a great advertisement for academic freedom.

The deeper ambiguity lay in Wisconsin itself. With no metropolitan centers outside Milwaukee, with relatively little mass production and few of the "new" southern and eastern European immigrants, the state could cling to an earlier vision of politics and life. Wisconsin Progressives, like others of their kind across the United States, held racial assumptions about "advanced" and "backward" groups. Sometimes, as in the writings of the Wisconsin sociologist E. A. Ross, these categorizations reached the level of a racist pseudo science.[25] Besides, Wisconsin simply could not defend its way of life from new and overpowering socioeconomic forces. The balance that LaFollette sought to preserve—between business interests and society at large, and between freedom and state control of the university—threatened constantly to tip toward vested interests.

World War I challenged Progressives to establish precedents for much thought and activity that was to follow. Wisconsin harbored perhaps more antiwar sentiment than any other state, by virtue both of its large German-American population and its Progressive–socialist political peace idealism. At the first outbreak of nationalist hysteria, Progressive superpatriots and political opponents of Progressivism made an unholy alliance to stamp out the Left. Wisconsin socialists, widely admired for their leadership of Milwaukee government and their principled positions, nevertheless found their meetings canceled "for reasons of public health," their newspapers' mailing permits revoked, and numerous vigilante threats voiced. LaFollette, now in Congress, heroically resisted the war fever. The university rewarded with venom his early contributions to campus life. A petition, signed by 93 percent of the faculty, assailed his political position—and, by implication, LaFollette himself—as a national menace. Richard Ely personally led a Wisconsin Loyalty Legion whose chosen task was to terrorize peace advocates by all legal means, and to damage the careers of those who defended the dissenters. Under considerable public pressure, university president Charles Van Hise nevertheless resisted efforts to have peace-minded faculty members dismissed. Other schools behaved far worse. But the university faculty set an ugly precedent, signaling the intense alienation that future opponents of war would experience within the university community.[26]

25. See Ross's rather startling characterization of "the idle, quarreling, sensual Afro-American," in E. A. Ross, *Social Control: A Survey of the Foundation of Order* (New York, 1920), 336.

26. Curti and Carstensen, *University of Wisconsin,* 2:113–22, 200–201, notes that President Van Hise was under severe pressure from visiting dignitaries, who complained of the lack of student patriotism. But they also note that prior to the U.S. entry into the war, Van Hise had given considerable ground to conservatives in the defense of academic freedom, condemning Ross for mentioning a local appearance by Emma Goldman (who spoke off-campus) and barring campus appearances by socialist lecturer and editor of the *Masses* magazine, Max Eastman, and socialist intellectual Harry Laidler. Curti and Carstensen, *University of Wisconsin,* 2:55–75.

Unabashed public dissenters gave intimidated university liberals new hope. The then-crusading *Capital Times* joined *LaFollette's Magazine* in opposing the war mentality. Socialists won over new voters and very nearly elected a second pro-peace Wisconsin congressman. Although much of LaFollette's middle-class, WASP support in the Republican party turned against him and his reform program, ethnic voters, farmers, and workers swung into his camp in increasing numbers. Predicting the future course of American liberalism, the old Progressivism split in two. The shape of Wisconsin politics, Herbert Margulies has argued, changed forever. And with it, the shape of university politics. The bitter war experience ensured the permanence of a political avant-garde, less respectable and more critical than LaFollette's early campus following had been. This avant-garde lived at the sufferance of university administrators, but repeatedly looked to the wider public to turn academic issues into political ones.[27]

Campus controversies in the 1920s and 1930s underlined these changes. As vice-president, Calvin Coolidge used his prestige to launch an attack on the surviving trickle of campus radicalism, including the purportedly dangerous University Socialist Club in Madison—actually a small, near-defunct group, by this time renamed the Social Science Club. Conservatives and the regents seemed eager for a war-style crackdown, and President Edward Birge sought to walk the narrow line between repression and a modicum of free speech. He denied the famed muckraker and Russia-enthusiast Lincoln Steffens the use of university facilities, and he forbade a speech on campus by the radical Scott Nearing. After the *Capital Times* rushed in to dramatize the First Amendment issue, prominent liberals from around the nation added their voices. Several years later, Birge quietly acceded to controversial speakers.[28]

Once more the university's traditions had survived. But trouble lay ahead. Alexander Meikeljohn, fired from the presidency of Vassar for his political heterodoxy, was hired by university president Glenn Frank to create an Experimental College. In a special program, some sixty male students (no females) lived together and for two years studied only the classics. The experiment gained early notoriety when a New York Jewish student, jailed earlier for a "pornographic" poem in a radical publication, was awarded a scholarship. As the depression struck, nerves frayed and the suspicious-minded looked around for signs of "revolution" on campus. When in 1931 a prankish undergraduate hung red underwear out the window of the Experimental College building, and his friends—tongues firmly planted in cheek—called students to "Rise! Revolt!," conservative paranoia flared. An obscure

---

27. See Kenneth Cameron Wagner, "William T. Evjue and the Capital Times, " Master's thesis, University of Wisconsin, 1949; and Herbert F. Margulies, *The Decline of The Progressive Movement in Wisconsin, 1890–1920* (Madison, 1968), esp. Chap. 7. As noted in "Cardinal Observes 65th Anniversary," *Daily Cardinal*, April 4, 1957, the *Capital Times* rescued the *Cardinal* in 1912, offering its own press to help the paper survive.

28. Curti and Carstensen, *University of Wisconsin*, 2:145–156.

state legislator, intent on making his career through attacks on campus "Reds," dominated public attention with wild charges. Even Glenn Frank, an urbane former publishing executive turned university administrator, was not beyond legislative scrutiny.[29]

The conservative charges fell wide of the mark. A handful of socialist and communist students attracted considerable support during the 1930s, but not because of revolutionary schemes or Marxist philosophy. Instead, they organized around popular issues and adapted themselves to the possibilities at hand. Almost immediately, their presence on the campus became a free-speech issue, with President Frank calling an all-campus assembly to denounce the physical assault on a socialist meeting by conservative rowdies. Later, amid congressional revelations about U.S. war profiteering that LaFollette had denounced, students broadly opposed any preparations for another war. The *Daily Cardinal* and President Frank went on record against campus military training, a 1935 student strike pulled thousands from classes, and Frank instituted a Peace Assembly the following year in place of a strike. Student opinion no doubt reflected popular Wisconsin sentiment. But the communist-influenced American Student Union also played a key role in propaganda and mobilization.[30]

Toward the end of the 1930s, fear of the Nazi threat divided peace advocates. Campus radicals turned to new issues. The Wisconsin Student Alliance, a liberal–Left formation, took a constructive approach to student problems. Investigating student work conditions, developing more effective cooperatives, analyzing university curricula and practices, lobbying state representatives about campus concerns, they made themselves an effective liberal lobby. The *Daily Cardinal,* increasingly sympathetic to the progressive–liberal Left, published a student housing edition that was distributed throughout the state.

Unlike the old days, when campus Progressivism revolved around professors and led to marches on the statehouse, the liberal and Left student politicos of the 1930s had seized a subtler initiative. Individual professors supported their actions, tolerating the sometimes irregular behavior of bright young activists and seeking to add wisdom to their commitments. The administration sought to chart a course between the young idealists and the state legislature. President Frank frequently reminded the press that the flame of radicalism could not be suppressed but must be allowed to burn—and burn out—in public. Supportive of Franklin Roosevelt's

29. The best account of Madison campus events in the 1930s is Reuben George Beilke, "Student Political Action at the University of Wisconsin, 1930–1940," Master's thesis, 1951. This account was checked against the memory of Fred Bassett Blair, a communist leader in Wisconsin. A later *Daily Cardinal* investigation, reported in Rita Middleton, "Cardinal History," April 4, 1957, noted that the most controversial moment for the paper in Meikeljohn's years was touched off by a letter from an avowed "ex-virgin" who "smile[d] at the notion that we have lost self-respect." A flood of responses followed. Radical politics inspired no equivalent excitement.

30. Beilke, "Student Political Action," 58–59, 93–97; Ralph S. Brax, *The First Student Movement: Student Activism in the 1930s* (Port Washington, N.Y., 1981), 33, 46, 64.

New Deal, he neatly deflected political attacks from the Right. At a time when obdurate administrators on other campuses acted autocratically and occasionally expressed sympathy for fascism, triggering strikes and riots, Frank could be viewed as coopting aggressive campus dissent. Ironically, Frank found himself trapped in a personal quarrel with the LaFollette camp, and was forced out. He had, however, established a precedent that would prevail until the darkest days of the late 1960s. As long as the radicals minded their manners, an unstated mutual understanding prevailed between them and university leaders. Madison, the tolerant, intellectual oasis, would serve various needs.

Under the penumbra created through decades of conflict and consensus in Madison, student radicalism became a permanent subculture. According to an unconsciously humorous quotation from the Madison Young Communist League (YCL) bulletin in 1939, the radicals sought to merge into the crowd:

> Some people have the idea that a YCL'er is politically minded, that nothing outside of politics means anything. Gosh, no. They have a few simple problems. There is the problem of getting good men on the baseball team this spring, of opposition from other pingpong teams, of dating girls, etc. We go to shows, parties, dances, and all that. In short, the YCL and its members are no different from other people except that we believe in dialectical materialism as the solution to all problems.[31]

Conservatives and not a few liberals saw in such phraseology a criminal deceptiveness, an "infiltration" of student organizations by subversives. Another interpretation makes more sense. Perhaps the lessons of confrontation elsewhere had been taken to heart. Moreover, some of the out-of-state radical students (often Jewish) had likely come to appreciate the value of a mutual toleration. They could work easily, in most periods, in student government and on the *Cardinal;* they could form or lead institutions such as the Green Lantern eating coop and the student film society. They never lost the differences that set them apart from the blond giants in the fraternity rush. But even the most resolute Marxist was susceptible to the congenial surroundings and the beautiful outdoors. Student life, too, provided a growing-up time, with interests considerably wider than politics. (The earliest activity I was asked to join was the "left-wing" softball game. "We have plenty of theoreticians," a campus radical leader shouted at me, "what we need is a second baseman!")

Madison had become comfortable for radicals, even as conservative legislators and regents sought to isolate and contain the "problem." As early as 1930, Madison had the lowest in-state and highest out-of-state student fees of any major U.S.

---

31. Quoted by Hal Draper, "The Student Movement of the 1930s," in Rita Simon, ed. *As We Saw the Thirties* (Urbana, Ill., 1967), 181.

university (a policy known in less polite circles as "keeping out the New York Jews"). But they could not stanch the flow of unorthodox out-of-staters. Major disillusionments, such as the 1939 Nazi–Soviet pact and the military character of postwar Eastern European politics, diminished the Left. The eclipse of the state Progressive party also undercut popular sympathies for many campus radical causes. But the revulsion against Nazism and the influx of European exiles reinvigorated the concepts of free speech and untrammeled thought. When the American campus became the prime political locus in America, Madison took second place to none. When professors, administrators, and students lashed out at one another in campuswide conflicts, all sides could savor the irony of familiar common interests that had made the scale of the drama possible.

Madison and the Historians

The historical bent of Madison radicals, and the scholarly prestige of the radical history prepared in this environment, also flowed from the school's political and intellectual development. Madison influenced dissident thought because the formulators stood close enough to Middle America to make their critique an immanent one.

The American historical profession, some wags suggested, had by the 1920s become one large *Turnerverein,* a play of words upon Frederick Jackson Turner and the *Turnverein* or German-American exercise club. Turner had in fact provided a *deus ex machina,* a functional hypothesis for the unique qualities of U.S. development, just as the history profession had taken shape and had sought to make its presence felt by the public. Hailing from the frontier town of Portage, Wisconsin— where in his childhood, Indians and their dogs trudged the streets, and tipis could be seen nearby—Turner united the Jeffersonian–Lincolnian optimism of pioneer democracy with the scientific method then gaining currency. He expressed a historic view of frontier democracy as the key to American uniqueness. If later generations of Madisonians repudiated the implications Turner seemed to draw, their own scholarly leap owed much to his use of data and his democratic impulse.

Turnerism led directly to socialist-minded history scholarship. Algie M. Simons, from Baraboo, Wisconsin, arrived in Madison during the golden era of Turner's influence, the early 1890s. Within a decade, Simons became the intellectual leader of the fledgling English-language socialist movement. He established in Chicago the premier journal of U.S. socialists, the *International Socialist Review,* in which he reprinted Turner's famed essay, "The Significance of the Frontier in American History."[32] No doubt it weighed in strangely alongside the ponderous Second International writings of Karl Kautsky or Anton Pannekoek, as a curious manifestation of what the upstart Americans took socialism to be. Simons's own *Class Struggles in American History* and (in expanded form) *Social Forces in American History* furnished thousands of socialist study groups with a basic lesson on

32. *International Socialist Review,* VI (December 1905): 321–46.

America's exceptional development. In his socialist Turnerism, the democracy of the grass-roots farmer had been disoriented by American political struggles (including the Revolution and the Civil War), which benefited only the nascent bourgeoisie. Now, as the industrial proletariat began to awaken to its role, the manufacturing elite was driving the family farmer to the wall. The once-edenic countryside had lost its dignity and cultural autonomy as well. The future of American civilization, argued Simons, depended on the success of socialism.[33]

This apocalyptic interpretation had a real attraction for the Texas and Oklahoma sharecropper, the Plains farmer, and the commercial townspeople passing through one last phase of Yankee perfectionism. *The Appeal to Reason,* which popularized Simons's ideas, reached close to half a million readers. War and repression decimated this radical following and eclipsed the agrarian–Marxist synthesis. By the 1930s, liberal revulsion at American lawlessness, dovetailing with communist popularization of Soviet Russia's rural collectivization, framed a pessimistic interpretation of Turner. As Warren Susman brilliantly noted, the frontier was now assigned general blame for American philistinism. By that time, the baton of Progressive history had long since passed eastward anyway. Turner himself had left Madison for the Ivy League in 1907. America's greatest citizen–historian, Charles Beard, in effect took over the great project of national self-interpretation until Madison's day came again.[34]

Beard was a powerful interim figure in more ways than one. He symbolized for more than thirty years the dissenting historian as scholar-*engagé.* Popular on the lecture circuit, on radio, and in magazines from the 1910s to the 1930s, he also authored (with his wife, Mary Beard) the best-selling history book, *The Rise of American Civilization.* As David Noble comments, the Beards' interpretation articulated the "Progressive paradigm" by which small-proprietor agriculture and, later, rapidly changing modern industry successively supplied the economic basis for a uniquely American nation-state, guided not by power and privilege but by democratic principle. Threatened by the undemocratic growth of European-style monopoly capitalism, the American system survived the Great Depression only to face the catastrophe of another world war.[35] A skeptic of aggressive foreign policy and growing state power, Beard was one of war propaganda's first victims.

33. See Kent and Gretchen Kreuter, *An American Dissenter: The Life of Algie Martin Simons, 1870–1950* (Lexington, 1969), and Algie M. Simons, *The American Farmer* (Chicago, 1902), for the most Turnerian version.

34. See Paul Buhle, *Marxism in the U.S.* (London, 1986), Chaps. 3 and 5; and Susman, *Culture as History,* 29–35.

35. Williams's assessment is certainly the classic one on Charles Beard's importance. See "Charles Austin Beard: The Intellectual as Tory-Radical," in Harvey Goldberg, ed., *American Radicals: Some Problems and Personalities* (New York, 1957); David W. Noble, "William Appleman Williams and the Crisis of Public History," in Gardner, *Redefining the Past,* esp. 48–49. See also Howard K. Beale, ed., *Charles A. Beard: An Appraisal* (Lexington, 1954), esp. George R. Leighton, "Beard and Foreign Policy."

Beard's prestige disintegrated when he attacked Roosevelt's war response to Pearl Harbor. A manipulative effort to resolve the social crisis posed by the depression, this premeditated strategy set America on the task of policing the world. Beard did not oppose the war against fascism, only the fundamental flaws its conduct exposed in the New Deal (and, by implication, postwar) program. But the progenitors of a new Cold War liberal and neoconservative history savaged him. Progressive history rapidly went out of fashion. Until the late 1960s, the Beards' textbook successors and mainstream historians generally would give American business and government their blessing while accusing radicals either of extreme irrationalism (Populists spawning anti-Semitism) or a weakness toward totalitarianism (socialists and communists supporting foreign revolutions). Beard had become, for most of these historians, an embarrassment.[36]

In essence, David Noble argues, a "counter-Progressive" historical scholarship had by this time become part of a wider liberal–conservative consensus. While Schlesinger penned *The Vital Center,* the theologian Reinhold Niebuhr repudiated his past radical commitments, declaring in *The Irony of American History* (1952) that radicalism had worked great mischief. The human possibility was more bleak than the Progressive historians, and other liberal–radical supporters of drastic change, had imagined. Spiritually based realism required an abandonment of well-intentioned U.S. isolationism, Niebuhr argued, and a moral (also military) armament against the culprits of disorder (i.e., the Soviet Union). Only such measures, whatever their side effects on individual freedom, could stem the menace to Western democratic pluralism. On that goal, presumably all Americans but the hidebound isolationists and communist-influenced liberals could agree.[37]

But not in Madison. Respect for Beard's courage, his antistate views, and his foreign-policy criticism helped produce a major dissenting historical perspective in the very depths of Cold War culture. One could criticize Beard properly, according to the Madisonian view, not by rejecting his criticisms or apotheosizing his worldview, but by moving on to a fuller understanding of the U.S. role in a complex world. From this perspective, Niebuhr and his political–scholarly kin ignored the ideological fixations of American political leaders that had prompted them to attack a prostrate Russia in 1917 and to ignore Russian calls for alliance against fascism during the 1930s. Cold War liberal historians' praise of Franklin Roosevelt as the ultimate democratic pragmatist in a world of absolutes contained the same logical lacunae. The maintenance of the U.S. overseas economic empire, most notably in Latin America, had been neither democratic nor pragmatic, nor even an assiduous *Realpolitik* adjustment to twentieth-century nationalist aspirations.

36. Noble, "William Appleman Williams," 52–54; see also the cautious treatment of Beard in Hofstadter, *Progressive Historians,* 438–39; and the bolder interpretation in James P. O'Brien, "The Legacy of Beardian History," *Radical America* 4 (November 1970).

37. Arthur Schlesinger, Jr., *The Vital Center: The Politics of Freedom* (New York, 1949); and Lemisch, *On Active Service in War and Peace,* 53–66.

While Cold War scholars insisted that Americans had to understand the importance of our pluralist legacy, Madison historians answered that their version was
only superficially pluralistic. The historic role of dissent, and its effective repression,
had been neglected.[38]

The three senior Wisconsin figures in the historiographic revival—Merle
Curti, Howard Beale, and Merrill Jensen—seemed at first glance throwbacks to an
earlier era. But by the 1960s they could be seen as prophets of a new historical
politics.

Of the three, Curti was by all odds the most influential. The son of a Swiss-
American pacifist, he had studied at Harvard with Frederick Jackson Turner (and
had been inspired by a Eugene Debs speech in Boston). By the time of his 1942
arrival in Madison, Curti had already made his name with sympathetic scholarship
on American peace movements and prepared his 1943 Pulitzer Prize-winning
Growth of American Thought. Optimistic about prospects for social change and at
the same time deeply suspicious of American militarism and the welfare state,
Curti attacked postwar liberalism for its obsession with the Cold War and its relative complacence at society's manifest limitations. He pioneered demographic
research, as democratic use of census data about ordinary people's lives. He encouraged scholarship on immigration, popular culture, and the unorganized working
classes, among other subjects scarcely studied. His presidential address to the 1953
American Historical Association convention, vindicating Beard and the Progressive
tradition, was remarkable for its boldness of purpose. It also indicated that support
for such unpopular views remained among at least a minority of historians.[39]

Howard Beale wrote a notable history of civil liberties and with the help of
his young assistant Herbert Gutman did the editorial work for the collective tribute
Charles A. Beard: An Appraisal. Beale's personal evaluation of Beard's "tireless
battle persuading his fellow citizens that the promise of American democracy could
be fulfilled, if only the lessons of history and philosophy were applied to public
problems," might easily be taken as the emerging credo.

Merrill Jensen, the last of the "neo-Beardian" Progressive historians to erect
a school of historical thought around his own work, traced the abuses of the state
back to the Constitutional Convention and the violation of autonomy explicit in
the Articles of Confederation. American democracy had been *fundamentally* dam-

---

38. Noble, "William Appleman Williams," 55–56.

39. Curti's broad interests in, and encouragement for, young scholars approaching such subjects as immigration history and popular culture should be noted. Rudolph Vecoli's unpublished paper, "Merle Curti
and Immigration History," has been especially helpful to my understanding. Vecoli, a Curti student,
is director of the Immigration History Research Center at the University of Minnesota and an outstanding immigration historian in his own right. I am also grateful for an interview with Merle Curti, October
17, 1987, for personal information on him. See also the respectful treatment in Robert Allen Skotheim,
American Intellectual Histories and Historians (Princeton, 1966), 149–72; in a less direct fashion, Curti
places his development as an intellectual historian in "The Evolution of American Intellectual History,"
OAH Newsletter, May 1984.

aged, by this reading, in the usurpation of the agrarian democratic impulse. Finally, a milieu of formidable intellectual powers and often unpopular ideas was filled out by the likes of the foreign policy historian Fred Harvey Harrington, the political historian William Hesseltine, and a keen, if disillusioned, former Marxist, Paul Farmer.[40]

Along with these historians, one historical-minded sociologist at Madison counted heavily. Hans Gerth, a refugee from Nazi Germany best known in academic circles for his translations of Max Weber, introduced a cosmopolitan learning and a depth of feeling for twentieth-century tragedy congruent to the historians' message. C. Wright Mills, one of Gerth's protégés, popularized the master's critique of the emerging corporate order. Gerth himself taught a sociological method utterly unlike the behaviorism that held sway in the field.[41]

The importance of these Madison mentors is clear from the scholars they helped produce. William Appleman Williams, John Higham, Harvey Goldberg, Jackson Turner Main (Frederick Jackson Turner's grandson), Charles Forcey, David Shannon, Herbert Gutman, Warren Susman, William Preston, Gar Alperovitz, George Rawick, and less-remembered figures set American history on a new path in the 1960s and 1970s, from the study of foreign policy and state repression to a "history from the bottom up" of working people, blacks, and others. *Their* students have become leading social historians, educational innovators, and scholarly critics of American foreign policy. The mixture of an old-fashioned pursuit of truth against the marshaling of the history profession by prestigious Cold Warriors, and newfound iconoclastic discoveries about America's unproud traditions, made for a heady brew. Those who quaffed it would never look at history and its uses through the same eyes again.[42]

The Politics of History

A curious anthology of American radicalism from 1957, edited by a recent Madison Ph.D. and future Madison luminary, Harvey Goldberg, prefigured the forms

---

40. Beale, "Beard as Historical Critic," in Beale, *Charles A. Beard;* interview with Merle Curti, October, 1987.

41. Arthur Vidich, "Hans Gerth: A Modern Intellectual Exile," in Joseph Bensman, Arthur J. Vidich, and Nobuko Gerth, eds. *Politics, Character and Culture: Perspectives from Hans Gerth* (Westport, Conn., 1982), 3–13.

42. See, for instance, the interviews with Herbert Gutman (by Michael Merrill) and William Appleman Williams (by Mike Wallace) in MARHO, eds., *Visions of History* (New York, 1983). (MARHO stands for the Mid-Atlantic Radical Historians Organization.)

It is worth mentioning that the other leading mentor to young labor historians, David Montgomery, turned from factory labor to historical labor at the University of Minnesota after a period of activity in the Democratic Farm Labor party. Another easterner, he too owed something of his intellectual education to the embrace of Middle America. See the interview of him (by Paul Buhle and Mark Naison) in MARHO, *Visions of History*.

that the historical criticism would take. Goldberg dedicated his book to the fearless muckraker I. F. Stone and emblazoned on it Andre Gide's aphorism, "The world will be saved, if it can be, only by the *unsubmissive.*" The heroes of the book were the unsubmissive members of the otherwise all-too-accommodating American history profession. The European radical, "consistently sensitive to the difficulties of challenging a class system, could be broken and yet rise again," generation after generation. His or her American cousin, overwhelmed by the system and the acquiescense of the majority to its values, had no such sense of continuity. The "soft center of personal gain" and the consequent corruption through perquisites had often broken the rebellious intellectual. In the Cold War era, most of another generation of scholars, including many who had so recently announced their rebellion against capitalism, had gone over to apologizing for the system. Against a political tide and moral temptations, the true (i.e., unrepentent) radical intellectual gathered a like-thinking circle and dug in for better times ahead.[43]

Madison's irony is that its own dissident circle had to come to grips with the deeper dualities of the Progressive tradition. LaFollette had denounced Marine deployments to Latin America more than a quarter-century earlier. Yet the frontier democracy proclaimed by Turner had, Williams and Goldberg argued, actually defined the twentieth-century pursuit of empire: "America's central conception of the world, or philosophy of history, has always rested on the assumption that there was enough at hand, or within easy reach, to meet and satisfy the needs and desires of all segments of the nation." International contradictions could be postponed, if not resolved, by further embrace of territory, taken easily enough from weak or preoccupied opponents, and the seizure justified as the spread of the most advanced civilization in the world. Delivered at the apex of internal crisis with no continental resolution (during the severe depression of the 1890s), Turner's formulations seemingly supported the expansionary faith among the emerging middle classes and their chief spokesmen, Theodore Roosevelt and Woodrow Wilson. European wars subsequently justified foreign policy crusades ending in American economic hegemony over the world. True radicals had somehow to wrench themselves free of *this* American consensus and locate their own vision of a better reality.[44]

American political and scholarly traditions could also be read in a way that was more congenial to the dissenters. Turner's conclusions arguably might have been pessimistic rather than supportive of empire. He simply could not envision democracy surviving without frontiers. Charles Beard took the same logic to demand that we look inward rather than outward to solve our national problems. Madison historians merged Beard and Turner, highlighting their Progressive faith that history is relative and due for perpetual revision by new generations. If the

43. Harvey Goldberg and William Appleman Williams, "Introduction: Thoughts about American Radicalism," in Goldberg, *American Radicals,* i, 8, 12.

44. Ibid., 4.

Madison intellectuals could build community links while carrying on a major reevaluation of foreign policy history, their personal sense of alienation from the larger America could be minimized, perhaps even overcome.[45]

The contradiction glared at times between a great university of far-ranging ideas and a national Cold War culture that sought to filter the flow of ideas. A few professors supporting Henry Wallace's peace candidacy in 1948 found themselves out of jobs, not so much fired as denied tenure. In the same years, several notable figures of the Left, including Gerhart Eisler and Howard Fast, were refused facilities to speak on campus. But thanks to a leftish bloc of opinion around the offices of the *Daily Cardinal,* to supportive professors, and to a shrewd and dedicated administration, the contradictions remained in a dynamic tension. Campus activists came out strongly for the defeat of Joseph McCarthy, in the Joe Must Go campaign discussed in several of this book's essays. The apparently benign presence of the Left at the university became itself a persuasive argument for free speech. As Howard Beale pondered several years after the worst effects of McCarthyism had passed, one could only speculate what might have happened if McCarthy had turned full blast upon Madison. That he did not was a tribute to his sagacity; such a crusade would have produced too many enemies in his own backyard.[46]

Even at the height of the McCarthy era, the university eased its posture enough for Owen Lattimore (who, as a U.S. diplomat, according to right-wing propagandists, had helped the nation "lose" China) to speak on campus. Many others followed. By 1958, the Anti-Military Ball—with its "Time Is Running Out" theme and its topical melodies "Grave New World" and "The Mushroom Cloud Also Rises"—had cracked the Cold War ice.[47]

In retrospect, these events had a subtle national importance. Madison's Socialist Club and *Studies on the Left* (both discussed in the essays) were arguably the closest U.S. counterparts to the contemporary British New Left. There, E. P. Thompson, Christopher Hill, Eric Hobsbawm, and others broke with the Communist party through a process of orienting themselves to English radical traditions. They would go on, individually and collectively, to rewrite British history while taking part in and even leading important social movements. American political activism revived from the Cold War doldrums in the civil rights movement. Nowhere but Madison did a fresh burst of *intellectual* energy so clearly mark off a new spirit from the old.

45. I wish to express my gratitude to Ron Grele, director of Columbia University's Oral History Research Office, for clarifying this point.

46. In addition to the essays below, the pages of the *Daily Cardinal,* especially during its years under Richard Schickel, offer the best evidence. See, e.g., Schickel, "'Is There No Way?' When Is a Marxist Not a Communist," October 15, 1952; and a blistering editorial in support of freedom of inquiry and teaching in history: "Compulsory Course Means U.S. History, Not 'Branded' Ideas," September 24, 1952.

47. "Pacifists Sponsor Anti-Military Ball," *Daily Cardinal,* May 2, 1958. See also the essays below, especially those by Nina Serrano and Saul Landau.

Studies, founded by graduate students under William A. Williams, appeared in 1959. Its landmark editorial, "The Radicalism of Disclosure," expressed the quintessential Madison faith in hidden truths to be revealed by the independent-minded scholar. "Objectivity," the students charged, had been reduced to "the weight of authority, the viewpoint of those who are in a position to enforce standards." Scholarly "dispassion" was a similarly opportunistic pose. Against the prevailing "intellectual racket," the editors insisted on the rebirth of the militant thinker "committed to the investigation of the origins, purposes, and limitations of institutions and concepts," for the "application of reason to the *reconstruction* of society." The bold action of a minority would help to reinvigorate intellectuals within and outside university walls who shared "a combination of scholarly integrity and commitment to the humanization of society.[48] Memoirs in this book show that the journal succeeded, during its four short Madison years, in creating a public presence for the new history. Growing doubts about the welfare state had accentuated a long-festering crisis in liberal thought at large. Madison thinkers gave these doubts a leftward spin.

Behind the struggle for insight into the operation of a total system lay a moral vision that Williams articulated and personified, a sort of scholarly counterpart to Martin Luther King Jr.'s contemporary moral appeal. "Few Americans," Williams wrote in *Contours of American History,* had yet begun "to explore the possibility that the frontier took men away from essentials," by which he meant away from an inner light that the frontiersmen, in their cupidity, had unwittingly helped extinguish. "The socialist," he concluded, "merely says that it is time to stop running away from life."[49] Americans could and did benefit from their imperial status. But it was a false gain, derived from a false view of the self in society. To become members of a mature civilization demanded a return to the common responsibility that liberal capitalism had eroded. It was a neo-Beardian message, delivered by the citizen–scholar incarnate.

Williams contextualized the deep criticism of U.S. society in this moral vision with a view of how historic elites had seen the nation and the world. Breaking with the older Marxist–Populist depiction of soulless manipulators, he manifested a sympathetic understanding, at least as far chronologically forward as Herbert Hoover, of their wrestling with America's problems and prospects. After all, their *Weltanshauung* (as Williams was fond of saying), or worldview, had persuaded many Americans in a cross-class bloc of relative or partial consensus.

Here Williams, heir also to the conceptual shortcomings of Progressive historians, ran into difficulties from which even his brightest disciples could not extri-

48. "The Radicalism of Disclosure," *Studies on the Left* 1 (1959), quoted at some length in James Weinstein and David W. Eakins, eds., "Introduction," in *For a New America: Essays in History and Politics from* Studies on the Left, *1959–1967* (New York, 1970), 7–9. The anthology contains many other important documents from *Studies.*

49. Williams, *Contours of American History,* 487.

cate themselves. The older Progressives, most notably the Beards, had always been weak on class, ethnicity, and race. They had viewed the Civil War, in particular, almost purely as a capitalist triumph over agrarianism rather than a struggle for race emancipation with decided black and radical involvement. Populist farmers they could appreciate, but they held a view of immigrant workers close to that of the mainstream historians. Removed peasants, pliable in the hands of new masters, these workers played little role in remaking America. Even unions, in the Progressive historical view, had been scarcely more than mechanisms for the integration of the working class into the industrial state system. In such an analysis, *only* the citizen, acting out of a combination of idealism and self-interest, could change the course of society.

Williams, a former civil rights activist, nevertheless retained the focus on elites. In his view, mercantilism or a colonial system of economic articulation gave way in the early nineteenth century to a feckless expansionism epitomized in the policies of Indian-killer Andrew Jackson. Without betraying their faith in the system, future rulers could not avoid the increasingly destructive effects of such expansionism, inasmuch as they accepted its role as the basic motive force of domestic well-being. The corporation, heir and modern avatar of the expansionism, demanded rivers of blood, the debauch of morals, and even the loss of real military security for the sake of continuation. The Open Door policy, for whose purposes the United States had entered World War I, blocked Third World revolutions; its advocates plotted the "rollback" of world communism, evaded the inevitability of world revolutions, and denied all responsibility in the name of a "freedom" defined by the free market. "Expansionism as escape" from a deeper reality, from the deeper truths of America, ultimately "meant nuclear war."[50]

The *Studies on the Left* intellectuals, excellent analysts of the corporate state, generally tended also to treat the manipulation of the masses by the American elite as smooth and almost (in a perverse sense) admirable. Indeed, when *Studies* moved in 1962 to New York City, it gained a prominent historical influence in Eugene Genovese, soon to be known as a keen interpreter of the southern slavemaster's *mentalité*. Such a perspective worked fairly well intepreting the elite's decisions on matters of foreign policy, where opposition often had little influence. It left much to be desired in portraying social dynamics, especially in periods of mass unrest. *Studies on the Left* broke up as the New Left became politically active in a massive way. The role of radical history remained undetermined.

To say that the weaknesses of this school of history brought another major Madison school into existence would be an exaggeration; but the two took shape almost congruently, interlocking patterns over twenty years of graduate student life.

---

50. Ibid., 484. Italics in the original removed. The fullest of "Williams School" scholarship on domestic policy is Martin Sklar's *The Corporate Reconstruction of American Capitalism, 1890–1916: The Market, the Law and Politics* (Cambridge, England, 1988). Sklar, as he notes in the Preface, originally coined the phrase "Corporate Liberalism" in 1960.

Herbert Gutman is as often associated with the second school as William Appleman Williams was with the first. Gutman's dissertation, begun in the early 1950s
but not finished until 1959, treated the subject that Williams's scholars found most
troubling: labor struggle during Reconstruction. Gutman confronted the thesis of
the Commons school, which had confined labor history to its institutional embod-
iment, by addressing the day-to-day life of a working class in turmoil. He struggled
with statistical and anecdotal evidence to discover subtle working-class and middle-
class alliances in small industrial towns and to reveal the immigrant patterns of
family economy and ethnic culture in the cities.[51]

As *Studies on the Left* found political inspiration in the doings of the British
New Left, so Gutman located methodological inspiration in that New Left's most
public leader. E. P. Thompson, author of *The Making of the English Working Class,*
made a trip to the United States in 1966, visiting Gutman in Buffalo, New York.
Thompson reinforced Gutman's determination to analyze "the processes by which
new subordinate classes are formed."[52] If the neutralization of class conflict through
various elite actions was the essence of the *Studies* effort, Gutman, like his English
colleagues, tried to go back to the beginning of the process and understand class
formation. The corporate state so well criticized by Williams's group might indeed
be the *outcome* of various social conflicts, but the process had been marked by
distinct and sometimes widespread challenges from below—in communities,
churches, and social clubs as well as in factories. Protestants, Catholics, blacks, and
immigrants of every stripe had contested the claims that emerging monopolies
made on the republican heritage. However often that heritage had been violated,
however it was misinterpreted, it retained a powerful meaning for a latter-day
democracy.

This scholarly strategy left hanging the larger political implications *for the
twentieth century,* but it recast the standard radical or Marxist view of nineteenth-
century social movements and, especially, labor movements. Marxists, too, had
focused on institutions, but had emphasized the contribution of movements
(largely led by socialists or, later, communists) that epitomized modern approaches
to class conflict. In so doing, the older Left historians had, like the Commons
school, criticized such movements as the Knights of Labor for being "utopian" or
backward-looking and for wishing to restore vanishing republican values. "What
does it mean," Gutman asked, "to talk about historical forces that workers faced?
We are letting in through the back door a notion of fixed and predetermined his-

51. Gregory Kealey, "Herbert G. Gutman, 1928–1985," *Monthly Review* 37 (May 1986): 23–26; and
E. P. Thompson, "The Mind of a Historian," *Dissent* 35: 493–96. A less pleasant side to the difference
between Gutman and the later *Studies* milieu lay in the bitter conflict (or competition) between Gutman
and Eugene Genovese. See the sensitive treatment of the conflicts in Ira Berlin, "Introduction: Herbert
G. Gutman and the American Working Class," in Berlin, ed., *Power and Culture: Essays on the American Working Class* (New York, 1987), 41–54.

52. Gutman interview, *Visions of History,* 194.

torical development." The notion of an "ideal type" of worker, against which American workers had to be compared, was not only misleading and condescending; it was also *blinding* the serious historian.[53]

The refinement and publication of Gutman's work took twenty years or more. Along the way, from published chapters of his dissertation to essays on black history, he made a solid name for himself. Critics could point to weaknesses, such as overgeneralizations on many ethnic and racial details, and a consequent difficulty in capturing the specifics of consciousness within cultural milieus. But Gutman made a larger point in behalf of the voiceless masses, and by the mid 1970s, his work had become a cutting edge of U.S. social history and certainly of radical history. His "Work, Culture and Society in Industrializing America," which dominated a 1974 issue of the *American Historical Review,* examined case after case of immigrant acculturation and resistance in the work process and the neighborhood, from the 1830s to the 1920s.[54]

Like Thompson, Gutman inspired students and spawned imitators for political as well as intellectual reasons. His efforts also sounded the note of consonance between Thompson's work and long-standing Madison traditions, emphasizing ("privileging," many would say) evidence over abstract theorizing. In some important way, the mixture of empiricism and romanticism in English radicalism had perhaps given Madison's Progressive heritage a new political and scholarly life.[55]

New Left activists would seem, superficially, to be the least likely devotees of Gutman's work. A general indifference (or hostility) to traditional working-class issues and a prevailing belief in what could be called Archie Bunkerism pervaded much New Left thought. But New Left intellectuals included many history students, especially at the graduate level. A residual Marxism and the urgent sense of a need for allies in the general public also conspired to restore working-class studies.

Radical America epitomized these latter tendencies. Although not founded to study working-class history as such, it adopted among its early mentors E. P. Thompson and C. L. R. James. It also sounded notes for "history from the bottom up," a phrase made popular by Jesse Lemisch, a colonial historian of sailors' impact on the American Revolution. James, author of *The Black Jacobins,* and James-influenced Madisonian George Rawick, had stressed a non- or anti-institutional approach to twentieth-century working-class history that favored Gutman-like themes of culture, apparent spontaneity, rituals, and race–class interactions. This

53. Best conveyed in Berlin, "Introduction," in *Power and Culture,* esp. 18–32.

54. Reprinted in *Work, Culture and Society in Industrializing America* (New York, 1977). Ira Berlin notes that this essay was by intent a response to the conservative and individualistic account of immigrant life in *The Uprooted* by Oscar Handlin, who won a Pulitzer Prize with his celebration of American assimilationism. Berlin, "Introduction," in *Power and Culture,* 38.

55. Gutman interview, *Visions of History,* 201. See also Bill Schwarz, " 'The People' in History: The Communist Party Historians' Group, 1946–56," in Richard Johnson et al, eds., *Making Histories: Studies in History-Writing and Politics* (Minneapolis, 1982).

touched a resonant chord with a part of the New Left, the more so as the end of campus rebellions appeared in sight.[56]

By the early and mid 1960s, a wider group of younger Madison radicals had also begun to doubt the ideal of the citizen–scholar.[57] That image relied too greatly on access to mainstream media, an access denied in any serious way to radical dissent. It also assumed a middle-class cultural propriety against which young people had been in apolitical rebellion since at least the advent of rock 'n' roll. The scholar–activist envisioned himself or herself as bringing information directly into the struggle. In Madison in the 1960s, this had been easy. In the wide world, for a short time anyway, a translation seemed possible via community tabloids, local labor movements, socialist women's organizations, and socialist–nationalist black groups. Historical knowledge may not have had the glamour or the immediate usefulness its proponents imagined, but sincerity and hard-working demeanor opened doors and minds to an extraordinary popularization of historical themes.

The doctrine preached had all the virtues of its faults. Redressing (consciously or unconsciously) *Studies on the Left*'s assumptions of successful elite manipulation, it showcased the struggles of the past in order to enhance prospects for struggles of the present. In emphasizing the rank-and-file character of historic movements such as the Congress of Industrial Organizations (CIO) during the unions' prebureaucratic days, it acknowledged the later process of bureaucratization—but only as an interim. Ahead, somewhere and somehow, radical democracy could be reinstated, through new organizations if not existing ones. Analogous lessons might be drawn from historic race and gender movements which had been ignored or regarded with insufficient seriousness. Any future insurgency, in order to succeed, had to offer a platform broad enough for the most oppressed to lead the way. This was the historical politics of the New Left writ large.[58]

---

56. Perhaps the best account of these trends is Jon Wiener, "Madison and the Origins of New Left History," unpublished essay. But see also two *Radical America* anthologies and their introductions: James Green, ed., *Workers' Struggles, Past and Present: a 'Radical America' Reader* (Philadelphia, 1983); and Paul Buhle, ed., *"Radical America:* A Fifteen Year Anthology," *Radical America* 16 (May 1982).

57. The absence of earlier historians was also a factor in the diminution of their influence. By the time of my appearance on campus (fall 1967), Beale and Hesseltine were long gone, Curti and Jensen had recently retired, Harrington had moved into administration (where he found himself, tragically, pitted against student antiwar demonstrators), and Williams was in his final academic year. By the following fall, literally nothing remained of the foreign policy historians' group, although a few years later one of their protégés, Thomas McCormick, would return as a professor. For the duration of the 1960s, nearly all the radical energy *among the history faculty* turned to non-U.S. history.

58. See Buhle, *"Radical America:* a Fifteen Year Anthology," for a variety of this material. By the late 1970s, the development of younger scholars in the seminars of Herbert Gutman and David Montgomery, among others, had outgrown the earlier influences of *Radical America*. Yet the journal has remained a popularizing outlet for women's history in particular. See also Green, "Introduction," *Workers' Struggles*. See also my evaluation of radical historians and other scholars affected most directly by the 1960s experience: "Conclusion," *Marxism in the U.S.*, esp. 264–274.

The hope for a major political connection between former students and the contemporary working class or blue-collar community could not be long sustained. Political tendencies divided or simply dissolved. Publications folded. The larger constituency fell away, no longer hopeful of social transformation in the foreseeable future. During the process of struggle and defeat, what had been distinctly Madisonian tended moreover to merge into wider tendencies and simultaneously narrowed to individual lives, individual experience. The "school tie" had nearly lost its meaning.

But not completely. Over the long haul, the entire experience from Madison to the outward diaspora had, for many participants, its own internal logic. Blue-collar life had many enduring qualities, by no means all of them negative. As the present grew worse, especially in terms of Left political initiatives, the working-class past grew more lustrous and fascinating. For the radical history graduate student of the late 1960s and early 1970s, this suggested an exciting intellectual challenge, a combination of detective-like search for clues and historical confirmation of anticapitalist sentiment. *Radical America,* one of the small handful of surviving journals from the heated 1960s, became, willy-nilly, a chief outlet for politicized versions of this history.

From a maturing but steadfastly radical perspective, class issues seen in this way linked closely with historical questions about the black community and about American women. The emphasis on culture (and where possible, consciousness) at the expense of institutions highlighted the themes this historical study undertook. Politically, in terms of solidifying a scholar–activist network, the larger radical history effort may have succeeded most significantly with these two groups because the short-lived undergraduate boom in black history and the longer boom in women's history met the scholarship and the scholar–teachers just appearing.[59]

Herbert Gutman's initiatives had another important role. "Public history," an idea advanced from the 1960s to the 1980s by the growth of National Endowment for the Humanities (and Arts) funds, urban–industrial museums, and a sort of nostalgic hobbyism stretching from the black community to labor unions, found a special constituency and a leadership core among radical historians. Perhaps few others cared about vanishing industrial memories quite so much as they did. Certainly, forums, exhibits, and above all, video and films made possible a quasi-radical, quasi-political intervention that would have been impossible on any other grounds. For many of these efforts, Gutman served as midwife, impressing on committees the importance of the scholarly and popular-scholarly work proposed for

59. Two contributions had particular importance in classroom use: "Women in American Society," described by Mari Jo Buhle in her essay in this book; and Harold Baron, "The Demand for Black Labor," *Radical America* 5 (January–February 1971). George Rawick's writings on blacks and labor epitomized the bottom–up approach: see "The Historical Roots of Black Liberation," *Radical America* 2 (July–August 1968), an issue of *Radical America* for which Rawick arranged the first appearance of C. L. R. James.

funding. He invested great quantities of his time in the American Social History Project, the producer of classroom films and textbooks.[60]

The overall political impact of these Madisonian initiatives remains difficult to determine. *Studies on the Left* led to the weekly newspaper *In These Times,* the largest-circulation independent socialist tabloid at the end of the 1980s. A certain historical inclination, an uncomfortableness with the New Left's direct-action legacy, and a tone of public argumentation reminded veteran readers of seeds planted long before. By contrast, other historiographical tendencies had become largely the pursuit of individuals or informal groups.

Scholarship, in any case, dominated radicalism after the political decline, as it had dominated radicalism before the mass excitement. The election of long-shunned William Appleman Williams to the presidency of the Organization of American Historians in 1981 offered a vindication, not only of "Cold War revisionist" (or "Corporate Liberalism") historiography but of Madison's decades-long radical history initiative. The truth, the apple, had not fallen so far after all from the tree of Bascom's and LaFollette's legacy.[61]

Perhaps the most persuasive evidence for Williams's importance was the treatment he received from the elite. For his message of revived democracy, Cold War liberal and conservative historians awarded him a crown of thorns. *The Contours of American History,* one of Williams's most powerful books, was greeted by the prestigious Harvard historian Oscar Handlin as an "elaborate hoax," the "literary striving of an unskilled freshman."[62] By the early 1970s, a former student, Robert Maddox, directed the splenetic *The New Left and the Origins of the Cold War* at his former mentor and received enthusiastic, front-page notices in the *New York Times Book Review.* In the 1980s, his most controversial years long past, Williams continued to be placed by the *New Republic* on the "Enemies List." By that time, twenty years after the House Un-American Activities Committee (HUAC) had attempted to get Williams to turn over the incomplete manuscript of *The Contours of American History,* the Internal Revenue Service (IRS) had at last

---

60. The influences of *Radical America* flowed into the *Radical History Review,* founded in 1971, with which it shared personnel and a number of writers. Over the course of the late 1970s and 1980s, *Radical History Review* became the chief outlet for considerations of "public history." The Temple University Press series in which the present volume appears is a further manifestation of the same tendency. See Sue Benson et al., eds., *Presenting the Past* (Philadelphia, 1986). See also, however, recent pages of the *Journal of American History,* edited by Madisonian David Thelen, for a sympathetic mainstream view of public history.

61. Christopher Lasch, "William Appleman Williams on American History," *Marxist Perspectives* 1 (Fall 1978), offered an advance view of Williams's vindication. Michael Meeropol, "Cold War Revisionism," in Mari Jo Buhle, et al, *The Encyclopedia of the American Left* (New York, 1990), overviews the subject.

62. Quoted in William G. Robbins, "William Appleman Williams: 'Doing History Is Best of All. No Regrets,'" in Gardner, *Redefining the Past,* 12–13.

ceased the protracted harassment that frequently followed a HUAC investigation.[63]

In a larger sense, the neoconservative counterattack at the end of the 1980s on women's, Third World, and working-class studies by Allan Bloom (with the assistance of his colleague, the novelist Saul Bellow) and Gertrude Himmelfarb, among others, was aimed at the very tendencies in radical history that Madison scholars had done so much to nurture. The conservatives' anger had intensified as Reaganism failed to displace the radicals from academic prestige and position. The rightward-turned New York intellectuals—now represented mostly in absentia by their younger members from the 1940s, such as Himmelfarb—thirsted for the revenge that eluded them.

Ironically, another scholarly revenge of sorts had by that time already taken place, against not merely radical historians but all historians, via the exile of the discipline from the epicenter of intellectual innovation. By the mid 1980s, semiotic-trained literary (or film and "media") studies had become the vogue, most especially in cutting-edge feminist scholarship. Intellectual mentors now seemed French rather than English or German—Lacan (and his various self-styled successors) more than E. P. Thompson or Karl Marx. In a world where "reality" so evidently lies in the eye of the beholder, and the representation of reality (including the representation or confession of the authorial standpoint) rules, history apparently becomes truly *passé*. The lives and thoughts of the masses, so recently discovered by scholars, seem least interesting for their historicity.[64]

The displacement of history contained at least two large Madison-linked ironies. George Mosse's examination of European cultural history had prompted a considerable body of young scholars to search out Freudianism, and to try out refurbished theories of the old avant-garde that—in a rush of post–World War I creative energy—had sought to abolish history in favor of art, the unconscious, and the present. Second, the historical study of U.S. commercial media and popular cultures (a study facilitated by the cultural ambience of Madison) had led a mini-school of Madisonians to the threshold of postmodern theoretics.[65]

From one standpoint, the limitations of earlier efforts demanded some dra-

63. Robbins, "William Appleman Williams," 13; Bradford Perkins, "'The Tragedy of American Diplomacy': Twenty-Five Years After," in Gardner, *Redefining the Past*, 25–27.

64. Joan Scott, "On Language, Gender, and Working Class History," *International Labor and Working Class History*, no. 32 (Fall 1987); and the symposium "The New Labor History at the Crossroads," esp. George Lipsitz, "The Struggle for Hegemony," and Mari Jo Buhle and Paul Buhle, "The New Labor History at the Crossroads," *Journal of American History* 75 (June 1988). For premonitions of this cultural critique in more straightforward cultural terms, see "cultural" works cited in note 4. See also Paul Buhle, ed., *Popular Culture in America* (Minneapolis, 1987) for essays by a number of Madison writers. And see Ben Sidran, *Black Talk* (New York, 1971), by a Goldberg student and long-time Madison musician, on music and black culture.

65. See "Introduction: George Mosse and Political Symbolism," in Seymour Drescher, David Sabean and Allan Sharlin, eds., *Political Symbolism in Modern Europe: Essays in Honor of George Mosse* (New Brunswick, N.J., 1982).

matic break, but a break with a twist different from the one that the American disciples of Jacques Lacan had in mind. Precisely within a circle of Madison graduates, including Joan Wallach Scott, Daniel Czitrom, George Lipsitz, Paul Breines, and Mari Jo Buhle, the effort to historicize contemporary cultural theory (or render historical study more culturally conscious) has recently taken hold. If semioticians have asserted the futility of documenting experience and have turned instead to consciousness embedded in language, cultural-minded historians insist on a meeting point between social experience and perception of that experience. This was not, to be sure, the meeting point perceived in the dominant discourse, or even by Marxists intent on finding some "objective truth," but something to be found through documentary investigation as well as speculation. Warren Susman had, in fact if not in postmodern vocabulary, been pointing this way for decades.

At the end of the 1980s, the confusing theoretical districts glimmered with at least a negative promise. The palpable decline of the West, "decentering" the familiar assumptions, had opened up possibilities ranging from sheer incoherence to a higher, vastly more democratic dialogue over class, race, gender, and nation. What historians could contribute to that dialogue had to be demonstrated, and convincingly. But their capability to add something of themselves, their scholarship, had been prepared by the decades of iconoclasm and resilient radicalism of Madison's historical training.

Madison Politics, Madison Life

A similar conclusion could be drawn for the avant-garde cultural–political life in Madison beyond the borders of historical discipline. Radical politics in Madison, intertwined with intellectual endeavors, ran the gamut of general hopes, disappointments, and unresolved future possibilities. In Madison, the "Sixties," as a sentiment or political mood, lasted longer than nearly anywhere else. A certain historical self-consciousness became a permanent part of radical discourse.

One might recommence the political saga of the Left with C. Wright Mills. Since his days with Hans Gerth, he had attempted to reinterpret intellectual traditions so as to cope with the bureaucratization of revolutionary and reform hopes of the world. In a section of The New Left, unfinished at his death, he stated his hopes for this intellectual effort:

> We cannot create a left by abdicating our roles as intellectuals to become working class agitators or machine politicians, or by play-acting at other forms of direct political action. We can begin to create a left by confronting issues as intellectuals in our work. . . . We must become internationalist again. For us, today, this means that we, personally, must refuse to fight the cold war. . . .[66]

66. Quoted in Irving Louis Horowitz, "The Unfinished Writings of C. Wright Mills: The Last Phase," Studies on the Left 3 (Fall 1963): 10.

Listen, Yankee may be credited with launching the first of the important Madison proto-New Left movements, Fair Play for Cuba, considered by Saul Landau's essay in this book. Logical steps followed as the evidence mounted up: the Bay of Pigs, the 1965 occupation of the Dominican Republic, and finally the war in Vietnam.

The importance of these issues for undergraduates grew slowly, and then caught fire all at once. Beyond intellectual circles, campus rallies for some years came and went, mostly crowds of a few dozen to a few hundred huddling around a speaker's podium or marching together to the capitol. Ironically, the only mass student disruption in memory had been a fraternity-row riot in 1958, powered by beer rather than political outrage. The 1967–1970 demonstrations described in the essays that follow had a precedent, if at all, in the antiwar student strikes of the 1930s, but perhaps not even there. Demonstrations against campus recruitment by the Dow Chemical Company, first in January 1967 and then again in October of that year, encompassed a political practice and principle that was distinctly new. The "black strike" of winter 1969, initiated by black undergraduates and their white allies to prompt university commitment to minority enrollment and community issues, offered a unique expression of consciousness in a school (and community) of minimal nonwhite presence. The Teaching Assistants Association (TAA) strike of 1970, in a city with few traditions of labor militancy, capped off the era of militancy with fervent hopes for broader mass coalitions in society outside the university.[67]

One of the poignant themes in the documents that follow is the radical disagreement over this politics, its strategic and tactical implications. From the New Left standpoint, simple exigencies compelled a break with long-standing traditions. LaFollette Progressivism and its liberal successors had been parliamentary; journalism, public debates, congressional and state legislative testimony by experts, and of course elections had provided the necessary means for expression. Direct action possessed rich traditions in America, but with few incidents in Madison's past. By the mid 1960s, civil rights demonstrations and antiwar meetings had begun to melt the insulation of campus intellectuals, so much so that the cozy prestige of the talk fest faded. Revered professors were elevated and removed almost to the status of intellectual monuments; students talked in a reverential but distanced sense about the "historic role" of figures such as Williams, even while attending their lectures. Then again, faith in the university slipped as the issue of academic freedom became less important than the actions taken with that freedom. Univer-

---

67. Despite considerable efforts, I have been unable to locate appropriate interviewees on the mixture of intellectual and political issues in the black strike, as I have nonwhite interviewees or essayists for the volume generally. I wish to thank Rhett Jones, on campus 1964–1969, for an interview on the self-perceived scatteredness of black campus life (especially among graduate students), even during periods of high militancy.

The Teaching Assistants Association also remains little discussed in print. An unpublished paper by Henry Haslach has helped me greatly in understanding the issues.

sity complicity with the defense and intelligence establishments became more embarrassing (or enraging) as American military adventures escalated. Unbeknown to all but the most perceptive observers, the stage for confrontation over the nature of the university was being set.

In the angry struggles to follow, means and ends frequently separated the intellectually like-minded. Sympathetic professors and even administrators found themselves in impossible positions. Symptomatically, the *Capital Times* felt compelled to denounce the campus antiwar activity its militant editorials had prepared the way for. On the other side, student protesters often seemed indifferent to the past contributions and precious achievements of the Wisconsin Progressives.

In the face of hysteria and divisiveness, however, the value of ideas and the milieu supporting them did not disappear. Intellectual work, most of all the study of history, lost none of its charm. Incoming graduate students and undergraduates struggled to establish new intellectual priorities for themselves and their generation. Certainly, many professors and some radical graduate students viewed the confrontational atmosphere as vitiating to learning. Perhaps it was, but never as much as the apathy and unrefined careerism dominating most other eras. For a brief time, thousands of students discussed ideas that otherwise had been confined to small circles of devotees and critics.

Indeed, the virtually continuous student strikes from 1967 to 1970 might be seen as a climax, amid national crises, to earlier Madison radical trends. The conventional wisdom of the 1980s, articulated by Senator Daniel P. Moynihan, is that the irresponsible protesters of the 1960s—radical and destructive outsiders to legitimate scholarly dialogue—impelled a beset American public toward the Reagan revolution (or counterrevolution). Sadly, more than a few commentators on the Left have joined in a veritable orgy of movement regret that threatens at times to overshadow larger regrets about the U.S. role in Vietnam and the campus contributions of administrators, ROTC programs, and scholars to the war. Unquestionably, there is a grain of truth in Moynihan's contention. A large number of liberalism's prestigious intellectuals subsequently moved to the Right on race, social policy, and a variety of other issues. There, save for a few momentary reversals, they have remained. Certainly the American loss in Southeast Asia, one indication of the gradual decline of empire, galvanized conservatism. But perhaps the larger premise of the argument is incorrect.

Kenneth Keniston, the closest academic observer of student radicals, argued that student dissenters not only enjoyed a *better* relationship with their parents than any previous generation but also took their studies, in the broad sense of intellectual growth, more seriously.[68] Appearances and publicity notwithstanding, the

68. Kenneth Keniston, *Young Radicals* (New York, 1968), 104; for reading habits of student radicals, see also Milton Lawrence Mankoff, "The Political Socialization of Radicals and Militants in the Wisconsin Student Movement during the 1960s," Ph.D. dissertation, University of Wisconsin, 1970, 153–154.

rebellion of Madison's youth in the 1960s was never so much generational as institutional or, even better, anti-institutional. The radicals of the 1950s, children of the Old Left, had, after all, erected the banners that their successors held high, not only political ones but cultural ones as well. Everything best in the historic campus experience led to expectations of a utopian leap, whenever great change seemed possible in the wider America. Naturally, many hoped that the campus would lead in the transformation. A strategy based on that premise might have been badly flawed, as several contributors to this volume argue. But looking back from twenty years of drift toward thermonuclear or environmental catastrophe, this youthful uprising seems also to have been a badly needed utopian eruption in industrial society at large. Was the moment squandered, or was it doomed by the overwhelming forces that took their revenge on the ideals of the age?

As this book closes chronologically around 1970, utopian striving and industrial conflict merged in the Teaching Assistants Association strike on campus that sought an unprecedented participation of students in the pedagogical process. Nothing less than a massive social transformation would have compelled the university to accept these conditions, and it did not accept them. From here on, campus radicalism became self-consuming.

A climate of violence mirrored, in a small but nevertheless damaging way, the massive violence America directed at Southeast Asia. Denied institutional power, segments of radicals turned their rage on available targets. Rock throwing ("trashing") became an expression of political rage. A small incendiary group, thought to be well tracked by the FBI, went another large step down this road, bombing the Army Math Research Center and causing the death of a researcher. This act, as George Mosse points out in his essay, had the characteristically idigenous quality of Americans from Left to Right taking violence into their own hands. The tragic fatality had been less than that in any one village in any one day of fighting in Vietnam. But the political climate of Madison changed overnight. Ultra-radicalism was reduced to words.

Ironically, the collapse of the violent Left redounded to the benefit of the mainstream's leftward edges. The same student milieu that reputedly torched a campus–neighborhood supermarket whose creation (and whose management attitudes toward students) had been seen as hateful, also elected Paul Soglin to the City Council.

Soglin, a former U.S. history graduate student, possessed the smooth edge that the community Left and its liberal allies craved. Madison mayor from 1973 to 1979 and elected again in 1989, he (and his adept staff of former anti-war protesters) crafted a coalition of students, liberals, and labor. Empowered, Soglin's team did much to effect a caring municipal social policy, from ecological efforts to funded daycare. They succeeded even more, perhaps, in the field of image making. Soglin's early administration, it was widely believed, had a foreign policy independent of the U.S. government. It welcomed ties with Havana, for one thing. (Only Burlington, Vermont, of the late 1980s, with political maverick Bernie Sanders in charge, rivaled the Soglin–Madison era in this declaration of peace with anti-imperial Latin Americans.) Meanwhile, Soglin's mustachioed police ceased to harass casual marijuana users. Madison's gay community flourished; one of its most prominent figures was a nightclub operator for whose "Oldies" nights Mayor Soglin sometimes served as disk jockey. But, to the outsider, perhaps the numerous women's softball teams made the deepest impression. Counter culture had been organized and reconciled with regional ways. Somehow, in the dragged-out and individualist 1970s, Madison made an adjustment acceptable to many segments of the unreformed "Sixites" community.

The fun finally ended. In a sense, Soglin's Madison had been too successful. Known as one of the several most appealing places in the U.S. to live and work, Madison became a magnet for new white-collar industry. Real estate boomed, aided by the continual expansion of the university and the state apparatus. The political leadership of a moneyed and decidedly antiradical sector consolidated its positions, and waited its chances.

The break took place in a seemingly unlikely sector for middle-class Madison, the labor movement. The *Capital Times,* edited in part by former radicals of the 1930s, increasingly felt economic pressure from one of the paper's owners, a conglomerate. Faced with a strike threat against attempts to automate, the paper locked out its union employees and provoked a lengthy conflict. Widely admired writers, along with decades-long veterans of the production staff, suddenly looked beyond their picket-line to armed guards and attack dogs. A boycott by many legatees of the LaFollette tradition followed, simultaneous with the attempt to fashion a new, progressive daily even as the *Capital Times* had been created two-thirds of a century earlier. This time, the capital requirements were too great. After twenty-seven months, the *Madison Press Connection,* published by the strikers, folded. In more than one sense, monopoly emerged triumphant. James Rowen, Soglin's chosen successor and a supporter of the strike, was opposed in his 1979 mayoral campaign by the entirety of Madison's major commercial media. A little known university professor, with ample funds from banking and business institutions, narrowly defeated him. The Left would not come close again to capturing municipal power for another decade.[69]

Pro-business, politically centrist city administrations to follow presided over a Madison transformed by sprawling suburbs and high-tech corporate headquarters dependent on massive automobile traffic. The five lakes that once girdled Madison with an arcadian beauty seemed increasingly to take on the aspect of traffic islands. Within a decade, the corporate strategy had over-reached itself, as public subsidies to downtown business developers hiked tax rates despite drastically declining city

69. Historical description on this subject, beyond the journalistic level, is scarce, but see my interview with Dave Wagner, a political leader of the strike newspaper *Madison Press Connection,* toward the end of the 1970s: "Workers' Control and the News: The Madison, Wisconsin, Press Connection," *Radical America* 14 (July–August 1980). I have also drawn on an unpublished account he provided of Madison journalism in the 1970s.

services. The 1989 mayorality contest coincided with a referendum on a proposed $92 million convention center, avidly supported by the major media. Soglin returned from retirement to campaign for fiscal restraints and controls on further growth, and won handily as the convention center went down to defeat.[70]

No one could say that the early radicalism (or radical liberalism) had triumphed, although the radical Labor Farm party's election of three candidates to the Common Council could form the basis of a sustained progressive bloc. A revived Madison Left needed a national context of vibrant social movements. Yet the city of Madison nevertheless remained, even apart from Soglin's return to power, a rather progressive spot, and a potential center of resistance to a new U.S. war in Central America. The Madison labor movement, long the victim of conservative building trades domination, became in the 1970s and 1980s a springboard for labor progressivism. David Newby, once the leader of a now much-reduced Teaching Assistants Association, came to power in the Madison Federation of Labor and continued on to the post of secretary-treasurer of the Wisconsin AFL-CIO. At the university, meanwhile, and in the face of all the difficult problems at hand, the balancing act between fearless free-thought and institutional accommodation survived as a perpetual academic–political vaudeville. Despite all the changes, Madison remained Madison, as new students—some of them the children of contributors to this volume—can testify.

Of course, the "big questions" posed by Madison's radical democrats become ever more relevant. The very basis for public life flounders in an increasingly class-divided society. Generations of corporate (and citizen) irresponsibility take their toll on an endangered natural environment. Meanwhile, the conspiracy to prevent public attention and engagement with foreign policy decisions is no secret at all, perhaps not even a surprise to a jaded public. William A. Williams's question grows more pressing: Can Americans, threatened most by the prospect of collective self-destruction, look inside themselves, search their traditions and their collective conscience, and make the choice for a less destructive, more cooperative order? If they can, they will owe something to the spirit of Madison rebels.

A few words on method. Fitting disparate stories together into a coherent pattern has surely been the most difficult task of this book. The collective approach to the problem of historical memory has its peculiar qualities, outside any fixed genre. The shape of particular contributions here depends less on some absolute standard than on the mentality of the writer and the circumstances of the writing.

Many of the contributions grew initially out of interviews that, as Sandro Portelli has argued, tend generally to emphasize a life "story" organized around

---

70. Richard Broun, "Left Turn in Madison as 'Red Mayor' is Elected," *The Guardian,* April 26, 1989. Also see the vivid nonscholarly account of local neighborhood and environmental degradation in Elizabeth Bardwell, *More Is Less: the Case Study of a City that May Be Growing Too Big for its Citizens' Good* (Madison, 1974), written by a prominent local political activist. Regrettably, nearly all pessimistic predictions have proved accurate.

some special sensibility that the interviewee, consciously or unconsciously, develops.[71] More or less straightforward essays, written at the editor's suggestion, articulate a similar coming-to terms with the writer's own passage from youth to adulthood, a recollection at various points, nostalgic, regretful, and cautiously celebrative. Still others, commentaries really upon the passing scene decades earlier, reflect the ambivalence of paths not taken by movements whose activists should have known (and done) better. Altogether, these encounters in exile reflect the exile of the spirit from a particular geopolitical site that has passed into history. At their most hopeful, they also reflect a psychic end of exile, a powerful sense of imaginative return.

In the folktales of a vanished medieval world, Walter Benjamin noted, death gave life its meaning, a summing up and a final note to experience.[72] We might almost say the same about two interviewees, the late Herbert Gutman and Warren Susman. A third, George Rawick, hangs between life and death even as these words are written. Rawick and Susman, who had suffered serious illness, spoke to me as if from that classic life's end vantage point. Gutman talked in haste, yet attempted to sketch out that part of his youthful past most neglected by his admirers and critics, so as to connect that hidden past to his scholarly present. The trio symbolize, I believe, the brilliance of a generation doomed to far less than they might have accomplished, doomed by the Cold War specter cast upon their younger years, and by the inability or unwillingness of the academic mainstream to comprehend the political essence of their scholarly commitment. Yet the three were *not* doomed, in the sense that they gave themselves to their work of democratic, radical scholarship, and they achieved great results. They contributed more perhaps than they appreciated, directly and indirectly, to the bearing of the undefeated radical scholar of the 1960s to 1980s, and to the wider perception among an educated public that "history" means above all the lives of ordinary people. This book is partly a monument to them and to their late colleague, the European historical giant Harvey Goldberg, too personally modest even to grant an interview.

71. Alessandro Portelli, "'The Time of My Life': Functions of Time in Oral History," *International Journal of Oral History* 2 (November 1981): 165–166.

72. Walter Benjamin, *Illuminations*, ed. and trans. Hannah Arendt (New York, 1969), 94–95.

Part One
Cold War Days

1 The Smoking Room School of History

WARREN SUSMAN

"By the time [Susman's] *Culture as History* appeared in 1984," writes popular literature scholar Michael Denning, "not only had his arguments and speculations come to shape American cultural studies, but the representative figures he wrote and spoke on . . . had become a sort of counter-canon of American studies."[1] And so it had. Susman introduced popular films into the college curriculum at Rutgers, where he spent nearly all his distinguished career, when this practice was considered daring. He trained his graduate students to write creatively about large areas of American culture, although (or perhaps *because*) he had difficulty writing out his multitudinous insights. Once his innovations had become commonplace, however, Susman's parental role in them grew indistinct. That was a personal tragedy, compensated in part by the wide reception given *Culture as History,* a volume of essays coaxed from him by the editors at Pantheon.

Denning says further that "if we wish to understand American culture less as the story of the hegemony of the middle class, than as the condensation of class conflicts—at turns mediated, or displaced by the new industries of culture—then we must pay close attention to Susman's practice of cultural history."[2] This most elusive element of American popular culture was also elusive in Susman's work. But he strived to deal with the difficult questions. In the interview that follows, conducted with Susman in New Brunswick, New Jersey, and written out in essay form, Susman subtly shifted the subject away from himself. Yet he speaks vividly about the collective Madison experience.

1. Michael Denning, "Class and Culture: Reflections on the Work of Warren Susman," *Radical History Review,* no. 36 (1986): 110.

2. Ibid., 110–111.

43

Madison was eye-opening for eastern intellectuals because it forced them to come into contact with Progressive, native traditions. The Madison campus was in the proximity of the statehouse. You couldn't avoid what was going on there. We were part of the last remnants of that old Progressivism in action. We knew the LaFollette family. And we learned practical politics in opposing McCarthy: The more one attacked him, the more one publicized him. I was on a committee to expose McCarthy. We used to have a twenty-four-hour radio program where people could ask questions. My job was to handle the sound system. In state after state I would take the calls. We were interviewed by the national media. We had trouble getting anyone to run against McCarthy. We spent a lot of time fighting him— and we lost badly.

I remember walking into town on Sunday morning, and seeing college students going to church. I was mortified. Incredulous. They did wild things on weekends, but Sunday to church. But I didn't feel strange being Jewish. There were lots of Jews around.

We were pretty solidly middle class; we had ambition, we valued intellectual life. For culture, access to Chicago was in some ways more important than Madison. We went to museums there; we went down to take in music, especially jazz.

The dichotomy between eastern intellectuals and midwestern Progressives is crucial in understanding [William Appleman] Bill Williams, in understanding the Wisconsin commitment to Charles Beard and the indifference to European history. We were enormously influenced by [C. Wright] Mills, and hardly at all by labor traditions and labor history, even though Herb [Gutman] did work on those strikes.

The History Department's big interest was in civil rights and civil liberties. There was always one prelim question, probably written by Bill Hesseltine, about the use of the army to deal with American internal political questions. The fear of totalitarianism came together with a fear of excessive government power of any kind. The department was rife with people who had been assaulting the Internal Revenue Service, restrictive city ordinances, and so on. One time a cop came to Hesseltine's class, and Hesseltine made the man wait out in the hall. The Police State was not going to invade his classroom!

On the strong side, this was a heroic 1950s attempt to make use of history so as to avoid war at all costs and to reach the men in power, as Beard and a few other historians had done, testifying before congressional committees or consulting with political leaders. The fear of war was rampant. [Merle] Curti and others studied how wars had corrupted the internal life of the nation. This concern also made for a sense of intellectual discovery—Williams discovering America, almost like Columbus. And there was also Gutman, working from [Howard] Beale's assessment of the breakdown of Reconstruction. [He] was very Madisonian in discovering data nobody else knew about, a Beardian piling up of data and local study, the way [Frederick Jackson] Turner and Curti had done. Until Curti's *Trempeleau*

County, the manuscript census hadn't been used since the early d
economists.

It made for a tremendously permissive atmosphere, with no s
great teachers. Everything, all the sources you wanted, were in the W
Historical Society, and everyone would meet there. Downstairs, on the
smoking room, we would gather, like some kind of magic, four or five times a
day. We would sit, talk, bring the books we found, with no faculty member present except, occasionally, Hesseltine. Those were the best talks I ever knew. I called
the group the Smoking Room School of American History.

But the Progressive history had no cultural depth. It assumed, in Beardian
fashion, that everything could be situated in terms of narrow "interest," not even
class interest; even more simplistic, that elites in particular get what they want,
rationally. Its fascination with elites tended to equate power with intelligence.

The problem of American history by the late 1920s and 1930s had been the
failure of anything in the American tradition to explain what was going on in the
world. Reaching out for an explanation, only European Marxism made sense—but
not enough sense. The failure to make sense of American phenomena in American
terms haunted historians. In that context, Beard and Turner looked like geniuses.
And Vann Woodward looked like a revolutionary by being just a little more
sophisticated. But Turner and Beard and Woodward do not really *explain* anything; the end of the frontier doesn't explain anything. Nothing explains what
happens after political Progressivism fails. If Progressivism is the fulfillment of the
old view, then afterward you have nothing. And we had nothing, in that sense.

We were all good at doing critiques of Turner and Beard. And we had a
terrible hunger for theory. The professors themselves were also tremendously interested in these questions, but embarrassed to admit it. Hesseltine talked about
"sociable and ineffectual history." We read what Frankfurt School material we
could get our hands on, mostly later. We learned a lot from Paul Farmer, a former
Marxist turned cynic, who taught the basic historiographical course.

Studies on the Left, which had the same desperate groping to get greater substance for what we did, was a continuation of what the best of Progressivism had
been. It was a muckraking journal on a higher level, to expose the corporate capitalists—even though the editors knew better than that. But *Studies* also was more
European than most American intellectual work; it had a kind of interest in social
relations that was more European. Although it took positions on many things, it
was not a call to picket the corner grocery store.

I can't tell you how important I found *Studies* even when I was upset with
it; it was terribly important simply because it existed. *Studies* sought to make scholarship activist without making it vulgar. It was thin because people were graduate
students, and who do you know working at that level who gets published? But it
was remarkable for the number of things that continue to have value. It asked
interesting questions. Its editors were relatively cosmopolitan intellectuals. The

reviews were good, a typical graduate student task. Its concentration on history blocked out many other fascinating people and currents, even on the local scene. It had little interest in arts and in culture. As a student publication it didn't last very long, but neither did publications on other campuses at the time, *New University Thought* or *Root and Branch*. That phase ended for *Studies* when Jimmy Weinstein took it east.

Of course, *Studies* owed its existence to the fact that there was not much political work to do. But Bill Williams had also created an intellectual excitement that would not otherwise have existed. He made intellectual work *seem* very important.

2 Learning About History

HERBERT G. GUTMAN

So much has been written about Herbert Gutman, in this volume and elsewhere, that little more is required but reflections on the following interview. *Power and Culture* (1987), with its compelling introduction and exhaustive bibliographical guide, supplies a near-biographical abundance of details. Herb Gutman seemed perpetually too busy (and perhaps a bit shy) to speak about himself at length; this interview was conducted in the CUNY Graduate Center cafeteria and amended in a private session in Rhode Island. Gutman's friends, students, and followers all wish now that he had further elaborated on one point little discussed elsewhere: his radical coming to consciousness and its continuing role in his life.

Mostly, I view my Madison experiences from 1950 to 1953 as genuinely liberating. My parents belonged to the International Workers Order, Jewish Division, the Jewish People's Fraternal Order. They were not Communist party members but [were] sympathetic. I grew up in the Yiddish Old Left and spent many summers at Camp Kinderland, part of the closed little Left world of New York. To protect myself in Queens, where we lived, I think I constructed a fantasy world out of my summer life as a way to avoid the ugly Queens reality.

I became political in the Henry Wallace campaign. I was deeply moved by it and have no regrets. I drifted about that time into a brief, intense if uneventful involvement with the orthodox communist movement. I also had a splendid undergraduate education. Then I studied at Columbia with Richard Morris and Richard Hofstadter for my master's. Drawn to the railroad strikes of 1877 by my radical preoccupations, I still knew very little American history.

My father-in-law used to say that when he came to the United States, he felt free for the first time. So he joined the Socialist party. Something like that happened to me in Madison. I began doing serious reading about Soviet Russia, especially books by its Left critics. Moreover, the Old Left at that moment had no real Madison presence. It spent much of its time in wasteful self-criticism. It looked inward, and had become a caricature of a serious political movement. It drove people away. In New York City, that had become clear. In Madison, it was banal and ridiculous. My Madison years were spent drifting away from the Old Left as a consequence of many experiences, often contradictory, among fellow graduate students and teachers. I was still attracted to the domestic *issues* pressed by the traditional Left and the historical questions posed by nondogmatic Marxists. Some of that still survives in my work.

At Columbia, I had started writing about the American working class. The Madison years made me understand that all my Left politics had not prepared me to understand America west (and even east) of the Hudson River. Not in the slightest. None of my preconceptions held up. The Progressive historians, my fellow graduate students, and the undergraduates helped me unload my dogmatic blinders.

Howard Beale, Merrill Jenson, and especially Merle Curti—that gentle and thoughtful man—offered me and others a critical American history, an analytical history that was deeply empirical. It was not strongly theoretical, not cosmopolitan. It worshipped Beard and Turner but was not deterministic. All three of my Madison guides were relatively new to Wisconsin, and they had revived the Progressive tradition in their own way. Jensen was already recognized as the last "Beardian" scholar of great consequence, with important fresh work on the constitutional period. Beale had been working on *Charles A. Beard,* a commemorative volume begun in the 1940s that higher-ups had tried to suppress because of Beard's opposition to World War II. The book finally appeared in 1954 with essays by Curti, Hofstadter, Max Lerner, Eric Goldman, and others, and a forward by Justice Hugo Black. I was a research assistant for Curti's essay on Beard as a historical critic.

Curti himself, of course, had written the history of American peace movements, a splendid history of education and a Pulitzer Prize-winning work on democratic thought; he would soon be doing his study of grass-roots democracy in Trempeleau County, Wisconsin. I was also very fortunate to have a Reconstruction seminar with Professor John Hope Franklin. He was the first black to teach history at the University of Wisconsin. I had never read Reconstruction historiography and it was a nightmare to me. I believed I could come back to that subject sometime later in life.

History was essentially past politics to these scholars. Grass-roots Progressives themselves, they had no patience with Stalinist "popular" vulgarizations. And they—all of them—had a deep commitment to civil liberties, to open discussion, in a time of liberal surrender and communist duplicity. That counted a great deal when so many intelligent people surrendered so easily to the 1950s and the "New America."

But they also remained "professors" in the old sense. There was little intimacy with the graduate students. I learned in a more active way from my own peers. There was a camaraderie of a liberal-Left sort that included Warren Susman (we used to joke that Warren had been born reading the *American Historical Review*), Bill Preston, Pete Forcey, and a few others. Susman pushed hardest. He was the most intelligent historian I had yet encountered. William A. Williams visited in the summer of 1952 or 1953. I was his teaching assistant in his introductory course. I heard him working out an alternative radical critique to sterile Stalinism. Many of us liked the good jazz then playing in Madison, and my wife and I went often with the Williamses. At that time, we shared a kitchen and a bathroom with two other couples, one from Rockford and the other from Eau Claire. We had to learn about America.

There were a small number of black graduate students. They made quite an impression on me. One of the ways the southern states got around the provision for separate but equal facilities was to send their black graduates north, to the Big Ten schools and elsewhere. Madison must have had forty or fifty in those days. I made two close friends, Vernon Jordan and George Cunningham, who must have been the first black graduate students in history since Benjamin Quarles had taken his Ph.D. in the 1930s. Anyone with any sense listening to them and others debate whether and when to return south would have known there was going to be a civil rights movement very soon.

Finally, we had some very lively undergraduates. The Ford Foundation began an experiment for smart kids to be brought out of high school so they could learn something before being sent to fight in the army. This group of real youngsters included Henry Wortis, Marty Sklar, Jeffry Kaplow, and Arnie Lieber. They were very funny, wonderful, free in their spirits, radical but a whole separate generation from the Old Left true believers I had known. I remember one of their apartments had a laundry room—they just threw their dirty clothes into the room—with a photo of Marilyn Monroe on the ceiling. Some of them were in my quiz sections. After I left Madison, they and others revived radicalism.

Apart from this group, I was especially taken up with the Italian-Americans from Kenosha and Racine, all from families that worked in automobile and mattress factories. I remember taking a group of them to see the film *Open City*. They had never seen an Italian film before. It was extraordinary watching them seeing Anna Magnani for the first time. I was learning more about America.

All this adds up. Selig Perlman—with whom I studied—wrote me a note saying that being an historian was an Anglo-Saxon profession. It was like being a literature professor. He urged that I do the safe thing and become an economist. Working class history was then taught in economics departments. I respected Perlman but rejected his advice. Too much happened in Madison. For me, Madison had opened new visions about the past, the present and the future.

3   WASP and Dissenter

WILLIAM PRESTON

William Preston is the village atheist in a stubbornly benighted land. He has been chair of the History Department at John Jay College, New York City, for some years, and is the author of *Aliens and Dissenters: Federal Suppression of Radicals, 1903–33* (1963).

By May 1950, they'd announced the teaching assistantships for the next year at Berkeley. I could have my assistantship if I signed a loyalty oath. So I basically said, "Up yours!" and headed for Madison.

I'd gone to the University of Chicago years earlier for a summer, which, given my WASP background, was like saying, "To hell with the Ivy League." Going to Chicago was to break away. I spent three months there, and I was psychologically ready to kill a Nazi. It was 1942, and I volunteered for the most colorful branch of the service, running around in tanks in Kentucky and Arizona. I turned down Officer Candidate School to be an ordinary soldier. Later I was part of the special assault unit on Omaha Beach, D-Day. My unit eventually was mostly wiped out. I made it through only until July 8 when I just about got killed.

The army probably fed my identification with the underdog. I got a strong dose of ethnic variety, in a unit recruited mostly from the Far West and Midwest. I learned something about class, a lot about stupidity in authority, and came out with a very resistant attitude toward higher powers.

I remember in that time also talking with my uncle, Roger Baldwin, the founder of the ACLU [American Civil Liberties Union], and Aunt Evelyn. My father had not been friendly with them for a good many years because he disapproved of their "radicalism." My aunt, Evelyn Preston, was the black sheep of our family. She had given away family jewels to the Communist party, and she married Roger and they had this nude beach up in Martha's Vineyard.

We had very little to do with the Baldwins when I was young. But one night, as our army unit was going through New York to sail for Europe, my sister said, "We're having dinner at Father's tonight." And there were Roger and Evelyn. And Roger asked me all sorts of questions about the army. I then recognized what he was like. So when I came back from the war, I got to know them.

When I went to Berkeley after graduating from Columbia University, Roger came out and introduced me to some important Free Speech people like Alexander Meikeljohn, the famous First Amendment figure. I told him that reading Big Bill Haywood's autobiography had turned me on. Roger said, "You ought to go up to Seattle and interview Ralph Chaplin [Industrial Workers of the World union leader], the old Wobbly." I did go to see him. And later I dedicated my *Aliens and Dissenters* to Roger.

At Berkeley I was rather disaffected. I had little contact with the professors, I felt lost in this big institutional program, the History Department was disappointing. There was a political resistance to the state loyalty oath and an additional regent's oath, but the major resistance was in the lower ranks, and not much at all in history. I wasn't sorry to leave.

Madison, I felt, was the one place with a tradition of freedom. I arrived in August 1950, and was met by the History Department with a "Welcome, glad to have you!" They obviously knew; but my refusal of the oath was not an issue in Madison. In fact, I was awarded two university fellowships. There was a certain amount of discussion concerning my master's from Columbia and the courses I'd taken at Berkeley. What *did* I want to do?

Most of my development, I believe, came in talks with Herb Gutman, Warren Susman, Pete Forcey, and others in the "Smoking Room School of History." Meeting them was a real intellectual occasion. I consider myself particularly lucky to have shared a class where Warren was the brilliant assessor of interpretations. I didn't think a lot about what our political positions were, but history was the most exciting activity in the world.

We were learning from [Howard] Beale, [Merrill] Jensen, and [Merle] Curti. We were also pushing beyond them, to a newer history. The professors used to feel—and Beale would say it—"You're a monk." They practically regarded my wife and two kids as inappropriate encumbrances. I had come to join a guild and should have no diversions.

And we were up to our asses in papers, seminars, and work. This was the first time I had ever run into such real intensity. If we resisted, it was perhaps because some of us were veterans. Once you've been pushed around by the army, the academic system becomes something you feel you can resist. We were older, more mature, and were not going to play the role of good, dutiful students.

On the other hand, the professors also understood our excitement and encouraged us. On one occasion, I recall, they scheduled a mini-conference with a paper by Susman as the centerpiece and me as one of the critics. It was entitled "Historians and Contemporary Crises," with a major attack on Arthur Schlesinger, Jr.'s, apologetic Cold War tract *The Vital Center* from a more Left, critical approach. We put the Red Scare in historical perspective, and more, at these conferences.

When we went away to historians' conventions and sensed the dead wood all around, we truly appreciated Madison. Curti, [Bill] Hesseltine, Beale, and others had a dedication to the profession. Jensen's intensity, his determination to carve out a whole new view of economics in the early republic, made a deep impression. But aside from Jensen, none of them really created a school of historical interpretation around himself, as Williams was to do. Beale, for instance, at the time was trying to get the Mississippi Valley Historical Society to open up its convention to blacks, by fighting out the issue of discrimination in cities like Louisville and Cincinnati where facilities were still segregated. But Beale was an odd man, and by the time I came to Madison, he had done his academic freedom books and was doing Theodore Roosevelt, whom I didn't respect at all. Incidentally, discrimination against women wasn't even on the agenda yet; there weren't many women in graduate school at the time.

With the help of the Smoking Room School, I found my way. But now I wonder—was it predestined? Programmed from my origins?

I had worked with Harold Serrett in my master's seminar at Columbia, and he, for some reason, wanted us to take up the history of religious movements. I picked the Mormons; even then, I identified with outsiders, and through them got a good sense of the political economy, here the giant trusts trying to bring a Utah sugarbeet industry under their control. Similarly, on arriving in Madison the Industrial Workers of the World (IWW) seemed a wonderful topic. I wanted to do the IWW history, but I could not get the kind of documentation I was hoping for. So I decided to come at it from the other end—government records—and the dissertation shifted to a new, different, and more exciting kind of history: the history of government suppression of a radical group. In the two years I wised up intellectually in Madison, I got ready for a frontier of my own. I was the first historian to use Department of Justice records to deal with repression of a left-wing union.

Those two years in the archives were, historically, my most exciting in the sense that the Wobblies' antiauthoritarian stance, their underdog attitudes, and free-speech attitude, appealed to my unconscious defiance of my own past. I was probably acting out a rebellion in a safe way, also settling a score for what happened in Berkeley.

After Madison, I got stuck at Denison University, when it was a small Baptist campus, volunteering as coach of the unofficial hockey team, siding with these athletic outsiders and playing for the fun of it. In 1967–1968 we had a peace movement and a strike over the Black Studies issue. I resigned; there was some follow-up, blackballing, that followed me around. Warren Susman said I would go down in history as the "Great Resigner." I then wrote a piece for the American Historical Association, saying you have to investigate the circumstances where people *don't get* jobs, not merely where they get fired. (My own destiny was John Jay College.)

Until Bill Williams asked me to head up the Committee on Freedom of Information and Access, I had never felt comfortable at a historians' convention. The Organization of American Historians then set up a Committee on Access to help historians fight government classification and secrecy. Perhaps that is another result of the Smoking Room School of History. Now I'm president of the Fund for Open Information and Accountability. FOIA began by forcing the release of some of the Rosenberg files; it has won an injunction against FBI destruction of files; we want the Freedom of Information Act to work.

Before Madison, I was "on the road." Madison brought it all together for me and made it coherent. I think I've been consistent to that vision ever since.

4 I Dissent

GEORGE RAWICK

George Rawick is, as he once told me in an interview, the descendent of radical rabbis and failed businessmen, also a personal survivor of Old Left movements that succeeded in their failure by planting seeds for the future. Unlike many contributors to this volume, Rawick is not a Madison celebrator. He is a born dissenter, from Madison as much as from his family or from the Left as currently constituted. He was expelled from the Young Communist League on trumped-up "white chauvinism" charges and later became one of the world's most distinguished scholars of Afro-American history, editor of nineteen volumes of slave narratives and one lucid monograph, *Slavery from Sun-Down to Sun-Up*. He was a premature New Leftist, thinking political and scholarly thoughts in the 1950s and early 1960s that would take a generation for others to work out. For his successors above all, he has been a beloved teacher and comradely guide—in the Madison tradition of the kindly curmudgeon. At a number of universities, especially Oakland University and the University of Missouri in St. Louis, he has taken many young radicals in tow. According to his own account, he may be the Madison exception that proves the rule. Yet the impression he left behind in Madison belies even that generalization. He shaped, and was doubtless shaped by, this reputedly unhappy moment of personal history.

I, for one, never found the Holy Land to be located in the Department of History of the University of Wisconsin–Madison, 1951–1957; particularly not in American history. Nevertheless, the university in general was a much more liberal institution than my undergraduate school, Oberlin College, which seemed to me to be the "world center" of hypocrisy, racism, anti-Semitism, and premature McCarthyite intimidation of leftist students and faculty. At least Wisconsin was strong enough to resist almost totally the McCarthyite onslaught, and the Wisconsin senator had less clout at Wisconsin than at virtually any major college or university in the nation. The recall campaign against Joe McCarthy was led from the university, and I am proud to have had a hand in it.

During my first year in Madison I did not receive a penny in financial aid from the institution, not even the waiver of out-of-state tuition. I managed to survive on summer jobs and by working on the mailing dock of the local Madison *Capital Times* almost forty hours a week, from 9:30 P.M. to 4:00 A.M. six nights a week, for $1.32 per hour. I barely passed my courses, found few of interest among the faculty in American history with the exception of Merle Curti and Vernon Carstensen. I read a great deal, passed a word or two with some of my fellow graduate students, who included Herbert Gutman, Warren Susman, Richard Kirkendall, Loren Baritz, and Gerd Korman—only Korman being someone with whom I was close—and wrote long and personally valuable research papers.[1] With the exception of the input of Merle Curti, the only great advantage that Wisconsin had over the University of Irkutsk in American history was the library and the great resources, particularly in labor and radical history, of the State Historical Society of Wisconsin. Whatever happened to me in my first year at Wisconsin was the result of my own hard work, ability to take a great deal of punishment, the friendship of Gerd Korman, and the subtle influence of Merle Curti, whose positive view of ordinary Americans and pioneering work in the new social history rubbed off on me, although at the time it didn't seem very important.

Oh yes. I cannot forget the small socialist society through which I met "Lefty" Yamada and Don Thomas, both members of the Young People's Socialist League, and John Martinson, a radical pacifist. Those three taught me a great deal, and reaffirmed my socialist antiwar position, which had led me to take a stand as a conscientious objector in the Korean war (I eventually was exempted on "psychological" grounds), despite the fact that my Trotskyist comrades had a line of going into the army and doing "opponent's work," as if the war in Korea was about to become another Bolshevik Revolution. I have spent a lifetime marveling about the fantasies of the American Leninist Left.

But the main thing was the hours and hours in the rich collections of the Historical Society, working on my master's essay, "Marxism and American Intellectuals in the Nineteen-thirties." While no major theoretical work, it allowed me to teach myself much of what I would need to know, being too young for the Old Left and too old for the New Left.

The faculty was made up of a bunch of what appeared to me to be weird old men, at least in American history, mostly Beardians. Most of these folks with their

1. Richard Kirkendall went on to become editor of the *Journal of American History,* Loren Baritz to dazzling intellectual accomplishments as a historian of education.

small-town midwestern and southern roots and their Populism prepared me to believe that Populism in America was more reactionary than radical.

At the end of my first year there was no suggestion that I might apply for financial aid. I was sure that I wouldn't get it from the History Department, as Howard Beale had declared in his overstuffed fashion, "Mr. Rawick, no one will get a degree from this department, no matter how brilliant, who persists in being an unwashed bohemian." Having no great desire to stay at Wisconsin, I left Wisconsin.

I managed to get a teaching assistantship at Western Reserve University, which paid for my tuition and about $14 a week beyond that. With that, I managed to find a room—quite literally a broom closet in an old house—for $7 per week, leaving me $7 per week for food, etc. The year at Western Reserve was the best year of my graduate career. I learned a great deal from Professor Harvey Wish about slavery, slave revolts, and black history. He was a great teacher and a fine friend.

Soon after arriving in Cleveland, I heard from Curti, who was surprised that I had not returned to Wisconsin. Eventually, he asked me to come back as his teaching assistant and arranged for me to be a Knapp Fellow at Wisconsin, which helped with room and board. Wanting to study more with Curti and looking forward to a standard of living that while at the poverty level was not starvation, I returned to Wisconsin after one year at Western Reserve.

This was a better year. Other than in Curti's seminar, and a seminar with a young, neoconservative historian by the name of Robert Lively who brilliantly took apart America's corporate economy from the perspective of Adam Smith, I spent my time in the Department of Sociology, meeting the requirements for a minor field and studying mainly with Hans Gerth, a brilliant German sociologist associated with the Frankfurt School. Gerth had been Karl Mannheim's assistant, was certainly a socialist, and was the outstanding translator of Max Weber's work into English. In many ways Gerth was extremely difficult as a person. This made it impossible for me to trust Gerth and led eventually, after I received my degree, to a complete severence of the relationship.

However, Gerth introduced me to the serious study of Marx, [Max] Weber, Rosa Luxemburg, and Karl Mannheim, and thoroughly transformed my thought processes. I think I became part of a rich tradition upon which I have lived ever since. And through Gerth, I met his former student and collaborator, C. Wright Mills, with whom I would work in New York City when he was writing *The Sociological Imagination*. I was becoming a hybrid sociologist–historian. Ultimately, the combination of Gerth and Curti would be a powerful one in terms of its impact on me, yet little was due to the institution or the group of fossils who dominated the Department of History at that time.

This second year at Madison was a better year. Loren Baritz and I worked together as Curti's teaching assistants in a big course on American Social and Intellectual History. I came to know a group of young radical undergraduate historians including Marty Sklar, Jeffry Kaplow, and several others. Ultimately, however, the experience of the year was coming to know and learn from Curti. His deep-seated commitment to American grass-roots democracy made an indelible impression on me. His presidential address to the American Historical Association in which he directly challenged the themes of his predecessors in the AHA presidency, Conyers Read and Samuel Eliot Morison, who had called upon historians to "enlist in the cold war for the duration," was one of the most remarkable experiences of my life. Curti, invoking the spirit of Sacco and Vanzetti and of Thoreau and Emerson, had declared, in the words of Emerson's Phi Beta Kappa address, "the scholar who walks without the people walks into the night." Despite the fact that I may have seen things in a more formal Marxist way than Curti ever did, my Marxism was forever marked by Curti—not only by a commitment to popular democracy but with the faith that American democracy was indeed "mankind's last best hope." Such a belief to this day enables me to have a specific faith in the American people as being able to create a new society that would be one in which Marx's deep commitment to human freedom would have a chance of becoming a reality.

At the end of the year I went back to New York City, engaged in socialist activities, did some teaching and research, and came back the next summer to work as Curti's research assistant. I also managed to pass my doctoral preliminary exams and then go back to New York and Washington to write my dissertation. When I returned to Madison in the late spring of 1957 to defend the dissertation, I found myself viciously red-baited by one of the members of the committee. Professor Beale at that time demonstrated that his civil libertarianism was real and strong. He demanded that the red-baiting questions be withdrawn or that he, Beale, would take the matter to the American Association of University Professors. Professor Beale and graduate student Rawick won the day; my attacker went on to be the chancellor of the University of Oklahoma.

In short, there were some good things that happened to me at Madison, many bad ones, and, in general, with the exception of Curti and Gerth and Beale's intervention at the end, it was an experience that tested my abilities to become stronger through adversity.

5 Parentheses: 1952–1956

JEFFRY KAPLOW

A Parisian historian turned art prints dealer, Kaplow is one of the distinguished expatriates from the profession. Actually, he still teaches now and then at the University of Paris, and he maintains a lively scholarly interest. His books include *Elbeuf during the Revolutionary Period* (1964) and *The Name of Kings: The Parisian Laboring Poor in the 18th Century* (1972).

I was fifteen when I arrived in Madison in September 1952. I was a New Yorker, Jewish (of the atheist, Yiddishist, and radical persuasion), a first- or second-generation immigrant (i.e., "American born," but brought up to identify with the stings and arrows to which [East] European flesh is heir). I was also an intellectual. I had done well in school and was sufficiently precocious to warrant high expectations for my future and to conjure up visions of the *naches* my success would bring to my relatives. Alternatively, this meant that I wore glasses and read quite a lot. I was a communist (by the lights of the CPUSA [Communist Party of the USA] and the Labor Youth League [LYL], its youth organization to which I had already belonged back in Brooklyn), and by virtue of having been brought up in its bosom by a fellow-traveling mother and other, more thoroughly committed relatives; and an overweight adolescent, very young for his years, far to the Left and exceedingly gauche.

Although I was a New York chauvinist who had hardly been outside the city two or three times, I quite desperately and for a variety of reasons wanted to leave home, high school, and Brooklyn. Dropping out would never have, could never have, occurred to me—that was for the *goyim,* our near but not too close neighbors, the Irish and Italian working class. Upwardly mobile young Jews went to college,

58

and the prestige of the city colleges having waned in the generation since the 1930s, preferably "out of town." My way of wanting out was thus highly respectable, one of those to which neither my mother (my father was dead) nor other members of the family council could object, especially when I came up with the means, in the shape of a Ford scholarship, to make the dream a reality.

And so off I went to the cow country, the green and generous land celebrated by my favorite local Madison disk jockey who, his daily program of poetry and jazz concluded, was forever returning to the mythic paradise of Waukesha. Whatever later came to be the perceived wisdom about expatriate New Yorkers, neither I nor anyone else I knew came on a mission of conquest to teach the hicks the big-city ethnic and Marxist truth.[1] On the contrary, I came to study in the university and to learn outside it, to live independently and to meet the variety of compatriots I knew existed somewhere out there. The politics were not intended, they just were. Like Mr. Arkadin's scorpion in Orson Welles's film, they were part of my nature. And Madison, so different from myself in every particular, and which older members of my milieu had indulgently labeled "liberal" when they learned that I was about to go there, turned out to be, for me, open, democratic, and infinitely liberating.

You will perhaps have noticed that in introducing myself as I was in 1952, I have not, except by indirection, spoken of my class position. Where did I fit into the scheme of things, I, whose mother was a seamstress and whose father had been a displaced intellectual become shopkeeper who failed miserably in each and every one of his undertakings? All that hardly made me a member of the working class: It is one thing to be a second-generation immigrant, but how could I, who had never known either the accumulated fatigue of factory labor or the fingernail grime of a hard day's dollar, be considered a proletarian? Yet to say that I was any kind of bourgeois, even petit, would be nonsense. My parents were, if not quite workers, certainly underdogs; I, by virtue of age and education, belonged to that crack in the social fiber so characteristic of the Jewish garment workers who constituted my larger milieu, in which what counted most was not what you did for a living, but what you thought.

I thought of myself as a proletarian because I had been taught to identify

---

1. Hostility toward out-of-staters was limited, although their presence, in large numbers, sometimes was used as an argument in the state legislature for cutting the university's budget. The feeling that non-Wisconsinites were perhaps a bit too visible in certain areas did come through once in a while: In the spring of 1954, the Joe Must Go campaign was inaugurated in the Memorial Union. Together with a number of friends, I had cut class to attend the setting up of the booth where the recall petition might be signed. A photographer from the *Wisconsin State Journal* took our picture, and the reporter asked for our names and home towns. "Irving Salz, New York," "Jeffry Kaplow, New York," . . . came the answers, until it became clear that we were all out-of-staters, with the single exception of a young woman from Black River Falls. The reporter eyed us with suspicion. "If I find one more New Yorker, I won't publish," he said. Whereupon a fellow Brooklynite, taller, broader, and perhaps capable of passing for a native more easily than the rest of us, identified himself as from Kenosha. The natural order of things restored, the article appeared the next morning.

with the heroic struggle of the workers of the world, led by the Soviet Union. I was a Stalin*ist* at a time when the word had meaning only for Trotsky*ites*. My vision of the world was faulty in its refusal to recognize the purges, the trials, the camps, the horrors of forced collectivization, and so on—all lies propagated by the bourgeois press, especially for someone who claimed to be a Marxist. The curious thing is that these ideological blinkers, while they made it impossible for American communists to analyze the reality of their own country (and thus contributed, along with the persecutions and the witch hunts, to keeping the party outside the mainstream of national life) did not interfere with our ability to recognize and deal with the issues of the day. We could not make the revolution we wanted, but we were rather better at realizing short-term goals. The conventional picture of communists of the 1950s shows them as opportunists subordinating all they did to the long-term objectives of the party. Nothing could be further from the truth. What we young radicals did in fighting for specific change on campus (discrimination in housing, the refusal of fraternities to pledge non-WASPS, the right of faculty and students to express dissenting opinions without being sanctioned) and in the community and world (for peace, minority rights, against McCarthyism) was done certainly from the perspective of a larger worldview, but equally because we believed in what we were fighting for. There was no conflict in our minds between reform and revolution, no fear that the obtaining of rights and advantages would dull the appetite for change of this or that group. Our own remained undiminished.

The first thing I did when I reached Madison was to make contact, how I have forgotten, with the campus chapter of the LYL. No one, I think, bothered to check my bona fides; of this I was happy because I had not been the most disciplined member of my Brooklyn club. I was then initiated into the team system of organization. Despite the fact that the university was the only one in the country then still to recognize the existence of a communist group on campus (all that was required was that two officers of the group make themselves known, be "open" members, in the jargon of the time—there was no need for membership lists, no limitation on the use of university facilities), one could never be too careful in matters of security at a time when the party that was our model was half underground (before being buried). So it was that the members, all twenty of them, were not supposed to know more than four or five of their fellows. (We did not get cyanide capsules to use in case of torture and interrogation.)

The urge to laugh now at our precautions is sometimes great, but the passage of time should not be allowed to obscure the real bases of our fears. If we wore them lightly, they remained part of our rational calculations concerning the future. Most of us, although proud of our convictions, did not want the world to label us, and in so doing make it difficult for us to pursue our careers. We hoped that our generation of Americans would indeed have a rendezvous with destiny, but, as individuals caught up in the prosperity and opportunities offered by the expanding economy of the 1950s, we assumed that the individual initiative shown in going to university and graduate school would be rewarded by success in our chosen fields. We did not disdain a little comfort while preparing for the *grand soir;* perhaps some of us even hoped to ride to the barricades in our Cadillacs, there to lead the people in the conquest of liberty and happiness. After all, we were part of the vanguard, by definition the elite of the society yet to come. We also expected to play that role, to some degree, in the here and now, and to reap its benefits.

Here I am being a little cruel. But the simple fact is that we perceived no contradiction between individual ambition and social commitment. To live poorly as a matter of principle, to share the discomforts of the masses (for whom, I wish to emphasize, we sincerely cared), was not our thing. We were Leninists, not *narodniki;* we did not so much want to go to the people as have them come to us. Neither did the tradition of religious witness and nonviolence, so fundamental to many of our successors in the New Left of the 1960s, mean anything to us. We tended to underestimate the importance of Gandhi (how little aware of the Third World we were, and blind to the significance of decolonization), and Martin Luther King, Jr., as a national leader did not yet exist. It was a tradition we might, in a pinch, respect, but judge it efficacious we could not.

A year or so later, when I came to share quarters with the two known members of the LYL in a storefront along the railroad tracks that quickly came to be known as the Glass Kremlin, I got to know a lot of members who were not in my team, although it was understood that I was never to ask for confirmation. Even so, I did not know all the members, and I remember my astonishment at learning, years later, that a president of the campus Young Democrats had been one of our own. Security, as full of holes as a sieve, sometimes worked, at least on us. The FBI, as we were later to learn (thanks to the Freedom of Information Act) kept rather better abreast of our activities. Despite our worries, we were not a suspicious lot, and on the one occasion when we had reason to believe that we had an informer in our midst—the single black, and to boot an athlete, we had managed to recruit—we felt more chagrin than indignation.

The Madison community was, in fact, hospitable enough. The rabid anticommunists were either few in number or to be found principally among those whom we called "jocks," not because they were athletes or even enjoyed spectator sports but because they constituted the great mass of nonintellectuals who were somehow not our peers. Our elitism kept us from feeling overly affected by what *they* thought, and we laughed one day on Bascom Hill when a hulking and somewhat hunched-over figure walked past our extended leaflet-bearing hands, saying, *sotto voce,* "Eat it, eat it."

It was the others, the intellectuals, a term understood to mean the serious and concerned students, who, together with a certain number of respected teachers, mattered. However much these people, mostly Roosevelt liberals unhappy with Truman, Eisenhower, and the Cold War, were opposed to our politics, they shared with us an opposition to McCarthyism, an opposition which was no doubt reinforced by geography. We were, after all, in the jaws of the whale, Senator Joe's home state. But our county was the only one to vote consistently Democratic, and our university was the true bastion of civil liberties. We, all of us, Reds and liberals alike, took at face value the plaque on Bascom Hall with its proclamation of support of "that fearless sifting and winnowing without which truth cannot be found," little concerned with analyzing the real history of its formulation. What concerned us was its application in the present, which meant the continuation of the Wisconsin tradition of social reform that had run from the Populism and Progressivism of Bob LaFollette and his sons to the reforms of the Roosevelt years. At each juncture, members of the university, like Richard Ely, John Commons, Edward Ross, and the professors of economics who had drafted national social security legislation in the 1930s, had played significant roles in providing intellectual backup to reforming administrations. This tradition, it is true, belonged more to the liberals than it did to us, who found it wanting in its lack of socialist inspiration. But we would nonetheless take our share in it.

The liberals saw in McCarthyism an infinitely greater threat to their heritage and freedom than could ever be constituted by what they must have felt was our naive, perhaps even reprehensible, faith in Stalin and the Soviet Union. This being so, we and they shared enough common ground to defend the university against political attack, ourselves against ostracism, and to maintain our campus as a place where radical ideas could be seriously discussed, and day-to-day reform stood some chance of success.

The discussion of communist and/or Marxist ideas seems, in retrospect, to have been a constant of my four years in Madison. Our team meetings were so many "educationals" for the study of the texts written by the leadership of the Communist party and the LYL, together with a little Marx or Lenin. Our predilection was for the study of American history, the main purpose of these discussions being to understand why the United States had not made its revolution—or more positively, why one day, inevitably, it would—and to identify ourselves and our ideas with our country. We were, beyond any doubt, too mechanistic, not at all dialectical, in our interpretations. Whatever our analytical shortcomings, we were willing to learn, and the many of us who were history majors were already benefiting from the work of certain of our fellow students, like Herb Gutman, and our teachers, notably Merril Jensen (whose defense of the Articles of Confederation and distrust of the centralized state rubbed off on us somewhere), Merle Curti (on the history of American culture, his concerns came closest to what today would be called the New History), and Howard Beale (the tradition of anti-imperialist internationalism in the person of the good midwestern bourgeois), all of whom posed questions that would help to widen our horizons at a much later date.

In public, there were endless roundtables at the student union, and the occasional political meeting we sponsored, generally to provide a forum for a communist leader of note. Herbert Aptheker came on more than one occasion, always equipped with extensive clippings from the *New York Times* with which to prove a point—the idea being that if an adversary could be used to add fuel to his fire, he must be right. These meetings were always well attended, perhaps because people were curious to know if communists really had horns or if they resembled human beings. (This is scarcely an exaggeration: I remember a survey carried out by the Madison *Capital Times* during those years, in which a large group of people were asked what communism was. The general tone of response was: "I don't know, but I think we should kick them out of Washington.") Their curiosity may not have been of the healthiest variety, but we certainly made the most of it to affirm our presence.

So there was a great deal of talk and a certain amount of show in our Madison days. For the rest, the times were not conducive to the mass actions and demonstrations that so characterized the civil rights and antiwar movements of the 1960s. If Madison in the 1950s was quasiunique in being the only university community not to brand us young Reds as pariahs, we were nonetheless constrained to work quietly. There was no other choice but to work within the framework of other organizations whose aims were in some way compatible with our own. The words used to describe this activity—"infiltration" and "burrowing from within"—have an essentially negative connotation and are, as such, unjust. For we were not so much using those organizations for our own ends as we were helping them fulfill their stated aims.

To some readers this will seem a bizarre assertion, yet how else can one describe what we did as members of student government committees to end discrimination in off-campus housing, or to force fraternities and sororities to accept pledges from among students whom we did not yet call minorities or ethnics but simply blacks and Jews? The same was true for the local chapters of national organizations like the NAACP [National Association for the Advancement of Colored People] or even, perhaps more paradoxically, the Young Democrats or the Students for Democratic Action. We disciplined young radicals lent these organizations and campaigns our commitment and whatever strength we possessed. There was no tit for tat, no advantage for ourselves as a specific movement, but "only" the satisfaction of helping to accomplish something we believed in. Nor was it, I think, dishonest of us to participate in organizations whose national directors made anticommunism their alpha and omega. Of course, we did our best to minimize that aspect of things while accentuating the positive. If contact with our fellow members caused some of them to come closer to our way of thinking, that was all to the good, but it was far from constituting our primary purpose.

Madison in the early 1950s was in many ways a haven in a hostile world, but even there we were on the defensive, it being up to us to prove that we were not conspirators bent on destroying all that was holy in the American republic— whereas the real threats to academic freedom, civil rights, and liberties came from the other side. Ours was a constant holding operation against consensus and conformity, and the silence to which they gave rise. Sometimes we were so busy defending ourselves and the freedoms that should have been, but were not, that we had no time, or inclination, for other matters.

Thirty years on, it is clear that our student generation was the point of transition between the Old and the New Left, and not just in organizational terms, due to the exhaustion of the Communist Party USA and the ensuing search for alternatives. We were still very much rooted in the classic socialist and working-class tradition, both by our origins and our ways of thinking (on the ideological plane, a form of economism was unquestionably our major fault). Our identification in the immediate past was with the labor struggles of the 1930s; we were too young to have experienced them directly, but we had parents, and sometimes older siblings, who had. A few years earlier, it had still been common among communist students to go into the shops, at least for a period before taking up further education or the practice of a profession. If this was not often our own option, we nonetheless aspired to be organic intellectuals of the working class, although we had not yet heard of [Antonio] Gramsci.

On the other hand, we were unaware of, or not overly concerned with, a whole variety of issues that would become central to the New Left a few years later. If we could be rightly proud of the attention we paid to the question of race (however inadequate our analysis), the same could not be said of gender. On this matter, we knew [August] Bebel and Lenin, but neither [Aleksandra] Kollontai nor the indigenous feminists of the nineteenth century. I caricature only a little in saying that our slogan was "equal pay for equal work," and devil take the hindmost. Sexual oppression was an epiphenomenon of exploitation, when and if we thought about it.

Ecology was a word we did not know, and our position on nuclear energy came under the general heading of the struggle for peace. If anything, we were in favor of its peaceful uses so that it could not be used for making war. Progress was an article of faith; nor were we wrong in holding that one could not stop the advance of science. What we failed to see was that the progress in question would not be automatic, nor would all of its applications be safe.

More curious was the way we handled foreign policy. It might almost be said that we didn't, beyond believing the opposite of what everyone else believed. For us, the Russians were the good guys (some of us had actually cried at the announcement of Stalin's death, and we felt a deep resentment when Mike Petrovitch, resident Kremlinologist, said, a week or so later at a lecture sponsored by the ROTC in which we were all obliged to enroll, "How pleasant it was to speak of him in the past tense"), and the makers of American policy, [John Foster] Dulles and Eisenhower above all, the baddies. We were convinced of the iniquity of the Korean war, but the truce proclaimed in early 1953 put the matter on the back burner. The simple fact is that there wasn't much we could do about foreign affairs, and that is perhaps why we largely ignored them, beyond trying to convince our contemporaries that there was no Soviet-led communist conspiracy to enslave the free world. We were also extremely parochial, except in the area of high culture, of music and art, where our concerns extended as far as Europe, if not farther. I don't think we either knew or cared very much about European politics other than in terms of Cold War superpower confrontation. Except for an occasional bow to the Chinese Revolution, the Third World and its anticolonial struggles were not much present in our consciousness; the first inkling of their importance came from the Bandung Conference in 1955, which also presented us, for the first time, with the unheard-of concept of nonalignment.

This catalogue of what we did not know or try to know is a full one, but so far from being a reason for negative judgment or a cause to say our collective *mea culpa,* it is a sign of the times in which we lived, and of how far we have traveled since. We lived in a small world, not just in a small town.

Mine was only one of several experiences on the Madison Left, and so, although I am convinced that what I have recounted here was to one extent or another shared by more than one of my contemporaries, I do not presume to speak for them. My Madison years contributed in every way—emotional, political, intellectual—to making me the person I am today. Given my origins, living in Madison was like discovering America, in both the literal and figurative sense. Like any discovery, *Mittelamerika* was a learning experience I did not always know I was undergoing. If the real effects showed up only in the long run, I was, I think, at least vaguely conscious of opening up to something new, particularly in the variety of people I met on and off the campus.

In those days, our activity was mainly confined to the campus: we out-of-staters did not acquire state citizenship and could not, as transients, participate other than informally in local politics; such participation came only in the 1960s. But we did have contacts with the locals, the residents of the East Side, the people who worked at Badger Ordinance and Oscar Meyer's with whom we sympathized and sometimes tried to help. Closer at hand, in classes and at the various places of residence, I got to know fellow students from a variety of small Wisconsin towns, who were far from being the unsophisticated bumpkins of popular rumor. (No doubt I was as odd to them as they were to me; I remember lodging for one semester in a fraternity house whose surplus rooms were rented to nonmembers. At one point, I was asked if I would like to pledge, to which I responded that I could not, given that forbidden "semitic blood" flowed in my veins. Their shock was considerable, and at least some of them, as they later told me, began to think that perhaps the requirement was strange, not to say discriminatory.) Students from the South were the first blacks, other than domestic workers, with whom I ever had any commerce. For the New Yorker I was, ethnicity was a central fact of life, and so learning, first, that there were Christians in this world with whom I might be friendly and, second, that their Catholicism or Protestantism was not necessarily their primary source of self-definition, was enlightening. I even discovered that not all Jews were on the Left.

In a word, I discovered a variety of people, a variety of opinions, most of them not my own, but nonetheless respectable, and could engage in a dialogue. I came to Madison the bearer of absolute truth, in which I too often sought refuge against the stresses and strains of a difficult adolescence. When all else failed, at least I knew what forces ruled the world and what the ultimate outcome of events would be. I left Madison a lot less sure of myself, and beginning to think that "inevitability" was something of an intellectual swindle. In the process, I also acquired a healthy distrust of authority, even, or above all, when exercised by Red diaper babies and *apparatchiks,* so often one and the same.

I would hate to think of this process as the acquisition of tolerance, too commonly a poor excuse for lack of commitment. Nor was it one of disillusion, although I certainly began then to lose some illusions about truth in general, official Marxism and the Soviet Union in particular. Years would go by before I could consciously draw the conclusions, but it was in Madison that a beginning of change was made. Because that change had begun, the Khrushchev Report, which coincided with my leaving Madison in February 1956, had considerably less effect on me than on many of my comrades. I had not wanted to believe in Stalin's crimes, or in persecution and murder as agencies of socialist power, but somehow I did not find the admission of their existence surprising. And so it was not necessary for me to throw up my hands in despair, put on sackcloth and ashes, or disappear in shame into the woodwork. What was important to me was less what had happened in the past than the potential for change in the present and future.

Had the Communist Party USA shown itself more open, more imaginative, and less sectarian in coming to terms with de-Stalinization, I would probably have followed the path I had expected to go and made the transition from the youth organization to full-fledged party membership. That that did not happen was more their fault than mine, so to speak. For a while, I felt a little like an orphan, especially from 1956 to 1959, when I was drowning in the politically stagnant pool of Princeton in the silent generation. But the end result of the process, if ever there is an end, was a return to politics in the 1960s, this time in New York City at the several universities where I taught, via a variety of movements for civil rights, for disarmament and against atomic testing, and, of course, the apotheosis of the campaign against the Vietnam war.

Madison, its classrooms no less than its politics, taught me to think critically and leave the slogans behind. In so doing, I lost my messiahs, but in all things essential kept the faith. Like the activists of the Radical Reformation, I abandoned the later glosses and went back to the Bible, but with the conviction that in the end, every person's conscience is his best and only guide. This the Wisconsin years did much to teach me. You can't go home again, and freedom being the recognition of necessity, I have never wanted to return to Madison—but it is one hell of a place to be from.

6   A Madison Bohemian

NINA SERRANO

Nina Serrano is a cultural and peace activist in the San Francisco Bay Area. She has won two international film prizes, published a volume of poems, *Heart Songs (The Collected Poems of Nina Serrano)*, and written and directed several plays. Currently, she produces a monthly radio program, cochairs Friends of Nicaraguan Culture, and works in marketing. She has four grandchildren and many works in progress.

It was a beautiful Indian summer evening in September 1953. I climbed down the airplane steps in Madison, Wisconsin, full of anticipation. It was my first plane ride. I was nineteen years old and running away to get married.

I'd boarded hours earlier in New York City, my home town. This was the farthest I'd ever traveled. I'd come to marry Saul Landau, a freshman at the university, whose letters said that Madison was a small city, very green, with lakes and trees.

When I graduated from high school the year before, there was some vague talk about going to college. But it was financially beyond my parents' means. My passion was the theater, and it seemed to me that the best training was in New York City, right where I was.

I moved to Greenwich Village to study acting and live the artistic life while surviving on a series of waitress, clerk, and sales jobs. I was a teenage bohemian, a nonconformist who dared to consider unpopular ideas. I loved the world of the arts and hated the commercialization of art and culture. I felt a deep connection to folk art and community art.

Right after high school graduation, Howard De Silva, a blacklisted Holly-

67

wood actor I was studying with, organized a reading of the letters of Ethel and Julius Rosenberg. The reading was performed at the New York City mass vigil in June 1953 to protest the Rosenbergs' execution as atom-secret spies. (Twenty years later, it turned out there was no such thing as atom secrets. The execution was part of the campaign to silence dissent.) In a period of fear and silence, the outspoken vigilers left an impression on me. De Silva was using theater as part of the bigger picture by empowering and mobilizing people to speak out, despite the armed police and the widespread anticommunist hatred. I was afraid, but this kind of theater appealed to me. Although two decades later I played Ethel, I always regretted turning down De Silva's offer to read the Ethel letters. As an eighteen year old, I felt too immature for the role of playing a thirty-eight-year-old mother of two.

I met Saul when I took a job as a drama counselor in a summer camp. By the end of the summer we were inseperable, until he went off to college. After two weeks, he sent me a one-way plane ticket. My first night in Madison, Saul and his friends sneaked me into their roominghouse. Women were not allowed. Actually it was "girls" who were not allowed. The world around the university seemed like a world of large children. Women had to be back home by 10:00 P.M., or maybe it was even 9:00 P.M. Virginity was the unspoken motto of the women's housing units.

Saul's friends were also from New York City, huddled together like refugees. But I was intrigued to meet his friend Bill, who was from a farm, as was much of the larger student population. At that time, about 70 percent of the state was involved in agriculture. Bill knew how to milk a cow, ride a horse, plant and harvest fields, hunt, freeze, and eat what he caught. I was impressed. My life on New York City's cement left me very separated from the basic stuff of nature.

We moved into a studio apartment with a hot plate and refrigerator on "fraternity row" right on Lake Mendota. I learned to cook hamburgers. The building was full of working people. The manager and her husband, a factory worker in the Oscar Meyer hot-dog plant, and her children oriented me to Madison. She taught me how to cook stews and to find work.

I landed a job waitressing in a Chinese restaurant owned by a university chemist who cooked. Norwegians, Finns, Swedes, and Germans had settled in Wisconsin only a little more than a hundred years earlier, and many Madisonians outside the university never saw any Asians. Despite my Caucasian features, skin color, and height, curious customers often asked, "Excuse me, Miss, are you Chinese?".

Soon after we moved into the apartment, the dean of men sent a threatening letter objecting to our living together. But we couldn't get married without parental consent because we were too young. So we cut a deal to have a religious ceremony held and conform to the state requirements later. The university, in its capacity as Big Brother, was appeased.

Life among the fraternity men involved lots of beer and Saturday night parties. During the football season, they built wonderful floats for great parades. I liked the carnival atmosphere, although I never did get to a game. The students appeared excited about football and the Military Ball, a spinoff from the ROTC (Reserve Officers Training Corps), a men-only program.

I experienced the university through the stories of my husband, his friends, and the fraternities until I found a job at the university information desk situated in an outdoor-facing booth in the Student Union building.

The foreign students stood out in a sea of blonds. Although New York City was a multicultural environment, I'd never met so many Middle Eastern, African, and Asian people. Among them were two out-of-place Afghan students. They were even more disoriented than I. Religious practice made them afraid to eat hamburger because they thought it might be made of ham. They survived the first few weeks on cakes and other desserts. I identified with them as a fish out of water, but they were afraid to speak to me. They frequently visited our one-room apartment, but I could never get a response from them when I joined the conversation. I was shocked when I found out it was because I was a woman and a friend's wife. Although I watched them change over the next few years, I learned a lifetime lesson from the experience, something about differences and something about the position of women in the world.

I was lonely. I joined a local theater group, the Madison Theatre Guild. I worked on children's productions, which was how I met a stage-struck high school student named Mike. Mike lived in the suburbs and attended a Catholic high school. Mike told me he was "gay" when he learned I was from Greenwich Village. Because "the Village" was famous as a symbol of nonconformity in a very repressed time, he felt safe to tell me. Besides sharing Mike's "secret," we shared our interest in theater, a kind of underground theater not so much because it was in hiding but because it was blacked out by mainstream media.

One of my acting teachers in New York had performed in Judith Malina and Julian Beck's Living Theatre production of Gertrude Stein's *Dr. Faustus Lights the Lights*. Although the play made no sense at all to my sixteen-year-old self, I fell in love with the repetitive rhyming, intoned language. It cast a spell on me. I would describe to Mike the wonders of the avant-garde New York scene, like the Greenwich Mews theater where color and racial boundaries were broken to cast actors. Often, after rehersals, we would talk before his dad came to pick him up. Mike introduced me to the works of the German playwright Bertold Brecht, who was a forbidden figure to discuss at his theater-minded school. Even his favorite nun would not allow it. Actually, Brecht was the director of a world-acclaimed theater, the Berliner Ensemble. Mike and I exchanged what information we could through my well-worn subscription to the United Nations theater magazine.

Meanwhile, the university information job led me to the pleasant pastime of visiting the Rathskeller in the Student Union. It was a lively cafeteria that looked out on the lake. My husband cooked hamburgers there for a while. It was the center of hot debates, philosophical wonderings, and conversational intimacies; roars of laughter or angry shouts burst from groups around the tables.

It was in the Rathskeller that I began the habit of reading the campus paper, the *Daily Cardinal*. I learned about the repression on campus and was immediately drawn to the underdogs, wanting to seek them out as the only visible signs of rebellion around. Their names were Henry Wortis and Arnie Lieber, the open members of the underground campus Marxist organization, the Labor Youth League (LYL). I asked around until I met them: both outstanding science majors from New York with broad interests. But I just met them, I didn't actually get to know them. My curiosity was keen. Perhaps it was at the Rathskeller or at a party that I met Cora Rubin (later Cora Weiss), a student activist and later a national peace leader. In those days, few students had their own cars, and certainly females didn't. I was impressed. She even had her own apartment, while most women lived in dorms or supervised housing. It turned out she was from a remarkable and wealthy family.This gave her more independence than any young woman I'd ever known. Cora was very commanding and purposeful. This was another rarity among young women. Her self-confidence and focus made her appear more adult. She offered me a job in the storefront office of the Madison branch of the Joe Must Go recall movement, whose headquarters were in Milwaukee.

I didn't type or have office skills, but this office fortunately was about organizing, not filing, mostly handling calls and drop-ins. It was decided that the infamous Henry Wortis and Arnie Lieber of the LYL were not to be encouraged to visit the office, as we would be tainted by association and this would make our work ineffective.

This was my introduction to the world of practical politics. It was a disappointing prohibition for me. When Arnie came in one day for leaflets, I felt guilty and flustered. It seemed cruel to separate him from a movement he felt so motivated to work for. Here was a person not afraid to stand up for his ideals, and even his sympathizers shunned him because of the guilt-by-association environment. But I kept my silence. I was so unsure. The one thing I knew was that it was dangerous to be called a communist. Anyway, I was beginning to feel a little oriented to Madison. Life moved quickly.

We moved to a university-owned, small, wooden apartment building for married students and graduate students. I was meeting mature unmarried intellectual women who were getting advanced degrees in science and anthropology. They were radicals. I found their talk fascinating and a change from the flow of younger male visitors to our home. I saw Saul's life opening up from his university studies. I longed for that stimulation and became a correspondence student through the University Extension Program.

The Spanish correspondence course demanded that you give back what it said in the book about Latin America. The correct answer was that there was a need for the United States to develop a larger middle class as the answer to the problem of impoverished masses and a small, wealthy elite. As I had grown up among Latin American immigrants, I felt I had a lot to say. My father immigrated from Colombia with his mother and eight siblings. My grandfather followed, and died soon after in New York. The family, except for my dad, returned to Latin America, and some of his brothers went to fight in the Spanish civil war. One was killed in battle the year I was born, 1934. Uncles, aunts, and cousins were always coming from Colombia to visit in the mid and late 1940s when political conflicts between the Conservative and Radical parties heated up. They would leave for home when the chaos died down. My grandfather had been a military man and a Radical party supporter, as were my uncles. My grandmother and aunt visited for months after my aunt was caught in a great shootout in downtown Bogota between the army and citizens in front of the bank where she worked. When I was in seventh grade, a large number of Puerto Rican students enrolled in my school. I was intimately aware that Puerto Rico was a U.S. colony. I felt that colonies, like youth, needed to be free.

There was no forum for my observations, questions, and conclusions in the correspondence course. I was glad of the opportunity to upgrade my Spanish grammar, but I disliked negating my brains for it.

The Joe Must Go office, meanwhile, dissolved in a sea of reactionary sentiment. I got a job slinging hash at a little breakfast place called Gary's, next to our house. I was in the swing of things, pouring out steamy hot coffee on freezing Wisconsin mornings, listening to workers' and students' comments over the morning newspaper while cooking up their eggs and hash browns, with three pieces of toast, butter, and jam. My boss, Gary, was for me the quintessential Wisconsin family man: farm-raised, fair-haired, with a friendly greeting for all, dedicated to filling the tummy of the folks. Sometimes Mike would come over to visit over the counter. One of Mike's other "older women" friends was a young woman director with the Wisconsin Idea Theatre. She was a breath of fresh air after the provincial Madison Theatre Guild.

The "Wisconsin idea" was an opening in a closed society. The idea was that "the boundaries of the university are the boundaries of the state." This meant creative arts projects were carried out in suburbs and remote rural areas. At that time, Wisconsin farms were frequently isolated and snowed in during winter. I loved the concept. I worked in some children's plays with her, although my pregnancy made me a cumbersome Cinderella.

We moved to a big flat as a good spot to make a nest for our expected baby. But to pay the rent we decided to rent out two bedrooms. A friend took one and said he would mention the availability of the other to Henry Wortis. At last a chance to know the most notorious person on campus, close up.

Henry brought conversations about Marxism and science to our dinner table, as well as late-night card games with his girlfriend, Jackie Cranach. The most popular game was hearts. One night, after a game, Jackie shouted angrily at us, "You're all New York chauvinists!" It took years before that charge made any sense to me. By that time, she was living in New York. Henry's presence made for intense debate and excitement, as did his world of secret meetings and endless observations of insects in jars. By the time he graduated, a few weeks before my son, Greg Landau, was born, we were convinced Marxists.

Natural childbirth was a new concept in Madison. St. Mary's Hospital refused to allow fathers in the delivery room. Although I'd practiced breathing exercises for a drug-free birth, the mask was over my face before I knew it, and the shot of Demerol sent me out on a cosmic float to unknown regions of psychic space. I came down to earth to find a baby boy, who kept me good company for many years.

I felt loneliness was at an end. I didn't know then that it is the human condition, a state I return to from time to time no matter how big the crowd.

Our little family left Madison for seven months, checking out the sites from California to New York and back to Madison. I was no longer a New Yorker but a Madisonian. My little boy wore red Bucky Badger sweatshirts.

A friend now headed up the student government Academic Freedom Committee. Knowing of my theater interest, he asked me to help produce something for Academic Freedom Week. I jumped at the chance to practice my art in a larger context, choosing *Inherit the Wind,* a play that deals with freedom of speech and thought, issues still being fought today. The play, set in the 1920s, focuses on the famous "monkey trial" debate between the legendary free-speech defender Clarence Darrow and the golden-tongued orator and former presidential candidate, William Jennings Bryan. They debated whether the theory of evolution or fundamentalist Christian doctrine should be taught in the schools.

Our production was a dramatized reading. The rehearsals and performance took place in a local church. Saul played the attorney Clarence Darrow and a black theology student played the golden-tongued orator. The Reverend Ed Riddick not only played Bryan but had a golden tongue, raising the cause of civil rights in our consciousness. The publicity for our show consisted of nothing more than the usual little mimeographed notices on university bulletin boards, but we had a full house and enthusiastic audience. This kind of theater I liked.

During spring break Saul, Ed, and another black student, Austen McClenndon, drove to Washington, D.C., to a civil rights conference. Austen's wife, Alma, and I were good friends through a third friend, Marilyn Weaver, a Wisconsin farmgirl who'd married into one of Madison's few black families. The Weavers had the market cornered on the janitorial business in town. All the Weaver brothers were known for their amiability. Alma, her infant son, Mark, and I with my infant son, Greg, spent time together babysitting or on park outings.

I took only a few credits, wheeling the stroller, bundled-up baby and dangling diaper bag, up Bascom Hill. There I'd wait for the sound of the bell and the stampede of exiting students. Among them was Saul, who would wheel Greg back down the hill while I went to class. Life was a race against time set to synchronized schedules.

Without Henry Wortis, political life lost some sparkle. We participated in ongoing LYL Marxist seminars that took place in members' homes. The discussions were dominated by male history students. In fact, few women attended, mostly wives or girlfriends. One woman stood out not only for her beauty but because she could argue with the best of them. Later, when she married, her participation diminished.

Our study groups were trying to figure out how to solve the world's social and economic injustices and understand how they came to be. What was society all about? What was Marxism? How could we change the world? We tried to work it out between ourselves with the help of some books. The classrooms and professors didn't offer much assistance.

We sometimes ate at the Green Lantern coop where there was a lot of complaining about ROTC. The steady members shopped, cooked, set up, served, and cleaned up after meals. The food was good, the prices low, and the company excellent. The camaraderie grew out of eating and working together. The Green Lantern operated out of the Grove Women's Living Coop, where women experienced more independence than dorm and sorority women. Grove coopers managed their own house affairs, though they had to conform to the university rules and regulations controlling the lives of women and keeping students at a childish level.

Many of the young men balked at the ridiculous demands of the compulsory ROTC classes, the shiny-shoe fetishes and prowar viewpoint. Saul hated it. The Quaker students and other religiously motivated students added a spiritual quality to the arguments against compulsory ROTC. So we picketed the ROTC headquarters and marching grounds. It was a scary experience as young warmongers and the top brass greeted us with hostility that smelled of violence. We stood our ground and returned with our picket signs and "buttons."

Today we would laugh at our buttons. They were really tags from a stationery store, with little strings for tieing on. We wrote in pen, "End Compulsory ROTC." We also wrote letters to the *Daily Cardinal*. It took years to win this struggle. Later generations picked it up, but their demand was to abolish ROTC on university campuses altogether.

In this environment of repression, a Green Lantern friend, Kenny, painted his car green and painted a feather on it. A hand-painted car was an oddity, and the green feather stood for Robin Hood and his philosophy of rob from the rich and give to the poor—and there was a rich-and-poor struggle on the campus. The rich were represented by the "Greeks" (fraternities and sororities), who dominated campus social and political life. The yearly Military Ball and the ROTC program were closely linked with their social scene. They defended the status quo, from crewcuts to curfews.

Soon after Soviet Prime Minister Khrushchev gave the 1956 report to the Soviet Communist party where he denounced the actions of Joseph Stalin, the LYL dissolved. This news came from the LYL national office in New York and did not respond to the condition of the group in Madison, which was active and growing. I felt disoriented. The idea that people in New York were making decisions for Madison seemed ridiculous.

On Greg's first birthday I enrolled as a full-time student in time for summer school. I took a class that proved to be the most utilitarian of all, Teaching Creative Dramatics for Children. I adored every minute of it as each class member carried out a lesson plan and the rest of us were students. The class gave me a methodology and a little practice. I even loved the textbook by Geraldine Brain Siks. I read everything in her bibliography I could get my hands on, learning that the leader of the child drama movement in the United States was Winnifred Ward at Northwestern University. I longed to study with her.

Eager to try out my newly found techniques, I found two teaching jobs: one at the the South Madison Community Center in the low-income part of town, far from the University, and the other, a Saturday afternoon class with the Wisconsin Idea Theater. The Saturday afternoon students were from middle-class suburbs. The South Madison Community Center children were from working-class families recently off farms. All the children enjoyed the opportunity for creative expression, and so did I.

But my youthful energies had their limits. I got the worst cold of my life from too much political activity, family responsibility, school, and teaching. I lay in bed reflecting on my life. I remember thinking I must be the luckiest twenty-three year-old in the world. My life was so full. I didn't know the most exciting part of my twenty-third year was yet to come.

I found myself closer to Ed Riddick's group. They were pacifists who had formed the Student Peace Center at the same church were we'd performed *Inherit the Wind.* At the time, their organizational techniques seemed so new and suited to my temperament. Everything was done by consensus. Feelings counted, not just well-reasoned discourses, like in the Marxist study groups. There were no bureaucratic trappings, like offices in New York making the major decisions, just direct action.

I was invited to chair the group, even though they understood I wasn't a pacifist. But in my heart I really was, and still am. It is a personal inconsistency too difficult to explain. We wrote a letter to the *Daily Cardinal,* and as chairperson, I signed it. I don't remember what issue we were raising, but it well may have been about ROTC, as we focused on peace issues.

It was published just as I was leaving on an overnight anthropology class trip to the Menominee Indian Reservation. My mind was full of child-care arrangements and the excitement of seeing how the indigenous people lived.

The reservation was a beautiful wooded area, dotted with small log houses. As an totally urban person, I felt quite alone away from my family in the company of trees. Mostly graduate students had come on the trip or people from other anthropology classes. I don't think I knew anyone except my professor, whom I admired greatly.

After my initial fear of the great outdoors, I began to notice that the group shunned me. My teacher took me aside and said that two members of the expedition were so angry over the Peace Center letter that they were planning to rape me. It is hard to imagine today that this threat evoked only fear. He suggested that I stick close to the professors and share their cabin. It became clear who my enemies were, as they taunted me throughout our trek through the Indian land. These two young men were more accustomed to rough terrain and more agile than I, and they made this field trip a torment. So I stayed very close to the professors, seeking shelter in their positions of authority.

I was happy to return unharmed to my own home. Given the degree of intimidation of dissenters and the "victim is guilty" view of a rape threat, I don't think the field-trip incident was ever mentioned outside an intimate circle, and perhaps not at all. I honestly don't remember because rape was a taboo subject even for a radical, a "bohemian." It was one thing to challenge foreign policy, the economy, and the legal system; rape was was too shameful to discuss in public.

Several exciting events also happened on campus. A group of us brought Carey McWilliams, author and then editor of the liberal magazine the *Nation,* to speak. This was a great victory for students because of university restrictions on outside speakers. The student response to the McWilliams visit was enthusiastic, and the struggle to get him on campus, encouraging and even revivifing. It seemed like the winds were slowly shifting.

Another editor, the economist Paul Sweezy of *Monthly Review,* came to speak off-campus; although he reached only the leftist students, his influence was profound. Most of us left his reception as subscribers to *Monthly Review.* For the next few years, articles from that magazine were often the center of lively discussion. (Sweezy's co-editor was Leo Huberman, whose book, *Man's Worldly Goods,* I'd found very moving in my teens. When I met Leo in the 1960s, a year or so before he died, I felt affirmed to find such a kindly and warm man.)

Perhaps sensing the shift in public opinion, Cora Rubin emerged with a pioneering idea. She thought that there was a revival of interest in folk music on campus and that by forming a folk music club we could invite performers who related to free-speech issues on campus without meeting the restrictions placed on speakers. Pete Seeger was the first guest. The concert played a pivotal role in my life. Outside, the Young Republicans picketed against the banjo- and guitar-playing singer. He was called a "pinko." Even as a young man, Pete was a legendary figure; he'd worked with Woody Guthrie and Leadbelly, the "greats" of the 1930s. He'd also been part of "The Weavers," a group whose songs were like a cultural oasis for me when I was in high school. "Kisses Sweeter Than Wine" expressed my teen sentiments. It was one of the few counterculture songs that made the mainstream charts.

Despite the picketers, the Seeger concert was a success, with a large and enthusiastic audience. The content of the songs spoke spoke right to my heart. I learned them, I think, from that one listening. Pete sang a satiric song about academic freedom based on a true event. He sang about integration in education. He sang songs that gave me strength and hope in the dark hours in the years to come, like "This Little Light of Mine." I've sung them to my children and my grandchildren and the thousands of children I've taught. It was the first time I'd ever heard

African songs and the nature of the struggles in the emerging African nations that were coming into being. He sang songs of women's liberation. The thaw was coming; after the concert, the world seemed friendlier. It had a magical quality. Pete stayed on our living-room couch. The next morning, toddler Greg crawled over to Pete's open guitar case and plucked a resounding note.

More of the younger leftist and liberal students who arrived on campus were guitar and banjo players. Bluegrass music and blues were strummed at parties and on the grassy lakeshore outside the Student Union. There were lots of opportunities for sing-along, hootenanies.

The Military Ball ("Mil Ball"), meanwhile, became more and more of a cultural offense. Our blue jeans were starting to be more popular than their khakis. Somehow the idea of an "Anti-Military Ball" took hold. I don't remember who thought of it. The Anti-Military Ball ("Anti-Mil Ball") was a dance with original skits and the first major countercultural activity of my time in Madison. I threw myself into it all the way, as did several others, staying up nights rhyming words for our show and learning the songs. I loved it. Putting on our entertainment was a thrill.

Our ball was as big as theirs in attendance, and I really had a ball preparing the theatrical element of it. I've heard that the tradition of the Anti-Military Ball lasted for years. The thaw had come. It almost felt like things were heating up.

Spring in Madison is like a great release from aching cold and barren trees. One balmy day, a former LYLer, Jerry, who'd graduated a year earlier, came to visit from California. He said he was working with a California group to organize a U.S. delegation to attend the International Youth Festival in Moscow to be held that summer of 1957.

He paid no attention to my little son, at which I took great offense. In general he was very negative. But, much to my surprise, he called me a "student leader" and invited me to be a delegate. I thought of myself as a "housewife," though I longed for other titles.

At first, it seemed impossible that I could go. But as I thought it over, the trip seemed very desirable, and that alone made it possible. Saul had no interest in attending because if he enrolled in summer school, he could graduate at the end of the summer. He offered to cash in an insurance policy so that I could go. I planned to bring Greg with me.

I had no printed information about the festival except that it was held every three years in a different country. Young people from all over the world came together to work for peace. Yet nothing could have pleased me more. The dates were for two weeks in August. I longed to see the world. I'd always planned to travel to all my favorite places in my elementary school geography book. Here was my chance to start. The only address I had was for the British Festival organizing committee in London. Jerry said I could leave from London to Moscow, as travel to the Soviet Union was still barely legal and difficult to arrange in the United States. It was only a year earlier that the U.S. State Department had allowed travel to the Soviet Union. It was considered quite suspect. Curiosity was almost a crime, but I was full of curiosity anyway. World cultures interested me.

I'd heard a lot of theory. I wanted to see socialism in practice. Peeking behind the Iron Curtain, as the Soviet Union and Eastern Europe were called in the press, was an exciting, if frightening, idea. Greg and I went downtown for passport photos. The photos later appeared in both Madison newspapers and *Newsweek* (with Greg cut out).

I bought three drip-dry outfits. They were the latest thing. I stopped at my in-laws for a week in New York to catch the train to board the ship to go to England. In those days, boats were cheaper than planes, especially on D deck (steerage).

Most of my family and friends were horrified or frightened by my trip. I boarded the cheapest ship to England, an Italian liner. I carried Greg in a sling, the latest form of baby carrier. Child backcarriers and "snugglies" were still to be introduced in the United States, though I was soon to see a universe of women carrying their babies in all sorts of marvelous things. In the 1950s, mobility for parents was not encouraged. The baby carrier broke as I walked up the gangplank, but it didn't discourage me from feeling like my life was just beginning. What lay ahead was a great adventure. At last I was fulfilling my dreams, though I felt a little homesick.

Chasing Greg around the upper deck, eating in the dining room, and meeting my fellow passengers, all going to foreign ports where I'd never been, lifted my spirits. The ship had a nursery. Life on board was a vacation, with no meals to prepare or clear up after, no house to clean. I looked out at the vast, endless, gray-blue sea. There was more to the universe than Madison, Wisconsin.

The trip to Moscow caused a small stir in Madison. But when forty-two of the U.S. delegates to the International World Youth Festival accepted the Chinese delegation's invitation to tour China's eastern seaboard from Peking to Canton Province, and one of them was a Madison student, it hit the front pages. Something like, "Forty-two Students Break Travel Ban," with my passport photo and a story.

Americans were then forbidden to go to China. By accepting the invitation, we were challenging the travel ban and asserting our right to travel. The FBI didn't take this news well. They harassed Saul in our apartment, insisting that he talk with them about my trip. He always refused. Phoning Saul from Moscow, I used up almost all my cash. I tried to phone from China, but it was impossible because of the estrangement between China and the United States. The FBI probably knew more about the trip, from their informants on our delegation, than Saul did.

Saul had already graduated and had moved out of the apartment and back to New York while I was still in China. Through the Freedom of Information Act, he was later able to see his FBI file, which I also read. It was the diary of my youth, as written by an ignorant, critical, and insensitive observer who always referred to me as the "subject's wife."

(According to Saul's FBI file, when he moved from our Madison apartment, agents went through the stuff left behind, old newspapers and the like. Actually, whatever they wanted to know could be learned by reading the books and articles or attending the lectures of those of us who went. Few publications were interested. They preferred to think that Soviets were bears and the Chinese inscrutable. Most of the delegates who went did so for the exact purpose of breaking the blockade of ideas.)

When I returned that autumn to New York, the Customs agents at the airport confiscated my passport, Greg's diaper bag full of soiled diapers, and books and a film. They were full of "propaganda" and had to be quarantined. It took weeks to get them returned, with the help of a lawyer who volunteered his professional service to fight for the right to travel.

I gave talks about my travels to community groups in New York City and taught creative dramatics in a neighborhood center. The FBI began harassing my in-laws. I received a lot of hate mail as a result of a painful interview with Mike Wallace that was reprinted in *Newsweek*. I was quoted in a way to make me feel foolish. My parents moved to another state.

I was also pregnant. Living in New York, Saul and I both missed Madison, our friends, studies, and the sense of community. New York was so big, dirty, and impersonal. In the spring of 1958 we moved back to Madison to resume our studies and enjoy the sense of community we'd missed. Suddenly, however, I was a notorious person because of the press coverage of the China trip. The chairman of the Speech Department thought that since I had a child and was expecting another, I was too "old" to be a student, suggesting I stay home and keep house.

I was twenty-three years old and still an undergraduate, but I ignored his advice and registered. It was true that my classmates were getting younger than me each year. (I didn't complete my baccalaureate degree until just before my fiftieth birthday.) But in the spring of 1958 I had enough credits to take upper-division classes that included graduate students. Classroom discussion was getting livelier.

While we were in New York, the Madison Left had consolidated into the Socialist Club. It was a much broader grouping than the old LYL, as there was no fixed truth or interpretation of text. When they invited me to speak on the World Youth Festival and China trip, more people attended than I expected, and they didn't all walk in with a hostile attitude either. In just seven months, things had changed. Civil rights movement activities were on the rise. Black students' participation in political life increased; on the whole, they were more action oriented than theoretical, which enlivened things a lot.

This second pregnancy didn't include afternoon naps because Greg was an active little toddler. I was often tired, falling asleep over my homework. Our circle of friends now included many couples with young children. Usually the husbands were graduate students, while the wives worked in offices to put them through school. We would cook meals in one another's houses, talking endlessly amid the kids and the clatter of dishes.

One couple was Anne and David Eakins. Anne and I hit it off at once. She was the missing element of my life in Madison, a "best friend." Anne was a child-centered mother of two adorable girls. She also studied music and was interested in education. I was in awe of Dave Eakins because he came from a ranch in California, like a cowboy. Both of them had been blacklisted in Denver where they were active in their meat-packing union, which was attacked by Red-baiting congressional committees. In the end, they were both fired and unable to find work. They came to Madison to prepare for new careers.

So often, at these couple dinners, the men would discuss history and political theory and the women their marriages, children, and the strain of trying to manage jobs or study. We never looked at feminist issues in the political and historical context we lived in. We took it personally, as individual luck or failure. Our husbands upheld the ideas of sexual equality and glorified women like Rosa Luxenberg, Mother Jones, and Krupskaya (Lenin's wife.)

Between civil rights, the Socialist Club, and such, the FBI visited our landlady. She evicted us when I was nine months pregnant. We found a great flat on the first floor of our old house. It was an enormous strain to pack and supervise the move. Right after my final exams, Valerie Landau was born, on a night when a happy group got together for spaghetti, card games, and Monopoly. An anthropology student babysat with three-year-old Greg so we could rush off to the hospital. Once again, the rigid St. Mary's Hospital policies were enforced. But this time I was in a double room with a very wise and mature woman. I found myself, too, a wiser woman.

It was a superwoman year: two children, classes, homework, housework, hanging out diapers that turned stiff on the line in the freezing cold. Saul was a teaching assistant, getting involved in professional conferences and his studies.

A Mexican family moved in next door. He was a postgraduate student in medicine and his wife, Bili, cared for the children. Bili and I became fast friends because of the children and language. She was home all day with the kids and no adult to talk with because she knew no English. Although her ideas were very traditional, she would push her stroller along with mine, just to keep me company, as I went from bulletin board to bulletin board putting up Socialist Club fliers.

The civil rights movement activities began with raising money on snowy street corners in tin cans to pay for legal fees for the students in the South who were arrested for nonviolent protest. There was a lot of sympathy for their cause. I remember raising hundreds of dollars in coins on a frosty afternoon. It was a shock when these heroic students arrived on campus wearing sophisticated clothes and with cameras dangling from their necks, smashing all my clichés about the "poor black students in the South." They brought with them high spirits and mobilizing songs and chants.

A black folksinger, Leon Bibb, passed through town. Anne and I were inspired by his performance. We organized a Leon Bibb children's concert in my living room. We sent out two hundred invitational postcards that we hand-addressed. This was a forecast of things to come. I'm still working with mailing lists to produce political and cultural events.

The new semester was permeated by our circle's excitement over a group of young writers in England. They were called the New Left Writers. They published a theoretical journal, *New Left Review,* and were also active in the theater. Joan Littlewood's group produced their works. I was excited to learn of a woman director; there were so few.

I enrolled in video broadcasting classes, which was a relatively new field geared to preparation for producing commercials, sitcoms, and other grist for the multinational entertainment industry mill. The course orientation conflicted with my view of art, education, and the role of media. I loved the video medium, but I couldn't get a good grade in the class. Perhaps because of my opinions? I couldn't hide them in my term papers or in the programs I would choose to produce because I cared too much. I cried when the teacher gave me low grades. Dave Eakins made me feel better, saying my ideas were good, but how hard it is to hold the minority opinion. His own experience had taught him that.

When the class assignment was to create an ad, I made a public-service announcement for UNICEF and the public library. When it was time for drama, I chose two New Left authors, Englishman Arnold Wexler *(Chicken Soup with Barley)* and Irishwoman Shelagh Delaney *(A Taste Of Honey).*

In those days the little theater plays were free, and all the fine foreign films I saw there were quite inexpensive. A rich cultural life was available on a student budget, and many of the world's greatest performers and lecturers passed through Madison.

It seemed like our English counterparts on the Left had picked up their shattered illusions from the Krushchev Report and moved on. Saul and several other graduate students were talking about putting together a new journal. It became *Studies on the Left,* and it dominated our living room and kitchen until it moved into Eleanor Hakim's bedroom, maybe a year later. "Ellie," as everyone called her, bedazzled me. She was the only woman the fledgling male editors had real intellectual respect for. I was flattered when she acted as if I was smart and what I thought was valid and interesting. She lived in the same building with other activists; they were English and theater majors or involved in literature. I loved the conversations about Brecht, Shakespeare, and Jean Paul Sartre. A trip to that building had my mind spinning faster than at the library where I tended to catch up with my sleep over required reading or research texts. The quiet of the stacks, where only the priviledged upper-division students could go, was the domain of professors and graduate students. Lee and Judy Baxandall and their infant daughter, Pamela, moved into Bili and Julio's old apartment. Almost immediately, exchange babysitting and idea sharing began. Lee translated Brecht and other fascinating texts. Judy read Simone de Beauvoir's *The Second Sex* and was convinced that women were indeed the second sex. At first I couldn't hear her: "Yes, yes in theory you're right, but what does that have to do with me and this effort I'm making trying to grow as an artist, raise children, and make pineapple upside-down cakes that don't come out looking like the ones in the cookbook? Besides, I still have a pile of ironing to do, an exam to study for, and all these people are coming over for a *Studies on the Left* meeting."

Ellie was nobody's wife. She held her own in any argument. Ruggedly independent, sensitive, and burning with intellectual passion, she disagreed violently with the prevailing English Department line on Henry James. She considered the department professors philistines. She refused to make any concession for the sake of a degree. As a student teacher, the students adored her, and she in turn gave them confidence and skill in written communication in her intensely supportive way. In the years to come, her innovative teaching methods helped many English as a Second Language and minority college students upgrade their basic English skills. Her real love was teaching literature. But when the budget cut in education hit the public colleges in the 1970s, basic English jobs were more available and literature jobs scarcer.

As a leftist, she followed no traditional path. I think she considered herself more a dialectician or existentialist than a Marxist. Dogmas didn't sit well with her. She accepted no compromise in the world of ideas. During one late-night conversation, I said, "Ellie, You're all alone out there." She nodded, accepting her fate. She wasn't a "joiner." Thin, small, and dark-complexioned, she always caught colds and bronchial infections in the winter. Despite this, we often stood on frozen street corners while she explained to me the dialectic within the plays of Shakespeare and Brecht. Snow collected on her dark lashes under her thick glasses. Her slender frame shook involuntarily in the cold. But there was so much to say.

I learned more from Ellie than from study groups or classes. She was humble, dressed in her younger brother's cast-off jeans, turtlenecks, and flannel shirts. Cascades of brown curly hair surrounded her face, which usually was encircled in cigarette smoke. She lived on black coffee.

Ellie was a tremendous correspondent who kept in touch with her sisters, brothers, parents, and many friends wherever they wandered. You could wake her up with a late-night phone call if you were scared, lonely, brokenhearted, or just wanted to talk.

In the process of putting together the first issues of *Studies on the Left,* she corresponded with many people. In her Madison years, she was always the first one to organize a softball game in the spring. It was a joy for her. A ball team was a team she could relate to and trust, not like the movements or political parties.

Ellie and Saul wrote an article on Cuba for the first *Studies* issue. Later in her life, she was enmeshed in the intellectual Cuban exile community in Paris and New York. Her sympathies lay more with the dissenters in socialist countries than with socialism. She was a purist, no compromise. Freedom or else.

Ellie died in 1985 when her generous heart gave out. Often she would point out during our twenty-two-year correspondence, that her fate was to be "all alone out there." She found no refuge in the women's movement of the 1960s and

1970s, preferring to publish her articles in small magazines for the broader intellectual community.

Her plays were produced in Off-Broadway theaters, leaving her broke and exhausted at the end of each of them, vowing never to write another until, of course, she found herself involved in rehearsals for the next one. Her last published piece, *The Domestic Baedeker of Gertrude Stein,* was published posthumously in *2 X 2.* The editors dedicated the issue to her.

Somewhere along the line, around 1957 or 1958, a new history professor appeared, William Appleman Williams. His impact was enormous. He wore a red vest—uncommon dress in a cowtown in the 1950s. Soon, many history graduate students could be seen in red vests. It was rumored that he was divorced and remarried. That, too, had an aura of the "shocking" and "new." His latest book was inscribed "To Corinne for all the reasons." Williams made history come alive. He described the depression of the 1890s in such graphic terms that when I see homeless men looking through garbage cans today, I remember his lecture. In time, his picture of the past became the future.

The civil rights movement was well under way, meanwhile. Students on campus were joining the Freedom Rides by boarding integrated south-bound buses over the Mason-Dixon line. It involved nonviolent training. The pacifist movement and civil disobedience were gaining ground and prestige. The Freedom Riders faced a lot of violence and were jailed. Major rallies in favor of racial integration were held on campus. Greg's picture, holding a picket sign at a demonstration, appeared in the *Capital Times.* When a student Freedom Rider didn't return, we marched down to the Capitol and were greeted by Governor Gaylord Nelson, who pledged his help and support.

Anne Eakins was especially involved in civil rights activities. She took a leadership role because she already had some experience from her union days.

There was a national boycott of the F. W. Woolworth store chain because the southern branches wouldn't serve Negroes at the lunch counter. We picketed the downtown Woolworth. While integration and civil rights might have been a big issue on campus, the town thought we were very odd to concern ourselves. They continued to enter the Woolworth store, turning down our leaflets, but perhaps hearing our slogans and chants. Activist circles broadened with the civil rights movement. Church and union members, the black community, and student groups were active in civil rights support work. Little by little, protest became more possible. It seemed the more freedom we took, the more there was of it.

In the meantime, the tight community of university leftist couples and young children was destabilizing. I can't remember which couple broke up first. But I remember that when the first couple separated, the wives began talking more than ever about the book *The Second Sex.* I was taking a class on Ibsen and Shaw from a visiting teacher. His lectures pierced my heart with the feminist messages of Ibsen and Shaw.

One day, around January 1959, a friend wrote me from New York about the young revolutionaries who had just come into power. I bought a copy of *Life* magazine and studied the photos. It was hard to understand what "revolution" in Cuba meant. In those days, living in Madison was a little like being "out of it." Periodicals and books were precious. We were so far from where events were "happening." New Yorkers had seen Fidel Castro walking through the streets of Harlem on the way to the United Nations.

Saul and I separated. It all happened just as the new edition of *Monthly Review* arrived, book length and all about editors' (Sweezy and Huberman's) trip to Cuba. I was curious.

I worked on a team-teaching project run by Harvard in the summer lab elementary school. It was the first in the country. I taught drama. The program included an arts staff; a dance teacher, an art teacher, a resident weaver, and me. This was extremely advanced for public education at that time. I enjoyed the adult interaction as teachers, something I missed and still miss when teaching in the traditional setting of one adult and a room full of children behind closed doors. The intermingling of the various disciplines was exciting also.

Saul left to check out Cuba, and give us a vacation from our domestic dissension. At the end of summer school, I took my whole two month's paycheck and went with my children and sister-in-law, Beryl Landau, to see Cuba for ourselves. The revolution was just eight months old.

It was a great experience. We landed at the Havana airport to be greeted by a rhumba trio, revolutionary soldiers, and graffiti: "Yankee go home!" This referred to the large corporations, like United Fruit. Beryl and I tried not to be scared. I think we were more excited than scared. The air was perfumed with tropical flowers, and the city was drenched in sunlight.

At first we were crowded into a hotel room more suitable for two than five. By chance, we met James Weinstein, one of the *Studies on the Left* editors, on the streets. His dad had holdings in a large Cuban grocery chain whose assests were frozen. He was compensated in Cuban pesos, worthless except in Cuba. He and his wife had rented a luxury apartment. They had paid for a month, but had to leave at once. Happily, we piled into the apartment; it faced the Carribbean and had two freshwater swimming pools. Beryl painted the sunset over the sea nightly.

I interviewed people for a film project and carried on the tasks involved in raising children and running a home. I went to plays, concerts, poetry readings, and art exhibits. Havana was full of artistic activity because all the exiled artists and intellectuals had returned. The society was wide open, liberated, and turned upside down.

Trained managers and technicians had also left. The young revolutionaries had to learn on the job how to manage factories, fields, schools, and hospitals—a happy chaos. Beryl and I went by train and jeep on a tour of the countryside. Our eyes were full of tropical beauty and our ears flooded with talk about coops, collective farming, and agricultural experiments learned from foreign advisers from all over the world.

Saul went to New York as a book editor and worked with the Fair Play for Cuba Committee. Our marriage was on shaky ground. He organized Cuba support activities and tours.

It was difficult to return to Madison alone and face another winter. Compared to revolutionary Cuba, our post-McCarthy thaw was an iceburg, and there was literally so much cold to endure. The winter lasted forever. I babysat a lot for Anne while she went to civil rights meetings. A black law student, Jim McWilliams, emerged as one of the civil rights leaders. Saul came to visit and invited Jim, Anne, and others to join a Cuba tour. I performed in a scene from a Brecht play for directing class. The Reverend Ralph Abernathy, from Martin Luther King's staff, arrived. He filled the Student Union theater to capacity. Danny Kalb, from our campus civil rights group, joined him on stage and played the guitar, Danny leading us all in singing "We Shall Overcome." Abernathy's speech met with a standing ovation.

Saul was in Europe. Our marriage was in question. The life of a single parent was particularly harassing and depressing. I barely attended classes. Beryl came to visit for a week, giving me pep talks. We vacationed at the Wisconsin Dells in a resort shack. I got back a little spirit and returned to Madison ready to audition for the Wisconsin Players production of *Summer and Smoke* by Tennessee Williams. I landed the lead role of Miss Alma. Ellie helped me learn the eighty-three pages of script.

The play went very well. I clipped my reviews. The production was technically a delight. But applause was not enough. By the end of the summer of 1961, I'd had it with Madison. I was twenty-six years old and still an undergraduate. I felt as if I'd been taking notes, listening to lectures, and worrying about unwritten papers and exams forever. I also vowed never to face another winter here.

A visiting San Francisco director passed through town. He brought photos of his productions at the Actor's Workshop. I thought, This is for me. I'd also seen a photo book called *I Am a Lover,* documenting the beatnik scene in San Francisco. It seemed a bohemian paradise.

Just as I planned to pack myself and my children up and head out for California, Saul returned. We decided to have another go at "marriage and the family." We piled everything into an old red pickup truck and drove to the West Coast. I left all the sweaters and coats behind in a dry cleaning shop because I never wanted to need them again.

I had arrived in Madison in 1953, to be a runaway bride at nineteen years of age. I left in 1961, at twenty-six, the mother of two. A lot happened in between.

7 A Journalist Among Historians

RICHARD SCHICKEL

Time magazine film reviewer, author of *The Disney Version* (1968), *His Picture in the Papers,* (1973), *D. W. Griffith: An American Life* (1984), and *Intimate Strangers: The Culture of Celebrity* (1985), among many other works, Schickel at first glance seems an unlikely candidate for this book. Looked at more closely, and with the help of his narrative, he becomes a natural. Schickel's militantly democratic cultural instincts, along with keen perception and hard study, readied him to interpret popular culture more than a decade before academics were prepared to bring it into the intellectual domain. Like an often forgotten pioneer of cultural studies, Gilbert Seldes (whose *Seven Lively Arts,* published in 1924, was arguably four decades ahead of its time), Schickel has taken the view directly to the masses via journalism and popular books. His iconoclasm has been earned through decades of close observation of commercial media.

The invitation is to autobiography, self-revelation. It is not my favorite form, as a reader or as a writer. I prefer to stand at a distance from any subject, describing, commenting, *kvetching,* and I have certainly never mastered the trick of distancing myself from myself. One result of that defect is that I really do not know, going into this piece, how I got from there to here—there being the University of Wisconsin, circa 1951–1956, here being "living proof," as the editor flatteringly put it in the letter soliciting this essay, that a "cultural critique" was under development in that rapidly receding time and place and that it has made some sort of mark in the world subsequently.

I hope he's right, and doubt he's right. But surely a very pleasant assumption—the assumption of coherence in one's personal history—is made here. And

85

a comforting one. For in your fifties you tend to search your past for evidence that you have arrived by some logical process, involving conscious, conscientious choices among readily definable alternatives, at your current condition. If you can trace your path to the present rationally, reasonably, then the implication that you can maintain similar control on the trail to the future, on which the ogres of old age inescapably lurk, is reassuringly proposed.

Unfortunately, my life as I look back on it does not support the assumption of intellectual coherence—or the hope of finding it in the time that is left to me. If that life contains any coherence at all, it is a purely emotional one. Which is perhaps the roundabout way of saying that the years at Wisconsin did not form me. Instead, they tempered certain basic instincts. Civilized me, perhaps. Rendered me fit for polite, liberal society. But they did not, I think, suit me for the society of this book, which I take to be a gathering of spirits both more radical in temperament and more ideologically intense than I am—or ever was.

My invitation to this party is, I suspect, based on my youthful success in assuming a false identity. For if I did not pass all my years in Madison in the radical intellectual or (if I may use the word somewhat anachronistically) counter-cultural university, I certainly spent the better part of them (in both senses of that term) there. Nothing duplicitous in that. I really felt I belonged there. Its population was smart—smarter than any group I had ever encountered in my short and sheltered life—and I was beginning to think I was pretty smart too. Ergo, this was the place for me, a sort of Zelig of the Left, happily taking on the colorations, political and otherwise, of my companions.

It was "otherwise" that in the end counted most with me. For though I look back on them with fondness and on the days we passed together with nostalgia, though I know that they helped to form values that have endured and in some measure shaped, if not my life, then my way of looking at life, I have come to recognize that politically I was merely passing through this community, that I was never deeply and truly committed to any of the large ideologies that moved—or perhaps I should say tormented—many of its members. Indeed, I have not ever found a community anywhere to the ruling principles of which I was able to commit myself fully. That, too, is inherent in my nature. It is either the ultimate radicalism or the ultimate foolishness. Or perhaps a little of both.

It was the entirely unprincipled achings of a huge yet curiously innocent and skittish ego that brought me, circuitously, to the counterculture of the 1950s and then led me forth from it and into the career I have since conducted. I was, I must say, an odd recruit for that community, for I was raised as the contented and cosseted only child of a suburban Milwaukee, middle-class WASP family, just prosperous enough to indulge the principal whims of their heart, which were centered on me. I learned early and alas permanently that a correctly ordered world was supposed to revolve around me. One form of their devotion was hanging on my every precocious word. When I learned that they (in particular my grandfather, a lawyer who revered literature) would applaud written expression—I worked on and eventually edited the high school paper—even more vigorously than they did my spoken sallies—because, of course, the ability to write has the force of a minor mystery, an ability to awe those who have no gift for it—my professional course was set for me. And my emotional course too. Even now, so many years and so many millions of words later, and after gathering considerable evidence to the contrary, some part of me thinks that if only I write well enough, I will earn, besides a living, a large increment of love.

I did not understand that at the time. And there was something else I did not understand either. That was that I was in desperate need of both a congenial literary form and suitable subject matter. This is not an unusual condition for an aspiring writer. If the need for approval is a prime factor in motivating him, the need to obtain it on his own terms is also hard, if secretly, at work in him. For all writing, from the humblest journalism to the most gnomic poetry, involves a reordering of reality in a form more pleasing to the writer—excluding what he cannot bear to contemplate, emphasizing what he most loves to hear himself talk about. Most writers are, in this sense, control freaks. I did not have the wit, or the gift, to remake the world entirely in a form over which I might have had absolute control—in other words, to write fiction. I did not have quite enough ego to do that. On the other hand, I had too much ego to be simply a passive, objective observer of the passing scene—in other words, to be a reportorial journalist. What I needed was a form that enabled me to assert myself without revealing myself—in other words, criticism.

But, again, I could not articulate any of that when I arrived on the campus one blustering January day in 1951, when a blizzard was blowing up (there was no symbolism, only typicality, in that storm). My intentions at that moment were exactly like those of my friends from high school, to settle into a major that would train me to earn a living (I was headed for the School of Journalism in the same spirit they were heading for the Comm School) and, of course, to join a fraternity.

Yes, really. Believe it or not. It may be that I was a little more articulate than most of my friends, and, I think, a little better read, thus a little more intellectually sophisticated than they were. (I owed this to the influence of that bookish grandfather of mine, who was also something of a political dissident, a Democrat in the days when they were the state's third party, after the Republicans and the LaFollette Progressives). But still, I had successfully, unhesitatingly conformed to their values back home, where I had been reasonably "popular" and part of the best crowd, and so it never occurred to me not to turn out for pledge week and not to accept the best bid I got, which turned out to be from SAE.

In a matter of weeks, it radicalized me, if so large a term may be applied to such near-comical circumstances. It would require the gifts of Tom Wolfe to record the empty haw-haw, har-har heartiness of life around the SAE [Sigma Alpha Epsilon] house. Suffice it to say that I took an instant dislike to virtually its entire membership. Their rituals were imbecilic, and the socialization they enforced on everyone, through fines and work details for slackers among the pledge class, were the height of hypocrisy (if their "brotherhood" was authentic, then why this element of compulsion?). Far worse, they were utterly determined to avoid contamination by any idea that might disturb the banalities and prejudices they had been absorbing since childhood and equally determined to impose their beer-puking, tit-mauling, jock-sniffing stupidity on others. Their aims, to be sure, were petty, and they imposed no physical threat on anyone, but still, the year and a half I spent—or rather did my best to avoid spending—in this company constitute my largest experience of a totalitarian society.

O lucky man! I hear the reader exclaiming—and correctly too. But it was quite enough for me. And quite enough to turn me into a virulent—and lifelong—opponent of fraternities and sororities. I haven't thought about them for years, but scribbling away here, I find the old outrage bubbling up. I still think they travesty the values of liberal education, and I still think they should be banned no matter what the cost in alumni outrage and student housing.

The Young Progressives did not rescue me (though reading John Dos Passos's *U.S.A.* probably helped) from my plight. Nor did some sly Marxist on the faculty subtly poison my innocent young mind, as so many on the radical Right at the time feared they would. And the Rathskeller radicals were all unknown to me. What happened was simply what is supposed to happen when you go off to college. I encountered a free university freely going about its business. It permitted me, gently urged me, to discover what education could be, ought to be—that is, a form of pleasure. I wrote my way into an advanced freshman composition course, in which, as I expected I would, I did very nicely. What was unexpected was the joy with which I found myself responding to the quite simple, but to me astonishing, play of ideas in my survey courses—Modern Lit, Sociology 2, Geology 1. It was the last, oddly enough, that made the greatest impression on me. Geologic time was made to seem, by a lecturer whose name, regrettably, I cannot recall, enthrallingly romantic, and my enthusiasm for this exotic subject startled and inspired me. It suggested to me that there must be realm upon realm of information like it—great stuff that had until now been not only beyond my ken but beyond my imagining. Now it was all here and handy, mine for the taking. Suddenly the alternately languid and anxious high school student, glumly grubbing his way through irrelevent chemistry and incomprehensible algebra, became an impassioned college student, eager to explore anything and everything. (Well, anything and everything that did not involve equations or 7:45 A.M. classes.)

My elated response to these first moments of higher education contrasted vividly with my despairing response to the first moments of fraternity life. But still I did not know how to escape its clutches. This was especially difficult because membership in it meant more than I had realized to my parents, especially my dad, who had attended Wisconsin briefly but had been forced to leave and find work to help out his family when his father died. I think he had hoped to live inside a college novel of the kind that was popular in his day and had been dismayed to find himself written out of the story in Chapter 2, before he had the chance to sing songs around the frat-house piano or take a girl canoeing on Lake Mendota. Later he would look at me in a sad and puzzled way and wonder aloud why I wasn't having more "fun" in college. I could never make him understand that I was having "fun"—more of it than I had ever dreamed possible.

It began on a trip to Europe in the summer of 1952. With my best high school friend and dorm roommate, Fred Leysieffer, I booked passage on a student ship, and on it encountered a famous campus figure, Jerry Schecter, who was working his way across by editing the ship's paper. He recruited us to help out, which we did both on the voyage out and the voyage home. Along the way he encouraged me to come out for the *Daily Cardinal* the next semester. He was a fellow of cheerful, insinuating enthusiasms, and since by this time it was clear to me that journalism school (in which I was enrolled largely because I had been awarded a little scholarship to attend it) was a terrible place to learn journalism, and that its trade school requirements soaked up time that could be better spent in English and comparative literature, political science and history, I was ready to try learning my future trade by other means, that is, by practicing it in what amounted to a semiprofessional atmosphere.

Schecter had not told me just how understaffed and otherwise hard pressed the *Cardinal* was. But its resources were so thin that I got a byline on my first story, written the first day I worked there, and after that I was rarely absent from its pages or its offices. For I instantly fell in love with the place.

It was all frantic, exhausting night work, with a hard core half-dozen of us putting out the paper with a little help from a slightly larger population of reporters and copyeditors who drifted in an out of our tiny, untidy (no, filthy) city room as their time permitted. To them the paper was just an extracurricular activity. To us it was life itself. We started turning up in the late afternoon, and started arguing editorial policy and writing immediately, grabbed pizzas or spaghetti at the old Italian Village next door, returned to edit and write headlines. Then, around midnight, a couple of us would head for the composing room to put the paper to bed. It was redolent of printers' ink and the molten lead being fed into the linotypes, and the experience of standing around the compositor's stone, under unyielding fluorescent lights, quite literally seeing your words hammered into their final place on the page, was also a romantic one. You felt connected to the most basic journalistic tradition, that of the independent editor, whose freedom was purchased by his ability, and his willingness, to do everything necessary to place his words, his views, before the public.

I had obviously, finally, found my true fraternity. Within a month or two, I celebrated that event by writing a column denouncing the Greek-letter fraternities (even though I was living in the SAE house by that time). The next semester I moved out and into an apartment Schecter and Dick Carter, another *Cardinal* editor, a wry, taciturn man who could actually run a linotype, were sharing on Francis Street. I don't think I ever again set foot in the fraternity house, and a year or so later, having been told it was against its bylaws to resign, I requested, and was granted, expulsion. By this time, Schecter having graduated—he was replaced in our menage by another *Cardinal* editor, bright, tough, funny Stanley Zuckerman—I inherited his job as stringer for the *Milwaukee Journal*. So after we had closed the *Cardinal*'s front page, I would write my stories for it—my first paid journalism—and then run them up to the telegraph office near the capitol—"NPR Collect," I would say, feeling very professional and foreign correspondentish, to the operator (the initials stood for "Night Press Rate") and then I would head home to Francis Street, where I would blearily try to catch up on my courses. Except, of course, one roommate or the other would usually still be awake, and sometimes a couple of reporters for the *Wisconsin State Journal*, who lived upstairs and kept the same hours we did, would drop in, and I would end up talking shop instead of studying.

Being true children of the 1950s, the subject of "selling out" was much on our minds, for we wished to do good and also wished to do well. How often and how earnestly we explored that conflict. What price working for Luce or Hearst or Scripps-Howard? Alternatively, could one find happiness in poverty at the *New Republic* or the *Nation?* Shimmering gloriously, and seemingly beyond reach, was the ultimate goal of every aspiring journalist in those days, the *New York Times*. We debated whether "objectivity," the great god of the journalism school, was possible or desirable. We read the great reporters' autobiographies—Lincoln Steffens, Vincent Sheehan (we knew enough to call him "Jimmy"), Eric Severeid—looking for clues to right behavior. John Reed was much in our minds. Television was not much in them, though we admired Edward R. Murrow. For, aside from his work, TV news seemed to consist mainly of guys reading wire copy to camera. We simply could not imagine what role there might be for guys like us in that medium.

But the *Cardinal* provided me with something at least as valuable as a working community. It provided me with that subject I had been unconsciously seeking as a writer. Please understand: Anything would have done, anything on which I could strut my stuff. But the tradition of the paper was a highly politicized one—it had always strived to be more liberal even than this very liberal university—and now, in the 1950s, it had an irresistible political issue, namely the general assault on civil liberties and academic freedom that was already generically known as McCarthyism. Since the man who lent his name to this "movement" was Wisconsin's junior senator, the controversy surrounding him, and all the issues he symbolized, was obviously more immediate and intense in his home state than it was elsewhere. And a university priding itself on its liberal tradition felt itself perhaps more threatened than other colleges did precisely because it shared its constituency with the man who had given his name to the darkest social movement of the time.

This was manifestly a matter to mobilize anyone's critical impulses, and here I was, in a position to exercise those impulses almost every day. Somehow it seemed that almost all the news we covered in some way or other touched on, or was touched by, the McCarthyite threat. The year I found my way to the *Cardinal,*

1952, was, of course, an election year, and the campus swarmed with speakers and
rallies in aid of Eisenhower and Adlai Stevenson, McCarthy and his opponent,
whose name also now escapes me. But at any time in that period famous liberals—
political, literary, academic—came to speak on campus and in the question period,
or in the press conference or interview they nearly always granted, they were asked
to comment, if not on McCarthy himself, then on some current investigation of,
or charges leveled against, someone or other by the radical Right. (I remember
Owen Lattimore, the Asian specialist whom McCarthy insisted was one of the people who lost China, and who had been hounded out of his State Department job,
receiving a standing ovation when he appeared.) Lesser numbers of conservatives,
like William F. Buckley, Jr., and Dos Passos, were also invited to the campus and
were always pressed hard, if not in outright hostile fashion, in the same forums. (I
remember haltingly trying to tell Dos Passos how much *U.S.A.* meant to me and
his impatient insistence—how many idealistic young men had by then tried to lay
their radicalism at his now reactionary feet—and being told I ought to consult his
later, tiresomely conservative fictions.) I also remember getting into trouble with
the administration—rightly so—when my boy-journalist questioning of William
Grede, a Wisconsin businessman who was then president of the National Association of Manufacturers, shaded over into heckling.

Beyond these weekly excitements, there were ongoing local issues requiring
our constant, humorless attention. Real and perceived threats to academic freedom
were constantly under investigation in our pages, and we were ever suspicious of
compulsory ROTC, athletic department shenanigans, parietal rules, the Young
Republicans, and, of course, Langdon Street. We were certainly against all the right
things, weren't we?

And beyond them, there were in those days two particularly vexatious issues
commanding a disproportionate amount of our time and patience. One was the
continued existence on campus of what had once been the Young Communist
League, now renamed (as I recall) the Labor Youth League. Its entire membership
consisted of two argumentative chaps, agreeable enough in manner, and doubtless
products of the surprisingly hardy New York Stalinist tradition, which somehow
survived, at least as a turn of mind, if not as a full-fledged ideology, all the assaults
of this period to resurface in new disguises in the 1960s.

Be that as it may, their chief activity was writing letters to the editor and
guest columns for the paper predicting the imminent triumph of fascism in America. Didn't seem likely to me, but then, what did I know? And anyway, our commitment to free expression obliged us to publish these screeds. Some among the
Cardinal's editors may have thought there was a germ or two of truth in their
social criticism. Some—notably Zuckerman, whose New York background was in
the anticommunist Left—actively deplored them. I was too dumb to see what they
were up to, which is what communists, even at this playpen level, are always up
to, namely, trying to embarrass the individuals and institutions committed to shel-
tering them, hoping we will betray them and thus fulfill their contemptuous estimate of liberal democracy. Since practically no one attended the LYL's meetings,

our coverage of them, together with the space we gave them for their commentaries, were their chief means of tom-toming their message to mostly deaf ears. The only ones attuned to it belonged to yahoo state legislators, who had their own long tradition of University of Wisconsin bashing to maintain. Periodically, the university's wisdom in continuing to sanction the LYL was questioned from the other end of State Street, but that was a relatively minor nuisance to the administration. The junior Stalinists were, I now see, much more dangerous to the newspaper.

For in this period the *Cardinal* itself became a major issue. The paper was not subsidized by the university. We depended for survival on advertising and subscription revenues, and we were losing money. (Indeed, in my last year there we were reduced to appearing three times a week instead of the usual five.) It was said that the source of our troubles was that our news coverage was too limited, that our interest in political matters prevented us from covering the stuff that really interested our readers—dances, intermurals, dorm elections, that sort of thing. Our critics were right, but for the wrong reason. Maybe we weren't profoundly interested in such matters, but we knew we had a journalistic obligation to them. The problem with discharging that obligation did not stem so much from political preoccupation but from the lack of space and staff to do the job.

Still, we were vulnerable, especially since we were governed by something called the Cardinal Board, which was chosen in the annual student elections. Because nobody but the Greeks paid any attention to this Mickey Mouse procedure, we were, in effect, governed from afar by our enemies. The board would never appoint Schecter or Zuckerman or me editor. On the other hand, they could never find anyone in their crowd with the talent or the energy to run the paper. They needed a Bill Buckley, but the best they could ever come up with were guys like Arlie Schardt, the sports editor, and Dave Kovenock, the business manager, the former amiable and competent, the latter disagreeable and competent. So we were ever at a standoff. Every year the board and the editorial staff entered into an unspoken conspiracy to find some amiable nonentity to be the official editor—he got to write editorials supporting the blood drive and encouraging the homecoming pep rally—while we activists ran the paper and spouted off as the spirit moved us. What we did not need in these tense circumstances was Stalinoid rant from the LYL, which many readers carelessly imagined represented our views.

We also did not need most of what I wrote. My memory of my copy—I have not read any of it, since I more or less heedlessly hammered it out, and am embarrassed to look it up now—is that it was very passionate and very simpleminded. I think, for example, that if I had been capable of developing a liberal, anticommunist position in my columns and editorials, I might have been able to defuse some of the tensions surrounding the paper. I think, as well, that if I had learned to temper my abrasive and arrogant manner in print, I might have served a similar end. But that never occurred to me. I pretended that I was operating out of high, uncompromising principle, and at one level I was: I certainly believed what I was writing. But at another level, two less admirable needs were operating: the need to trumpet my independence from my middle-class background and the need, quite simply, to be the center of controversy and thereby call attention to myelf.

Probably these needs operate in most college radicals; manifestly they mightily moved the radicals of the 1960s. But, as it turned out, certain fringe benefits derived from my posturings, which have proved invaluable to me. One of these was facility. The naiveté and simplicity of my thinking may now embarrass me—especially my efforts as a drama critic (a job I simply arrogated to myself), which were remarkable for their pretentiousness and pomposity—but it did represent a primitive attempt at the analytical mode, and thus it did establish the habit of mind on which my livelihood, and ultimately my identity, has since depended. I didn't learn how to write on the *Cardinal*. It would be nearer the truth to say that I learned how *not* to write there. By which I mean, finally, that my ineffectiveness showed me that observations filtered through ideological preconceptions, even benign ones, were bound to falsify response—particularly if they were expressed in ways that were dictated primarily by egocentric, if not downright egomaniacal, needs.

The *Cardinal,* of course, was part of, in a way the voice of, a particular university community—that radical-intellectual community of which I spoke earlier. In my active years on the paper there was no time to participate fully in its wayward life. One had cups of coffee with it between more pressing errands, one solicited pieces from it, and received a certain amount of friendly criticism from it. But then the *Cardinal* years came to an end, and I had a leftover campus life to kill—a senior semester and the year of graduate school I undertook mostly because I could not bear to abandon the comfortable, familiar life I had made for myself in Madison. Now I had time, and the need, to explore this community and allow myself to be absorbed into it.

It was not their politics—all the main points along the Left continuum were represented here—that drew me toward them. Rather, it was an attitude they all seemed to share, a kind of passionate sobriety about ideas that did not preclude a certain playfulness—anyway, a naturalness and ease—in their relationship to them that I had not known before. (I took up ideas as if they were sacred artifacts that became yet more sanctified by my interest in them.) This crowd would turn up at our corner table in the Rathskeller, fresh from a seminar with Hans Gerth or Merle Curti, full of the issues and ideas that had occupied their last two hours. More important, their talk was informed by writers like Camus, Orwell, Edmund Wilson, a dozen others who were not yet formally taught at the university, writers in whom I began to see the critical sensibility operating at levels to which I had not previously been exposed. And their excitements were infectious.

I don't mean to imply that I instantly determined to become a critic because I happened on *Such, Such Were the Joys* or *Classics and Commercials* at this moment. But here were forms—the essay and the review and the essayistic review—that felt right to me in some way. I loved reading these pieces, and it seemed to me that I might be able to learn to write them. Moreover, I saw that essays could carry material of the kind our conversations carried—historical references, social and psychological observation—that it was adaptable to all kinds of subjects, and, above all, that it was a very flexible form. It could be abstract or it could be personal; it could be journalistic on one occasion, more reflective or academic on another; it could shrink down to a column or two, expand to book length if need be. In other words, it perfectly suited someone who had already had, as it happened, enough harum-scarum daily political journalism to last a lifetime, and was now learning in graduate school that he did not have the patience or the love of research for its own sake that a scholarly career required. Here was something that one could write against deadline (even then, a necessary goad for me) and appear in the public prints, but could yet sustain a certain weight of research, reflection, and personal commentary.

Two other points need to be made about all this. The first is that I was beginning to understand that writing of the kind I was learning to admire had nothing to do with showing off, smarting off. In other words, George Jean Nathan, or Addison De Witt in *All About Eve,* were not appropriate role models. The other is that both the company I was keeping and the hopes I was beginning to entertain for myself encouraged me to rejoin, at a somewhat more sophisticated level, the university that had so inspired me when I caught my first glimpse of it in my first year in Madison, the liberal university, using the "L" word in the large, rather than the narrowly political, sense.

But there is something more I need say about this new community of mine, something about the uniqueness of its composition. For its singularity deeply informed my sensibility as a writer, my choice of subjects and my choice of tone. About half its population was drawn from a Midwest previously unknown to me, the small-town Midwest, and they were thus much truer products than I was of the now-dwindling Populist tradition of the region. A generation or two earlier, many of them would have returned home, I imagine, to teach or edit weekly papers or practice law and go into politics. Some of them might have moved on to similar roles in state and national politics. This ideal of "service" was, I think, still operating, unacknowledged, within them, but it was leading this generation toward Ph.D.s and college teaching. The other important segment of this community were the "New Yorkers," if I may borrow the Langdon Street genteelism for Jews. It was not entirely a misnomer. Most of them were, indeed, from New York, and they brought with them the nervous energy, and the slightly paranoid edge and the propensity to visible mood swings—from a kind of free associational and absurdist wit to sudden glooms—that that city imparts to its natives. Wisconsin, Michigan, North Carolina, at one time Alabama, were the liberal state universities that young people of this kind had been drawn to for many years—good, relatively inexpensive schools, to which lower-middle-class families could afford to send children who might, in any case, have been barred by the restrictions then in force at the Ivy League colleges.

This odd mix was a good one, mutually informative and mutually balancing. The midwestern WASPs had a certain phlegmatic quality about them, a sense that most crises were not terminal, that the seasons, the world, would roll on in their accustomed ways, McCarthyism or no, Cold War or no. The "New Yorkers," on the other hand, bristled with the nervous energy that was the heritage of their city and, yes, their Jewish leftist backgrounds. What they had learned at their mothers' knees was that you really could not count on anything, that cataclysms—indeed, holocausts—could and did happen. If the WASPs had a healthy sense of security about history's reliable course, the Jews had an equally healthy sense of its unreliability. Both groups were right and wrong in approximately equal proportions, I now think. And I learned about equally from both of them. Calm reflection and urgent reflection are not, I discovered, mutually contradictory; they are mutually informative.

But the truth is that the "New Yorkers" bedazzled me in ways that my own kind did not. They talked with such tumbling eagerness about ideas, and with such knowingness, with such a range of casual references. What particularly impressed me was their habit of applying their knowledge and their critical faculties to popular culture. Raymond Chandler and Dashiell Hammett were on their reading lists too. And the movies and sports and comic strips and jazz were on their minds. In their company I think I began to perceive dimly, not quite consciously, what might just possibly become my largest subject as writer. Anyway, I don't think it was entirely accidental that my only official extracurricular activity in my last year on campus was helping to organize a film society where we showed the Marx Brothers and Leni Riefenstahl and yes, *Ecstasy,* which, naturally, financed most of the year's activities for us, since the sight of a major movie star naked was not then the commonplace it has since become.

Certainly it was no accident that I headed directly for New York when it became completely clear to me that I would never be temperamentally suited for academic life. I had learned not just to admire its children, but more or less to hold my own with them. And I had learned that, like the unexamined life, a life without Jewish hubbub—that compound of dispairing wit, guilty intelligence, self-mocking self-examination, and realistic idealism—is not worth living. Let me put it as simply as I can: It is impossible for an outlander to imitate the spirit, the soul, if you will, of a Jewish intellectual. But I did find it possible to ape something of his rhythms and habits of mind. The born fellow-traveler was born yet again in this period, and has stayed close to this caravan—within hailing distance at worst—ever since.

But yet there are strange turnings in its road that I find hard to comprehend. For example, in his correspondence with me, the editor of this volume mentions the sense he gathered from the interviews he conducted with Herb Gutman and Warren Susman, just before their tragically untimely deaths, that both felt they had been prevented from developing as far as they might have by their lack of

"European-style preparation," and by their failure to develop the "intellectual-methodological sophistication." I do not know Gutman's work (though I did know and admire him in college). I do know and admire Susman's work (though I did not know him in college), and I am dismayed at this report. I must wonder if they did not, out of modesty or some deeper discontent, misunderstand the problem confronting them, all of us of the 1950s generation, who have since attempted to grapple critically with the American political and popular cultures.

As I look back upon our intellectually formative years I see, or think I see, that we were all teetering, all unknowing, on a historical cusp. In that period, modernism, which the academic community was only belatedly, tentatively beginning to embrace, was about to be set upon, and routed, by postmodernism's unkempt hordes. And I am inclined to think that none of us was adequately prepared for this onslaught. I am speaking both politically and culturally, but let me make my point initially in political terms.

McCarthyism, our great touchstone issue in the 1950s, represented, I think, the first primitive stirrings of the postmodernist politics that have become, in less than three decades, our only politics. There is, finally, only a difference in manner between McCarthy diving into his lawyer's briefcase to pull out spurious documents "proving" communist penetration into this or that government agency and George Bush at the flag factory. Or, more to the point, perhaps, Bush's repeated implication that somehow membership in the ACLU constitutes a form of socially subversive activity. All the politics between McCarthy and Bush partake of the same spirit, whether we are talking "Camelot" or the cap-and-bells posturings of the 1960s radicals or Reagan's conduct of the presidency. As everyone is aware, this is all a politics of images, not issues.

But it is also something else: It is nonnarrative politics. Until the 1950s, each new political generation wove a piece of its own into a historical tapestry, a tapestry that had as its hopeful theme, its story if you will, the halting progress of mankind toward some imperfect but yet encouraging enlightenment. In the years since then, that tapestry has been abandoned. Images of the kind I just mentioned are not woven into a sometimes murky but essentially comprehensible tale; they are slapped helter-skelter into a framework containing a work in postmodernism's most characteristic form, a collage. And the aim of a collage is not to stir reason, but to stir feeling.

It may be merely coincidence that the rise of television as our basic means of mass communication coincides with the rise of postmodernism as the organizing—or disorganizing—principle of the elite sensibility. Or it may not be. What we can surely say is that the decline of traditional narrative in politics coincides with the decline of traditional narrative elsewhere—in the novel, in painting, in theater, in the movies, even on television itself, which today offers fewer dramatically comprehensible fictions than it did in its early days. We must also understand that the decline of narrative urgency permits a certain drift on the part of narrators. They are free now, as they formerly were not, to pause and rummage through every level of culture—high, low and in between—in search of images that, when juxtaposed, will create Wow effects, knock your socks off. But that do not necessarily enlighten us—rather the contrary. Or move humankind's story along.

It follows from this that postmodern or postnarrative culture, like postmodern or postnarrative politics, cannot be apprehended, let alone significantly altered, by the application of traditional liberal or conservative standards. For it is profoundly a reactionary culture in the crudest meaning of that term. That is to say, its sole aim is the creation of sensation, simple, visceral responses, which may seem to some of us beneath criticism, but may only be beyond the reach of the critical tools that were handed on to us in the 1950s.

What I am saying is that the dissatisfactions that men like Gutman and Susman felt at the end of their lives, the dissatisfactions I feel with my own critical–historical work, arise not from our lack of "methodological" sophistication, our inability comfortably to apply, let us say, the ideas of the Frankfort School to the American reality. These dissatisfactions arise instead, I think, from our uneasy sense that the Frankfort School has nothing useful to tell us about that reality, that, God help us, Freud and Marx and the rest of the twentieth-century pantheon may be equally irrelevant to our enterprise.

I was, I believe, luckier than many of my academic contemporaries in that my self-absorption, my catch-as-catch-can education, my hasty passage through several university societies, above all the fact that my sensibility is writerly rather than intellectual, combined to leave me bereft of theoretical ambition, for that matter bereft of theoretical interests. I have never set out to make a cultural "critique" and am unaware of ever having consciously committed one. My interest is only in the discrete object and its immediate context. It is all I am prepared to handle, all I can handle, all I want to handle. For these finite needs, the tools one finally took away from the university of the 1950s, the open, honorable, and responsible attitudes about the world of ideas that one is surprised to find one absorbed quite profoundly there, after all the shouting died, are entirely sufficient. Indeed, one need only read Susman's marvelous collection, *Culture as History,* published just months before his death, to see how well thematic modesty becomes a man in a world where inflated ambition is often equated with actual achievement. And to see what uses rigorous specificity can have in prizing at least some limited, but highly suggestable, meaning out of the confusions of our culture. I felt that Susman's superlative work did honor to the heritage he and I shared, and that he needed to do no more to claim our deep respect.

In the year that he published his book, I happened to publish a book too. It is the one book of mine that is not an essay. It is a formal, full-scale biography of a once great, now quite ignored American figure, D. W. Griffith, the man who essentially invented the craft of motion picture direction. I struggled with the thing for years, despaired of it, despised it, yet finally saw it through to publication. Lost in its toils, I could not recall why I had undertaken this task, or what I had once hoped I might accomplish by it. It was not until I was finished, and was checking the footnotes and bibliography, that I realized, finally, what I had been doing all those years. What I had been doing in my way was, of course, what Susman had been doing in his way, what I sense the others of our time and training continue to do. That was paying my dues, and my belated tribute, to the highest ideals of my youth. These, I now saw clearly, encouraged not grand visions but simple, even glancing, observation, not sweeping theory, but unambiguous factuality. Above all, they encouraged the search, against the odds, for humane narrative coherence—a sense of a meaning, not The Meaning—in a life, and in life. If we are to reclaim the world for reason, these are the values that must be patiently reasserted. They are not, of course, the values of the radical university. They are values of the liberal one, that university that claimed my first, and now my final, allegiance.

Part Two
From Old Left to New

8   From Liberal, to Social Democrat, to Marxist: My Political Itinerary Through Madison in the Late 1950s

BERTELL OLLMAN

Warner Brothers scripted a film about Bertell Ollman's life a few years ago, based very loosely on his whimsically autobiographical *Class Struggle Is the Name of the Game: True Confessions of a Marxist Businessman*. In the film, his real-life wife would conveniently die, and he would—in a bungling professorial manner of a Marxist about to learn better—make sexual approaches to a female buyer at Bloomingdale's. Luckily for himself, his wife, and perhaps Warner Brothers, the film was never made. Bertell Ollman is a prominent figure in political science, author of *Alienation* and other works on Marxist theory, co-editor of the *Left Academy* series, principal in one of the most important academic freedom controversies and libel suits of recent years, socialist boardgame inventor, sometimes humorist, and persistent social critic. When he looks back at his intellectual–political origins in Madison, he finds more reasons to laugh.

I came to Madison in the fall of 1955, after a year and a half at the University of Wisconsin extension in Milwaukee. I was raised on Milwaukee's north and west sides, the only child of Jewish immigrant parents who worked in factories nearly all their lives. My mother was in the Amalgamated Clothing Workers, and my father was in the Brewery Workers. Trade union newspapers were an important part of my early reading, especially since the only book in the house was an old copy of *Reader's Digest*. My parents desperately wanted to enter the middle class by opening up a little grocery store, a wish I considered crazy even before I wholly understood it. They had little formal education. My father had been expelled from school in the sixth grade for wrestling with his teacher, and my mother completed only two years of night school. Still—maybe I should say because of all this—I was supposed to become a doctor. From my earliest years, I recall that I helped make all important family decisions. No doubt this had a lot to do with building my self-confidence and in giving most of my relatives the idea that I was a spoiled brat.

There was something special about Milwaukee in those days. We still had a socialist mayor, Frank Zeidler. No one could think socialism was a dirty word. You could see the differences between Milwaukee, with its long tradition of social-ist mayors, and Chicago, just by comparing our beautiful, park-dominated lake-front with the high-rises that spilled into Lake Michigan on their end. Socialism was also associated with clean, honest city government. There was a feeling that even if socialist ideas hadn't changed the world, they had counted for something.[1]

Moving to Madison was the most dramatic change I've ever experienced in my life. Before that, I had never really had contact with anyone from outside Wis-consin. In Madison I got to know people from all over the world. Ideas were impor-tant for many of my new friends. They had known other ways of life. All of a sudden, nothing could be taken for granted. My appetite for the exotic and for controversy had been whetted.

My first term in Madison, I joined eleven or twelve organizations, which struck the half-dozen Jewish boys from Milwaukee with whom I was living as pretty funny, especially since they included both the Arab Student Association and the Israel Club. I found it equally odd that in the midst of so much stimulation, they could remain aloof.

It was at the end of my first term that I joined the Student League for Indus-trial Democracy (SLID). There was a big snowstorm that night, and when I arrived at the organizational meeting announced in that morning's *Daily Cardinal,* I dis-covered I was the only one there besides the organizer, Gabriel Kolko, then a grad-uate student in history.[2] I'm afraid Gaby didn't have much choice. By a unanimous vote, I was elected president of the new organization. Afterward, I went home and announced to my friends that I had joined another club, but that this time I was president. When they stopped laughing, I added that they had also become mem-bers because I was using the money I owed them from poker to buy them all membership cards. So began the SLID chapter at the University of Wisconsin. In the years to come, more than one successful Republican lawyer did his best to hide his youthful membership in our social democratic organization.

SLID started with seven or eight members, and eventually got about twenty-five, all undergraduates like myself. Two years later, I became vice-president of the

---

[1] Milwaukee remained a bastion of socialist politics long after the Socialist party had been reduced to a marginal organization on the national scene. Frank Zeidler was perhaps to Milwaukee what a Norman Thomas in office might have been to the United States: more honest, moral, and truly concerned than Democrats or Republicans, but unable to effect more than superficial change.

[2] Gabriel Kolko, who with the *Triumph of Conservatism* became one of the best-known radical historians, has remained a leading scholar on American domestic and foreign policies.

national organization, edited a few issues of the official journal, which was published in New York, and made contact with people like Andre Schiffrin (leader of the other main functioning chapter, at Yale, and president of national SLID) and Aryeh Naier.[3] Though we shared many ideas, there was a clear distinction between SLID and the Socialist party. SLID was an educational group raising basic questions and giving people a chance to hear a variety of answers. One of our most successful forums was on Israel, where the speakers were the president of the Arab Student Association and a leading campus Zionist. This was a sizzling confrontation, possibly unique, and highly educational. SLID also related to leftist liberals and independent socialists. National leaders with whom we identified included people like Norman Thomas, Walter Reuther, and Paul Douglas.

We passed out a lot of pamphlets and even sold a few. At that time, a soapbox was set up outside the student union every Friday at noon. I spoke frequently, mostly in favor of socialized medicine and against McCarthyism and Russian communism. Maybe it's nostalgia but I think these were the best lectures I ever gave. At the girls' dorm where I worked, I was known as the "Red waiter" because I was always talking to the girls about politics. Talking with people who don't agree with me and drawing them toward socialism has been an important activity of mine from that time to this. Of course, in those days I was about as radical as European social democracy. I've moved a long way leftward since.

Professors who influenced my thinking in those years included the economist Selig Perlman, a social democrat who regaled us with stories about conspiring in the forests against the czar before the Russian Revolution. And Hans Gerth, who delivered a fascinating monologue in the Rathskeller on life and politics in Nazi Germany. But it wasn't until William Ebenstein, a political science professor, introduced me to Erich Fromm's *Sane Society* that I began to call myself a socialist.[4]

I learned even more from fellow students, from my roommate, Gar Alperovitz, then president of the Student Union, who already had the wonderful knack of being able to speak to anyone in their own language. Isadore Silver, who was president of Students for Democratic Action, seemed to have read everything that was written on current affairs. Sadoun Hammadi, then president of the Arab Student Association and later foreign minister of Iraq, provided some balance in my view of the Middle East. I also learned a lot about Marxism from George Rawick and especially from Gabriel Kolko, who was already a very sophisticated thinker.[5]

[3] Andre Schiffrin is director of Pantheon Books and has been active in various progressive causes; Aryeh Naier is one of the best-known international civil libertarians, working in Amnesty International and similar organizations.

[4] Selig Perlman is best remembered as a prominent author in the John R. Commons multivolume *History of the American Labor Movement,* a curiously conservative argument for the "wage consciousness" (rather than class consciousness) of American workers; William Eberstein was the first political science professor I had who did not caricature socialism.

[5] Gar Alperovitz, author of *Atomic Diplomacy,* has been one of the most prominent policy theoreticians in the liberal wing of the Democratic party, but has recently moved farther left.

One of SLID's main activities was debating the communists. The Labor Youth League (LYL) started a series of open discussions on Marxism, and we went to present another view, turning the sessions into a debate. The next year, we had a formal debate with them on the question "Does Marxism Have More Holes in It Than Swiss Cheese?" (The title was my idea.) I knew little about Marx at the time—my main sources being Kolko and the early Sidney Hook, Socialist philosopher long since turned Cold Warrior. Fortunately, the LYL-ers didn't seem to know much more. I recall that one of their main points was that you had to eat before you could screw. A decade later, I met one of the LYL-ers I had debated, who had since become a successful psychoanalyst, and apologized for all the stupid things I had said about Marxism. "No," he said, "don't apologize. You were right and I was wrong." We had changed sides.

When I think now about all the debates we had with the LYL, I am more than a little embarrassed. There were a lot more pressing problems. The LYL had only three public members and probably a dozen or so secret ones. Still, it was in these debates that my real involvement with Marxist ideas began.

We also shared a culture with LYL-ers at the Green Lantern eating coop— my uncle had been a member back in the 1930s. Most of the best folksingers and musicians, Ronald Radosh among them, were LYL-ers. Often on Fridays there would be a party at the "Little Kremlin," a house where several LYL-ers lived, and upward of a hundred people of various political allegiances would gather to sing. I was always a little jealous that social democrats didn't have such a rich folksong culture.

The fact that there was an LYL chapter at Wisconsin, the only university to have an officially recognized communist group at that time, is something we all felt proud of. Our civil libertarian commitment to defend them and the absolute freedom to speak and read anything one wanted led to a much publicized battle with the American Legion. In 1956, the American Legion came out with a demand that the university reduce its stock of "commie books." After doing some on-the-spot research, the state commander of the Legion concluded there were too many communist titles in the library, adding that this went counter to the "American way of life." SLID wrote to him asking for a definition of this prhase so that we would know how to be better Americans. He answered that he really didn't know what the "American way of life" is, but that we could be sure of one thing, that he was ready to give up his life for it. After sharing this gem around the rest of the campus, SLID called an open meeting to discuss the Legion as a threat to American democracy.

It was very lively. Several state officers of the Legion attended, including someone called the Americanism Commander. So did about fifty students, and the discussion went on late into the night. The next day, the *Cardinal* carried a headline suggesting that a riot had taken place, which led to a call from the dean protesting my treatment of the visiting Legionnaires. A few years later, of course, the administration's sensitivity would be tested by some real riots. Not to be deterred, we planned a big book burning in front of the library. Dressed in Legionnaire, Nazi, and KKK [Ku Klux Klan] costumes, we hoped to show what it was exactly that the Legion was asking the university to do. At first, lots of people agreed to participate, but the uptight editor of the *Daily Cardinal* said the action was unbecoming, and frightened off most of our supporters. In the end, I and a couple of others were left holding the matches. We didn't light them.

I was also active at the time in Students for Democratic Action, a liberal educational group, and in the Young Democrats. The president of the state's Young Democrats was a close friend of mine and a member of SLID; I was on the state council of the Young Democrats and wrote a column for their newsletter. In my last year at Madison, we succeeded in getting the state Young Democratic convention to pass a number of resolutions nationalizing most of the big industries in the country. Copies of our resolutions were sent to Democratic legislators at state and national levels, demanding that they be translated into the laws of the land. We are still waiting for their response.

Mock United Nations were also big events at Madison in those days. Over a thousand students from many different colleges participated in these role-playing extravaganzas. In a mock UN conference at the University of Indiana, I headed the Russian delegation. At the Wisconsin mock UN some months later, I found myself at the head of the American delegation. Maybe it was the insights acquired by making such a shift in perspectives, but all of a sudden most of the world's major problems seemed terribly easy to solve. The U.S. delegation simply admitted how wrong our government had been in the past and adopted new, more humane policies. When people got over their shock at our change of heart, the joy was general.

A pet project of mine at the time was the establishment of a World University that would promote international understanding as a means to world peace. I wrote an article on this subject for SLID's magazine, gave a few talks at Madison and elsewhere, and even delivered a petition to the UN calling for such a university. Prejudice and hatred based on misunderstanding, I was convinced, underlay many of the major conflicts in the world. If the people of the world, especially future leaders, could only get to know one another better—I guess this is really the kind of university that I would have liked to go to. In the years to come—as part of my growing realization of what capitalism and imperialism really are—I came to see that knowing "us" better could have the very opposite effect. We are led by a pack of wolves whose interests are really different from everyone else's. In which case, promoting international understanding, where this means something more than simple tolerance or knowing what a nuclear war would bring, is pure propaganda or even positively dangerous to world peace.

On the Left and among liberals, Joseph McCarthy was a great uniting force. When he died in the fall of 1956, I decided to go to his funeral outside Appleton, hoping to write an article. I lost my ride home from the cemetery and was forced to hitchhike back. The hearse that had just dropped off McCarthy's body picked me up and took me back to Appleton. At the time, this seemed to me to be an act of vast historic significance: the old reactionary going to the soil, while from the soil, riding into the City of Man, comes the young radical—grinning from ear to ear—to stake his claim on the future. I never did write the article; but the *Cardinal* reported on my ride in the hearse, which led to my being harassed by a bunch of Young Republicans, who viewed this as a form of desecration.

What did it all add up to? When I came to Madison, my first career choice was the U.S. Foreign Service, but I dropped this as I gradually came to understand that the government (and system) I would have to defend was indefensible. More important than particular individuals and books in bringing me to this conclusion were the great variety of viewpoints and the encouragement to think for oneself that were the hallmarks of university life in Madison. I didn't start calling myself a Marxist until some years later, after I had been to Oxford and read a lot of Marx, but the beginnings and early stages of this transformation and for whatever else I have become, both politically and academically, took place at Wisconsin.

9 From the Labor Youth League to the Cuban Revolution

SAUL LANDAU

Saul Landau has long been a scholar in residence at the Institute for Policy Studies, Washington, D.C. He is also a noted documentary filmmaker and author of a number of books on foreign policy, including an outstanding early book on the New Left, edited with Paul Jacobs, *The New Radicals,* (1966) and an important work of investigative journalism (with John Dinges), *Assassination on Embassy Row* (1980).

When the plane landed at the Madison airport in September 1953, Henry Breitrose, who had attended the same high school as I, said, as we looked around, "I've never been to this part of New York before." A joke often covers nervousness, but for Henry and me, Madison was just about the right distance from New York City—1,000 actual and cultural miles. Like other New Yorkers from the province of the Bronx, I grew up believing that the United States contained Catholics, the majority, and Jews, the minority. In Madison we met not only Protestants en masse, but people who lived in and even owned their own houses, not tenants in fifty-family apartment buildings.

Wisconsin had a charged atmosphere. Joe McCarthy was the junior senator and still in his ascent in the fall of 1953. But Madison, the capital, was also the heart of the anti-McCarthy movement in the state. Another transplanted New Yorker, Cora Rubin (Cora Weiss after marriage), had organized and coordinated the Joe Must Go movement to recall McCarthy. She had recruited well-known political people like Gaylord Nelson and William Proxmire, who later became senators, and freshmen like myself, who volunteered to deliver petitions to people who wanted to sign the declaration calling for a recall election. My wife, Nina

Serrano, worked as a staff person on the campaign. I still remember a man who punched me in the nose when I delivered a petition to his house.

The Labor Youth League [LYL], the unofficial communist youth organization, could function on the Madison campus because of the courage of one sponsoring professor necessary for status as a campus organization and because of the tradition of academic freedom. In the home state of Joe McCarthy, the last open chapter of the LYL continued to play some role in the lives of students and faculty.

Years later, distinguished Left scholars like Gar Alperovitz and Bertell Ollman, not members of the LYL, could look back on their Madison experience and evaluate—I think positively—what benefit they derived from the lively debate that surrounded the LYL.

I was recruited to join the LYL by the student who rented a room in our house. Henry Wortis was a senior and easily handled my devil's advocate political arguments and then would leave copies of the *Daily Worker, Masses and Mainstream, Political Affairs,* and the *Guardian* in the bathroom. In addition, several other radical juniors and seniors engaged me in provocative conversations, some of them members of the LYL, some just bright people who refused to accept the prevailing Cold War and anticommunist framework or mythology as the proper context for understanding the world. Henry Wortis, Gene Shapiro, Alan Blumstein, Marty Sklar, Arnie Lieber, Doris Jackson, Jeff Kaplow, Carl Parrini, and my wife, Nina, were some of those who formed a core of students who helped shape my thinking and that of others in the mid 1950s. Later, a formidable group of graduate students, who came mostly to study with William Appleman Williams, gave me a rigorous education.

It was Henry, however, who convinced me to actually join the secret—and thus exciting—campus chapter of the LYL. The *Worker*-in-the-bathroom ploy was obvious but effective. On Sunday mornings, however, Henry would put on his trenchcoat, ask me to feed his dog if, for some reason, he didn't get back in time, and then mysteriously leave the house, often turning his head several times to check that no one was following him.

Once in the LYL, which was divided into cells so that an individual would know only the names of those few students in his own unit, I began to learn not only the ABCs of Marxism and Leninism but the basics of organizing in the political and cultural arenas. Secrecy was maintained because the party leadership believed at the time that McCarthyism was just a short step away from full-blown fascism and that therefore members of even the unofficial party youth organization had to be protected. There were practical reasons for maintaining this kind of security. Thousands of professors, media and entertainment workers, union leaders, government employees, and just plain working people had been fired from their jobs because one of the congressional witch-hunting committees would visit a community and an informer would surface to name names of communists. Graduating students were rejected from graduate school and medical school because of membership in "subversive organizations." The Smith Act trials of communist leaders, the FBI persecution of suspected or actual communists, the 1953 execution of the

Rosenbergs—all provided evidence for what party leaders saw as an increasing level of repression.

When I joined the LYL, I had every reason to expect that membership would directly affect my ability to get a job or pursue a professional career. So, joining meant a real commitment, or a ridiculous level of naiveté. I suspect I had both the commitment and the naiveté, and, with hindsight, that many of my activities as an LYL member would make fair soap-opera material—or even stand-up comedy for a political audience. For example, we met in Madison's small black neighborhood. This was done, of course, to make us inconspicuous. The LYL members were mostly white, Jewish, and from New York. There were blacks and non-New Yorkers also, but the cultural tone of the group carried that strain of arrogant imperiousness that is easily acquired in the New York streets and schools.

We also took seriously our commitment to the working class, and in order to provide it with information and analysis that it needed to have, we would appear at 6:00 A.M. outside the factory gates of Oscar Meyer or Ohio Chemical to hand to the entering laborers copies of the *Worker* or *Guardian,* or occasional pamphlets written by Communist party theorists. In retrospect, I'm surprised that no one punched us out or even hurled insults at us. I suppose that the workers must have in some way appreciated that young students standing in the subzero cold to hand them newspapers must have had some deep interest in reaching them. Sometimes, a worker would even thank us and say that he or she had actually read some of the material and liked it.

Another LYL activity was campus education. This involved bringing communist speakers—or progressives—to campus. We invited Herbert Aptheker, Annette T. Rubinstein, Meridel LeSueur, A. B. Magil, Joseph Starobin, and others.[1] We also engaged regularly in free-speech fights and received threats from Korean war veterans, some of whom looked as if they had not only killed before but could again. And we "controlled" some campus liberal activities—which didn't mean very much when you consider that in order to protect our secret identities we had to act like other people who led organizations, like Students for Kefauver or the Campus Peace Center.

The LYL provided us with the opportunity to acquire a special education and a good sense of discipline. We had internal study classes. We read the Little Lenin Library and discussed theory with the more advanced people, who included Wortis and the brilliant Marty Sklar.

[1] Annette Rubinstein, a Left literary critic, had been an editor of *Mainstream* (1945–1946), the unsuccessful attempt of literary-minded intellectuals to break from the narrowness of the 1930s leftist traditions; A. B. Magil, a sometimes editor of the *New Masses* (which merged into *Masses and Mainstream*), was a political leader of Left-leaning Jewish movements; Meridel LeSueur, one of the very few noted literary figures of the 1930s to remain close to the Communist party during the 1940s, had written several novels about blue-collar women's life in the Midwest during the depression; Joseph Starobin, a leading Communist party functionary and later historian of American communism, was among the earliest to break with party orthodoxy on questions of polycentrism.

You had to read the newspapers carefully, and relate your daily activities to the larger world. I began doing well in school because I could go into a history or political science class and write more coherent essays than I could have without the cement of Marxism.

I never felt attracted to Stalin, although I was convinced, by my reading and my colleagues' arguments, that U.S. Cold War policy was based on a fundamental lie. When the "good guy"—Stalin—was shown to be the "bad guy" at the Twentieth Party Congress, and the invasion of Hungary occurred in 1956, we were confused and had to reevaluate. We retained our critique of American policy, while we changed our attitude toward the Soviet Union. The LYL, like its Communist party parent, lacked an ideology that provided coherence in the late 1950s.

The LYL on the Madison campus dissolved after Pete Seeger came to campus. The university's Music Committee declared that the LYL was a political organization and therefore could invite only speakers, not singers. We answered that Seeger would lecture on folk music, singing only to illustrate his points. Seeger laughed when we told him, and did what he does best. He got a packed crowd because of the controversy. The Music Committee people sat around with stopwatches and determined, correctly, that Seeger's singing time far exceeded his talking time and that this meant that we had intruded on the sacred monopoly of the Music Committee. We had a great concert, but LYL was no more.

William A. Williams's reappearance on campus in 1958 provided a new intellectual inspiration. He offered a fresh look at U.S. society and history without a Cold War or anti-Soviet attitude. His neo-Beardian midwesternness meant to some of us a legitimizing sense of "real" American, not New York Jewish. His basic method meshed with ours and expanded our way of thinking about history and ideas.

George Mosse was also a good teacher, an important professor, and he enjoyed the stimulation provided by leftists. We also learned a great deal from Merrill Jensen and Bill Hesseltine. Hesseltine forced people to define their positions and to write well. He wouldn't let students get away with anything. Jensen was also a stickler for proof. These professors didn't agree with us, but they welcomed a challenge they didn't get from most graduate or undergraduate students. By 1959, the Left history clique had an impact on other graduate students, so there was an exciting atmosphere of debated challenge. On the other hand, we still tended to think of the anticommunist Left as The Enemy—people like George Rawick, whom we learned to respect later on. The lines blurred a bit with the formation of the Socialist Club. We had to modify some of the holdovers of Communist party sectarianism. Other Left—nonparty—activists like Bertell Ollman found out we weren't so bad either.

We joined together to do battle against the Right, with a common policy of antimilitarism, anticapitalism, and a mildly critical approach to the USSR, one that was slightly tolerant of those less critical. Everybody shared a sense that a new era was beginning, a "thaw" in the Cold War.

We were not a big part of the campus. The majority were agriculture and engineering students. As a history teaching assistant in 1958–1959, I had students who could not identify Hitler. Most of the agriculture, engineering, and pharmacy students were not just apolitical but downright disinterested, turned off to learning anything outside their chosen vocations, acquiring a good husband or wife, and getting a steady job. And there was the fraternity–sorority crowd. We were address-ing ourselves to perhaps the other thousand or so students, and about 20 percent of them were responsive.

The liberal–left students enjoyed an active cultural life. I remember reading Marxist cultural critics, [Georgi] Plekhanov, [George] Lukacs, and [Theodor] Adorno, after first turning on to the literary criticism in *Masses and Mainstream* and discovering interesting class analyses of literature and music. Later, we held Anti-Military Balls in 1959 and 1960 with comic skits, which we wrote. One author was Marshall Brickman, a talented musician and a very funny young man.[2] Nina [Serrano Landau] played a big role in local theater. I acted in Eugene O'Neill's *The Hairy Ape*.

We all discussed theater and movies, read literature and that genre of literary criticism that attacked the existing criticism. And I thought about becoming an actor or a playwright, which is, in part, how I got into movies.

Meanwhile, in 1959 we organized the *Studies on the Left* editorial board, made up of young Old Leftists and new people who had come onto campus. We made fund-raising trips to Chicago and New York, raising $5, $10, or $20 from person to person. We sweated to get that money; there was part of me in that magazine. We decided who not to include through an ideological perception. We still had one foot in the Old Left and didn't invite anyone from SLID or the Trotskyists.

Studies seemed at first broader, more cultural, than it would later become. I argued for cover art and a nice photo for the Cuba issue, and I had an eye for sharp writing. We didn't know how to take it further than we did in the cultural area. In the end, Jim Weinstein, who more or less took over the leadership of the mag-azine after three or four issues, aimed it in other directions.

■■

I left Madison for Cuba in 1960 because my marriage was breaking up, and I wanted to get away from graduate school. I hadn't been knowledgeable or even interested in Cuba before the revolution. I didn't even know much Spanish. But this was a revolution that answered the dreams of the New Left without abandon-ing the Old Left.

When I came back to Madison, I gave a speech to a big campus audience. Bill Williams provided the introduction. Being on the same platform with him

[2] Later famous for his collaboration with Woody Allen on *Annie Hall* and his own film work as writer and director.

was inspiring to me. We began the student Fair Play for Cuba Committee, which gathered some support on a number of campuses. I wrote the national newsletter from Madison, traveling around to organize other chapters.

In 1960, I met C. Wright Mills, by accident, in a Havana hotel lobby. Mills never said anything of interest about his Madison years, perhaps because his collaboration with Hans Gerth had soured. He and Williams had little interest in each other. Still, Mills, like Williams, had an important influence on both the New Left and those who moved from Old to New. I remember reading *White Collar* when it came out. *The Power Elite* seemed even more interesting. We ran to *Monthly Review* to get Paul Sweezy's critique of *The Power Elite*. We probably agreed with Sweezy; but *The Power Elite* made us feel fortified, reinforced by data.

And also by example. Mills began a new phase with *The Causes of World War Three,* like a pamphleteer, the Tom Paine of the New Left. He came from a moral sense, unlike the Old Left, which, by contrast, seemed strictly political, economic, Marxist.

Mills wasn't really very political at all. But he had a job to do, and he did the job. When we reprinted his "Letter to the New Left" in *Studies,* I remember we distrusted a lot of the stuff in it. But we admired it too. *Listen Yankee* helped mobilize pro-Cuba and anti-intervention support.

After leaving Madison in June 1960, I drifted away from *Studies,* from some of my old friends, into more cultural work. I was told that a U.S. marshal with a government subpoena was looking for me to testify about my Fair Play for Cuba work before the Senate subcommittee. So I agreed to go to Europe with Mills, as confidant and personal secretary of a man who knew time was running out on him. Mills had suffered a serious heart attack in the fall of 1960.

I had the idea that I would shed Marxism and become a Millsian. After a while, I discovered that Mills didn't have any alternative to Marxism, except that men of goodwill and determination can do the right thing. I did help him get out *The Marxists,* not a heavy book, but one link between Marx, Lenin, and the New Left.

I've thought since about what Madison did and didn't do. I still have friends from Madison who influence me. I had two children born there. I got a good education, which would have been less good if I hadn't been involved in the LYL and the Socialist Club. I learned how to read literature, to see film and theater critically, which enhances my own aesthetic sense. I acquired a general worldview that has stayed with me, for which I'm grateful.

Most important, I got a historical grounding, at a time when history seemed about to be erased. A peculiar conjuncture of graduate and undergraduate students with some older historians, Marxists or not, gave us a chance to look at the world with a coherent view.

Williams's critique of the American men of power helped put history back into the Left, in a new way. I don't know if Bill Williams understands how much we appreciated him.

10 *Studies on the Left*

JAMES WEINSTEIN

The weekly tabloid edited by James Weinstein, *In These Times,* is the first social-ist newspaper in the U.S. since the 1940s with anything like a mass readership (currently around 35,000). That fact speaks, no doubt, to the problematic quali-ties of American intellectualism. But it also points to Weinstein's determination and his political skills. He traces his intellectual–political life here. He passes eas-ily over his willingness to give up, or at least postpone, his own considerable scholarship for his commitment. His *Decline of American Socialism, 1912–1925* (1967) was the first socialist history that looked closely at the grass-roots press and the remarkable political recovery the socialists staged in the last half of the 1910s. In so doing, he overtuned existing scholarly orthodoxy in any number of ways. He has continued to overturn orthodoxy, political–journalistic this time, by add-ing a scholar's vision to his weekly editorial sweep of the news.

I wanted to be an electrical engineer when I entered Cornell in June 1944. So my first semester I was a chemistry major. Then, as the war was still going on, I knew I'd be drafted, so I took fourteen hours of Russian, hoping to get into naval intel-ligence. I was drafted into the navy, but didn't get into the language program because my high school principal told the FBI that I had been a member of Amer-ican Youth for Democracy (AYD).

In the navy I learned electronics, but when I returned to Cornell, I was inter-ested in history. So I became a government major—because that was the field with the least requirements.

I met Warren Susman in a constitutional law class, and he became my best friend. The connection between an intelligent approach to politics and a sophisticated understanding of history was already in Warren's mind, and in mine. We took courses with Paul W. Gates, treasurer of the New York Wallace for President Committee, and with Curtis P. Nettles, who was then ranting against the Truman Doctrine. Like Warren, I became active in the Progressive party—and in the Young Progressives—on the Cornell campus. I also belonged to AYD—a Communist "front" group—on campus and later joined the party.

I then went to Columbia Law School for a year. I quit in 1950, partly because I decided I didn't want to be a lawyer and partly because the FBI was harassing me about my roommate's connection to Julius Rosenberg and I assumed I would have trouble getting through the bar. After I quit school, I went to work full-time for the Young Progressives and then worked in a series of radio and television factories in the New York area, including David Bogen Co., where I was a steward in the International Brotherhood of Electrical Workers, then Emerson Radio, where I ran ritually for office in our local of the International Union of Electrical Workers.

My four and a half years at Emerson were the most carefree I can remember. I was the happiest worker in the plant. Interesting work—I was a troubleshooter. I liked my fellow workers—mostly women. And I had no responsibilities. It was the only time in my life that I would wake up singing, eager to pick up my riders and drive through the Holland Tunnel and get to work—where I spent most of the day dreaming about what to eat for dinner. I couldn't understand why most of the workers, particularly the men, were always trying to figure out how to get out of the plant.

Then one day in 1956 it suddenly occurred to me: I was going to be thirty years old that July. Am I going to spend the rest of my life working in a factory? I asked myself. That was the day I was proletarianized. I finally realized what was going on in my friends' heads. But unlike most of them, I had alternatives.

Entirely fortuitously, this coincided with Nikita Khrushchev's speech to the Soviets' Twentieth Party Congress, and with the Soviet invasion of Hungary. I had been a member of a Communist party group at Emerson. Even before the Khrushchev speech, it had disintegrated—it simply stopped meeting because it seemed to have no point or direction. It seemed to me in the light of international and local events that we didn't know what we were doing. The Party Congress and the invasion confirmed everything that we didn't want to believe about the communist movement. So I quit the party at the same time that I quit work and went back to school to study history at Columbia University.

I did so because I had always been interested in history, but also to try to find out what had gone wrong with the Left. Originally, I thought I'd do my dissertation on Representative Vito Marcantonio, the head of the American Labor Party (ALP) in New York and the most outspoken leftist in Congress. My interest was partly personal. I had been active in the ALP on the West Side of Manhattan, and I knew "Marc" through friends. But as I looked into this, I concluded that he was really unique. He didn't represent a milieu or historic movement larger than himself, and I was not intersted simply in a biography, but in a political history with some wider meaning for an understanding of the Left's predicament and its alternative possibilities.

Then I stumbled across some material on the old Socialist party during World War I that completely contradicted what we had been taught in the party about its predecessor. I dug into that and ended up doing my master's thesis on antiwar sentiment and the Socialist party in 1917. That, in turn, led to further research and to work that eventually led to the writing of *The Decline of Socialism in America, 1912–1925,* which initially was to be my dissertation but ended up being a book.

Somewhere during this process, we moved to Madison, Wisconsin, in part because of my work and in part for family reasons. My then wife, Jackie, came from Wisconsin, first from Alma, where her family had run the *Buffalo County Journal,* and then from Madison, where her mother worked as a proofreader on the *Capital Times* and *Progressive* magazine. From 1956 (when we were married) on, we went to Madison every summer to visit. Jackie had gone to the university there and had been a close friend of Marty Sklar and Saul and Nina Landau since they were undergraduates together. I met them all in 1955–1956. We all were former party or LYL members. (I had been organizational secretary of the Manhattan LYL.) And Marty and Saul, along with David Eakins and others, were historians and students of William Appleman Williams, which is how I came to know him.

In New York, Jackie and I had also become active in the reform movement of the Democratic party in 1959. We lived on the West Side and joined the FDR-Woodrow Wilson Club in the old Fifth District. In 1960, I was instrumental in pushing through the nomination of Manfred ("Fred") Ohrenstein for state senator. As a reward, he appointed me his campaign manager. His election, along with that of William Fitts Ryan for Congress, was a signal victory for reform in New York. But Fred had high ambitions, so he fired me the night he won the election, explaining that while he was grateful for all I'd done, I was too far Left for a man of his ambition. He didn't want me to hold him back (he's still in the state senate).

That summer we also went to Cuba, where my father had a 20 percent interest in a chain of supermarkets. After the revolution, he couldn't take money out of the country, so he asked us if we wanted to go down and spend it. I had never had an interest in going there before the revolution, but we jumped at the opportunity to see what was going on, and went for three weeks. The revolution inspired us. When we came back we thought, Why do we need all this political tsuris in New York? Why not do something meaningful? So we picked up and moved to Madison, where *Studies on the Left,* with which I was already marginally associated, had begun publishing.

When we got to Madison, not much was happening politically, but intellectually it was the most stimulating experience of my life. It was a time and place of tremendous intellectual excitement and growth, and the core of it was among historians. Williams was at the center of much of it, as were his graduate students, especially those involved in *Studies on the Left.* But we didn't know what we could do with our left-wing politics, or even if we knew what we believed, how we could make sense of it to others. My main interest initially was the history of American socialism, Sklar's was the history of ruling-class ideology and power. For me, the two were different sides of the same coin, each shaping the other. In my work, they came together in my second book, *The Corporate Ideal in the Liberal State, 1900–1918*, which I started working on while still in Madison.

Though Williams and I became friends, we were never close. We saw one another from time to time over breakfast at Rennebohm's drugstore. Most of my time was spent at the State Historical Society, where I sat and read old socialist and labor newspapers all day, or at home writing on alternate days and weeks. My ideas developed as a result of my research and through discussions with my fellow *Studies* editors, especially Sklar, Landau, and Dave Eakins.

I was still in New York (I was listed as New York editor) when the first issue of *Studies* came out in 1959. I got to Madison just after the second issue was published and joined the resident board. It was that I had much more political experience than the other editors, most of whom were eight to ten years younger than I was. But Marty and Eleanor Hakim were the key people on the journal while it remained in Madison. Marty was the historical–political guru, Ellie was cultural editor.

Marty made many important contributions to the journal. He played a major role in identifying intellectuals as our political constituency and in seeing intellectual work as an activity vital to building a viable Left. The greatest weakness of the New Left was its belief—false, as was clear even then—that it had no roots, that it was unencumbered by the past experiences of the Communist and Socialist parties. We attempted, instead, to understand our roots and transcend them, which only a new understanding of our history—and that of the nation—could make possible.

Studies was not directly a part of the New Left. It started publishing before SDS [Students for a Democratic Society] was organized, and it had few, if any, connections to the civil rights activity that began in the South in the late 1950s. But we quickly recognized the potential in the various New Left activities. And we also felt strongly that for the new movement to succeed, it would require an understanding of what had brought the Old Left to grief and a theoretical basis for a new socialist politics. We represented a break with the Communist party's use of theoretical constructs simply as rationales for the current party line. We saw that as ideological. And, of course, we also appreciated the impossibility of avoiding the fatal errors of the past without an understanding of the reasons for past failures.

It's hard to say who read *Studies* outside Madison or what its influence was. We did have friendly relations with many SDS leaders. And after the journal moved to New York in 1963, Tom Hayden, Staughton Lynd, Norm Fruchter, and Stanley Aronowitz joined the board. We knew many movement people read the journal, and we were very much at home with SDS and such groups as the Northern Student Movement. This was true even though we insisted on the need to understand our place in the history of the Left, while Hayden and most other SDS leaders believed thay had no connection to the Old Left.

In New York, Hayden used to tell me that he attended editorial meetings of *Dissent* and that Irving Howe kept asking Tom how he could be an editor of a journal that was part of the Soviet world. Like most SDS-ers, Hayden thought this was a joke. They saw little or no connection between their politics and those of people like Howe because they didn't want to get hung up on ideological disputes and backbiting. We were not seen in the same light because even though we had come out of the communist movement, we now considered the party to be irrelevant. We were looking for roots, but not in the factional wars of Trotskyists, Shachtmanites, and communists, which was the world in which Howe and company still lived.

Although there was a loose intellectual community around *Studies,* the journal played no role in bringing people together into organized groups. We hoped that *Studies* would have an effect on the general orientation of Left intellectuals, and it may have had some impact. But I was surprised and disappointed at how little it seemed to influence the political behavior of people active in the 1960s. Ultimately, it seemed to have had little effect on the thinking of those involved in the movement, or even on the intellectual currents among academic Marxists. On the other hand, that seems always to be the case when one works on publications. I had the same sense of detachment when putting out *Socialist Review,* and we have it now—at least when we are working in our office in Chicago—in publishing *In These Times.*

11 The Intellectuals
and the First New Left

JAMES B. GILBERT

Jim Gilbert's *Writers and Partisans* (1967) was the earliest and one of the best of the intellectual histories to examine the New York intellectuals in the wake of Daniel Aaron's *Writers on the Left* (1961) treatment. Gilbert has subsequently placed himself as a distinguished scholar and an equally distinguished teacher at the University of Maryland, College Park. His other books include *Another Chance: Postwar America, 1945–68* (1981) and *A Cycle of Outrage: America's Reaction to Juvenile Delinquency in the 1950s* (1986).

I got to Madison in 1961 as a result of advice, ambition, innocence, and several fortuitous events. While I was at Carleton College in Minnesota in the late 1950s, I experienced a sharpening of the undirected anger I had always felt as an adolescent. Some of this had derived from family situation, some from the boredom of growing up in suburbia, and some from the strongly felt but unfocused protestantism I grew up with. My home town, after all, was located only about two or three miles from Park Forest, Illinois, site of the new society that William Whyte studied and satirized in *The Organization Man*. I was torn in my reaction to this specter of gray flannel suits and "koffee klatches," not knowing whether its sameness offended my snobbery or provoked my vague worries about things like McCarthyism. I emerged from high school without serious political opinions, however, other than an intense dislike for fraternities and sororites (which reminded me of the country club life that dominated my small town) and a very strong desire to break away from home.

Once I left, in the fall of 1957, these feelings assumed a political form—although, in retrospect, had this been another place or time, they might well have found a different expression. At Carleton College, I had a political awakening of sorts. This was principally intellectual. For the first time in my life, I encountered alternative ways of thinking about American society—from books and from people who expressed various forms of opposition to what I had always believed to be permanent truths. This occurred in an academic atmosphere that crackled with the electricity of a small Protestant college, devoted to ideas of social service and moral rectitude. It was a perfect place for a young radical.

I also had a very strong reaction to several events. The first was the launching of *Sputnik I,* which I suppose shook my confidence, although it's hard to say what confidence that might have been, except in the absolute and total superiority of American society. The second event was the downing of the U-2 spy plane over the Soviet Union. The fact that it happened, and that the United States was guilty of what it accused the Russians of doing for years—spying—was immensely distressing. My reaction was to focus on the premises of much of what I had only half believed.

Also at Carleton, I encountered a number of fellow students fast becoming radicals. The leader of this group eventually joined the American Trotskyist movement and is currently its head. Our politics at the time were pretty naive, I suppose. They were half outrage and half enthusiasm, without much intelligent structure. Our cause at that moment was the Cuban revolution, probably, again, because Castro was such an extravagant personality, so different from anything we knew about or understood, and so contemptuous of the values that we thought we were abandoning.

My radicalism was cemented, for the moment, after I went to Cuba for a week, as part of the now famous Fair Play for Cuba trip of 1960. It was a tour that shook me deeply because it confirmed my suspicion that much of what I read in the newspapers was biased and misleading—blind to what was happening in that nation. I was also scared, half believing that something ominous would happen to me either there or when I came back. In fact, nothing of the sort occurred: only a suitcase lost by the airline between Chicago and Miami, and a very funny and puzzling fight between the organizers of the tour and Scott Nearing, who debated endlessly over whether taking a bus trip to Cienfuegos at Christmas was a Stalinist act because it deprived Cubans of transportation to visit their relatives. It was my real introduction to sectarianism.

My decision to go to Madison came partly as a result of my trip to Cuba. I had met a number of students from Madison on the tour, and they struck me as intelligent and politically committed. I would not have gone, however, had I not decided to abandon my English major in favor of American history. The reason was obvious to me: I felt that if I could understand the past, I might be able to change the present and the future. That grand choice made, Madison was one of the institutions anyone might have selected, since by reputation it had one of the strongest history departments in the country. Naturally, there were other factors. One was a *Time* magazine attack on William A. Williams during the summer when I was making my decision. In those days, I was prone to applaud anything *Time* didn't, and so I began to read Williams on my own, and liked his work very much. So I went. I suppose I thought of myself as a serious radical in those days.

When I got to Madison and passed through the first shocks of graduate school, I gravitated to the group of radicals around the Socialist Club. I was known to almost everyone at first as a Trotskyist—that's the only politics I really knew at the time—but even then I believed it was a curious position. I'll probably never forget the first Trotskyists I met, including Ray Dunne, one of the original leaders of the Minneapolis Teamsters strike in 1934, and a famous radical. What I remember most from that evening was a woman in the party, at whose house we met after a political speech. I asked her what she thought I should read about Marxism, and she said: "Buy this pamphlet by Trotsky on fascism." I was pretty nonplussed because I didn't see the connection, but I bought it anyway.

My immersion in the radical politics of Madison came in two waves. Perhaps foremost, there was the Wisconsin historical tradition, upheld and nourished by a remarkable group of scholars. These men had been educated in a tradition that had deep roots in American Progressivism, and they exhibited its curious but attractive secular religiosity, its antiestablishment anger, its faith in the power and possibility of government, and its firm belief that intellectuals ought to serve the state and the nation. To a very great extent, most of the professors I knew subscribed to some variant of this philosophy, and we all imbibed a respect for this Turner–Beard school of writing with our first swallows of historiography. The best representative of this school was, of course, William Appleman Williams. But others shared the perspective, and we were indebted to them all.

Once in Madison, I quickly became friends with graduate students in the Socialist Club. Many of them were studying history; a few were also active on *Studies on the Left.* I was most impressed by the fact that so many of them were New Yorkers, Jewish, and "Red diaper babies" (although I didn't know what that term meant). They were everything I was not—and I have no doubt they often looked upon me with some suspicion. After all, I was a midwesterner, a Protestant, a suburbanite, hailing from a small liberal arts college. Which brings me to what I think was most impressive, interesting, and permanent about Madison: the social and cultural politics of the Left and the way it intersected with and sustained the older Progressive traditions of Wisconsin historiography. This movement created a hybrid, enormously creative view of American politics, culture, and history.

At Madison, there was no such thing as the New Left. It was 1961, and the glimmers of such a movement were hidden from most of us. Nonetheless, at that point I think I was spiritually much closer to the New Left than as it eventually developed in the late 1960s. I certainly shared much of the anger and disillusionment that drove that later student generation. But the Left as it existed in 1961 was cautious, intellectual, and a bit cynical about picket lines, demonstrations. Like many of the later New Left, I came from a family and a town and a culture where demonstrations *never* occurred. When the New Left appeared, marked by risk taking and a kind of jubilant activism, I was too old or too established or perhaps a bit too cynical to join full-time. Had the movement begun earlier, I might have been much more active.

As it was, I encountered sons and daughters baptized in the Old Left. Their inherited political consciences had been suddenly reawakened by a burst of activism inspired by the Cuban revolution and particularly by the momentous civil rights agitation in the South. I also met a substantial minority in the Socialist Club interested in defending the Soviet Union. The funniest and strangest result of this was a debate between members over nuclear testing. Some members tried to convince a skeptical majority that Soviet tests had a peaceful effect. A friend stood up, and in a burst of well-directed irony, asked if socialist fallout hurt you less than capitalist fallout.

By and large, the Socialist Club was a social center, an umbrella organization to sponsor speakers and hold political rallies. It was not, especially, an intellectual center. Serious intellectual life went on in classes or wherever your friends were, and that, most likely, was the Historical Society during the daytime or the 602 Club at night. Like the Socialist Club, this local bar was something of a social club, but most notably it was a place where several editors of *Studies on the Left* discussed the journal and political and cultural ideas.

Although I had abandoned literature for history in coming to Madison, I certainly did not give up my fascination for writing or for political and social theory. For me, Wisconsin was an eclectic feast with a broad menu of ideas—from debates left over from the 1930s to neo-Marxist theories that ultimately became the intellectual undergirding of the New Left. These theories came all at once, and in an extremely compressed fashion. I quickly realized that in order to understand the new theories I encountered, I had to learn about the old ones. And I couldn't have chosen a better place because the radical politics at Madison were still dominated by arguments from the days of the Popular Front. Thinking back on it, I suspect that this was a great advantage. One of the serious problems of the New Left was that it lacked even an elementary familiarity with the history of the Left in America. This was not so much a factual amnesia as a failure to understand, at an emotional level, the meaning of that history. The New Left was born innocent. Only in its decline did it rediscover the Old Left—and then with fatal results. I think some of our revisionist historical theories and the internecine struggle between radical fathers and mothers and their college-age sons and daughters had much to do with wiping out that historical sense to leave the impression that the only valid radical politics were those that began in the 1960s.

At Madison in 1961, the most important intellectuals on the Left were James Weinstein, Marty Sklar, and Eleanor Hakim, all of them associated with *Studies on the Left*. Among them they represented three very different approaches to scholarship and radical politics. Nonetheless, they collectively replicated a portion of New York intellectual life that was enormously fascinating to me. Weinstein was engaged in revising the history of American socialism and communism, and although this was a more or less practical task of analysis, deeply imbedded in the Progressive historical tradition, it involved rethinking the 1950s, and especially, the 1930s. Sklar, although he was most engaged in historical revisionism, particularly of the Progressive era, read widely in European social theory: Marx, Weber, Hegel, and so on. He also loved to discuss American philosophy. Hakim focused primarily on literature, and specifically on Brecht, although she had very broad literary interests.

The issues that most engaged the *Studies* intellectuals were the same problems that had divided New York intellectuals for a very long time. Farmed out to Madison, as it were, these ideas became an important background for the development of the New Left.

Whatever the New Left became in the mid 1960s, because of the shattering impact of the war in Vietnam, emerged from the belief that terrible inadequacies existed in the assumptions of the Old Left and modern American liberalism (sometimes it justifiably equated the two). The fact that the worst charge one could make in those days was that an opinion was both liberal and Old Left was a sure indication of the rejection of both traditions—this despite the fact that almost everyone belonged in some measure to both camps.

It was always my greatest concern to try to find a third way, to use history to explore roads not taken, decisons not made—in other words, to create a radical present. This was not a unique effort; almost everyone who fancied himself or herself a revisionist historian, or even a revisionist intellectual, hoped for some such discovery. Indeed, the New Left emerged in part for this effort to find out what had gone wrong in American history, both in terms of living it and writing about it.

I think that the best work done by the *Studies* group turned on precisely these questions: How could sorting out the past alter the present political and cultural impasse? Could the grip of old mistakes be broken? Could the study of history, in the broadest sense, generate the power to change the present? A similar impulse guided the reading, translation, and commentary on European socialist and communist traditions. The purpose was the same: to discover a theory of socialism that made sense in the exciting but confusing days of the Kennedy and Johnson administrations.

Some of the best work that *Studies on the Left* published was written by Marty Sklar, Williams, Eugene Genovese, and Weinstein. Generally, what I liked most were the editorials, and I read them as avidly as I had once read the opening statements in the *Monthly Review,* because they seemed action oriented.

If I were to add up the impact of these contributions, plus those of Eleanor Hakim and the influence of endless discussions that all of us had on contemporary and historical events, I would have to conclude that they left us stymied, up against forces that seemed so large and inevitable that nothing could be done. If, as I came to believe, politics and culture were dominated by the general evolution of American capitalism, which was so successful as to suffocate any genuine opposition and even turn potential opponents into unwitting servants of power, then not much could be done. Of course, I never articulated such a belief, nor did anyone else, but it was a conclusion that lurked just below the surface. All our explanations were deterministic in this sense. History was therefore really a blind alley to a better future.

That is one reason many of us were so excited by opposition to the war in Vietnam. Here was an event that seemed to be a major turning point, an exception that might change everything. I certainly felt that we might be able to push history in another direction. But nothing in our theories told us what to do. We learned from the Women's Strike for Peace demonstrations. We learned from students at Berkeley and Michigan. We copied some of the tactics of the civil rights movement. Most of all, we learned the exhilaration of action. This point suggests the major fault line in the history of the radical community at Madison and explains its quick evolution from a rich intellectual world to the explosive activist center it became in the late 1960s. What every editor of *Studies* lamented—a separation between theory and action—was, almost by definition, exacerbated by what occurred. Our history writing and thinking and our actions each seemed to go their separate ways. When the Vietnam demonstrations began, a number of Old Left intellectuals declined to participate or were inconspicuous. They did not see their role as offering leadership to a generation of student radicals. That fell to the most vocal, most activist, and, of course, younger students.

At this point, any question about the weakness of a cultural critique almost answers itself. A European *cultural* critique was certainly missing in Madison, except insofar as it was studied and repeated by students or professors such as George Mosse. But a European *political* critique was also missing. In the long run, this was probably not a bad thing. To have operated from a European intellectual framework would have meant making the intellectual contortions that have often characterized the American Left, without much benefit. Undoubtedly such ideas are fascinating and have had an enormous influence, but borrowing theories from other cultures is an extremely complex and often misunderstood process. It does not involve simply picking up ideas from one place and putting them into a different context; it implies a high degree of selection and transformation. To put the problem in the form of questions: What theories should we have—could we have—borrowed? Would they have been understood here in the fashion they were intended in Europe? How would they have been altered by our attempts to apply them?

These are questions of enormous importance, and ones that I don't pretend to be able to answer adequately. But it does seem to me to be a fatal assumption that we can shop for theories and apply the best ones to our own situation. I would argue, on the contrary, that borrowed ideas look feasible only because we read them through our own cultural biases.

This leads me to a principal point. I do not believe that the Left suffered from an absence of theory—political or cultural. Nor do I believe that an ideological infusion would have changed us very much. In fact, the most successful borrowing of European cultural theories in Madison occurred in historical seminars, where some of the future leaders of the new social history adopted the techniques and ideas of the French Annales school and British social historians.

More serious borrowings, in terms of strategies, ideas about political parties, probably would not have worked or would have resulted in intellectual contortions. One preposterous example of this occurred after I left Madison and was teaching at Columbia University in 1969, the year after the devastating antiwar demonstrations. At an international students' meeting (which was held up for a long time while the group debated the "elitism" of appointing a moderator), a German speaker convinced the gathering to march to the Mexican Consulate, after assembling representatives of the American working class, to protest brutal treatment of strikers in Mexico City. I can't remember what the original purpose of the conference was, beyond some sort of solidarity with European student movements, but no doubt many of the participants were shamed into believing that they ought to act like European radicals. This meant pretending that American workers could be brought together for such an occasion.

So the experience of Old and New Left at Madison renewed the old American problem of discovering the resources for change in our culture. That was a task that hisorical revisionism (and the early New Left) set for itself, but one that eventually dissipated during the wild skirmishes of the late 1960s. What we missed along the way (I certainly did not understand it at the time) was a clear accounting of what we meant by change. From this perspective, the most revolutionary leader of the 1960s was not Fidel Castro or Ché [Guevara] or any of the others whose posters stared from our walls, but Martin Luther King, Jr. He merits this description not only for the amount of social reform he helped direct but because he based his movement in a lucid understanding of American culture. He recognized the remarkable and revolutionary power of southern black culture—and, by definition, he understood what almost all the whites who opposed him missed: The very abjectness inspired by oppression can be a powerful weapon.

I think we all yearned at that time for a European cultural critique and a European political critique because we overlooked such insights, because we were impatient for dramatic change and sometimes failed to see it when it came. We doubted the ability of American society to generate its own theory of culture because we doubted the capacity of our society to express profound change in anything but apocalyptic terms. This living on borrowed theories and exalted expectations has always been risky because of the failure to recognize what it is that can and cannot change.

The most serious problem at Madison was not, therefore, theory or even practice, but communication. After the mid 1960s, a new group of students (plus some reborn leaders from the earlier period) became more influential. *Studies on the Left* moved to New York. There, activism, not debate, or even the historical revisionism of the earlier generation, was the order of the day. The positions that many of the

older generation of students had arrived at, painfully and with a great deal of
hesitation and qualification, were the beginning assumptions of the new student
generation. They believed us when we declared that liberalism was a corrupt tradition and that American socialism and communism had deeply flawed and troubled pasts. But they believed these things too literally. It is one thing to decide
that the history of the American Left and the history of American liberalism are
marred by self-deception. It is another thing to dismiss the past as of no importance, to call for a completely new politics. The most painful lesson to be learned
from this experience is that, instead of calling for something entirely new, the New
Left was, ironically, behaving just as American reformers have often behaved: as
moral extremists. What happened at Madison, then, was the eventual collapse of
a fruitful political–cultural amalgam whose premises were historical, to be replaced
by a new politics and a cultural revolution based on moral vision and not much
else.

The effect of this experience in my life has, of course, been enormous. The
intellectual and political life at Madison was always exciting, always changing.
They were years of enormous hope—despite the wrenching we felt because of Vietnam and the grave failures of the Great Society.

But the most important influence on me was probably the self-deceptive optimism I held about the future of the university. The mid 1960s were flush times
for higher education: it seemed that limitless building and expansion would continue forever. No one worried about finding a job after graduate school because
there seemed to be plenty of positions in academia. A test of these optimistic times
were the teach-ins centered on Vietnam. They were important because they seemed
to indicate a renaissance of ideas in American culture, and, of course, a central
position for intellectuals in that awakening. Consequently, it meant a great deal to
me that my professors had something to say not only to one another but to a wider
audience.

This was only a brief, optimistic interlude. I realized this when late one evening, toward the end of my days in Madison, a shifty-looking man in a trenchcoat
knocked at the door of my university-owned house and asked to speak to me. He
claimed to be from the FBI, and gradually he revealed his purpose. He wanted me
to write monthly reports on the activities of the Socialist Club. His argument was
that this sort of work had begun under Franklin Roosevelt and was therefore a
good cause. At first I was furious—then paralyzed. I could have written to the
president of the university, himself a distinguished historian. I thought of writing
to the *New York Times*. But I didn't do either. In the long run, I learned a great
deal from this incident. It shook my faith in the university, which I concluded
probably knew of such activities. But, most important, it underscored the fragility
of radical dreams at Madison—something that was to become apparent in the
whole student movement shortly thereafter when, in a larger sense, reality was only
a knock on the door away. Finally, my frustration in not knowing where to turn
underscored the fundamental problem of the New and Old Left at Wisconsin.

Despite our contributions to historiography, to issue-oriented activism, we had still not developed a politics of social change. In our rising impatience and accelerating demands for a better society, there was less and less a strategy for living in a world of compromises, institutions, and alliances. Inevitably, the romantic heroism of revolutionaries in faraway places seemed more relevant than close-to-home political movements that proved so unwilling to bend and accommodate new ideas. It was on such issues, eventually, that both New Left and Old Left rose and fell.

12 New York Meets Oshkosh

LEE BAXANDALL

Lee Baxandall, now editor of the naturist quarterly *Clothed With the Sun*—published since 1981 in Oshkosh, to which he has returned as local iconoclast and publisher of school materials—has many books to his credit. They include *Marxism and Aesthetics: An Annotated Bibliography* (1968); *Radical Perspectives in the Arts* (1972); *Wilhelm Reich's Sex-Pol, 1927-34* (1972); *Marx and Engels on Literature and Art* (a 1974 collaboration with Stefan Morawski), and *World Guide to Nude Beaches and Recreation* (1980). He has had two of his plays, and translations of Bertolt Brecht and Peter Weiss, with New York productions.

I was born in Oshkosh in 1935, less than a hundred years after an ancestor, a farmer turned timber cruiser, and a man who became the first Wisconsin governor in 1848, had laid out the survey lines for the white immigrants, dividing up the natives' communal hunting and foraging range. At first, the city was called Athens. Then, requiring an improved claim to its choice location, it was renamed for an unhappy local Indian who had a plausible title to being a chief. Oshkosh later killed a man in a drunken brawl, but by then he had signed over this land where the Fox River flowed into Lake Winnebago to the land speculators who, 150 years ago, doubled as surveyors and politicians.

In Oshkosh, European antecedents were quickly forgotten. German woodcarvers and masons imposed a few dim memories on the new city's look. The rest was wide streets and big backyards, wooden boxes, and whining sawmills. The latter quickly transformed the forest primeval to enormous heaps of sawdust by the Fox River. These, in turn, caught fire every few years, sending sheets of flame through the clapboard worker housing and up Main Street. Devastation. What the culture of hard work hadn't eradicated, the sparks of the factories in the forest did away with.

I did not come from a radical background. My parents liked anyone and anything Republican. They subscribed to Henry Luce's publications. They went along with the churches' claims because they felt it was a way to explain the comforting, lovely regularity of nature.

Confirming their duty to the child, Sundays they took me to the Congregational church. There my happiest moments were in relaxed sports chats among my more athletic friends, while the adults sat silently elsewhere in pews. One church friend loaned me the recently published *Kinsey Report,* a meaningful moment. And in the church book nook I found Paul Blanchard's devastating portrayal of church exploitation of the religious believer, *American Freedom and Catholic Power.*

I was secure in my parents' affection. But I was bored and alienated by Oshkosh. I had no way to tell how much or what it meant. My independence was assisted by good fortune with the Boy Scouts. I got to be an Eagle Scout, specializing in stamp collecting, birdwatching, and "Indian dancing." The Scouts introduced me to skinny-dipping, and I became our Scout naturalist and program director. I was also on the Oshkosh High School debating club and senior class president. To amuse myself and friends, I learned hypnotism.

On gaining Eagle rank, I was sent east to represent the Upper Midwest in Scouting's Report to the Nation for 1951. Twelve of us were brought to Washington where we were put into photo opportunities with President Truman, General George Marshall, and a host of other dignitaries. There I was, sixteen years old, shaking hands with Harry Truman, who didn't look me in the eyes. That bothered me.

We also toured the Pentagon and FBI headquarters. J. Edgar Hoover autographed his photo personally to me, although he didn't find the time to see our Scout group. Senator McCarthy's office wanted me at an anticommunist chicken dinner. I was curious when our chaperon said I couldn't accept this invitation.

Back in Oshkosh, a history teacher gave me Upton Sinclair's *The Jungle.* Its behind-the-stockyards story of meatpacking in Chicago was an inspiration. The baseline skepticism with which I walked through my small-town experience was put to a test as the junior year debate question targeted Senator McCarthy's ethics. Initially I had no opinion and looked up his record. McCarthy was not on the up-and-up, I concluded. He switched parties to get elected, and he took a gift house from a Milwaukee industrialist. McCarthy's ferocious attacks on so-called communists were beside the point; McCarthy himself lacked integrity.

I intuited, however obscurely, that truth, warmth, and real excitement lay elsewhere. I didn't have that thought in focus, but while I was a high school senior, I had published in the *Octopus,* Madison's campus humor magazine, a fantasy about Abraham Lincoln's statue's sex life.

How Long Does It Take to Get to Which Madison?

At first, Madison was joining a fraternity for the instant conviviality and beer parties. I kept a raccoon in my room at Delta Tau Delta. After learning in my seminars on Henrik Ibsen the anarchist challenge, "He is strongest who stands alone," I resigned from the fraternity with a speech attacking its conformity. Frat brothers called it a breach of standards to resign, and so they "expelled" me.

Madison was also joining the Reserve Officer Training Corps [ROTC]. In ROTC quarters I read words attributed to President Eisenhower that I have never forgotten: "Leadership is getting others to do what you want them to do because they want to do it." Neat! Decent! Democratic as you can get, I thought. But it cuts two ways: How *rational* is the decision to accept leadership? I quit.

Madison was also theory to explain my senator. A concept for McCarthyism was provided without *ad hominum* attachment in the freshman sociology lectures of Howard Becker where I grasped the practice of demagoguery. Now I knew why I'd rejected my use of hypnosis as demeaning my subject friends.

And Madison was appreciating Thorstein Veblen, a midwestern, Norwegian-American pioneer of the sociology of the American personality. I was one-quarter Norwegian—my grandfather a river hog who rode and piked the logs down the rivers to New Orleans each spring, then worked his way north following the harvest, like any migrant worker today.

Veblen offered concepts to explain adult behaviors, both constrained and flamboyant, that I'd seen and disliked as a kid. His idea of "conspicuous consumption" translated for me as the Midwest's worship of Cadillacs, banks, ownership of whatever—the suffocation by possession that I knew and rejected.

Literature was my chief study, and I eventually found a radical classicist Madison example in recently emigrated Alban Winspear, whose *Hermes the Thief* is a model of the political–economic analysis of myth. The professors available to me, however, observed the formalist etiquette of New Criticism. Insistent on reviewing the sociocultural prerequisites of literature and aesthetics, I sought the despised anthropological, sociological, and Marxist texts in hard-to-find magazines. I deflected my seminar professor Frederic J. Hoffman's distaste.

In the German Department, Jost Hermand, a quiet and prolific scholar from the German Democratic Republic, inspired me, as did Walter Hoellerer, a guest professor of poetry from Berlin. Peter Jenkins, also from Europe, was later to become a prominent British economics journalist. For us, he served as president of the Socialist Club. It was the year I drew the attention of the campus FBI informant because I lived near the wrong people and had written a letter to the campus paper objecting to the atmospheric tests of atomic bombs. Jenkin's confident Fabian way with political economy was an encouragement as I read Isaac Deutscher, recommended by all *Studies* editors.

I also came upon other obviously exotic vital types, who encouraged my adventuresome instincts and grew to be friends. In my freshman dorm, Bennie

Carruthers kept late hours, smoked unusual cigarettes, and sometimes went to class. From the New York streets, Bennie had a role in John Cassavetes's *Shadows*. He clued me to hipster attitudes. I began to comprehend social alienation as "Benito" lived it and relaxed with it.

Milt Polsky was no hipster. He took me to his grungy room to hear Leadbelly sing. My range till then was from Presley, "You Ain't Nothin' But a Hound Dog," to Grofe, "The Grand Canyon Suite." Never anything like the anger and roughness in "John Henry" or "If I Had a Hammer."

A campus LYL-er was the sensitive future physician Henry Wortis. I didn't know him, but his younger brother, Avi, talked about their dad's encounter in therapy with the great Freud. This awakened my interest in a radicalized psychology of consciousness.

In Oshkosh I'd seen only one film that stood above the Hollywood attractions. Another, deploring anti-Semitism, *Gentlemen's Agreement*, was screened for the schools, which was reason to skip it. But the marvelous French *Volpone* taught me how to regard avarice with a cynical eye. It also raised my expectations for cinema, and now in Madison I went to the Film Series. Its impressario was Henry Breitrose, another easterner. He was buddies with all the vivacious people I was getting to know. I wrote program notes on Eisenstein films when they were shown in the series.

Studies on the Left

The path of my experience and interest led inevitably to the irrepressible group that founded *Studies on the Left*. In 1959, as they moved to conceive, fund-raise, and write the first new radical scholarly and political journal in twenty years, they were glad to find an in-stater eager to connect to global forces and explanatory schema.

Housed in neglected two- and three-story clapboards, we were studious and very purposeful. Internal émigrés camped in a Siberia dreaming of a better future. The present, we all knew, wasn't a problem, but neither was it attractive. We could cope. None of us would flunk, none go hungry. There were taverns, mentors, sexual and intellectual liaisons. Life was pretty good even when we didn't clean or cook much.

I met such unanticipated colleagues as Saul Landau, who wanted to be a playwright and would become a radical filmmaker and administrator–author at the Institute for Policy Studies in Washington. His teenage bride, Nina Serrano Landau, raven-haired and black-skirted, journeyed to a World Youth Festival in Moscow and on by rail to Peking. No one else in our generation had put politics to the test of travel. Nina led me about the Madison of the easterners. She understood my excitement when I returned from seeing Brecht's *Threepenny Opera* and its star, Lotte Lenya, on the New York stage. Nina helped me find the later Brecht, and my passion for drama theory and performance blossomed. Having a son, Gregory, Nina was a radical empowered woman with limited tolerance of student habits and pretensions, and was a match for Saul's cool.

From Colorado came a phlegmatic, lanky ex-union organizer and current graduate student, Dave Eakins. Dave had two lovely girls with his wife, Anne, and provided labor authentication to *Studies*. Anne later married Jim Williams, a black graduate student who would be hired as a lawyer representing the State Department in trust territories.

A current workingman on the *Studies* board was Martin J. Sklar, who carried brick hods and was revered for his theorization of corporate liberalism and its roots in the Wilson administration. Marty smoked a pipe, which, with his deliberate and friendly manner, lent a guru aura, while his black wife, Dorey, embodied his irrevocable commitment to a racially integrated society. Marty's gears ground slowly, belieing his influence. Only in 1988 was his thesis published!

Ronald Radosh didn't make it onto the *Studies* board, although he obviously aspired. As an associate editor of *Studies*, over the years Radosh was often ridiculed for rigid orthodoxy. Years later, he reemerged as an equally maladroit apologist for the U.S. State Department. Ironically, Radosh is the one writer near *Studies* who has lately been propped up within the penumbra of the New York intellectuals.

Stephen Scheinberg from Chicago was yet another history graduate student. Steve stood by helpfully and with some amusement as radical perceptions rooted in my mind. We laughed a lot. He nominated me to the board along with Matt Chapperon, perhaps a weird joke or balancing act, because it turned out Chapperon was the next husband to my then-current wife.

Carl Wiener and his wife, Ruth Feinglass, became close. Rumpled and sardonic, gentle Carl was the archetypal European cultural historian of our generation, although he didn't join the *Studies* board. Ruth's father was president of the furriers' union in Chicago. She played Gruscha in my production of Brecht's *Caucasian Chalk Circle,* giving the role its motherly bite.

Eleanor Hakim was another culture type on *Studies*. Short, thin, and frail, pale skin and big eyes behind thick glasses, with black, straight, long hair, Ellie was a Ratskeller habituée. Ellie would assure you in a low, agreeably controlled voice that she had not long to live. She cultivated an existential correspondence with the New York editor Emile Capouya. Ellie apparently did not think much of my priorities, writing an obliquely countering essay on Brecht for *Studies*.

Ellie would invite for coffee. Her North Lake Street apartment was the cramped but welcoming center of *Studies* socializing, along with the "602" University Avenue tavern. She later got to live in Paris. And she died young.

In this grouping, which forty years earlier would have been counted on the ethnic Left of the Socialist party, I represented the cultural additive. I suppose I also played a role something like that of Granville Hicks twenty-five years earlier.

Not only did I direct and translate Brecht, I presented his theories to the Socialist Club and reviewed books on him for *Studies*. I was contributing to the *Drama Review* and other journals on political theater. In the summer of 1960 I went to Cuba, writing for the revolutionary cultural supplement *Lunes de Revolucion,* then describing the culture of Castro's Cuba for *konkret* in Hamburg.

The *Studies* editors gladly accepted my photograph of the First Declaration of Havana for the cover of the second issue of *Studies,* and my translation of [Ché] Guevara's essay on development of the revolutionary war. But I sensed limited enthusiasm for "culture." Later I would research the Left socialist speaker–organizer Louis Fraina, who around 1920 wrote brilliantly not only on politics and economics but also on modern dance, drama, art, and literature. Fraina was likewise suspect for the scope of his intellect and interests.

Easterners had some advantages. I had others. I had a sense of belonging, born to univocal customs altered only with reluctance. I could measure society, and myself, with a framework in effect constant, far different from the cosmopolitan streets where each day was a new occasion for predation and amnesia.

■ ■

Encouraged by the growing quality and quantity of radicals on campus, I staged Brecht's mammoth *Caucasian Chalk Circle* in the tiny Play Circle of the Student Union. It came across effectively, amusing and entertaining.

Meanwhile, I translated Brecht's *Mother*. With politicos Scheinberg, Sklar, Landau, Chapperon, and then-wife Judith Woelffer from the Socialist Club, I staged a reading of his *The Measures Taken*. My idea was objectively to present and judge its Stalin-era revolutionism. But when the play was over, we found graffiti on the outside of the theater that stigmatized us as Stalinists!

On April 9, 1960, we presented an "Anti-Military Ball"—countering the ROTC official one—with a skit I co-scripted with Marshall Brickman and Danny Kalb. The cast was the formative *Studies* group, more or less. We satirized the elaborately duplicitous invasion of the Bay of Pigs by the corporate liberals. We turned the breaking newscasts overnight into dialogue.

By this time, I had a two-year old daughter, a disintegrating marriage, and a retreat in the basement of the apartment next to the Landaus and other easterners, where I was reading Paul Valéry, Arthur Rimbaud, and Bertolt Brecht, writing plays, poems, and essays, and resolving more clearly every day not to compromise my life. A divorce decree put an end to my agony. On the next day, I flew away from the United States for the first time, to Cuba for the summer, to see what revolution really might be about.

I was totally impressed with the creativity of this Latin revolution. Still, I visited the American Embassy to get its current view of events. All I heard were canned propaganda statements in defiance of the obvious reality. For me it was an eye-opener, comparable to the visit to Harry Truman.

All in all, 1960–1961 was a splendid peaking of opportunity. I shared evenings with the *Studies* collective, advanced my theatrical knowledge, wrote on Brecht for *Studies,* and published his play *The Mother* with Grove Press and *The Baden Learning Play* with the *Drama Review.* I was productive and competent, confident that I was hitting my stride and could contribute as a politically informed theater worker and author on varied topics. I was ready to leave Madison.

13 Another Madison Bohemian

ROZ BAXANDALL

Roz Baxandall teaches U.S. history at SUNY, Old Westbury. Her *Words on Fire* (1988) is both a biography and an anthology of Elizabeth Gurley Flynn's writings.

I, Miss Rosalyn Fraad, no Ms then, didn't imagine riding the rails, halfway across America, being inalterably transformed by the University of Wisconsin. There, the permutation to political activist–intellectual percolated. In Madison, at the tail end of the 1950s, I met Lee Baxandall, who would become a lover–associate–husband of seventeen years, and my current closest friends and co-conspirators, Wini Breines and Liz Ewen.[1]

My first year in Madison, I lived in a dormitory dominated by midwestern sorority girls, quite a strange environment for someone from a communist cosmopolitan culture who had been systematically sheltered from American mass media. I expected the opposite and had gone to Madison because of its progressive reputation. My roommate and suitemates were terribly sweet and welcoming, which made them hard to dislike. They were from Chicago and very aware of being Jewish and celebrated holidays and used expressions like "m.o.t." (member of the tribe), perhaps that day's equivalent of "jap." I'd assumed I was Jewish, but my parents were atheists and my family celebrated only Christian holidays, even having Easter egg hunts. As a kid I lived with Catholic relatives and even knew my Hail Marys. These midwestern, *nouveau riche* gals were my introduction to American Judaism. They made no pretense of intellectual interest and stated openly that they

[1] Wini Jacoby Breines, who now teaches at Northeastern, and Elizabeth Ewen, who teaches with me at SUNY, Old Westbury.

were seeking a "Mrs. degree" and looking for eligible, meaning "rich," Jewish fraternity boys. These soon-to-be sorority girls didn't look like me either, but they were generous with advice on how to look "sharper." I was flat-chested, gangly, with stringy straight hair and I had no sense of style. They were petite, round, and busty, with short, curly hair that was set nightly; they wore girdles and gobs of makeup and had wardrobes of matching cashmere outfits. I didn't reveal my own socialist culture because I didn't realize I had one; in addition, the remnants of McCarthyism muzzled me.

It took me a semester to find the Rathskeller, which was the American version of an underground European café. There I encountered folks who I at least wanted to emulate; they were older, and unconventional, but they attracted me. "Rat" habitués drank 3.2 percent beer, smoked cigarettes, and hung out at tables for long periods, appearing wise, and they were oblivious to the rest of the cute campus coeds. Ratskeller life and the heavy talks carried out there were as or more significant than the formal classroom education.

Mainly graduate students, these "Rat dwellers" were serious theorists who undertook the reevaluation of American corporate liberalism and Marxism–Leninism in order to bring about an American socialism. Growing up a "Red diaper baby," I caught their key phrases and listened intently, hoping to understand more. I was a Marxist by heritage and heart, but I had a lot of learning and catching up to do. I tried to "ooh and aah" appropriately, but I was too young and unseasoned to be taken seriously.

There was also an arty set, many of whom were politically "progressive" as well. They drank, smoked dope and chewed peyote, and hung out in the Rat as well as the 602 Club, Lombardy's, or Glen and Ann's late at night. These bohemians—that was their identification then—hid slouching behind dark sunglasses, in black turtlenecks often adorned by Russian or Mexican motifs. The girls, often theater majors, were *zophtic,* full, bra free; they wore long, layered multicolored skirts and heavy, dark eye makeup and looked pale and sickly, quite a contrast to the blonde, spunky midwesterners who dominated campus life. I, being a hotheaded, enthusiastic Manhattanite fit into neither category, but aspired to beatnik cool.

These bearded men, many of them accomplished folksingers, several from New York City's Music and Art High School (Marshall Brickman, now of Woody Allen fame, Eric Weisberg, who cut a few Weaverlike hit records, and Ronald Radosh, now a Cold Warrior, who played a mean banjo), and Bob Dylan, undiscovered at the time, who came down from Chicago and played with a harmonica around his neck, had hootenanies outside on the patio by the lake, a warm-weather extension of the Rat. Other notables were history majors—Mosse, Curti, or Williams graduate students—and later several of them became editors of *Studies on the Left.* The historians and folksingers were tall and skinny, frail in comparison to muscular midwesterners, and dressed as modified hoboes and lumberjacks. I and other females of my age group copied their unisex dress with occasional colorful ethnic trinkets and weighty silver earrings. This dress was freeing and vanguard 1960s.

Before I knew about Allen Ginsberg and the "beats," I recall these folks dramatically reading unrhymed poems and sketching in pencil or charcoal. Some dropped out of school to write, paint, dance, or act. Their writing and art was passed around like *samizdat* and printed in the *New Idea,* a political, cultural magazine, which had poems, artwork, and historical articles. The University of Wisconsin's Creative Writing Department partly supported it, and parties to raise money were also held. Their avant-garde performances of modern dance and theater, notably Brecht, and reinterpretations of American classics were innovatively performed in the smaller university theaters. Intense controversy followed the performances, so others became involved in the ongoing drama. Many of the rehearsals were public events, and I recall commenting on a dance work in process and during the performance feeling that I had a stake in the outcome.

These seedy souls whom I admired lived in groups off-campus in two- or three-story houses with wooden porches, and ate communal dinners. Women did most of the cleaning, but I remember men who cooked well, and others who shopped and did laundry. In fact, domestic chores and daily life were shared more or less equally at college, as men and women were engaged in the same educational and social endeavors. Only after college did this sexual reciprocity break down. We were the first generation of coeds who shared daily life before marriage. Living together resembled working and playing as partners; no one did much cleaning or laundry. The women's liberation movement came about in part because we had experienced similar gender expectations at college and took it for granted, only to be shocked that in the work world and marriage, women were treated as inferiors. Having once experienced a relative equality, we rebelled and were indignant at the injustice. Of course, there were exceptions; a female couldn't legally live off-campus until age twenty-one, but there were ways around this.

Some saw this little band as an invading, agitating force. In fact, there was a stink for a while, carried out largely as a paper war in the *Daily Cardinal,* the campus newspaper of record, about too many New Yorkers at the university and too many particularly in the Rat. "New Yorker" was shorthand for out-of-state bohemians and Jews. Wisconsin residents resented that their tax dollars subsidized the tuition of these dangerous elements. Most of the New Yorkers were Jews, but we didn't have particularly strong cultural or religious identification. This was my first experience with anti-Semitism, but I never remember Judaism being discussed explicitly; in fact, ethnic and religious and sexual differences were minimized, as they had been in my family. Only racial differences were consciously expressed.

Blacks, in comparison to their small numbers at the university, also hung out in the Ratskeller, but they weren't mentioned in the *Cardinal* discussion of outside elements. Madison had a large number of foreign graduate students, many from Africa, and they had an important radicalizing influence. These students came from political cultures and had a well-articulated, anti-imperalist interpretation of the American Empire, which we incorporated. Interracial dating was taken for granted. I remember my mother visiting and observing that this was unusual—and maybe even being hesitant about it; but we felt it natural rather than daring. I was friendly with several Ethiopians, who were knowledgeable and far more forward sexually than most of the white boys, which I admit I liked, although I knew I wasn't supposed to.

My earliest rebellion was sexual. The ritualized kissing and petting scenes just before curfew (for women, 10:30 weekdays and 12:00 weekends) in front of my dorm sickened me. The mass make-outs were extensions of the noisy frat beer brawls to which we felt superior. At our parties, usually potluck suppers with some political purpose, we served beer and cheap wine. Most women pretended to be virgins, but to me, admitting you fucked was a red badge of courage. Sometimes I would come in at 10:30 and then climb out the window and spend the night at my boyfriend, Neil Cohen's,[2] house. Occasionally there was bed check and a friend would call me to come back. High drama. After my freshman year, I lived in a house where you could cook, and the majority of the girls, as they were called then, were liberals. Another trick for staying out all night was to say you were babysitting, and I did babysit for radical couples with children. Somehow this made me feel like an important part of their families. Later, I duplicated a dorm key and came and went as I pleased. When I was a senior, however, someone told the housemother I had my own key. She disliked me and had always suspected something, and now she had me. She said girls were concerned that I was giving Gilman House, our dorm, a cheap reputation and said I could no longer stay in the dorm. This would probably mean being kicked out of college altogether. I was scared.

During this ordeal, I had to talk to the dean of women, Martha Petersen, later a president of Barnard and in the 1970s the first female on an important corporate board. She was a tough lady, and we hit it off. She suggested subtly that my parents write to her stating that financially I needed to work and had their permission to work as a live-in maid or babysitter, and this would constitute approved housing. Eleanor Hakim and Helen Kramer, the only two females on *Studies on the Left,* agreed to let me live with them. Ellie was business manager of *Studies,* and did a great deal of the scut work, for which she wasn't given ample credit. On the journal they were almost good enough to be men, but therefore treated as flawed (asexual) females by the male board. Ellie was a literature student who had taken a leave from formal studies and was more interested in art and culture than most of the board members, who were historians. Ellie had a bohemian frailty and sensitivity I admired, but didn't want to emulate. Helen was respected because she was a hard-nosed economist. I never lived with them. I moved in with Lee Baxandall and made no bones about it.

---

[2] Neil Cohen was the editor of the *New Idea* and now is a lawyer and editor of *The Law Reporter.*

In my sophomore year I became pregnant by my boyfriend, Kim Willenson.[3] I had an abortion in Milwaukee. I pretended to be rather blasé about it, telling my roommates proudly that I'd have to miss morning classes for an abortion, but I'd be back in the afternoon. The doctor's office was a seedy abortion mill, and after the unpleasant ordeal, I went to the bathroom and sat there sobbing. The nurse came in and told me to hurry up—other patients were waiting. That afternoon, in class, I remember aching and feeling faint and fearing I'd be taken to a hospital and booked on criminal charges for I don't know what. Nevertheless, I acted stoic and nonplussed, which I thought was sophisticated.

There was some political activity, but of an undramatic sort. In my sophomore year, there was a peace church organizing to test segregation in housing. We would go out to look at apartments listed as vacant, first as an all-white team and then as a racially mixed team. Consistently the interracial team would be told the apartment was already rented. We would write up reports, and a lawyer would file a brief. I sensed I was engaged in important activity, but the spark and group solidarity were missing. At this time I was reading about slavery and Jim Crow, and in this action I felt the coming together of theory and practice. This church also espoused world peace and brotherhood through everyone speaking a universal language, issues that seemed wholesome and correct, but lacked an urgency and active roles for participants, so they hardly consumed me, as the women's liberation movement later would.

Other political events, perhaps as they are preserved by newspaper clippings and photos (I have some), stand out. We picketed vice-presidential-hopeful [Henry Cabot] Lodge; our signs questioned his civil rights policy in particular. I remember that supporters of Lodge and Richard Nixon in 1960 seemed extremely subdued compared to our rather raucous antics. We shouted and danced and made our signs, all different; they sat and listened politely to Lodge.

The Military Ball was a major campus event, and even if you wanted to ignore it, the floats and marching bands spread over the campus. Our reply was the Anti-Military Ball, which became a ritual for us arty "pinkos." In 1960, Lee Baxandall, with a little help from friends, wrote a three-act musical comedy, the vice-president character played by a black. A ditty I still recall is "Look beneath the bamboo trees there you'll see the red Chinese." My job in this production was working the lights. When I thought the audience's attention was waning or a piece was going on too long—many of the pieces were mixtures of ad-libs and set lines—I'd dim the

---

[3] Kim Willenson was an editor of the *Cardinal*. In this capacity, he supported the right of the Labor Youth Leagues (LYL), the youth section of the Communist party, to exist, although he wasn't personally sympathetic. The LYL had been booted from all other campuses at this time, so this was an important last stand. The Right attacked Willenson so brutally that he enlisted in the army to get some distance on it all. He came out radicalized and got a job on the *Capital Times*. He is now a *Newsweek* bureau chief and recently published a book on Vietnam.

lights. The director, Lee Baxandall, thought I violated the integrity of the production and had no right to show such initiative, but I felt if others could add lines, I could subtract light. In retrospect, I don't remember women having key roles in this event, but then the focus was on the military. In fact, many of our activities were reactions to mainstream campus events; the Left would not be the center of the campus life for another few years. Peace and racial discrimination, as racism was then called, were key issues. We were clearly outsiders, and liked it that way— night people in a romantic underworld. We didn't yet see ourselves on center stage, calling the shots.

Academic life was exciting as well; several professors loomed large and further united our socialist, bohemian band. George Mosse, who taught European intellectual history, was a performer and challenged our North American-centered education with knowledge of the European giants. Mosse lectured in the auditorium, pacing back and forth and making intellectual debates come alive. He was warm and encouraged you to learn more. I remember getting the courage to ask him who Dilthey was. His booming reply was, "How can you have lived so long and not know Dilthey?" William Agard, who taught Greek, was another model; he was so steeped in ancient Greece, he danced through the halls singing Homeric rhymes, like a sole survivor from ancient times. He rattled the archeological bones and made the world of Plato and Socrates come alive by connecting classic art, politics, and daily life. William Appleman Williams, another professor with an aura, introduced historical methodology, sending us to the primary sources. He managed to milk every innuendo from a letter or decree, reading in more than the document seemed to say. As a professor, I now expose students to original manuscripts, still using Williams as the beacon. Mosse is my model for an exciting lecturer, and, like Agard, I try to steep myself in the material I teach.

I majored in French and history and was a true francophile, France representing everything I wanted to emulate in art, philosophy, and daily life. [Simone de] Beauvoir and [Jean Paul] Sartre were my models for a political life and a companionate marriage. I spent my junior year in Paris sitting where they sat and reading their diaries, books, and journals. When I returned to Madison, Germaine Bree had joined the Humanities Institute, and I volunteered to work for her so I could prolong my French fix. Bree knew [Albert] Camus intimately and talked about the French existentialists as if they were next-door neighbors. She was also a thrilling professor and added a personal touch to the existential literature we read. In retrospect, she was the only female professor I wanted to emulate.

Just as I was leaving Madison, Paul Breines was elected president of the Socialist Club. For me, that meant a new generation, be it male, had been handed the Red throne. Paul had been a frat boy, was athletic and handsome in an all-American way, and appealed to "pinkos" and coeds alike. Maybe the midwestern masses would join our small band of outcasts. The dawn contains in it the brilliant noonday sun, and still there is something special about beginnings. Maybe Madison just seemed wonderful in the late 1950s and early 1960s because of the mass social uprising that followed. Is everyone nostalgic about their college years as they hit middle age, whatever that is? But, then, perhaps those formative Madison years are better in retrospect than in reality. Hegel knew, "the owl of Minerva only spreads its wings at dusk."

14　Civil Rights and History

HARRIET TANZMAN

Harriet Tanzman is an archetype for the rank-and-file scholar as activist. She has
been documenting social movements in which she took part almost from her
earliest fieldwork days, and she has pursued the material into the archives themselves, overseeing its processing. Civil rights scholars of the future, and the militants who most need that scholarship, owe her a debt unrepaid by grants, fellowships, and the usual scholarly trappings. She continues to be active in political
and social movements through a labor–media group. She lives as a freelance
writer in Brooklyn and works at the Henry Street Settlement Senior Center.

When I left home to go to the University of Wisconsin in September 1958, I
anticipated a stimulating campus and a community in which I'd find others with
values similar to mine. It was still the McCarthy period, and the 1950s were a
difficult time in which to grow up if you had any conscience about issues of war
and peace, racism and inequities. I grew up in Far Rockaway, New York—then a
lower-middle-class community with a majority of Jewish families, a minority of
black and Irish families, and a few Puerto Rican families. My high school was
tracked; I, along with many other white teenagers, was on the "honors" or college-
bound, track. Most students of color and some poorer white students studied
homemaking, shop, and commercial courses. Some people I encountered, particularly some adults, were prejudiced toward black people. This bothered me; but I
did not act against it.

　　Many of the adults in the community were striving for a better material life
for themselves and their children. My extended family was "different": The adults
got together and engaged in lively and thoughtful discussions of politics, from a

Progressive perspective. A few relatives were active in unions or in trying to free Julius and Ethel Rosenberg. I grew up feeling different from many classmates. I felt less isolated, and much more a person who could make some difference, when I joined "Ban the Bomb" demonstrations at the UN in the mid 1950s, which were sponsored by SANE [Committee for a Sane Nuclear Policy] and other groups. I looked forward to going away to college and chose the University of Wisconsin partly because of its liberal reputation.

Madison from 1958 to 1964 was a stimulating place, through its faculty, student body from all over the country and other countries, and campus political groups. I enrolled in integrated liberal studies, a two-year program, which at that time gave you all required courses in a historical perspective. The whole program had only two hundred students, out of an undergraduate campus of thirty thousand. We got a chance to know teachers and students the way we would have in a small college. One outstanding professor taught a course on medieval society, and brought the manorial system to life through a detailed depiction of the social and economic system on a manor, including relationships between workers and owners. There were no books available with this perspective; his lectures were the substance of the course. History became a key subject for me, though I chose comparative literature as my major in my junior year.

My out-of-classroom education was at least as important as classes in understanding and trying to "change the world." During the late 1950s and 1960s, the Socialist Club reached many students with its speakers from unions, leaders of Left parties, journalists, and scholars who had traveled to China and Cuba. In the heartland of the state that spawned Joseph McCarthy, we heard many voices of dissent, with no state or university censorship. We heard Anna Louise Strong, Harry Bridges, Pete Seeger, and Gus Hall—chairman of the Communist party of the United States—whose speech brought an overflow crowd to the Student Union's Great Hall in the late 1950s.

One speaker who challenged my views and changed me was Saul Landau, then graduate student, who had traveled to Cuba, in the year after the Cuban Revolution of 1959. He returned to campus and spoke in depth about the changes Cuba was experiencing—ending the corruption and misery the people had lived through under [Fulgencio] Batista. A new society was being built by all ages, including the youth, who were teaching literacy all over the island, and the neighborhood people in their organizations. I had previously believed some of the media coverage that depicted Castro as a dictator who was out for power and had sold out the revolution. When I changed my view, I came to question our government's role in trying to overthrow Cuba's government in the Bay of Pigs invasion. I found myself becoming more and more critical of U.S. policies toward other countries and the media's coverage of world issues.

My one American history undergraduate course, U.S. Foreign Policy from 1890 to the Present, deepened my consciousness of the U.S. role in the world. William Appleman Williams was the professor; he taught us how to examine documents critically, beginning with the mid-nineteenth-century Monroe Doctrine, to understand the values and point of view of the writers. I was influenced by the awareness of the Monroe Doctrine as a statement by the U.S. government that Latin America is in its sphere of influence, not to be economically or politically controlled by European powers. Williams gave us a vivid look at the 1890s as the Age of Imperialism, particularly with the U.S. role in the Philippines and Puerto Rico.

With this awareness, one could go several ways—become a scholar and professor and influence students, or become an activist working against U.S. foreign policy and other issues. Or both. I came eventually to choose the latter, though I was interested in teaching comparative literature until I was in my early twenties.

The 1950s and the early 1960s were tumultuous nationally, with the beginnings of the civil rights movement in the South and its continuation in northern cities and on campuses. I identified with the youth "in the streets" in the South, fighting racism. When I was a high school freshman, *Brown v. Board of Education* was decided, and young blacks were walking amid jeering white mobs in Little Rock and other southern cities to attend previously all-white schools. I had many questions about how this could happen—and why.

By the early 1960s, Madison hosted the Freedom Riders, "sit-in" demonstrators, SNCC [Student Non-Violent Coordinating Committee] organizers, and Freedom Singers. All came to tell us of the emerging struggles against segregation, and of courageous steps taken to try to register to vote or to organize. I was living in Groves Cooperative, a house run by the students, made up mainly of easterners, with some students from the Midwest. We ate at the Green Lantern, in the basement, with over a hundred men and women from different countries, including some activists in the Socialist Club and some people who had been active for change in their own countries.

I was particularly affected by a visit to the campus of Diane Nash, chair of the central committee of the Nashville Student Movement.[1] She was originally from Chicago, and as a Fisk student in Nashville experienced a southern version of racism for the first time: segregated public facilities, segregated schools, institutionalized segregation throughout the city. She gave a stirring speech describing the city's segregated institutions and the strong, nonviolent movement that resulted in integrated lunch counters and took on interstate travel and other issues. When a bus carrying Freedom Riders trying to integrate interstate buses was attacked in Birmingham by a mob, paralyzing one Freedom Rider for life, the bus company and its drivers refused to continue. The Riders left, but the Nashville students sent eight blacks and two whites to continue the ride to Jackson from Birmingham.

Diane Nash's presentation conveyed the spirit of resistance. I was afraid to go on the Freedom Rides, and to risk jail in Parchman Penitentiary. But the decision to work actively against segregation on the part of students my age in the South

---

[1] Diane Nash was a leader of the Nashville sit-in in 1959–1960. In the mid 1960s, she became a SNCC organizer; still later, she was active in the antiwar movement in Chicago.

had a great impact on me, and on many others like me. I felt strongly about issues, but until 1960 I mostly educated myself and discussed issues with friends. I wasn't a participant in the struggle. In the summer of 1961, C. Clark Kissinger, head of a newly formed SDS [Students for a Democratic Society] group, rounded up a small group of people to support a strike by Volkswagen mechanics. We were on the picket line at 6:00 A.M. for several weeks of the strike. It was the beginning of a change on the campus, from words to action, in line with our beliefs in the necessity of changing oppressive conditions.

I also took a survey of African history class, the only one then offered on Africa. Philip Curtin was the professor. It was a time when many African countries were winning their independence from Europe; when the Congo's great leader, Patrice Lumumba, was assassinated; and when the campus had African students from Nigeria, Algeria, and other countries. We read a great deal from assorted readings, since there was not a good single text on the subject. One source I remember was the nineteenth-century missionaries' writings, used to teach history in a West African country. We examined its cultural biases and the colonial way that history was presented. The class, and meeting and becoming friends with several African sudents, taught me about other struggles. One friend, Larbi, came as a teenager with ten others from Algeria during the revolution being waged there. I learned of his participation as a child in the revolution against France.

When I graduated from Madison, I spent a year in New York, working and becoming active in helping to plan an early trip to Cuba for the summer of 1962. I returned to Wisconsin in 1963, and decided to major in social work, hoping to be in a field where I could help people. I had passed up the opportunity a year earlier to work for a doctorate in comparative literature on a teaching fellowship. I wanted to work at a more practical profession.

In 1963 I marched in Washington with 200,000 people for civil rights, human rights, and justice for blacks in the South and in the rest of the United States. A few weeks after that moving experience, four children were assassinated in a Birmingham black church. The pressing issue appeared, and still appears to me, to be the racism of this country.

I became active in forming and working with a Congress of Racial Equality (CORE) group in Madison, made up of students and townspeople, black and white. It was headed by Silas Norman, a graduate science student from Augusta, Georgia.[2]

Meanwhile I was disappointed with my social work studies, and by my field placement in the Youth Division of the Probation and Parole Department of the state, where I counseled girls on petty crimes. I felt I was doing "Band Aid" work and not dealing with the causes of their problems. Our CORE group increasingly took up my time and energies; my roommate and I lived with a mimeograph

---

[2] Silas Norman was a SNCC fieldworker in Selma in 1964. He continued to be active in the Alabama SNCC, 1965–1966.

machine on the dining room table, went to many meetings, and tried to help plan a way of working against employment discrimination and other problems facing black people.

On November 22, 1963, I was working at Probation, counseling a young person on why she shouldn't shoplift. During my lunch break, I heard the news that John F. Kennedy had been assassinated in Dallas. It was a shock. Though I was critical of his administration, I thought the assassination meant a step to the right, and that the murder was done by right-wingers.

National and world events seemed to be developing so quickly. Different speakers I had heard asked for more help, in person and by donations, for the southern movement. I decided to leave school to work, if possible, through SNCC, in a southern community. I quit my studies with no regrets, and headed to Atlanta, where I worked in the SNCC national office from November 1963 through January 1964. I lived with two Madison friends, Dick Krooth and Annie Baxandall, who were supportive and involved themselves in the Atlanta civil rights movement. The "Wats line reports" we received at SNCC from field projects in southwest Georgia, Arkansas, Alabama, North Carolina, and Mississippi presented a stark picture of the conditions under which organizers were working to build local leadership and struggle for civil rights. Reprisals, ranging from shootings to losing jobs to jailings and beatings, were a daily occurrence, and very rarely picked up by any but the Left press, such as the *Guardian*. Reports were also compiled of mass marches to courthouses, demanding the right to vote, of organizers on foot and muleback, working for under $10 a week—doing the day-to-day organizing work.

I primarily typed in the office, and eventually participated in the renewed sit-in movement, begun during Christmas by SNCC fieldworkers. Atlanta had an image of a liberal city, and when Oginga Odinga, Kenya's foreign minister, came to visit the city as a guest of the mayor, SNCC decided to show him and the rest of the country that beneath the liberal image was the same segregation as in the rest of the South.

Our target was lunch counters at first; as we sat-in, we were joined by militant teenagers from the city and some college students. My one arrest, at a Toddle House restaurant, was an experience for me in the power of people united. Forty of us were put in a black women's cell on a Saturday night with women arrested for alleged prostitution and other crimes. All of us sang freedom songs all night, and found encouragement in the voices of supporters outside the jail, singing. I felt a sense of strength and power in our protest—in our songs.

Late in January, I ended my stay in Atlanta to return to Madison for the spring semester. Due in part to the repression against civil rights activists, exemplified in southwest Georgia where black and white SNCC workers were charged with insurrection by the state, new white organizers were not being sent into different states to organize. It was also much more dangerous for local people to be seen with white Freedom Riders than with Black workers. John Lewis, then chairman of SNCC, suggested that I come to Mississippi for the Mississippi Summer Project in

June 1964, when massive numbers of young people, black and white, would be recruited to help in Freedom Schools, with voter registration, and in building the Mississippi Freedom Democratic party. I decided to go.

Returning to Madison, I picked up on activities in the local civil rights movement. By then a "Friends of SNCC" chapter was formed, in part by Dion Diamond, a SNCC worker then in school at the university. That February, an old conviction was upheld for Dion, and he had to serve time for civil rights organizing in an infamous prison in Louisiana, interrupting his semester. This made many of us more determined to work for change, in Wisconsin and in the South.

In 1963–1964, a new history professor, Harvey Goldberg, was lecturing to three hundred to five hundred students, many of them auditing his classes. Of the three history graduate courses I took that spring, his was the only one I attended and found relevant and stimulating. He was scheduled to teach modern French history, his specialty, but changed it to a class examining revolutionary change in a series of countries including Iran, India, China, and Poland. He conveyed a strong perspective that changes were possible but that they were and are the responsibility of all of us, as well as an understanding that we in the United States need to be informed about our neighbors on all continents—their needs, their struggles, their problems. I don't remember the content of the course; primarily, what I was left with was a strong humanist and socialist view of the world, and a confirmation of the direction I was already taking, that it is up to each of us to shape the changes we see as necessary to change U.S. foreign and domestic policies.

That spring, our CORE chapter—composed of poorer community people from south Madison including blacks and a few whites, plus some women from the middle-class white community, and students—took on a campaign against Sears, Roebuck, whose board of directors was controlled by H. L. Hunt, the oil billionaire. Sears refused to hire blacks in sales positions. We had hundreds of people on picket lines, and a sit-in was staged inside a Sears store, where there were some arrests. Several of us headed south after that spring. We had lost interest in further studies—and wanted to participate full-time. Silas Norman went to Selma, Alabama, and eventually became head of a project there. I went to Mississippi, then worked in Alabama for a year, then back to Mississippi for a year and a half in a rural community. I stayed in the South for five years. In the late 1970s, when I had finished my master's in history, specializing in women's studies, I decided I wanted to write about southern history, during the civil rights period and in the decades before it.

The orientation toward a historical perspective, the need to analyze and understand the process of change, the growth and development of movements in the context of economic and social forces—these I developed in Wisconsin. I have also produced slide shows, some in the late 1970s about a strike I supported in California, and one on Eddie Carthan, a Mississippi black mayor who faced opposition and harassment for his devotion to the people of his community.

In my last semester in 1964, I also began to organize against the Vietnam war, inspired in part by Harvey Goldberg's class. John Coatsworth and I organized Madison's first antiwar demonstration May 5, 1964, as one of many campus demonstrations around the country. We brought out a hundred students and community people, and John gave a strong speech against the war. It was a good beginning of what grew into a very strong campus movement.

In 1967, I returned to Madison to speak at a statewide antidraft conference called by SDS. I was working full-time for the Fort Hood Three Defense Committee, named for the three GIs who were the first to refuse to go to Vietnam, and who brought a suit against the war. I hoped that I, too, could reach some students and encourage them to "carry it on."

15 A Way of Seeing

ELIZABETH EWEN

Liz Ewen, who teaches American Studies at SUNY–Old Westbury, has been a historian of both mass consumption (*Channels of Desire: Mass Images and the Reshaping of American Consciousness,* [1981]), and immigrant women's lives (*Immigrant Women in the Land of Dollars: Life and Culture on the Lower East Side, 1890–1925* [1985]). Her son, Paul, currently attends the University of Wisconsin.

I grew up on Long Island, New York, in a radical but not communist family— the daughter of a WASP anarchist and an Italian mother. In high school, I always felt caught between being a "typical" suburban teenager and a beatnik. I spent time in the Village and became somewhat active in civil rights and SANE [Committee for a Sane Nuclear Policy].

My decision to go to Madison for college was part of this split. I heard from a friend who was already there about the intellectual and political life of the campus; she also emphasized the "cute boys" roaming around. Two in particular caught her eye, Danny Kalb and Gene Dennis. In September 1961 I got off the plane in Madison wearing a prim little dress. I met Danny that very day; Gene Dennis became my first husband. It was sort of prophetic.

As soon as I got to my dorm room, I changed into dungarees and a workshirt. I went over to the Student Union terrace, with its lovely lakefront setting, and I fell in love with Madison. They were people dressed exactly like me, playing guitar, singing folksongs, or talking politics. I could see intellectuals wandering around, spouting texts, reading Marx.

I lived in a private dorm with a mixture of New York beatniks and Wisconsin girls. Unfortunately, women couldn't get apartments the way men did—it was still the university *in loco parentis*. Dorm rules said you had to be in by 10:30 on weekdays, 12:30 on weekends. My friends and I immediately figured out how to break the rules. The "dorm mother" got very drunk by 9:30. My room was on the first floor, so we snuck out the window and spent a lot of time on the streets or in Mifflin Street apartments. One time, a bunch of Wisconsin girls turned me and my friends in to the dean of women, Martha Peterson. She said that by existing rules she had to "campus" us (not allow us out on weekends) for six weeks, but it was perfectly all right with her that we did what we were doing.

Tension prevailed between us and the sororities. The dorm I lived in was next to a sorority, and we made loud fun of the songs they sang. Since I had my own friends and culture, I never felt I was in hostile territory. Moreover, because of the expanding movement, many sorority women later became political. We felt we were into organizing, not magnifying the differences between ourselves and the mainstream. I don't remember a feeling of hostility as such, even though fraternity boys had broken up a Fair Play for Cuba demonstration the year before.

By my sophomore year I had discovered [George] Mosse, [Hans] Gerth, and Germaine Bree. And I had political friends like Elliot Eisenberg, who developed in me an insatiable need to study Marx. For a long time, I felt I was majoring in Hegel and Marx. We had two kinds of study groups; one on the Marxian classics and a less formal one that sprang up around the classes we were taking.

We developed ideas, both positive and negative, about what a professor should be. We would choose our courses with a kind of litmus test, whether the professor could teach us something or we should argue with him in class. Elliot Eisenberg was from the Bronx, a drummer, open and full of life. Paul Breines was an early friend, a little older. So was Donald Bluestone, who had more books than anyone, and crazy systems for organizing knowledge and a total dedication to politics. He and Richard Ward put out an early national peace and anti-imperialist magazine, *Sanity,* peddling it door to door in Madison.

I also had girlfriends, interested more often in avant-garde literature than politics. A lot of us were into the taking of risks, figuring out ways to defy the rules without getting into too much trouble.

It was obvious that within the Left, in lots of ways women weren't equal to men. In the Socialist Club, for example, men did most of the talking. But, still, the general atmosphere wasn't oppressive. I remember feeling respected. Frequently I gave presentations to largely male Marxist study groups. I remember Mosse read an exam of mine and said, "Very good for a girl." I responded, "Very good anyway!"

It was a time of changing student generations. Many of us younger students felt that the Old Guard, people like Marty Sklar, had become sort of father figures, whom we idolized intellectually, but didn't follow politically.

Then, too, we had Germaine Bree. Few women were professors at that time; even fewer seemed to have a life outside the academy. Bree had written on Camus and Sartre, knew the French intellectual scene from the inside, and was very beautiful. My friends and I had all read Beauvoir and knew about existentialism. We didn't so much learn from Bree as attached ourselves to her. We found out about her personal life. We took her classes and followed her around like a bunch of groupies. Her *example* was very important.

I married Gene Dennis, son of a former general secretary of the American Communist party, before the end of my freshman year. Yes, I was recruited into an Old Left organization. But even the Old Left in Madison had what I would now call an embryonic New Left consciousness. The Madison branch wrote position papers defending the Chinese Revolution, Malcolm X, and the necessity for mass action. We acted within a number of organizations. Soon we were militants and fighting the national organization and developing a political hostility to most of the tenets of the Old Left.

These years were extremely political and intense. Among my tasks was to become involved in CORE (Congress of Racial Equality). In the fall of 1963 we discovered job discrimination against blacks at the Sears store in Madison, and the first mass action I helped to design and participated in was a shop-in. After exhausting legal channels, we decided on direct action. While a large picket line sang civil rights songs outside the store, about forty people were sent to various departments inside the store. They would, for instance, pretend to try on and buy twenty different dresses or pants and then ask the salesperson if the store discriminated. All this climaxed with civil disobedience in the shoe department. Aside from Ken Knudson's tax protests, the first political arrests I knew of in Madison took place here.

Sears changed its policies, and we received a lot of media coverage for the demonstration. Although some people in the community viewed us with hostility, others welcomed the activism. A crossover between community and campus people was created that had not existed before. The campus supported us warmly.

In early 1964 we organized a civil rights demonstration with perhaps 1500 people, against Barry Goldwater when he came to town. The period for mass action—for direct action—had started.

The intellectual and political climate also changed. Being an intellectual earlier meant something like being a talmudic scholar. The civil rights movement did more than anything to change that; it caused people to join activist organizations, to *do something*. Being active now meant as much as the printed word.

Although [William Appleman] Williams and *Studies on the Left* had provided an intellectual understanding of the crisis of American society—the functions and limitations of what we called corporate liberalism—both Williams and those *Studies* people still left in Madison seemed rather remote. Harvey Goldberg emerged as more important; he personified the spirit of activism, he lived in the student community, and he went to the Penny University, a coffee house, with his student friends. I remember attending Goldberg's class by accident his first semester; there were thirty of us. One hundred registered for the second semester. It went on from there. Goldberg made you feel that *revolutionary* history—France in 1789, Russia in 1917—was part of the present, part of your life.

I remember when John Kennedy was assassinated in 1963. The news came two minutes before Goldberg's class. He made an appeal to the community and invited the students to leave the classroom with him and go to the Rat where we could talk as equals. The Socialist Club had become part of the past. When Marty Sklar advised Paul Breines not to go on a Freedom Ride, one tradition had come to an end and another had to go beyond it.

The civil rights movement had another important impact. It took people off the campus and into the community, especially during the summer. People went south, or got involved in the Northern Student Movement, where they got experience in direct action and organizing. I spent one summer taping, photographing, and working with California migrant workers. Many of the people I stayed with had been organizers for forty or fifty years. Some had IWW [Industrial Workers of the World] pasts.

I began to appreciate the history of radicalism in the United States, and I became interested in American history—a jump, to say the least, from Hegel. I also worked in a Freedom House in Chicago where I learned the strategy and tactics of direct action in a poor black community.

Direct action also speeded the disintegration of the Old Left. The Communist party, for example, had been against the anti-Goldwater demonstration. We prided ourselves, meanwhile, on our nonsectarianism. Many Communist party-related people admired people from the Young Socialist Alliance (Trotskyist) because of their abilities and personalities. We lived across the street from each other anyway, and played poker together. We would hear about totally sectarian attitudes communists and Trotskyists had toward each other on the East and West coasts, where you couldn't speak to a person from the other group. That seemed ridiculous. When the Committee to End the War in Vietnam began, and caught the campus by storm with its educational and activist plans, the radicals all had the same position (immediate withdrawal) against the liberals (a negotiated settlement) on the war. There was a sense of connectedness in the Madison Left, with a growth of Left-leaning neighborhoods, where you'd walk down a street and feel a sense of common bond. There was goodwill among radicals that I've rarely felt in the Left since then.

The *Madison* Left— that's the point, anyway. Even if people belonged on a national level to other organizations, those took second place—were subordinate, in a sense—to the larger Left community. When the Committee to End the War in Vietnam became national and bogged down in sectarian infighting, we ignored it.

I've always thought it interesting that SDS [Students for a Democratic Society] was never a large organization in Madison. We didn't need it. We had our own *ad hoc* organizations that planned teach-ins, door-to-door campaigns, sit-ins, strikes, and so on. I remember in 1968 a group came to Madison from Columbia SDS and tried to take over. They caucused and carried on in a sectarian manner.

The result seemed like a primal scene, a violation. There was also very little Red baiting, except from outside the Left. At one time in 1965, twelve people received subpoenas from the Senate Internal Security Committee. I remember going home expecting a letter, but I received none. This one time I benefited from sexism. But, by mutual consultation, no one honored the subpoenas.

Around 6:00 P.M. every day, a right-wing Madison radio commentator would broadcast the activities of the Left, especially those with communist backgrounds. He broadcast names, addresses, and daily activity. Although we expected reprisals for a while, nothing happened. In Madison, at least, that type of McCarthyism was dead. The University of Wisconsin had a tradition of fighting McCarthyism and its forerunners. This heritage created an open space in a closed society. It meant that doing radical intellectual or political work was a possibility. This break from McCarthyism made the role of ideas extraordinarily important in Madison.

We were fighting for the right to be intellectuals, even against the university, which we saw as sometimes degrading education. We had professors with radical pasts and radical ideas: Williams, Goldberg, Gerth, Mosse. Although we fought with our professors, they supported us and expected us to fight. When I went to Rochester in 1969, one of the first things I noticed was the difference in expectations of the faculty. Madison was special in the sense that your political and intellectual work didn't have to be separate. The fight for the mind was as important as the action in the street. This wasn't true in other places.

Madison was also flexible. Look at my history. In New York I would have been typecast as an Old Leftist. Madison allowed me to immerse myself in the Old Left, to learn how to become a New Leftist in the Old Left, and finally in 1965 to break with the Old Left without losing my friends or my ability to do political work.

I still feel Madison was a great place to be in the 1960s. In post-Reagan America, it's important to know you were once at a place you could experience at its best. When so much written and said about the New Left make it sound artificial—all style and no content—I have a memory that confirms it was social, intellectual, personal, and political—it was real.

I lived in Madison eight years. It took me seven years to recover from the culture shock of leaving. Madison gave you a way of seeing. It's not surprising that my friendships from Madison have lasted in a way none of the others have. Madison is a bond between people. It is also a vision of a radical community.

Fred Harrington, Charles Vevier, and William Appleman
Williams, Madison, 1962(?). Photo courtesy Thomas
McCormick.

Warren Susman, Judy Gutman, and
Herbert Gutman, Madison, May 1951.
Photo courtesy Mrs. Warren Susman.

Nina Serrano (Nina Serrano-Landau) as part of a U.S. student delegation that
broke the travel ban to China, 1957. Photo courtesy Nina Serrano.

Eleanor Hakim, Madison, 1960. Photo credit: Lee
Baxandall.

Greg and Saul Landau, Madison, 1959. Photo credit: Lee Baxandall.

Bill Lee and Mike Lebowitz read *Studies on the Left,* Union Terrace, 1961. Photo credit: Lee Baxandall.

Madison radical community protests electoral rally for vice-presidential candidate Henry C. Lodge on Wisconsin Capital steps, October 1960. Photo credit: Lee Baxandall.

Dick Ward, Steve Scheinberg, Madison,
October 1960. Photo credit: Lee Baxandall.

Lodge rally, Madison, October 1960. Photo credit: Lee Baxandall.

Jim McWilliams, Steve Scheinberg,
Madison, October 1960. Photo credit:
Lee Baxandall.

Rosalyn Fraad Baxandall and Lee Baxandall, 1961.

Demonstration in solidarity with the sit-in movement to desegregate lunch counters at Woolworths, Madison. Photo by Nina Serrano.

Paul Breines and Winifred Jacoby (later Breines), 1961. Photo credit: Lee Baxandall.

Organizing for trial resulting from Traux Air Force Base demonstration, Madison, November 1965. (l-r) Evan Stark, Bob Cohen, Betsy Fromer, Bortai Scudder, Stanley Grand. Photo by Lea Zeldin, courtesy Evan Stark.

Paul and Mari Jo Buhle, Madison, 1971. Photo by Paul
Richards, courtesy Paul Buhle.

Shawn Bayer, Paul Buhle, Paul Richards,
Spaight St., Madison, 1970. Photo credit:
Mari Jo Buhle.

Harvey Goldberg, Madison, 1980. Photo by Dave
Hasenberg, courtesy *The Daily Cardinal*.

George Mosse, June 1961, at his picnic
for his Seminar on Marxism. He is
watching the Marxists of the Heart at
play. Photo credit: Lee Baxandall.

Part Three
Conflict
and Consciousness

16   In Exile

EVAN STARK

Evan Stark was the orator of a critical era in Madison. Neither physically magnetic nor golden-tongued, he echoed through the handy bullhorn a soulfulness that touched ordinary students unknown to (and even fearful of) the Left. He made them dream, and he made them righteously wrathful. More like turn-of-the-century anarchists, who could rouse a crowd of immigrant workers with a few roaring phrases, and less like LaFollettes, who successfully built institutions to support their beliefs, Stark passed swiftly from the Madison scene. His influence remained for years in the widened circle of antiwar sentiment. He had coaxed quiet opponents of the war into doing what they had wanted to do but had not recognized themselves as capable of doing.

Stark finally received his Ph.D. in sociology from Madison in 1984, after a decade directing Yale research programs in health, job stress, and family violence. He currently teaches public administration at Rutgers University's Newark Campus, co-directs the Domestic Violence Training Project, and is chairman of his neighborhood Ward Committee.

I was not made in Madison. But when I came, I was in pieces. A clumsy gas balloon lifted from a Bronx play-park sex-gang fantasy life, I set down hard in "the tradition of the new." There was an extended moment during the 1960s, with May 1968 as its zenith, when alien intellect took root in native-born activism and re-emerged in one of those rare conjunctures of theory and practice from which revolutions come. For me, encounter with exiles had begun years before at Brandeis, culminated with Hans Gerth at Madison and in forms of resistance and imagination that let me embrace alienation as my true home. That summer of 1959, I was a million miles from stickball, in Waltham, built in the shadow of a great underwear king to whom my grandfather was just another bolshie greenhorn at a machine.

Abe Sachar had been chosen, over Albert Einstein, as president of Brandeis. Now, a regular Captain of Erudition, he bartered radical genius in the marketplace of McCarthyism, where it was cheap. Even as critical theory concentrated at Brandeis, it continued to reflect its ambiguous origins, resistance in hiding. These were the 1950s, and we were twenty years old, surrounded by sexy bohemians, avantgarde architecture, and unmade beds, things rare in the suburbs. Yet, behind the new glass and the glitter, the subtext was fear. Our teachers talked and dressed as if the Fuehrer (or Joe McCarthy) had come personally to run them out of their homes in the middle of the night.

The mentors of the radical generation to be came to Waltham to play Sancho to the Harvard Don. For me, the best were Norman Mailer, Malcolm X, Paul Goodman, and James Baldwin, but especially Mailer. Each had made personal estrangement the center of his identity and had improvised a mode of speaking— we called it lecturing in reverse—that let them make their points by negative example. They assaulted every tenet of our taken-for-granted world, then took our wiseass jibes full on, only half responding, until our nasty questions hung before us as points of intimacy, alienation as a form of connections. The seed was planted. If I could let my sense of always being "in the wrong place at the wrong time" into full consciousness, it might prove my greatest asset.

Had I my own historical address, I might have been more cautious about this stuff. But I saw myself only in passing, the way you glimpse a defaced poster in a subway station from a speeding train. I wore my public identity like the dog tags we'd been given in grade school, wondering whether my "achievements," like the tags, would survive the bomb blast.

Was this the "pursuit of happiness"? Said my college counselor, "You use happiness to avoid facing yourself." This strengthened my conviction that the self I was avoiding was unmanageable—or worse, not worth managing. "Oi America!" Hans Gerth moaned in the very first class we had together in Madison. Then, rising slowly from the chair, a lion rudely awakened, he roared in endless sentence polemic: "Our playground directors train ten year old girls for the competitive pursuit of appearance values by writing on the blackboard 'Gina (the daughter of an Italian tavern keeper) is the best dressed girl in the playground.'" I came to Madison feeling perpetually absent, hearing about myself from a distance. The sociologist Erving Goffman coined the word "nonperson," and Clark Kerr called us affectionately "the walking wounded."

Not that I was unself-conscious. Mastering self-reflection was a key to classroom (and bedroom) success. And I wanted success badly. Again, it was Gerth who put it straight:

> The rebelliousness of our most highly educated youth seems to me
> readily understandable. It is an expression of the profound agony of

youngsters taught to consider what Freud called the superego a superfluous overhead. Under the universal atmosphere of drift and aimless-
ness, in a world of "operators," they strive for "success" (whatever it
may be) and one man is the other man's wolf, as Hobbes had it.

Yes, we turned out like a pop Left collage, not Yankee symbols of the American
dream. But this I attribute to the shallow payoff (we expected better) and the
insulation my peer (and academic) culture imposed. The feeling that "nothing was
good enough" found its rationale in critical theory where things that seemed or felt
good paled against their ideal form, sex against Eros, politics against revolution.
Incredible perhaps, but I simply had no idea that the style I worked so hard to
perfect in the early 1960s would leave me pursuing failure, like a wind-up doll
pointed at a wall. We were hardly "refuseniks." We presented ourselves cordially
to John Kennedy for a peace tea at the White House, and I wore my tie to be
beaten at Woolworth counters in 1962. That I was yearning to live my alienation
is public even then, I know only from dim memories of sexual and political irresponsibility. As I argued that H. Stuart Hughes should condemn U.S. action in
Cuba (even if it meant "throwing" to Kennedy the Senate race he could never win),
I felt an affinity with "the beats" well deep inside.

The radicals whom Hans Gerth helped to start *Studies on the Left* had come
to Madison in the late 1950s mainly as "Red diaper babies" or members of the
Labor Youth League. Their Popular Front sentimentality made them ripe for bed-
time stories about native Populism, though they could hardly fathom the current
descendants of "midwestern tradition" who inhabited fraternity row. Gerth was
close to this group intellectually. But in us he found another kind of recognition.
We were compatriots in exile. As he insisted:

> It is the age of the superman and batman on TV and of "The Fugitive"
> as *the* neurotic personality of our time which these hundreds of
> thousands of academic youth feel "alienated" from. They are driven
> into exile by adults and learn to think of themselves as voluntary expa-
> triates and lost generations . . . and they protest in their agony against
> the insensitivity and hard rubber callousness with which the victors of
> World War II tighten their helmets and prepare for the "eternal peace"
> without resurrection.

Initiation

When I arrived in Madison in 1963, the civil rights movement was passing into a
phase of creative militancy. Nationally, the New Left was still confined mainly to
an elite stratum of crewcut jacket-and-tie "leaders" who thought each of their
"shocks of recognition" should be heard around the world. To me, the Port Huron

Statement seemed saccharine, patronizing, and unbearably social democratic. In Madison, the statement attracted the Old Left *Studies* crowd, Marxist academics whose search for a class of activists could not be interrupted for leafletting and the like. Women were active to any extent only in SNCC [Student Non-Violent Coordinating Committee] and CORE [Congress of Racial Equality], and the great "mass" of blonds were not politically active at all. Nationally as well as locally, there were only inklings of another level of political activity among those who were less ambitious than the elite students—hence more angry than disillusioned—and for whom the poverty of college life was no brief interlude.

In Madison in 1964, student activism centered on civil rights "organizing." We got Sears to integrate with a "shop-in" that made them rude to and fearful of any black, or any non-straight-looking student, who used the store for months. At the Republican State Convention in Milwaukee, a Madison activist was pushed down. When she refused to rise until the offending guard apologized, we surrounded her for safety. In Madison, the *Capital Times* headline was *CORE Stages Sit-In*. I was shaken. History, it seemed, knew us better than we knew ourselves.

I became sidekick to Ken Knudson, Madison's anarchopacifist loner. The Peace Center, which he and Clark Kissinger had maintained to do antidraft education (a popular pamphlet was their "Advice to Young Men on How to Get into the Army") suddenly emerged as the major stimulus for civil disobedience in Madison, presenting a program of "direct action" that evoked the enthusiasm, if not the participation, of large numbers of students. In October 1965, in an effort to confront federal lawmakers directly, we presented a "citizens arrest" warrant to the commander of the Truax air base, Colonel Arrowsmith, and blocked the entrance to the base with the inadvertent help of assembled newspeople. Then there was the Anti-Military Ball of 1965, the event of the radical social season, attended by thousands. All this was oddball to the sectarian Left. CORE was, to them, on the margins of "real" politics because civil disobedience supposedly "alienated" the "masses" and because the majority of CORE's members were older blacks (many of whom had come to Truax from Alabama and Mississippi) or women from "town." Perhaps most threatening to the sectarian groups, we had fun.

From 1964 to 1966, the campus Committee to End the War in Vietnam (CEWV) provided a loose but important framework for antiwar protest. A coalition of campus groups, dominated alternately by local supporters of the Communist party and Socialist Workers party, the CEWV organized campus teach-ins, maintained antiwar booths, aggressively recruited in the dorms for "classes" in Vietnamese history, held periodic soap boxes and rallies, and maintained contact with the national antiwar movement. When the State Department "Truth Team" came to campus in May, 132 faculty members signed an ad of greeting and were joined by graduate students at a coffee-and-cookie reception. That evening, however, about 300 of us took over the Truth Team presentation, an action that— thanks to a report in *Time* magazine—prompted similar protests by antiwar groups wherever the Truth Team appeared. Our proposal for the Truax action on the International Days of Protest was, however, predictably voted down in a CEWV meeting.

Whatever the formal status of this activity may prove to have been on the long march to socialism, it had tremendous personal importance for me. My new friends were both political and unapologetic in their aggressive demand that program and tactics directly extend personal need and imagination. Because of this, in my first talk to a peace rally, on Hiroshima Day, 1965, I finally felt confident enough to carry out my sense of alienation. As I began to see it, the problem was neither to stir liberal guilt and appeal to principle nor, as my "Marxist" comrades insisted, to touch every "interest" so that "coalitions" would form. The problem was to use the deep feeling of "*un*beauty" as a weapon, to correct alienation comically so that they became a point of connection rather than isolation. Certainly, we had to call attention to the real violence of the Cold War. But this violence rested on another violence, which hurt me even more personally:

> a violence which reaches the heart of my generation like the headlines of the newspapers no longer can, a violence that forces us to choose again and again between our need for personal freedom and integrity and loyalty to our government, a choice no man [*sic*] should be forced to make, between a death of courage, truth and dignity, between giving up the need to be whole, and isolation from the mainstream social and political community.

Of course, by this time, Berkeley had erupted. SDS had already brought thirty thousand of the five million students in the United States to Washington in an important demonstration against the war. But for me, these events were less important than the fact that somewhere between Gerth's critique and the living imagination of black and student activism, I was finally finding a point from which to talk in my own voice. The more aware I became of my alienation (*i.e.,* of the political implications of my cultural estrangement), the less interested I was in formal consciousness, politics, or responsibility. Expressionist writer Hugo von Hofmannstahl said of the German youth movement in the 1920s, "They seek not freedom but connection." Things were a bit more complicated for us. There was no way I could return to the Bronx where patient, arthritic grandparents waited on street benches for rumors of itinerant surgeons risen from the ranks of the *cheder,* or to Westchester where my Catholic buddies worked construction gangs building edifices for children they quickly forgot they had once wanted to have. For the Frankfurt intellectuals, the "quest for community," preached by the likes of Madison historian William Appleman Williams, was pure mythology. But what if, rather than agonize in the abyss of our fragmentation and build a political movement (and program) whose conventionality was simply an extended defense mechanism, we actually *chose* alienation? I concluded the speech:

America's community has become 80 million isolated TV viewers, sipping cocktails and Cokes and watching, with the aspirin bottles near, as those to whom they pay their taxes bring them closer each day to nuclear death. Indeed, as Mr. Bayer assures us after each exhausting newscast, "Relief *is* just minutes away." . . . Disloyalty not community is the basis of our society: it is the basis of our market; of our international relations . . . our heroes, our weapons, like our cars, our women, our treaties and our "facts"—all are "dynamically obsolescent." . . . And so we have learned our lesson well—too well, some now say—and we have made disloyalty into our creed. But we are disloyal not because there is so much to oppose—there *is* more than ever—but because with its vast stretches of free land, riches, its doctors, lawyers, scientists and their machines; with its movies and its higher learning and its sports and its glamour, there is so little of our community left to support. We are not proud to be Americans, and we are becoming alienated in the most profound sense. We can no longer love our country and remain honest men.

Academic Life

Since I'd suffered college as my bohemian interlude, I went to graduate school directly. Maurice Stein, the Brandeis sociologist and author of *Eclipse of Community,* told me he'd learned more by listening to a man named Gerth for an hour once at a sociology convention than in many terms with [Robert K.] Merton at Columbia. "And," he added, as if this fascination was insufficient, "He was [C. Wright] Mills's teacher." I set out to Madison with visions of apprenticing to a radical guru at a midwestern *studium generalis.*

The Madison student Rathskeller was built defiantly by LaFollette and his German constituents during Prohibition. Outside, on the patio stretching to the edge of Lake Mendota, depressed graduate students in English sat, like great elephant seals, staring at the hefty blonde coeds skillfully maneuvering their craft. There, I met my first "real" sociologist. "You'll like it here, Stark," he promised with a transplanted wise-guy contempt. "We'll bust your ass, but it'll do you good." The football lingo was apt. During the next two years, the statistician player–coach of "the largest sociology department in the world" communicated with us twice, to remind us to join the department team and to sell us T-shirts at a special discount apparently subsidized by the same National Institute for Mental Health grants that paid our way to games (i.e., "conventions"). We were an army platoon from a third-rate 1940s film learning to take whatever was dished out.

Hans Gerth was my oasis. If the up-and-coming faculty lured their graduate students with fellowships, Gerth got us with talk—constant, unremitting talk. It was how I imagine the medieval scholars to have worked, like learning before books, moving from illustration to illustration until the dramatic weight of events themselves made one definition after another clear. Other students in sociology found Gerth's classroom style intolerable, especially his outbursts of emotion, the difficulty in taking notes or outlining what he said, and most of all his indifference to bells (he often went twenty or thirty minutes over time). I was fascinated by his singular attention to his own inner voice, undistracted by routine.

What I hadn't bargained for was Gerth as friend, playing the benevolent patriarch with whom one must constantly travel so that nothing important (including the car keys) will be lost. While faculty and radical students debated whether it was politic to use "imperialism" in our antiwar propaganda, in class Gerth would present "imperialism" as a series of lived experiences and from the vantage of the victims of "progress." In private, at his house in the evenings, we would work together on a paper often till morning, sometimes actually putting down on paper no more than a sentence or two. I was the chorus to Gerth's monologue, which was punctuated by bursts of rage and hypnotic poetry readings from ancient books in a language whose meaning I caught even when the words were obscure. In the morning classes, I was able to incorporate the flow of imagery with relative ease into my store of political examples. I could keep no distance in the evenings, however, and none was demanded. I was bewildered at why I should have been chosen for this strange ritual and found myself searching through my autobiographical baggage for experiences to serve as countermetaphor to Gerth's treatment by the Nazis, his neglect and harassment by colleagues, his wife's suicide, his second life in another language, and his sense of "betrayal" by former students. Was it only a matter of time before he perceived my own inadequacy?

I suddenly felt an overwhelming compulsion to cover the distance between my hidden experience of the world and the historical motifs Gerth represented through his life. He was a living newspaper, moving with studied melodrama from theory to personal memory to the latest "headline" and the story "behind the news." Then we ended at the single line where we had begun. "Write this up, Stark," he would say when it was time for me to go. For a few weeks, I tried following his instructions literally, painfully reconstructing the evening monologue around an incomplete passage on the First International, Friedrich Sorge, or the Claflin sisters in late-nineteenth-century New York. But I finally sensed the more general meaning in his parting words. This was my initiation into political thought. Gerth meant "writing it up" to be my life assignment.

Gerth's reputation was ambiguous, and so was my status as his student. Though he was neither a team nor a conduit for research dollars, his Germanic presence lent intellectual credibility to the otherwise lackluster pursuit of professional careers. Einstein once summarized the theory of relativity for Marlene Dietrich in one sentence. "Think of when Geneva stops at this train," he quipped. Gerth lacked the time or patience to make things this brief.

What Franz Neumann said of university life under Bismarck, that it "excluded the study of social and political reality," was true of Madison sociology from the mid 1950s on. If, in the Second Reich, this was because "speculation and book learning" prevailed, here the situation was reversed. Social science meant data methodology. Nor was this because the department was politically conservative. To the contrary, a number of the senior people had been communists in the 1940s and, more important, had pioneered the study of race relations and class inequities when these topics were *verboten*. But a healthy suspicion of the "unproven"— often linked autobiographically to disillusionment with Soviet Marxism—had degenerated into a virtual veto on larger questions. Several men (there were no women in the hundred-member department) had been fired from other jobs because of their stands; others were pathologically shy; and for still others, genuine concerns had become so complicated by ambition that there was little coherence left. So a secure consensus arose that real value lay not in what was proved but in the mastery of techniques with presumed utility to prove anything—save anything that could not be counted—and in the "significance" of the "readout." Providing radicals toed the methodological line, they would be accepted, even defended if the need arose. As the orgy of trivia became less shamefaced, the younger faculty took the initiative. The course on theory became a rote lesson on "theorems"; the language requirement for the Ph.D. was eliminated (with Gerth the sole dissenter); the old-fashioned master's thesis was transformed into an empirical paper; and required classics were replaced by more current readings on "the controversy in functionalism."

Gerth brought to Madison precisely that historical comprehension and theoretical commitment from which academic sociology was in hot retreat. For two decades, Gerth was watched and kept from promotion by chairman after chairman. When Mills took the Weber essays Gerth translated as class handouts to Oxford University Press, Gerth asked that his "assistant" be so listed. Though he could not read German, Mills was furious at this neglect of his career and threatened a suit if Gerth failed to apologize. Oxford turned to Madison's current sociology chair, and that southern gentlemen reminded Gerth of his duty as an "alien" in 1945. Gerth bowed low. Still, though Gerth would chide his former student for calling the middle class "*lumpen* intelligentsia," borrowing without footnote from Paul Sweezy, and for "never learning the language of Karl Marx," he would quickly add, "He died of a failure of heart, not of nerve." In the 1950s, after the publication of their collaborative volume on social psychology, *Character and Social Structure,* with McCarthyism spreading like pollen in the Wisconsin air, even Merton's introduction couldn't stop Madison's empiricists from relieving Gerth of the social psychology course. And so, on into the 1960s, when the class we designed on the Sociology of Film—we concentrated on the historical basis of key aesthetic images—was taken from us and rotated among the "younger men" as Sociology *Through* Film.

Thought was a job in Madison, not a quality of being. My efforts to make Gerth "popular" were fruitless. Gerth needed friendship too badly to mince words on its behalf. I tried introducing him to Maurice Zeitlin, local antiwar activist and sociological notable. "Hans," I began, "Professor Zeitlin wrote *Cuba: Tragedy in our Hemisphere.*" Zeitlin (who smiled at everything) smiled. "Tragedy?" groaned

Gerth, already pivoting to walk away. "Why there's nothing at all tragic about it." And that was that.

The picture Gerth left me with made even his recurrent fears about "going too fast" sound prudish. Beneath every paradox, Gerth detected the same compelling contradiction, the absolute need to break with the terms of the present and the absence of any means to do so that was not illusory or barbarous. While our "native" intellectuals monitored the grand designs of diplomats and rebel leaders, Gerth directed attention to the layers of human significance beneath the seemingly banal and evasive features of everyday experience. For him, the national agony was illustrated as much by the housewife secretly shedding her "unwept tears" in a suburban cinema as by Secretary of War James Forrestal's scream before throwing himself from a Pentagon window, "The Russians are coming." Critical thought was neither a weapon nor a morale booster for Gerth. It was simply a way to pose reality in its full complexity as a problem to be solved by our collective self-invention.

Departure

By 1967, I was a "student leader," one of a rare breed of postadolescent gunfighters whose artillery consisted of rhetorical flamboyance mixed with Jewish humor and an almost inhuman capacity to attend meetings and walk the picket line after debating through the night. I was reified like a campus queen (and felt as isolated), doing radio and TV spots, talking at "bagel" breakfasts and unitarian services, even getting anonymous love notes ("I was the one holding the candle when you read *Howl* at Hillel on Sunday"). In 1966, the FBI elevated my security status to "dangerous subversive" and officially targeted me for harassment, under its clandestine Cointelpro Operation, as a potential "terrorist." I was followed, and reports on my activity were collected from campus and city police, reporters on the *Daily Cardinal,* the manager of the Student Union, and several patriotic members of the Sociology Department. Actually, my ascent had little to do with subversive intent.

Early in 1966, the university decided to turn student grades over to the government to determine eligibility for the Vietnam draft. As a result, about a hundred of us decided to occupy the administration building, against the pleas of our radical leaders and the heads of various student organizations. Our act was designed to be exemplary and limited, but by evening, as if they had simply been waiting in the wings for the drama to start, almost two thousand students had joined us and the administration abandoned any thought of using force.

During the next several days, William Appleman Williams, William Taylor, and other radical faculty came to talk to us, then left after promising that their group would win faculty support for our demands. When the faculty refused to meet "under duress," we agreed to leave. As the crowd moved tiredly home, I realized that the only professor acutally to sit-in was the old-line liberal Gerth. Perhaps he was there because he was treated like a student by his colleagues, alternately patronized and bullied; perhaps he felt he had to be there when *his* students got the trouble he was chronically waiting to return. Or perhaps he simply wanted the company.

The faculty turndown was inevitable and brought thousands of students into the night, looking for a spot to rest their anger. I held the crowd at bay with a talk on the medieval *studium generalis,* while our scouts found an unguarded site. But my leadership had less to do with speechmaking than standing at the center of huge ballrooms and facilitating a mass conversation among the thousands sitting on the floor.

By next morning, dozens of faculty had climbed through the windows of Bascom Hall to join us, just watching and sharing their own stores. Ralph Hanson, campus police chief, put his crowd-control equipment under our command. Everyone who came near seemed to sense immediately that we had secured this space to try on our skins, and they were seduced by this. Whatever would be charged in the official postmortems, we took their buildings for the same reason the Reuther brothers occupied Dodge Main: to give our capacity for autonomous social cooperation a direct political expression. Irony put us in the administration building. It would never have occurred to us to talk about the sort of society, education, or life we wanted, in class, and these discussions pit our collective integrity against the invidious distinctions (in sex, lifestyle, etc.) around which our official education was constructed. We left Bascom Hall when the discussion was done. But we had been closely watched. A year later, when we sat-in again, they broke our heads, less because of what they feared we would do *to* their buildings than because, by becoming our kinds of adults *in* their building, they put their obsolescence on public view.

Everything was different on campus when the administration brought Dow [Chemical Company] to recruit in October 1967. A new chancellor, William Sewell, had been picked largely for his progressive views—his son had even been arrested at Berkeley. A social science methodologist with not a whit of administrative skill or experience, he lacked even the patronizing aura of conciliation that surrounded his predecessor. Sewell remained incredulous when we put documents on his desk showing that his dean of students, Joseph Kaufman, was meeting with city police behind his back to plan a possible "occupation." Just days before the "Dow incident," Sewell assured me in private that as long as there was no violence on our part, the police would never be used.

The vast majority of students had long since recognized the futility of symbolic protests on a campus where 90 percent opposed the war. But when a group of "concerned black people" pulled out of the planned protest, the Trotskyist-oriented leadership of the CEWV opposed direct action, calling instead for a day of "peaceful and educational" leafletting. A parallel leadership had meanwhile developed, partially rooted in a newly revived SDS chapter and partially in the increasing numbers of students drawn to direct action and antidraft work. When SDS proposed that Dow be blocked, the planning meeting of three hundred was split, but by midnight the one hundred remaining agreed to my compromise proposal; peaceful picketing on Tuesday and then civil disobedience on Wednesday. I oriented the flier toward direct action:

> We must move from protest to resistance. Before we talked. Now we must act. We must stop what we oppose.
>
> We must enter the arena of action to make the kind of history we want.
>
> We will enter a building in which Dow is recruiting and stop them.

Over five hundred students met on Bascom Hill. Soon after the rally began, about a hundred "jocks" approached and began tearing signs and pushing through the crowd. I took the bullhorn and spoke extemporaneously on "Why the Wisconsin Football Team Was Losing." I drew a parallel between the plays called into the team from their coach on the bench and the spoon-fed education in class. Both created a "spectacle" that locked our energy and imagination in tight, making us feel overwhelmed by our capacities and clumsy as a result. Tomorrow, I promised—not realizing the impact of what I was saying on young athletes desperate for self-confidence to go with their strength—we would have a real chance to use our energy to "shatter the spectacle." (I finished with a story of a young black player from Galveston who had been admitted to the university despite an achievement score of only 8. After an outstanding first year, he had been a day late for practice the second, missing the team photograph, apparently because his mother was sick. The man was kicked off the team—which meant out of school—and returned to a world that had suddenly become totally alien.)

The city police arrived shortly after we entered the Commerce Building the next morning. After an abortive charge, led by Dean Kaufman wielding an axe, Chief Hanson urged me to talk with Sewell, and my "bodyguards" (both now prominent sociologists) kept the police from grabbing me as we moved through the crowd. Hanson begged Sewell to avoid a "bloodbath," and so did I. But the man had frozen still into his role, and his face was as pasty as that of the heart attack victim he would tragically become shortly after. Once the beatings started, a law school dean rushed into Sewell's office to phone an ambulance. He was still riveted, just staring at the wall.

When the police finally broke through, they met a cordon of athletes who had been counterprotestors just twenty-four hours earlier. I remember Kim Wood, a fullback on the team, talking calmly to a policeman who was vainly trying to beat the 250-pound senior with a stick. After we left the building and were fighting the gas, I did an odd thing. Having gone to wash out my eyes in the social science building, I suddenly thought, "Why not check the mail?" The hall upstairs was empty. But faculty members were clustered at the windows in the offices overlooking the melee, occasionally cheering a student they recognized. I slipped in next to them for a few minutes, realizing the irony of this "participant observation." Then I returned to the street.

After things settled, I visited the wounded in the hospital. Then I left the city, resigning from school just hours before we would be officially suspended. I was afraid and undoubtedly shared some of Gerth's most paranoid fears about what might come next. Years later, I still wake occasionally in a cold sweat and try to shake the picture of police coming up the stairs toward my room, beating my friends bloody on the way.

After the letter inviting him to Frankfurt sat unopened on his desk for a year, Gerth finally agreed to go, as he put it, "to show them what it had once been like." Left-wing students there insisted that he make history a footnote to Marxology. When he refused, they "turned off the lights," and he retired. He died soon after.

I would like to believe that the marvelous conjuncture between theory and practice that I felt through our encounter in exile bore political fruit. By once again showing that the outcomes of confrontations with the state are always a question of "we shall see," the protests that circled the globe between 1966 and 1970 rescued the Marxian dialectic from the idealist heights to which it had been chased by the Nazi war machine, as well as from the prevalent sectarian view that history was merely the "inevitable" product of economic circumstances.

Wherever I travel, I meet veterans of the Madison sit-ins. And the same sense of recognition binds us, however much we may have grown apart in other respects. It is a sense of having once been so filled with collective imagination and personal possibility in a space from which authority had been cleared that inventing the future came almost as an afterthought. These "moments of autonomy" are rare in a person's life, and they can easily dissolve into nostalgia. But having experienced this sense of my capacities, of *our* capacities, I always know when I am settling for less. And whether I respond with muttering dissatisfaction, a quiet longing that I keep to myself, or an angry refusal that once again gets me labeled "subversive," I feel my alienation authenticated and know I can stay sane for at least another day.

17 The Intellectual New Left

STUART EWEN

Stu Ewen brought Herbert Marcuse into the critique of advertising, in *Captains of Consciousness: Advertising and the Social Roots of the Consumer Culture* (1976) and expanded his critique in *Channels of Desire: Mass Images and the Shaping of American Consciousness* (co-authored with Elizabeth Ewen). His examination of media and experimentation with print (a long-running mini-poster series, *Billboards of the Future,* owed its inspiration to him) and video, led him to *All Consuming Images: The Politics of Style in Contemporary Culture* (1988). He chairs the communications program at Hunter College, New York.

I feel like I grew up in a secret organization, unaware of the secrets myself. While the moral values were liberal, opposed to social injustice and racial prejudice, there was little discussion of politics. Until I grew up, it never occurred to me that my parents were leftists. I think my parents had been terrified by McCarthyism and the execution of the Rosenbergs. Only later did I discover some hidden past commitments. In 1970 my father called me aside and in hushed tones told me he had something to give me; he pulled out a Modern Library edition of *Capital*—a good Charles Kerr edition that I still have—and gave it to me for safekeeping. It was like pulling a family secret out from behind the back of a drawer. Despite the secrecy, however, something was percolating. All three children turned out to be radicals of sorts, a bit anarchist in my case.

Before coming to Madison, my main "political" involvements were in the area of counterculture. In high school I was taken with "the beats," and very moved by black music (rhythm and blues) as well. The music was inspirational and at the same time taboo. My parents and other adults of their generation reacted badly to it, adding to the appeal. Other bits of early politics? The high school I attended had no doors on the boys' toilet stalls, a practice common at the time to discourage masturbation and other forbidden activities. I and some friends were outraged by such a system of moral surveillance and discipline. We organized a movement to get doors installed. It was a Situationist-type impulse, with kids making curtains and creating good slogans. The principal of the school refused to budge. It only served to make me more aware of the politics of daily life—how authority operated at all levels of existence. This reinforced a lesson that cultural questions could be very incendiary.

Another involvement was more conventionally political. Though there were few blacks in my high school, in my senior year discussions between black and white students began to open up in response to the civil rights activities in the South. At that time, a guy named Lincoln Lynch had begun organizing to integrate housing projects on the south shore of Long Island. He was with CORE [Congress of Racial Equality]. A group of students, black and white, formed a Committee for Civil Rights. We talked, and collectively we began to acknowledge that some-thing was wrong in American society. We also got involved in sit-ins at Long Beach, to open up housing to blacks. There were arrests. Doing something moral meant going against the law—an important lesson.

I got to Madison in September 1963 with that kind of sensibility—not being an "outlaw," but being against the law. I went to Madison because I had heard good things, and I needed to get away from home. It was also a place I could get into; my grades weren't particularly good. Madison also was intriguing because it was so unlike New York, yet there were enough New York kids so that I wouldn't feel too strange.

I first lived in the Elm Drive dorms, at the most distant part of the campus, near to the Agricultural School. I smelled cowshit every morning—amazing to a kid from the New York suburbs. I was placed in an athletic scholarship dorm, with big midwestern guys on my floor, mainly football and basketball players. I made friends right away. I was a good talker, and there was a mystique around me because none of them had even been to New York or even known a New Yorker. The only kindred "weirdo" was Dave Wagner, a poet and likewise an oddity there.

I was into an eighteen-year-old misanthropic mentality, threatening people, putting firecrackers down the toilets, and earning a kind of perverse respect. After half a year, the dorm authority and I had had enough of one another. I was relieved of my dorm contract and moved into an apartment on West Johnson Street with an eighty-six-year-old man named "Rip," who was a retired traveling salesman from the horse-and-buggy days. For me, it meant freedom. I was on my own at last.

I got involved with a bunch of people who were marginally leftist, primarily into beat literature, existential acting-out, drinking, causing trouble, provoking fights, working on our mystique. We were the Outsiders. In the midst of this, we heard something about a political action that was about to take place, and we thought, "We'll go there." This was a demonstration against Sears for racist hiring policies. A Sears shop-in was aimed at disrupting store activities and hurting their business. We had a great time. It mobilized a political sensibility and a love of political theater. I started getting interested in campus politics, but at a distance. On the intellectual side, I started reading Marx, which was exciting. Elsewhere, I attended meetings of the Socialist Club, which seemed to me pretty uninspiring; mainly boring debates between liberals and leftists over policy questions.

I learned a lot from several people. Pallo Jordan was very impressive and important for me. A black exile from South Africa, he seemed to know a great deal about politics intellectually and from experience. He knew Marxism, but was no stuffy Marxologist. He could rap rock 'n' roll for hours. This was a discovery for me: The links made possible through culture. There were also people like Don Bluestone and Dick Ward, who knocked at my door at Rip's, selling subscriptions to *Sanity*. We would sit and talk politics for hours, though they had never before met me. I was being organized, and learning about being an organizer.

In spring 1964 a friend, Steve Fraser, told me about an upcoming activity to begin down south in the summer. It was being organized by SNCC [Student Non-Violent Coordinating Committee], and it promised front-line experience in the civil rights struggle. We both applied to the Mississippi Freedom Summer project, but were convinced we wouldn't get in. Steve said, "It's going to be harder to get into than Harvard," which was a big joke for both of us. We didn't think about really being there, in the South. We wrote to the umbrella group—COFO—that was organizing the Freedom Summer. We had to write essays about why we thought it was important to get involved. We were both accepted, and that June we went down as civil rights workers in northeast Mississippi (Columbus) and then, for me, Tupelo, Mississippi. I ended up staying for nearly a year, becoming one of the few whites to be part of the SNCC staff.

It was a political education that changed who I was. It taught me how to be an organizer, walking door to door and talking with folks who gave me more than I could give back. It was also a life of relative danger, not part of my suburban upbringing. I was in a war zone, a world of guns and shootings, being tailed and threatened. Our Freedom House was burned down one night. There was time spent in Mississippi jails. Being young, and without too many obligations, living such a life seems sensible and possible.

I returned to Madison in the spring of 1965 as someone for whom politics and action had become central. I remember only a few others from Madison who had gone south at the same time, so I was one of a very few in Madison who had that experience. I felt I had made some very heavy life commitments, and I had brought back some practical lessons that were transported to student politics: how to do organizing, talk with people I didn't know about political issues; how to put out publications, newsletters, leaflets, and propaganda. At this time, the idea of developing what we'd call an "alternative media" proved very important. In mass media America, opposition politics had to be cultural politics.

Within a few weeks after getting back to Madison, I met Liz [Elizabeth

Ewen] on a picket line at an all-night vigil to protest American bombing in Vietnam. Liz, Pallo Jordan, and I kept ourselves warm that night by writing antiwar
lyrics to old rock 'n' roll songs. I also met lots of others. I met Bob and Vicki
Gabriner, who had been active in the west Tennessee civil rights movement. They
were assembling an archive of civil rights papers for the Historical Society, and I
had an extensive collection of memos, position papers, leaflets, and letters. I also
met Paul and Wini Breines through Liz; and I became connected with Russell
Jacoby, who had just arrived in Madison that year. My involvement with Paul and
Russell was rooted in our common interest in Herbert Marcuse and our conviction
that repressive ideology permeated the realm of everyday experience in American
society. Products of suburbs in the 1950s, we all had been raised in an environment
that betrayed the conformism underlying the postwar American dream.

Bob Gabriner, Paul, Russell, and I formed the Ad Hoc Committee for Thinking (ACT) in the spring of 1965. We wrote and passed out leaflets with commentaries on the politics of everyday life. They were short, in the vernacular, and always
signed simply *ACT*. We bought a cheap mimeograph and became cultural pam-
phleteers. We might write about how, in Madison, the urinals flushed automatically, commenting on the machine taking over the functions of the body; or we
might put a leaflet on the desks of a lecture hall where a bad professor was about
to hold class, with a message beginning, "Your Professor Does Not Really Exist."
We were bound by a sacred oath of antiauthoritarianism. The Old Left types felt
all this was a perversion. Politics, according to them, wasn't about such questions.
But even if ACT was a fringe activity, it made a very visible point about everyday
life and politics, and for the most part there was a strong and spontaneous positive
response.

In ACT we were excited by this response, but nervous as well. On the one
hand, ACT was seen as something that could become bigger. Lots of people were
eager to get involved in countermedia activities. On the other hand, ACT had been
a precious activity for the four of us. To expand it might mean the loss of that
preciousness. Fortunately, the former impulse prevailed. We called a public meeting to discuss how more people could act on ACT. Fifty or sixty people showed
up, and the discussion quickly moved toward starting a newspaper. There was great
excitement, and *Connections,* Madison's first underground paper, was born. We
were part of a movement begun in 1965 when the *East Village Other* [*EVO*] began
publication. At the heart of *Connections* was the idea that a newspaper could be
created that was totally different from newspapers that had previously existed.

Gabriner and I became co-editors among this group of newspaper people with
no experience whatsoever. If all you've got going for you is your imagination, you
don't pay attention to the formal rules. This was our strength. Gabriner and I went
to New York and talked with Alan Katzman, editor of the *EVO,* and he gave us
a "Dick and Jane" lesson in putting out a paper. He also explained that in photo
offset printing, you can print any image you want. As a group, the people around
Connections developed an idea of countermedia, not only on the level of ideas but

in terms of form. The paper was experimental at all levels. There were very talented people involved; a coalition of artists, writers, and technicians. A former Miss Wisconsin contestant, Abby Debuhr, was art director and did some wonderful things with layout. We raised about $145, mostly from sympathetic professors, and printed a first issue of eight pages (5,000 copies). The issue was pretty bad, but it was a phenomenal success anyway. The idea and the moment were right for each other. We were into the theater of distributions; we had hawkers with T-shirts, lots of energy, and it cost only 15 cents. By the second issue, the paper was very good, terrific; a good-quality newspaper with excellent and innovative graphics; part of a new journalism inventing itself. Our layout included "Colloidal Essays," double-page spreads with little messages throughout, illuminated texts, and so forth. The paper was irreverent, containing essays and images on the politics of sex, religion, music, or hamburgers. The juxtaposition of clashing images was also used a lot. The paper was establishing itself in Madison, and by the fourth or fifth issue we were able to rent a storefront.

Gabriner and I worked as co-editors for a while. After about six months, we had a split based on differences of personality and approach. I had a lot of weird ideas that had given shape to the paper's countercultural style, but I wasn't good at making things happen. Gabriner was a "city desk" type; he could make it happen. I then became a subeditor, and finally left the paper.

While I was involved with it, however, the paper was an exciting and important activity for me. I recall, for instance, an issue that Liz and I did a good deal of work on. It was on Chancellor Robin Fleming, and the issue offered a general critique of liberal administrative types. Fleming was leaving Madison, about to become president of the University of Michigan. We interviewed various people who had worked with him and who saw him as representative of an administrative personality. The whole issue tied these interviews together as a medieval legend, held together by a poem. It was extraordinary, and we printed about 12,000 copies, taking half of them to Ann Arbor with a guerrilla theater dramatization of the life of Fleming. The response there was great. This kind of thing has had a tremendous impact on what both Liz and I have done since.

Madison didn't force the dichotomy between being an intellectual and an activist. For me, it's comfortable to be both, to know that you can't be one without the other (not successfully anyway). Having run into activists who didn't think at all and—even more depressing—Marxists without any political experience, reinforces my sense of Madison's importance. Outside the United States, you find the integration of intellectual and activist more often; Madison is one of the few places that provided such an opportunity for an American. It's a basic commitment to an identity of critical thought and engagement. It is also a spirit, an era that still lives with people.

18   Memories from the Periphery

MALCOLM SYLVERS

Malcom Sylvers has achieved the rare feat of becoming not only a teacher in two cultures (as he indicates below) but also a scholar in two cultures. Professor of History of the United States at the University of Venice, he writes often in Italian on U.S. radical themes. He published *Sinistra politica e movimento operaio negli Stati Uniti. Dal primo dopoguerra alla repressione liberal-maccartista* in 1984.

Since 1971, I have been teaching American history in Italian universities, first in Trieste and since 1982 in Venice. In Italy it is quite common to identify faculty colleagues—other than by politics and publications—through where, when, and with whom they studied. Given not only what the University of Wisconsin objectively is and was in the 1960s but also its reputation in general in Italy, it has always been an immense source of pride for me to indicate that I was a graduate student in history there, first in 1961–1962 and then in 1966–1969.

What I think about Madison, what I remember about it, and what it has meant to me cannot be separated from my having left the States. On reflection, the period I spent there was an essential moment of my identity as an American, intellectually and emotionally. It is, however, easier to describe where Madison fits into my development than to analyze what it actually was in those years. Oral history and written memoirs, as we well know, often reflect considerably more the moment they appear than that of which they pretend to speak. And just as ex-militants tend to justify their role in past movements, so immigrants—of whatever sort—have the habit of remembering the "old country" in a much more rosy and heroic light than is often justified.

The left-oriented graduate students in American history were one of the main forces intellectually and politically in the Madison student movement of the 1960s; but those of us studying European history were connected with them because the Left really was—to use an abused term—a community with a great deal of exchange. My first year there, 1961–1962, was important to me for a very particular reason: I met the well-known Italian historian Girogio Spini—a specialist in early modern Europe and Italian Protestantism, and the author of an excellent work on American historiography of the seventeenth and eighteenth centuries—who was substituting for George Mosse in European intellectual history. Through him I began my professional association with Italy, which even then was mixed with a political interest. But in a more general sense, the early issues of *Studies on the Left* (the Madison period) had appeared, and many of the themes would remain central to the U.S. Left: the nature of American imperialism, the State Department and its relationship to the ideology and praxis of the labor movement, black radicalism. I also remember articles on the relationship of Marxism to ethics and science, the dilemmas present in the writings of Hemingway and Brecht, pieces by Sartre and C. Wright Mills. But over everything was imprinted the influence of the Cuban revolution, its then "nonideological" character, and its message that revolution was possible notwithstanding the disparity of forces. If, however, Caribbean socialism was for the Madison Left something of an example as to what courageous minorities could do, it also played a role in the formation of a sectarian approach far from that of the leadership of the Cuban revolution.

After I left Madison, I studied for a few years in Italy—in Florence mostly with Spini and the brilliant communist historian Ernesto Ragionieri—and then in France. I returned to Madison in 1966 and worked in Harvey Goldberg's seminar in European social history; I was also, for a time, one of his army of teaching assistants. His lecture course was one of the central events, or happenings, of the Madison Left: few things I remember so sharply from those years as Agricultural Hall packed (including the balcony), Goldberg lecturing when it was spring and autumn with the door open in back of him and the leaves in view. He conveyed to the students—including graduate students—a sense of European history as a constantly mounting romantic rebellion; in later years, I came to see his approach as much more imbued with a Populist spirit, maybe even a Popular Front spirit, than a method of analysis of class forces. Perhaps he gave us the impression that history in Europe was more glamorous, that in the States something essential was missing. It definitely was not easy to put it together with the research and teaching going on in American history. Was the latter our reality and European social history a form of escapism, something we studied because we could not find it in our own country?

Yet Goldberg's seminar and course were also a path for us, through the use of documents, to an understanding of the activity of the lower classes. And it gave his graduate students a chance to meet European scholars passing through who were Goldberg's friends or associates. In this sense I also benefited from working closely (also for a time as his assistant) with the Reformation specialist Robert Kingdon, another fine scholar and teacher.

I also remember vividly the Madison period of Georges Haupt, the historian of European socialism, who substituted for Goldberg on various occasions. He taught us all so much about history (above all, on the methodological level), about politics (he arrived in Madison after the French May explosion in 1968), and about life itself (what experiences had he not had?—extermination camp, a doctorate from Leningrad, an important role in an East European Communist party, beginning again almost from scratch in Paris—and how he was envied by other academics for them!). Even his courage at lecturing the first time in Madison with his rudimentary English was a lesson for us. How hard he tried to make us understand that, besides studying and being political, we should also enjoy life. Alas, to many of the Puritan Left, among which I must place myself at that time, his desire to go boating and to buy finely tailored clothes, and his willingness to associate with non-Left women—to name only a few of his sins—seemed inappropriate or even sacrilegious.

European history at the University of Wisconsin was then a crossroads where one could relate to many stimulating people. From each I think I managed to absorb something about the technique and the seriousness needed to become a historian and the inextricable link between politics and history. Some of them, like Haupt, I would see again when I returned to live in Europe, but the Madison experience was sufficiently strong that it would always be a little difficult for me to relate to these people as fellow professors and scholars.

During the last part of the 1960s, the American involvement in Vietnam seemed a clear confirmation of what the Left graduate students and professors in American history had been working on since the early days of *Studies*. How much the student and black protest movement in general felt the need to understand American oppression by delving into the past is, however, a moot point. The image that most comes to my mind of the student Left in that period with regard to the past is that of an outlook similar to the Communist Party USA in its time of maximum expansion: a search for heroic examples, as opposed to the Gramscian nexus of how present situations derive from past experiences. If we history graduate students were a little more sophisticated in our approach to the past, this may have not made much difference in the movement as a whole.

Political protest and activity on the campus for the graduate students proceeded, if I remember correctly, along two separate lines. There was, first, participation in the broad Left political activity with the innumerable meetings and demonstrations; the conflicts with the police, the National Guard, and the sheriffs; and with the representatives of the armed forces and monopoly capitalism (not only Dow Chemical) who came on campus to recruit. Alongside this were the activities of the History Students Association, which to its credit tried to deal with questions of curriculum and hiring-and-firing procedures; especially how it tried to get the department to "take a position" on a number of political issues—an activity that bourgeois liberal professors in American universities, even if they were against the war, as most seemed to be, simply were not used to. Much petty conflict was provoked by our attempt to be "members" of the department, but it did show that being on the Left did not necessarily mean a disinterest in scholarship or the institutions connected with it. I wonder, in fact, if this aspect of the student movement—the attempt to carry through "a long march through the institutions"—has been sufficiently looked at.

In 1969–1970 I got a job at Stout State University at Menomonie, an agricultural area in northern Wisconsin. For me, that year was a continuation of the Madison days. Paul Faler, a graduate student in American history (now a professor at the University of Massachusetts, Boston, and author of an important work on Lynn, Massachusetts, in the early industrial revolution) was hired with me, and together we tried to build an antiwar movement. It was not an easy task in a college where students came mostly from farm backgrounds, largely out of contact with "opposition" ideas. Moreover, the campus had a number of white Vietnam veterans, most of them not in a mood to listen to criticism of the war.

If Paul and I made an impression, it was not particularly because of our organizing ability, but simply because we spoke in a language that could be understood. Paul was really good at this. I remember the teach-in of the October 1969 Moratorium, apparently the spark that convinced the administration, at this early date, not to renew our contracts. Although many were shocked, Paul managed to defend, in a credible way, not only that the United States was wrong to be in Vietnam, not only that it should withdraw unilaterally, but that it would be lucky to be allowed to do so without first paying reparations!

Following the Kent State killings, Stout saw demonstrations. I remember the final one, held in June, which also served as a farewell for the two of us after various petitions by the students failed to reverse the administration's decision to sack us. It was held at the main intersection in Menomonie (population 8,000). Paul invited those present to look around. On one corner, he said, was the supermarket; on another, the chamber of commerce; on a third, the district attorney's office; and on the last, the university. He concluded the lesson on the local power structure: "That, comrades, is America."

The Menomonie adventure was closely watched by our Madison friends and reported on by the student newspaper, which, I think, ran a series on us called "Marxism in Dairyland." The title may have actually revealed the irony often heaped by the Madison Left on less activist areas, an attitude that was anything but politically productive. The short period at Stout was, however, a practical lesson in the protective value of a vigorous bourgeois liberal presence for radicals, of the need for what Italian communists call a "strategy of alliances." In Madison, we on the Left received protection from many liberals whom we often considered to be our enemies. They may well have been true in the long run, but for whatever reason they gave their protection, it was necessary in providing the Left with a political milieu in which it could exist. In Menomonie this was desperately clear. We were almost totally isolated in the community and among the faculty, where the liberals really were of the inconsequential and spineless type. Placing those in Madison on their level, we certainly were schematic, omitting what [Palmiro]

Togliatti called the necessary "differential analysis": not knowing how to appreciate and work with dedicated liberals may well have limited Left influence in Madison. In any case, back in Menomonie we received support from the local area ACLU [American Civil Liberties Union], but this group was rooted neither in the town nor on the campus. It may be of some interest to note that the national professional academic organizations were of no help.

The following year, something similar was repeated for me at California State University in Chico; there, however, a small group in the department originating from Madison did put up resistance to my severance. It is hard today not to muse over the thought that had I not been fired, I might still be in Menomonie or Chico, as opposed to Venice. A friend in Chico who supported me then in the departmental skirmish is fond of saying that had he succeeded, it would have been forever a crime on his conscience.

After this second firing, or "nonrenewal," in two years and not having found another job that pleased me, I took off for Italy in 1971, utilizing contacts I had made when I had studied in Europe in the mid 1960s. On my way to Europe, I taught in the summer session of the University of Havana and got a close look at what happens—not all negative—when a revolution moves into an "organizational phase" beyond its initial enthusiasm. I wondered how much the organization or even regimentation then going on—necessary, I think, in a revolution in a poor country with strong enemies close by—had been understood by the student Left.

Paradoxically, working in an institution in a foreign country and not having regular contact with other Americans (for this reason, I don't think of myself as a classic expatriate) had the effect of drawing me closer to America, or anyway to a certain idea of America. As I settled into life in Italy, my interest turned sharply toward U.S. history, specifically to the working-class movement as an element of national history, perhaps as part of a personal search for identity. To this is also related my growing interest in the political thought of Thomas Jefferson. Although the Marxist influence on me was more and more directly Italian, this path led me back to Madison, as I tried to come to terms with the work of many historians connected with the university, persons whom I had known but whose writings I had never studied.

In Italy, the somewhat naive "history from the bottom up" school has had many adepts in the field of American studies. Correctly attempting to break away from the institutional party or trade union history that, at least until recently, also characterized the study of the European lower classes. Such an outlook, it seems to me, condemns working-class activity to a subaltern role; although it accentuates moments of rebellion and cultural autonomy, it basically accepts as permanent that the synthesis—hegemony—will always be carried out by the ruling class. In this it appears to be somewhat connected to the Madison version of consensus history (Williams, Weinstein)—well known and appreciated in Italy—where the ruling class manages to flatten out the historical panorama, rendering all opposition voices insignificant.

The change in my historical interests toward the United States paralleled my political evolution. Already in the late 1960s, while in Madison, I had a sense of our limits as a student Left, primarily based on my experiences in Europe. This increased after I returned to live in Italy, as I moved closer to the Italian Communist party (PCI), of which I have been a member since 1972. Basically I began to feel that related to our inability in America to build a mass movement rooted within the society was not only that we had no sense of what the politics of such a mass movement could be but that we often felt extraneous, separate, different, and maybe even a little better than the society as a whole.

The reality of widespread bourgeois hegemony had thus led politically to a situation where those who had broken out of the ideological web in which the American people were entwined came to see themselves as an elite, and to behave as such. Seeing young American military personnel in Italy—sailors from the Sixth Fleet in Trieste, air force people in Vicenza or hiking in the Dolomites—one easily gets the impression that the Madison experience, although a genuine moment of the country's experience, surely was a very small part of its reality. The pluralism and ghettoization in American life, which the ruling class is so good at utilizing, is striking when viewed from Italy where society remains rather homogeneous. The American system—whether by design or through a natural process—manages to place the domestic Left on the margin of society; and once there, this Left has no difficulty convincing itself of its moral and intellectual superiority.

In such a situation, Left politics in America, at least that of the student Left of the 1960s, often seemed less moved by the need or possibility to change reality than of acting as a moral witness in the name of values unrecognized by the majority. Thus the sectarian push where what is most essential is to have the correct line and much less important is who, if anyone, is following you. We seem to have had difficulty understanding that history is made by the broad masses, who necessarily operate within the country's major institutions and ideological currents and that our task was—to put it crudely—how to get them on our side and prevent their discontent from once again being hegemonized by the bourgeois liberal reformers or, even worse, by the Right.

The desire for purity led to the call to separate the university from society: Given the overwhelming strength of U.S. capitalism in all institutions, we simply could not imagine a relationship between capitalism and the university that would mean anything but the latter aiding the former in the oppression of the world's people. Such a generally correct analysis is, however, too drastic, since in a guerrilla-like way, certain positions, due to the contradictions of American pluralism, can be and have been conquered, thereby permitting (even if in a limited sense) the use of the university in a critical way. The main point is that this analysis left us with no alternative except the impossible one of reconstructing the university as an ivory tower. Some were even ready to believe it a victory if only Dow Chemical could be forced off *our* campus.

Related to this attitude of facing politics abstractly was our absolute lack of advice to those undergraduates who became radicalized. What could they do once their political and ideological outlook had been transformed? What could it mean to the life of the Stout State students, who were mostly on their way to becoming shop teachers in small Wisconsin towns? It may not have been our fault that we had no answers, but the fact that we did not, circumscribed the movement.

I have often wondered how much consciousness each of us had during those days. Some were foolish enough to believe that we were building a revolutionary movement, and some senior members of the History Department understood so little of historical development that they feared we were right. Those of us who were more mature politically seem to have been swept away by the enthusiasm of the base, or were perhaps afraid of trying to impose their will. [Antonio] Gramsci's comment on the years of the factory council movement—that "we were only another element of the general disintegration"—seems appropriate. The least was that, once again, other forces would be able to utilize—but perhaps "manipulate" or "hegemonize" are more correct words—Left agitation for their own ends.

The Madison history graduate students and the Left faculty in the department were nonetheless engaged in a monumental and essential, if possibly fruitless, attempt to contribute to a realization that societal and historical problems do not begin with one's own physical existence and that one component of the process of liberation is to understand the past. The banal cultural anti-Americanism of some Europeans affirms that the United States does not have a history because it is a young country. While this is of course ridiculous, many Americans seem to act as if it were true.

While I think I have learned a great deal politically, intellectually, and personally from Italy, certain cultural roots have very definitely remained with me. And a part of my American background composed of individualism and an empirical approach was constructed or at least strengthened during the Madison experience. If in the States it is all too easy for me to appear to be an "Italian," it seems to me that whatever the value of my criticism and contribution in Italy, they are related to my specifically American perspective.

A plethora of American research institutes and European intellectuals are always telling us that Italy—flexible, warm, nonjudgmental, the home of the Mediterranean diet, etc.—is one of the countries where one lives best. An ordinary Italian may be amused or enraged by this evaluation, as he or she tries to renew a driver license or take care of aging parents or sick children or simply work seriously in an institution like a university, connected with the state apparatus. It is nonetheless an extremely vital country with a genuinely amenable style of life, culture, and climate. Perhaps more important, it is very much on the periphery, and for someone with a broad historical perspective, this counts. For this reason the memory of Madison in the 1960s is important: However much the University of Wisconsin may have been only a piece of American reality, it was very much at the center of the Progressive ferment in a critical period of the nation's history.

19   Radicalized History

PETER WILEY

For most of his post-Madison life, Peter Wiley has been an editor and journalist. *Leviathan* (1969–1970), one of the most stylist New Left experiments, tragically disappeared with the movement that had given it inspiration. "Points West," a longstanding syndicated column co-authored by Wiley, had wide readership in commercial newspapers from the Rocky Mountains to the Pacific Coast. Wiley has also written *America's Saints: The Rise of Mormon Power* (with co-author Robert Gottlieb, 1984), among other books. He lives in San Francisco and meets with a poker group composed largely of former Madisonians.

My parents were involved in local politics in New Jersey when I was growing up. Hence one might argue that it was an understandable decision on my part to attend graduate school at the University of Wisconsin in 1964. The political world I entered in Madison, however, was fundamentally different from the placid and commonplace one I grew up in. My father was active in the Republican party—in its moderate wing—in a suburban county, my mother in the League of Women Voters. Politics were discussed nightly around the kitchen table. My parents disappeared regularly in the evening to attend political meetings. Around election times, my brother and I were recruited to hand out leaflets door to door or at the local commuter railroad station. I even saw Richard Nixon campaigning in the 1952 election. And I can remember carefully examining the signature on the postcard he and Pat sent to my father, thanking him for his support. I was disappointed. It was a fake, stamped on by a machine.

Religion captured my interest as a teenager. At a religious conference during my senior year in high school, I heard William Sloane Coffin, the Freedom Rider and Yale chaplain, speak. The details remain vague, except that he discussed the civil rights movement, about which I knew nothing. Beyond his forceful personality, I found the idea that there was a connection between Christian values and political activism intriguing, though beyond my imagined range of experience.

By the time I reached Williams College, my interest in religion had dwindled. There was nothing more deadly than being compelled—chapel attendance was compulsory—to attend the local Episcopalian church and hear the pasty-faced young Ivy Leaguer who served as chaplain hold forth on little or nothing. Compulsory chapel and later the fraternity system became the principal targets of our youthful campus activities. Both were soon abolished.

The intellectual atmosphere at Williams, at least in the classrooms, was for the most part stultifying, and there was never more than a handful of political activists. The few activists worked to abolish the House Un-American Activities Committee, supported H. Stuart Hughes when he ran in Massachusetts on a peace platform for the U.S. Senate in 1962, campaigned to ban the bomb, and supported the civil rights movement. We were intrigued by the Cuban revolution, had our doubts about John Kennedy, were alarmed by the Bay of Pigs invasion and scared by the Cuban missile crisis, and were vaguely aware that something was going on in the jungles of Southeast Asia. We read and discussed everything we could get our hands on: the history of the Russian, Chinese, French, and Cuban revolutions, and Marx, Engels, Trotsky, Fromm, Fanon, Isaac Deutscher, E. P. Thompson, William Morris, Leo Huberman, Paul Sweezy, Paul Baran, Edmund Wilson, Dwight MacDonald, Paul Goodman, Daniel DeLeon, the *Nation,* the *Partisan Review,* the *Realist,* the *Militant,* the *Weekly People,* the *National Guardian,* the *Peking Review,* and books and articles by a young historian named William Appleman Williams.

During my senior year, I read an article in the *Militant* about a coal miners' strike in eastern Kentucky, which included an announcement that there was going to be a conference for students in Hazard, Kentucky, during spring vacation. Three of us went to Hazard and found a world of poverty that we had so easily overlooked in the slums of the New York metropolitan area. Impressed by the deeply engrained activist traditions of the miners and their families, I returned to Kentucky that summer to help put together a broad-based community organization that contested the local political machine and the federal bureaucracy for control of federal funds allocated for Appalachia by the Kennedy and Johnson administration.

I had planned to enter graduate school in history at the University of Wisconsin in the fall of 1964. Despite my growing estrangement from academia, I was eager to find out what a campus with a political reputation was like. I moved into an apartment west of the capitol and quickly fell in with a group of people that included others who had been organizers, particularly in the civil rights movement in the South. We found ourselves back on campus, but out attention was still riveted on politics in the communities where we had worked. During my first semester, for example, I returned to eastern Kentucky, catching a ride as far as Louisville with a friend who was headed back to a civil rights project in Fayette County, Tennessee. In the spring I traveled to San Francisco to raise money for work in Appalachia. Those of us who were graduates of the movement enjoyed the self-congratulatory mystique of the Organizer and the sense of superiority that this mystique implied. Student politics, by contrast, seemed very emphemeral.

With the Free Speech Movement in Berkeley, students had begun to engage *student* political issues *on campus* and to move beyond merely providing support for off-campus activities, such as the civil rights movement. Vietnam, the issue that would eventually galvanize the new student movement, slowly moved to the fore. I had been amazed when, sitting in a barber chair in Hazard, Kentucky, in the summer of 1964, I read about the U.S. bombing of North Vietnam. By 1965, the full import of events in Vietnam began to dawn on us.

■ ■

Since we now view 1960s radicalism through a lens distorted by the sectarian episodes that eventually helped wreck what we called the movement, it is hard to imagine the congenial and exciting atmosphere of student political life at a place like the University of Wisconsin. It is also hard to grasp the naive sense of optimism, the feeling that through a number of significant developments—the civil rights movement, the student movement, efforts to organize the urban poor, campaigns on the Left of the Democratic party—the country seemed to be witnessing the first stages of the emergence of a mass-based left-wing movement, perhaps even one calling for a new, American kind of democratic socialism. Political activists brought an entirely new dimension to academia and a new meaning to education. As history students, for example, we were not simply examining historical phenomena in a typically detached academic manner while accumulating course credits and footnotes. We were engaging history, grabbing it with two hands, and using our knowledge to try to shape, in whatever minimal way was possible, our own future and, we believed, the future of the country. For us, history became a continuum that connected with the present and rolled on into the future.

Part of Madison's charm, and the day-to-day substance of our communality, was our social life, the bars, restaurants (such as they were), and assorted hangouts where the community coalesced and carried out its rituals of love, debate, intrigue, and entertainment. My favorite was the 602 on University Avenue where radical students, young faculty members, never-to-graduate students, and various ne'er-do-wells and bohemians gathered in the afternoon and evening for a beer. Dudley, the owner, was a congenial soul, but Mitch, one of his regular bartenders, was a diehard patriot who was easily riled when we turned the news on the television and yelled our irreverent comments at Lyndon Johnson, Dean Rusk, and other medial personalities. On Friday and Saturday evenings, Madison's tiny, invisible gay community congregated at the front of the bar, gathered around a young man known as Silver Toes. There were also the cheap movies at the Student Union; the pinball machines, pool tables, and Plaza Burgers at the Plaza Bar; and many hours spent lounging at the Rat, in the cafeteria or on the terrace during the warmer months. Our social axis ran from the apartment houses east and west of the capitol through the University Avenue hangouts to the campus. The dormitories, the beer bars of State Street, and Fraternity Row were a separate world with which we had little contact.

On campus there were other events, such as the Anti-Military Ball, which was put on by a handful of anarchists the night before the ROTC ball. The best of these was centered on an elaborate play written by Tina Hower with the assistance of Carole Deutch, Vicki Gabriner, and Jo Stickgold that was called *The Wooing and Winning of Globelle Power.* It featured the conflict between Uncle Sam and a black-pajamaed Led Menace for the hand of Globelle Power, a dingy Statue of Liberty who wandered around with a flashlight. The slogan of the Anti-Mil Ball was "Anti-Militarists Have Balls," an apt indication of the prefeminist nature of our politics. Later, Barbara Garson's *MacBird,* the retelling of *Macbeth* using thinly disguised characters from the Kennedy and Johnson administrations, was a campuswide success. *Connections,* Madison's underground newspaper, played a central role in defining issues and the political culture on campus, while *Radical America* provided an outlet for more scholarly and analytical work.

I began work on a master's thesis on the impact of mechanization on the United Mine Workers (UMW) union. I was looking for some meaning to the events that had had such a disastrous impact on the lives of the people of eastern Kentucky. I was intrigued by the way in which the UMW leadership abandoned their members in the coalfields of southern Appalachia in favor of a stable relationship with the big coal operators in other coalfields. I had begun to develop a general sense of how unions had become distinctly junior partners in the corporate attempt to control the workforce, rather than the countervailing force described by the liberal economist John Kenneth Galbraith.

In the History Department, groups of students coalesced around their favorite professors, including Harvey Goldberg, George Mosse, William Taylor, and William Appleman Williams, each of whom had his own view of student activism. When Williams attended public meetings, such as the early teach-ins on Vietnam, he was a commanding figure. At one of the first teach-ins, a Captain Bollenbeck, a regular attendee and a lone voice representing the American Legion point of view, got up and impugned the patriotism of antiwar activities. Williams responded by reviewing his own career as a U.S. Naval Academy graduate and a commander of a destroyer in the Pacific during World War II. The audience went wild.

Like many others, by 1965 I found myself drawn into the activities of the antiwar movement. After drawing large numbers of students to the original teach-ins, the Committee to End the War in Vietnam bogged down in an unproductive conflict over whether "Stop the Bombing" (advocated by the Communist party types and their liberal allies) or "Immediate Withdrawal" (advocated by the Trotskyists and their allies) was the proper slogan for the movement. Many students, turned off by male power plays and endless squabbling at meetings, soon moved to other organizations—such as the fledgling Students for a Democratic Society (SDS) chapter and the newly formed Wisconsin Draft Resistance Union—or stayed away all together.

Numerous political approaches were being experimented with, but it was clear, particularly as the draft brought the war home in a real way to male students, that great numbers of students in the dormitories and even the fraternities were not getting the antiwar message because of the social exclusiveness of the Left. The isolation of the Left was aggravated by the cyclical nature of student politics. A pattern of confrontation, mass participation, and return to passivity began to develop with the draft sit-ins in the new administration building in May 1966. Dramatic action and the use of police to break up demonstrations would lead to days of intense mass meetings. Then, after a time, things would return to more or less normal. The student movement would once again become the sole province of its self-appointed leaders. The students appeared to be returning to their old routines, although it later became apparent that even those routines were gradually changing. There was more dope, more off-campus living, and more cultural estrangement then before.

To deal with the pattern of action and inaction that seemed built into student politics, a group of us began to organize an educational effort directed at students who lived outside the social world of the campus Left. Teams from the antiwar movement held regular meetings in the dormitories to discuss the war. These meetings focused not only on what was happening in Vietnam but on the ways in which the war highlighted the nature of the American political economy. Vietnam was neither a mistake nor an abberration, we argued. It was an outgrowth of an expansionist foreign policy that was inherent in an economic system seeking global hegemony to protect its markets, investments, and sources of raw materials. National liberation movements, such as the Viet Minh and later the Viet Cong, were viewed by American policymakers, we explained, as the cutting edge of a global movement that could eventually undermine the Pax Americana and threaten the world economy, which was dominated by the United States. We found it particularly effective to use the statements of President Eisenhower when he explained the relationship between supporting the French in Vietnam in the 1950s and the need for tin and tungsten from Southeast Asia and for markets for America's ally, Japan. Students were also tantalized by his remarks about how Ho Chi Minh would have won a free election in Vietnam.

This work led to other efforts. Through SDS's Radical Education Project, run by Jim O'Brien, we put out one series of pamphlets including an annotated reading list for those interested in the issues of the war and American society. Another critiqued conventional academic approaches to American history and the books handed out for freshman orientation, such as Eric Hoffer's antiactivist panegyric, *The True Believer*. The Physics Department unwittingly donated paper, and we did our printing either on the SDS press in the *Connections* office or late at night on the Sociology Department's mimeograph machine.

By 1967, a group of us felt that the time was ripe to discuss the issues of socialism. The student movement had shied away from a clear definition of its goals, using instead compelling but vague terms such as "participatory democracy." This was because many student leaders were not socialists. If they were, they were either loyal to one obscure Marxist sect or wanted to avoid the ever-present Red baiting and the sectarian conflicts of radicalism's past. A few of us, who at this point knew that we were not long for the world of the university, were eager to force the question of where the radical movement was ultimately heading and to find a way to link university politics with potential constituencies outside academia. We naively envisioned the possibilities of building a mass-based socialist movement and wanted to put that question on the intellectual agenda of student radicals. To this end, we organized a series of symposia under the auspices of the Socialist Club, named after an earlier organization on campus. The first of these events was well attended, but in the end they, too, proved consistent with the episodic nature of student politics and were another idea with little staying power.

As the draft became more of an issue, we were forced to look at the role of the modern university in the larger social system. In May 1966, a group of 165 teaching assistants moved to form the Teaching Assistants Association (TAA). Our immediate concern was that, as TAs, we were being called on through the marking system to make decisions about who would and wouldn't stay in the university, which was the same as deciding who would and wouldn't be sent to Vietnam. In the long run, we saw the TAA as a union that would, we hoped, avoid the shortcomings of the established unions. We found it encouraging that the organization grew out of a draft protest because it established a direct link between unionism and political activism. We wanted the TAA to remain independent of established unions. And beyond the traditional collective bargaining issues of wages and hours, we argued for an organization that would examine the role of the university in the larger society and would strive for TA participation in shaping the content of courses and curricula. Some of the founders had been influenced by Harvey Goldberg's extensive lectures on European syndicalism, others by studying the Industrial Workers of the World (IWW).

In essence, throughout all our activities we had been arguing for an education in everyday living, for a direct link between thought and action. We recognized the political and intellectual limitations of academia, limitations brought home time and again by the political weakness and timidity of the faculty. Madison's splendid isolation on the northern edge of the prairies reflected the conventional isolation of the academic world from the worlds of politics, production, trade, and war. Conventional academic life in the humanities was a process of studying phenomena that were treated as if they existed apart from the social reality of the students and the world they were entering, phenomena on which the student was to reflect, but not act. We had been busily building a parallel educational system that would encourage students to look at themselves and their institutional environment as a prelude to entering the larger society as activist citizens. The sheer volume of our work and our output in the form of meetings, publications, and symposia are hard to imagine in the context of the contemporary university. From bars to eating places, Madison was a self-contained world, a place where our social lives dovetailed pleasantly with our educational and activist pursuits, providing a reassuring sense of community.

■ ■

When I left Madison with a Master's degree in January 1968, I was still undecided about my future. I moved to San Francisco, carefully avoiding Berkeley. But Madison remained, and remains, with me. In San Francisco, Madison graduates formed the core of a group of people who put out the New Left analytical review, *Leviathan,* in the late 1960s. Today, some of these same people and a number of others remain in close contact in the Bay Area and with Madison activists from as far afield as Lusaka and Tokyo. We never experienced the Big Chill, and though our lives are less flamboyant and our aspirations more limited, we remain dedicated to the ideals that informed our activism in Madison.

Madison was a transient experience, but a singularly important one. I arrived a committed but aimless radical, disaffected by a return to a privileged environment. Madison proved to be an exceptional educational experience, due to our own efforts and the efforts of a handful of teachers, such as Harvey Goldberg and William Appleman Williams, who went beyond conventional notions of education. When I left, I felt that my values had been anchored and my commitment strengthened and that I had a clear sense of what to do next. Only later would I have time to reflect on our shortcomings and illusions, to gain a fuller understanding of why a movement that started with such promise would go into almost total eclipse five years later, leaving a complex, but nonetheless real, heritage.

20 Madison and Women's History

MARI JO BUHLE

Mari Jo Buhle teaches in the History and American Civilization Departments at Brown University. Along with *The Concise History of Woman Suffrage in America* (1977) and *Women and American Socialism* (1981), her books include *Women and the American Left: A Guide to Sources* (1983). Her most recent area of interest has concerned the historical relation between feminism and psychoanalysis.

I spent my first year or so in Madison, 1967–1968, working full-time at the State Historical Society of Wisconsin, researcher on the six-volume History of Wisconsin series, as labor history researcher, studying materials and preparing notes. When not at work, I pursued my growing interests in the Frankfurt School and, especially, Herbert Marcuse's *Eros and Civilization*. I read it several times. The Frankfurt School helped frame one of my interests, the reasons why Americans seemed to lack so thoroughly any sense of "negative thought" or of dialectics. I was fascinated with American Positivism and Pragmatism, and their origins in the ideas of the 1830s–1850s. This study also returned me to my earliest intellectual concern and one that would recur repeatedly over many years: the nature of self-consciousness.

I grew up in a small, predominantly Eastern European (now mostly black) factory town north of Chicago. My grandparents came from Poland. My father, who began work at the hardware foundry as a delivery boy at age fourteen, had become a self-taught products engineer. My mother, daughter of a tavernkeeper, had aspirations to become a high school teacher, but gave them up to marry early. They were very much part of a fading but energetic Polish-American culture that revolved around its rituals (polka, weddings, funerals), institutions (ethnic and neighborhood bakeries and clubs), and lifestyle (fishing, card playing, and drinking). I was an only child, born when my parents were in their forties, so I grew up with a peculiar sense of generational distance yet sharing a vanishing historical scene. My earliest education, in Catholic grade school, remained part of a less nostalgia-provoking lifestyle also fading away: obsessions with death and salvation, with classroom unruliness, world communism, and diagramming sentences.

Through a fluke of high school hiring policies, I had a few bohemian teachers, some outstanding and some offbeat (I met one of them, a gay hipster, by chance in San Francisco years later). It was quite a change from Catholic grade school. Perhaps they helped inspire my interest in psychology. At some point, I abandoned my earlier hobbies for the "science of the mind." Quickly exhausting the holdings of the public library on that subject, I joined a science seminar and used Abbott Laboratory's far larger holdings. Personality theory and parapsychology competed for my attention until I settled on psychoanalysis.

When I attended the University of Illinois in Champaign, I pursued the study of culture and personality, a middle ground between psychology and anthropology where cultures were largely classified as to childrearing practices. This method, soon after outmoded, remained at the time a prestigious remnant of Freudian influence over the academy. Russian authoritarianism, for instance, might be explained by swaddling procedures for infants—whereas American problems, infinitely less severe, stemmed from the disintegration of the patriarchal family! *Intellectually,* in working out systems of thought, this sort of study was very helpful, despite its ideological overtones.

Meanwhile, as a part-time job, I worked for an academic psychologist on questionnaires framed to update Theodor Adorno's Authoritarian Personality "F" (for Fascism) Scale. The update was, in fact, very progressive: Through forty-some pages of "pretest," it captured detailed racist responses of the subject and related them to general authoritarianism, support of U.S. militarism, and so on. As I now see it, we were looking for something like "false consciousness," which is to say an absence of self-consciousness in some vague democratic or even perhaps class sense. My professor–employer was, in fact, one of the early and rare faculty members at Champaign–Urbana openly against the Vietnam war. At any rate, I had a very odd introduction to the Frankfurt School. The only Adorno textbook in our classrooms, *The Authoritarian Personality,* was discussed mostly for the author's ability to locate authoritarian qualities in Stalinism. Adorno's negative dialectics, his milieu, and the implications of their work for the fast-approaching generational politics remained utterly obscure.

I barely escaped becoming a psychologist rather than a historian, largely by virtue of my misplacement in a psychology department where experimental, positivistic science virtually excluded all other approaches. Shortly after marrying, I gave up my original career aspiration, without altogether losing interest in the important questions that had taken me into the study of psychoanalysis. I also moved, intellectually, to the Left (but without becoming involved in the antiwar activism of SDS, which dominated protests but had a male intellectual and middle-class character that left me uncomfortable). History courses helped me sharpen my ideas about classes, social movements, and U.S. foreign policy.

At the University of Connecticut, where I started graduate school in history, I learned to become a scholar. My professors, especially the Wisconsin graduates, cared deeply about method and had a crypto-radical approach that hardly any of their students, graduate or undergraduate, appreciated or even recognized. Perhaps for these reasons, they encouraged me enormously. I heard later that in other schools, including Madison, women history graduate students often had a hard time with professors (including some "radical" professors) who regarded women as future dropouts to motherhood. At Connecticut, I got the opposite message. For that, I remain deeply grateful.

I began graduate school in Madison in January 1969, with an intent to study intellectual history. I turned first to the history of Wisconsin radicalism, in a pursuit of *mentalité*. I studied the Milwaukee socialist Victor Berger's avowed racism toward blacks and, scarcely less, toward recent eastern and southern European workers. Then I wrote a seminar paper on the positivistic general perspective of "constructive socialism," the reformist politics of the Milwaukee Left. At that point, I was reading, casually, *New Left Notes,* the weekly newspaper of the Students for a Democratic Society, which came into the house. I was struck with the first stirrings of debate over women's status and role in the New Left, partly because I had accidentally discovered, in the basement of the Wisconsin State Historical Society, a full run of *Socialist Woman/Progressive Woman,* 1907–1912. The nature of the dialogue had scarcely changed! The strategic questions, such as women's participation in the same or parallel movements, had come around again. The very character of a sort of materialist feminism of 1910 had its direct parallel in the early writings of Margaret Benston and others seeking a "political economy" of women's status.

In some ways, this discovery was, for me, a big step forward. In other ways, it was only a sidetrack to my earlier questions about consciousness and self-consciousness. The wealth of material and the precisely strategic questions plunged me into the discovery of forgotten history and the creation of a narrative. But these questions, which marked my dissertation (completed in 1974), were hardly cultural at all. I would have to retrace some of my steps later.

At any rate, in 1967 I wrote a seminar paper, "Women in the Socialist Party," which appeared in a special "Women's Issue" of *Radical America,* edited by Edith Hoshino Altbach, and in the early women's liberation book *From Feminism to Liberation* (1972) that came out of that issue. But my professor at Madison wasn't so pleased. He called the topic of "socialist women" a "granfaloon" (borrowing from Kurt Vonnegut), that is, an imaginary category that could not *possibly* be written about seriously. I held my ground, although it nearly cost me future teaching assistantships (and possibly did cost me fellowships). Luckily, all hell had begun to break loose in the university. Research discrepancies such as mine suddenly became a very minor matter compared with student and teaching assistants' strikes. Besides, I soon had more good fortune. William O'Neill, whose *Everyone Was Brave* offered an early history of woman's rights in the United States, had an ambivalent approach to the subject, and we budding women's historians would have an ambivalent relationship with him. But he tried to be encouraging. More important, David Thelen, a young historian who had graduated from Madison and was now visiting professor (and who would later become editor of the *Journal of American History*), taught a seminar on the Progressive era. From him and my classmates, I learned a great deal, but felt the encouragement to go much further myself.

At this juncture, more or less, my ideas about women's history began to take shape. The need was in the air. Invited to teach a section of O'Neill's History of American Radicalism, I offered women's history. Suddenly, I found myself surrounded by wildly energetic young women, who argued vigorously over the relative radicalism of Emma Goldman or Susan Anthony, and asked me seriously if they should consider marriage. I had never seen this level of energy in any class. Many of them worked hard on the course, disproving (for me, anyway) the prevailing myths about the anti-intellectualism of the student protesters. They were the soul of youthful, counterculture feminism.

The imperative of women's history struck others as well. I began to co-teach a Free University course on women's history. I also spoke, on Wisconsin Public Radio's studio network, to women who gathered at the local stations and called in their questions. With seeming suddeness, I deepened my scholarly relationship with two fellow graduate students, Ann D. Gordon and Nancy Schrom, who had been thinking somewhat along the same lines.

Two of us had been drawn into the writing of a special 1970 *Radical America* issue on radical historiography. Through many study classes and private conversations, especially in the Historical Society corridors, we had set ourselves to discover what had been radical in U.S. historical scholarship and what agenda lay ahead. We, two women of the group plus Nancy, outlined a task that quickly outgrew the pages available for the special issue.

The task was to summarize and synthesize EVERYTHING important that had been written on U.S. women's history. Each of us took a century (Ann Gordon the eighteenth, myself the nineteenth, and Nancy the twentieth). I recall ransacking the basement stacks in the Memorial Library, where books were essentially boxed with the old Cutter System classification, and I went through the metal boxes book by book, kneeling over to take notes on each one. And we engaged in frantic discussions, for which there never seemed enough time: we began to speak unnaturally fast so that we could convey all the information and develop our conceptual ideas in common. A few paragraphs from the resulting "Women in American Society: An Historical Contribution" summarize the synthetic view:

> The rise and fall of concern for women's history has followed the intensity of organized women's movements. Not since 1920, when the suffrage movement ended, has there been the interest evident today. As

women were forced back into individual lives, understood through the personal lens of psychological adjustment . . . history as a study of their collective experience over the centuries no longer seemed to explain their condition. Historians, always more interested in writing about the powerful, studied a history without women. Only social scientists documented the changing presence of women at fixed times in a variety of situations, but their fragmented analyses did not provide a way to understand the totality of daily life for women. Neither did these evaluations describe the overall changes in society. But today, women with renewed caste-consciousness are returning to historical questions in a search for their collective identity and for an analysis of their condition. . . .

Faced again with the task of defining women's history in relation to the re-emergence of women as a collective force, we find it essential to define what we understand to be our past. Through a historical critique we can begin to transcend the imposition of contemporary institutions and values on our lives. Without such a critique our view of daily life remains at the level of individual reaction to what strikes us as intolerable. Our analyses tend to document our feelings of subjection rather than the underlying historical conditions of the subjection of all women. . . .

That women have not had access to the means of social definition and have not lived and worked in the spheres of reward and recognition is obvious. They have lived in what Simone de Beauvoir has described as the historical anomaly of "The Other." The problem remains: as objects, do we have a history, properly speaking? As long as historical enquiry is constrained by equating initiative and mastery with life, the lives of women are, at best, a "situation," as Juliet Mitchell has noted. The seeming timelessness of women's lives may describe one source of the lack of female consciousness though long periods; the processes affecting their lives are frequently slow and without immediate impact of their awareness. But to assume that their lives were, as a result, without time and without change, ignores the role that the subjection of women has played in world development. Historians' chronic blindness to that fact prevents them from probing the fullest meaning of history. If we can succeed in defining the "specificity of their oppression," we will as well have moved closer to realizing the dynamics of all historical development—a prerequisite for changing it.[1]

This was, so to speak, a manifesto on women's history, and although it addressed women's history only in the United States, it had a certain international

1. Mari Jo Buhle, Ann D. Gordon, Nancy Schrom, "Women in American Society: An Historical Contribution," *Radical America* 5 (July–August 1971): 3, 5–6.

significance (aided by an Italian edition) as the earliest document of its type. Arriving at the right moment, moreover, it met—through reprinting as a 50¢ pamphlet by the New England Free Press—the rush of women's history courses. Over the next half-dozen or so years (i.e., until substantial textbooks became available), it sold more than 10,000 copies. My file copy, stamped "Libertaria Bookshop, West Green Road, London," is a reminder of the document's outreach.

The theoretical approach had been inspired most clearly by a historical adaptation of existentialism or, more precisely, Simone de Beauvoir's reflection on womens' status as "Other." We sought to understand the historical character of the Otherness. And, like black historians or labor historians, especially in a few years when Herbert Gutman's work became better known, to discover specific moments when the sense of subjectivity had been recuperated by the subject. We wanted to know, What were the preconditions for those moments?

One might ask today, Why did this task shape up in Madison? In part, this was a matter of personalities. In part, it was a matter of sources. But the particular intellectual stimulus of Madison's graduate student community had a great deal to do with the effort we put forth, if not the methodology. It is interesting to note how little influence the Frankfurt School would have on women's history in these days. We had first to work out other problems.

In the waning days of my Madison sojourn—not long after my share of writing, then illustrating "Women in American Society" with an old picture of my mother and a snapshop of the three authors, among other drawings and photos— I got a chance to put to work my powers of historical reassessment on a maddeningly finite task. An editor at the University of Illinois Press asked the two Buhles to edit the classic six-volume *History of Woman Suffrage* down to a neat and readable one volume. It sounded easy. And the project had the virtue of steeping us in the original self-documentation of women's history by women suffrage leaders, as well as the literature of and about the surrounding reform milieu. Like most such projects, the detail work dragged out terribly and proved almost unendurable. It also reinforced a sense of how radical the nineteenth-century pioneers had been, and how much of the early-twentieth-century activity had depended on that tradition, exhausted by 1920.

This insight, embedded in *The Concise History of Woman Suffrage* (1977), had the special virtue of warning against the sort of intellectual smugness apparent in the modernist critique of sentimental women's literature, or of the historians' smugness about the various failings (mostly on race and class issues) of suffrage leaders. The intense historiographical emphasis in Madison had helped me understand that the burning truth of one era (even my own) might well become the discarded hypothesis of the next, and that varieties of approaches to women's emancipation had earned respect in their own right.

■ ■

The next few years saw an acceleration of methodological discussion among radical historians, many by then finishing their dissertations and embarking on teaching careers. In 1975, at a sort of "countersession" to the Organization of American Historians meeting in Boston, I tried to summarize how far we had come. My approach was thoroughly rooted in Progressive (i.e., Madison-style) history, and I think women's historians from other parts of the country were amazed to hear Charles Beard and James Harvey Robinson evoked. We were attempting, I noted, to recover the Progressive traditions through a polemic against consensus history, but also to transcend them:

> When we first began our efforts in the late 1960s, often from scratch and in isolation, we . . . had grown within the mold of the time. I remember the excitement when discovering Mary Beard's work in those early days and her warning that oppression was a bad model for writing history. We accepted her premise that women were a *force* in history but did not feel comfortable with her standards, which as Berenice Carroll has pointed out, were "taking men as the measure." We were less interested in the traditional dimensions of "civilization" accepted by Beard and very disdainful of anything smacking of compensatory history. Consequently our own first efforts took us outside the usual parameters of historical study in search for a distinct method (and subject) for women's history. I genuinely feel that many of us laid out the framework for something which isn't too well shaped or filled in yet (perhaps because we threw so much of our energies into teaching rather than writing). At any rate, many of us were searching through history for signs of women's consciousness through their own self-awareness of themselves as a sex . . . we were always looking for women's own perception of changes.[2]

Writing *Women and American Socialism* forced the two tracks of my work more closely together. I had to begin afresh with my dissertation notes, recasting the themes from an intellectual history of strategies to a basically cultural study of different radical women's milieus and how distinct historical experiences shaped responses to political opportunities. I was responding, most directly, to the work of Nancy Cott, Carroll Smith-Rosenberg, and others in the formulation of the concept of women's culture.[3]

But perhaps I was also beginning to respond, although not yet consciously, to another aspect of the questions of subjectivity. *Women and American Socialism* sealed off one part of my Madison life, in the sense that the monographic project conceived there has been completed. Another part remained to be explored. One

2. Mari Jo Buhle, "Recent Contributions to Women's History," *Radical History Review* 2 (Summer 1975): 5.

3. Among the early writings: Nancy F. Cott, ed., *Root of Bitterness* (New York, 1972); Carroll Smith-Rosenberg, "Beauty, the Beast and the Militant Women: A Case Study in Sex Roles and Social Stress in Jacksonian America," *American Quarterly* 23 (1971).

could hardly have imagined, in the late 1960s, that "I ♡ Adorno" bumper stickers would appear on campuses twenty years later, or that *Village Voice* journalists would describe themselves as "Adorno Heads." Part of the charm of the Frankfurt School had been its apparent impenetrability, its enigmatic style and meaning. Actually, hostile critics of mass culture as they were, the Frankfurters offered in advance the perfect framework for vernacular postmodernism. Instead of central-izing signifiers by authoritarian commands, fascist or communist, late capitalism evidently diffused meanings, liberatory and regressive, into every vacant space of the hypertrophic commodity-culture system. Not surprisingly, cultural criticism itself became both more prevalent and more insular in the university system. By way of French intellectual imports, it commanded high theory and higher prestige for the once disregarded subject of feminism and psychoanalysis. Here, many unan-swered questions of my intellectual awakening returned. What Madison taught me was a historical approach to research and intepretation of the subject.

21   A Madison Communist

PAUL RICHARDS

Paul Richards is a native Californian. He received his Ph.D. in History in 1978, and is author of *Critical Focus: The Black and White Photographs of Harvey Wilson Richards* (1986). He is a veteran of the civil rights movement and the Vietnam War anti-draft movement in California and Wisconsin. Currently he is a general contractor in the San Francisco Bay Area.

I entered the Communist party at Berkeley in 1965 when I was classified I-A by my draft board. I came to Wisconsin in August 1967 as a party person, and officially transferred. I was one of two open communists on campus from 1967 to 1971.

I had attended Berkeley from 1961 to 1966, so I went through all the civil rights agitation, the Free Speech Movement, the Committee on Agricultural Labor, and the Vietnam protests. I was a political veteran in the sense, also; I had served two months in jail on civil rights charges and done two years of antidraft counseling and some fleeing from I-A status—including a trip out of the country for three months.

But I was part of the New Left generation in another way. Somebody told me in Berkeley, "You're a natural leader." It made me sick to my stomach. I felt like Bob Moses pulling out of SNCC, saying, "A pox on leadership." I came to Madison determined to study, thinking I would go to jail at any minute and determined to learn until then. I had heard about the State Historical Society of Wisconsin from historian Leon Litwack. When I found out that the History Department had no labor history program, I was very discouraged; I should have broken a window or something to express the kind of anger I felt. But the economic historians made it possible for me to get in touch with the really good people, the historical archivists like Josephine Harper of the Historical Society, the real jewels of the earth. They helped me find what I wanted, more than any professor or other graduate student did.

My main problem in orienting myself was that when I came out of Oak-land—in spite of traveling halfway round the world to Siberia and Africa—I didn't really see that the whole world wasn't like Oakland, in some ways almost a Carib-bean town. I went to school in Oakland a minority white, but there were also minority Mexicans, blacks, Japanese, Chinese, Filipinos, and others. No matter what happens in the papers and at the symphonies to define "culture," no culture dominates the streets; there are always friendships, relationships, across race lines. When I went to Madison, I had to perceive there were virtually no black people around, and with so few blacks on campus, no way to overcome the racial polar-ization. I became friends with all sorts of people, but it was happenstance. The dominant racist assumptions made me homesick, which may have been an escapist view.

One experience really contradicted the liberal image of Wisconsin for me. A black man knitted a sweater for my son when he was born; the man was just nice, and we became friends. Being disabled, he worked for Goodwill Industries, where he got involved with a seventeen-year-old white girl, for which he was accused by her mother of statutory rape, and got five years in Waupun Prison. That wouldn't happen in California. To me that was like a southern lynching. When my mother remarried a black man, they had to leave California to get married; but that was in 1946!

Madison also seemed very *eastern* to me, which was of course the opposite of what easterners thought. My mother is Jewish. But here I saw Jewish New York culture—not a few people, but enough for a social force—for the first time. I also remember going through Minneapolis and seeing just two kinds of people in the airport, straights and freaks. For the first time, I met people who didn't like their parents. I felt as if I had stepped into a closet. So even if I had a hard time dealing with Wisconsin, I don't think of it now as a bad experience—more like, "Hold your nose and take the pill."

Being a home-town boy from an Oakland Old Left family, I never felt I could move in Wisconsin the way I could in California. So all my political work was around the campus. I worked with the various Communist party-oriented groups, the American Institute for Marxist Studies (AIMS) and what we called the Marxist Forum, an organization to present speakers. It was strange to be one of the two open communists. In one sense, I could have been anywhere in the United States: Madison was irrelevant. You push the newspaper, you try to get converts involved in local peace and labor movements, and you work in liberal electoral campaigns. I was a classic communist, but on campus.

The handful of people we recruited were all Wisconsin people. The party grew because of good cadre, good outreach, becoming relevant to people's lives, and offering an oppositional stance you could take and not sink with. It was pretty much the same for young workers we reached in Madison and Milwaukee, an advanced consciousness over the New Left, even if we didn't understand America. We shared many Old Left illusions. But if Americans are trained to hate and kill communists, these communists were the opposite of the image, just average people who try to do good in their situation.

On campus, a huge Left activity existed in general, and we were just a voice, hardly heard at all. We did get big crowds for our forums. We would have five ten-minute speakers, representing different viewpoints, in order to bring Marxism into open discussion. In Berkeley the W. E. B. Du Bois Clubs had things on science, philosophy, every subject people were trying to understand; a place where my whole worldview had come together. I wanted to re-create that, to have somewhere people could talk, even if they disagreed.

Part of the trouble came from conflicts in the sectarian Left. I had never been called "Stalinist" before—it wasn't a West Coast term—or I never heard it. One Independent Socialist member, in particular, baited us at meetings and finally called me "Hitler." The Jew came out in me: I never was a tough guy, but I called him on the floor and asked if he wanted to go outside. That was the last meeting I ever chaired. I decided I was not constituted to withstand or dish out that kind of abuse.

Then again, the party wasn't much help. The forums were not normal procedure, which was one of the reasons I was forced out. They confounded all my efforts to recruit people through educational activities and fun when in 1969, they ordered me to set up the Young Workers Liberation League (YWLL)—the new party youth organization—on campus. That would have torn me out of all the relations I had established, and set me up for trouble. Meanwhile, for two years I had also been engaged in intraparty struggles over national program and politics, and had even been singled out as an "ultra-Left" (which meant more critical of U.S. trade unions and more favorable toward Third World revolutions than the party leadership). So this was the last straw. I said, "See you later." To my surprise, the local party club stayed, and became the YWLL.

Quitting the Communist party happened on one of those days I will never forget. I was walking down State Street and saw myself in a storefront window. I could look at myself as another poor *schmuck* American rather than some great savior and organizer, with the personal responsibility to make the revolution in America. It took me back to the days of cutting school at 2:00 in the afternoon with nothing particular to do.

Pretty soon my contacts with the real New Left excited me because it brought me out of postparty isolation. I felt positive and wanted to meet new people. I remember after I left the party, I chaired a campus meeting on civil rights and talked about my background. It was one of the few moments I can remember when lots of blacks were in the same room as political whites, probably during the Black Strike or shortly after. I recall a desperate cry from some eighteen-year-old white,

"We have done everything and nothing works." I responded, "We haven't done anything. We've never gone to the white community and faced racism, to fight it in our own culture." All the black people applauded. I felt that even what I had done so far was nothing to what had to be done, and what could be done.

During the summers, the School for Workers would bring workers from around the state to live in the dormitories. Some of us would go to the dorms when they were drinking beer, walk right in and start talking about the Vietnam war. These experiences were really wonderful, the most I could ever do to meet workers from the heartland. We didn't do it on a sneaky basis; we came right in and said, "We're opposed to the war." People came up, their faces livid, and said, "My cousin just got wounded." We had to keep talking, making correlations between imperialism and their condition in the working class. Pretty soon it was, "Have another beer." People would cry about it; the whole thing was very moving. I remember I developed a sort of understanding—much as I was opposed to the war, I couldn't hate these people who supported it.

Intellectually, the New Left solidified my learning. I always knew W. E. B. Du Bois was held in high esteem. I studied him with Litwack, and found a man who had a fresh view of America, a view not tainted by self-interest or self-serving. I admired the ends to which he put his scholarship, and I found his observations well advanced of any Marxist writer he had come across. I instinctively felt the official communist view—in which Du Bois "evolved" or matured into Marxism—completely condescending and wrong. Writing an essay for the *Radical America* issue on radical historiography helped me elaborate my idea that the term "Marxism" is reductionist if not applied to *Black Reconstruction,* one of the few great books of American history.

The economic historians solidified my learning too. When I got into economic history, I went to my adviser and announced, "I am a Marxist." His response was: "I don't give a damn. I just want the facts." It was a challenging response, the hallmark of my graduate education.

Politically, the New Left still gave me problems. One of my most striking experiences was going to the famous 1969 SDS [Students for a Democratic Society] convention. I felt very weird, which I told someone, and got the response, "Your problem is you don't have the will to struggle." But I went there as a student, someone whose family was made up of workers, someone who had worked in warehouses and other places, and who knew he was now a student in a university. Here the SDS convention was talking about "Which Road for the Proletariat?" Everybody was a Marxist theorist, or believed he was, which surprised me because I had been part of groups where political people actually read Hegel and had been communists for decades. I felt sorry for these poor students mimicking some behavior from somewhere with no reference to themselves. The convention was dominated by the "We're Not It" phenomenon, which left me very disoriented. I felt sympathy, but what was *I* doing here?

Some similar problems applied to the Teaching Assistants Association (TAA). I had practically grown up with the longshoremen's union, so the work that the TAA did to organize seemed natural and exciting to me. I loved the TAA strike of 1970. But I couldn't believe that the emphasis got transferred from a critique of mass education to wages and better job security. Perhaps in this case I knew too well what was going to happen. In spite of all the New Left claims, when you get down to dealing with the paycheck the leadership follows the art of the possible, which reinforces the economic solution. The TAA faced the same old problems of the Left, and didn't have any better answers.

At another level, the problems of the university—of any university—came out in the case of my friend Robert Starobin. He met his wife at my father's house. He was almost like a member of the family, a fellow Red diaper baby. I knew him also through the Free Speech fight in Berkeley. He was a very uncomfortable fellow, but eager to help me when I was getting set up in Madison. He pulled some strings to get me a teaching assistantship in his Black History course. That was a happening, with more students than had ever attended a history course. Bob didn't let any laziness on my part slip by, however; he was very demanding. I had to increase my standards of work because of him. Also, he wore a suit and tie. But he had a consciousness of himself that just wouldn't quit. He identified with the students; he never identified with the club or the history profession, and that made him unacceptable.

I remember when I quit the party, he came to my house and said, "Welcome to the human race." The entire time I had been in the party, he hadn't made a single remark or shown any prejudice to me, although I found out later his family had suffered, in his childhood, from McCarthyism and from Communist party leadership machinations. What he said shocked the hell out of me, and put into words that reflection of myself in the storefront.

I had an inkling, even then, of him as a tragic figure. I didn't want to impose on him; he had such strong demands on him from every direction, and he took them so seriously. I wasn't stricken in the same way, but I understood his bitterness about the Left too. His suicide stands as a living prod to me, a person of similar background. In a certain sense, it was an appropriate act; I forgive him but I don't forgive the world that made him so miserable. The level of insanity in this country, the anticommunism, the racism, the treatment he suffered at the hands of the university and the movement, doomed this promising brilliant person.

22   Neighborhood Politics

MICHAEL MEEROPOL AND
GERALD MARKOWITZ

Michael Meeropol, an outstanding political personality despite his modesty, notes below that he is a son of Julius and Ethel Rosenberg. In *We Are Your Sons* (1980, rev. ed. 1987), written with Robert Meeropol, and with numerous speaking engagements, Michael has practiced a unique public scholarship. He has also taught, for many years, at Western New England College, and lives in the Berkshires. Gerald Markowitz, whose books include *Democratic Vistas: Post Offices and Public Art in the New Deal* (edited with Marlene Park, 1984) and *"Slaves of the Depression": Workers' Letters about Life on the Job* (edited with David Rosner, 1987), teaches history at John Jay College, New York.

Who We Were and Where We Came From

Jerry was twenty-two years old when he and his wife, Adrienne, arrived in Madison in 1965. Michael was twenty-three when he and his wife, Ann, arrived in 1966. We (Jerry and Michael) were New Yorkers, in Madison to go to graduate school. We considered ourselves radical politically as well as academically. We were both "Red diaper babies." Michael is the older son of Julius and Ethel Rosenberg, though at that time he was enjoying the anonymity of his adopted family's name.[1] Jerry was a close friend of four years whose father and mother were both long-time members of the National Lawyers' Guild. Adrienne was also a Red diaper baby (her father edited a Hungarian language left-wing newspaper), who had, as an

---

1. For Michael's family's story, see Robert and Michael Meeropol, *We Are Your Sons* (Champaign, Ill., 1987). In the latter pages of the book, there are some scattered references to Michael's teen and young adult years, including some pages about his and Ann's life in Madison. On Red diaper babies, see, for example, Jonah Raskin, *Out of the Whale* (New York, 1974).

infant, been wheeled in a carriage next to Michael's as her mother conversed with her neighbor and friend Ethel Rosenberg.

We had both been involved in politics in high school, participating in local demonstrations against bomb shelters and picketing Woolworths in support of the first sit-ins in the South. Michael had briefly been vice-president of New York High School SANE [Committee for a Sane Nuclear Policy]. When Jerry went to Earlham College in Richmond, Indiana, his political activities continued. Within the first week, he was part of a group from the college and town that went to integrate the local skating rink (the first and last time he skated). A small group continued to demonstrate and raise issues at the college, holding vigils against the early escalations of the Vietnam war and protesting U.S. intervention in the Dominican Republic in 1965.

A graduate of the Bronx High School of Science, Jerry thought at first of a major in science, but by the end of his first year he had become a history major, engaged in independent study attempting to support his gut-feeling view that the United States had entered World War I for economic reasons. Impressed by Jerry's thoroughness in developing his position, but totally unconvinced of his radical "Beardian" economic determinism, the professor remarked that a new book had just been published by a historian at the University of Wisconsin that was "more Beardian than Beard." The book was *The Contours of American History* by William A. Williams. Though the professor's characterization of the book could not have been more wrong, the description intrigued him, and he told Michael about it. During Jerry's sophomore year, which was Michael's junior year, they began to read *Contours*. Michael first read *The Tragedy of American Diplomacy* in its 1962 edition and shared it with Jerry while they and Adrienne worked together at a summer camp in 1963. Williams's more sophisticated nondeterminist analysis, which still emphasized economic interests, led Jerry to search for a more systematic Left approach to history than the economic determinism with which he had arrived at Earlham. Madison thus seemed a perfect place to go for graduate study because Williams was there and because Left intellectual and political ferment was so strong.

Meanwhile, Michael had been involved in politics at Swarthmore, participating with a branch of SDS in Chester, Pennsylvania, as well as on campus. His crude economic determinism had been sorely tested in his junior American history seminar, and his desire to find validity for his radical inclinations in his major course of study, economics, had been virtually fruitless. All the economics he studied seemed to demonstrate the falsity of Marxism (as he understood it), and this was not successfully countered by some brief appearances at the college by Harry Magdoff (not yet with the *Monthly Review*) and an abortive effort to read *Capital* as part of a Marxist discussion group. Two years at King's College in Cambridge, England, gave him time to read seriously the works of Paul Baran, Paul Sweezy, and Josef Steindl. He met and attended lectures of the great British Marxist Maurice Dobb, and was supervised by the brilliant Joan Robinson and the equally brilliant but then unknown Bob Rowthorn. He also met and shared ideas with fellow radical students. This Cambridge experience left him confident that a Marxist approach to economics had validity. In 1966, he was ready for graduate school at an American university. He chose Wisconsin because one of his teachers from Swarthmore had told him of the interdisciplinary graduate program in economic history. His experience at Swarthmore had taught him that mainstream economis at a U.S. university would be a waste of time but he needed a Ph.D. in the field if he were to teach. The graduate program in economic history would permit him to combine his interest in economics and history, and to do research that permitted more institutional and historical forces to influence his economic analysis.

Though concerned to protect his anonymity, Michael cared little that he was a Red diaper baby. It was unremarkable to Jerry as well. Both of us were radical, unafraid to admit it.

We were neither members nor supporters of the Communist Party USA. On issues such as Soviet international policy, we were more supportive of the Chinese and Cuban pro-Third World approach. On issues of Soviet internal policy, we had escaped from our uncritical Stalinist apologism for one-party dictatorship. We believed in the SDS participatory democracy ideal. Our most important ideological commitment, which Michael expressed in a document he convinced Jerry and another friend to sign, was to systematic efforts to persuade more "average Amercians" about the validity of radical interpretations of, and solutions to, our problems, both internationally and domestically. The method we chose to begin to implement this commitment was a proposed third political party for the 1968 elections. Though the proposal was published in the SDS newsletter *New Left Notes,* when Michael traveled to a national meeting in Cleveland during the Thanksgiving weekend in 1966 and talked up the idea, it got literally no support.

What We Saw/Learned/Did/Thought in Madison

We had come to Madison because of its tradition of academic excellence and political activity. We found a vibrant, if at times confused, radical community that excited and stimulated us—and repelled us at times. During Jerry's first year there, the Johnson escalation of the war in Indo-China had already occurred, and the first teach-ins were held. From the time of Michael's arrival till both families left in 1970, the war remained a desperate focus for almost all the political activities we engaged in.

More out of economic necessity than choice, we found apartments several blocks apart on the near East Side. Although this area later became predominantly populated by students and young faculty, in the late 1960s few students were living there. The population was very mixed: blacks and whites, working class and middle class, mostly tenants but with a good sprinkling of homeowners as well. In a sense we lived in two different worlds—the university and the community—and we quickly became aware of how separate and alienated they were from each other.

Adrienne had begun to teach art in the Madison public schools before Ann and Michael arrived; Ann, after a year and a half of graduate study, also went to work in the schools. Their contacts and our neighborhood encounters helped solidify our views (already partially formulated) that if the Left could not adequately communicate to nonuniversity Madison residents rational reasons for getting out of Vietnam and radically transforming our country, then our hopes for a new, humane, peaceful, and yes, socialist society would be doomed. But university-based radicals did not initially focus on the problems or issues of the residents of the near East Side, and university activism was not understood by the ordinary people of Madison. In part, this resulted from the way local and national media misinterpreted and smeared us to the American people in general and the residents of neighborhoods like the near East Side in particular. We also felt that the media's success was to a significant degree the Left's own fault.

There was an unfortunate strand in the New Left that dismissed ordinary citizens, which included the white working class, as too nationalistic, too chauvinist, racist, anticommunist, and most important, *bought off* by the affluence of 1960s capitalism. The university-based radicals, by their actions if not explicit thought, communicated (with some help, creation, and misplaced emphasis from the media) contempt for the average American.

As an example of how the Left's failure to reach out to the unconvinced actually worked against their effort, we recall a major "action" that occurred on the campus of the university in the fall of 1966. This was the effort by the Madison Committee to End the War in Vietnam to "confront" Senator Edward Kennedy, who had arrived in Madison to give a speech. The audience was filled with radicals, who interrupted his speech before it began with catcalls and insisted that he "talk about the war." Kennedy was smart. He asked the leader of the group to come on stage and asked point-blank: "What would you do in Vietnam?" Here was a chance to reach a gigantic audience. What was the answer? "Immediate withdrawal." That was a fine demand, but it wasn't the kind of answer that would reach out to people. With 20–20 hindsight, we felt a better answer would have been: "Our government must immediately stop lying to us about how we got involved, why we are there, and what we are doing there. Once political leaders stop lying, the American people will insist on the right course." That might have provoked a dialogue with Kennedy and the audience about the nature of the lies the government was dealing out. Instead, Kennedy laughed off the "absurd" idea that "immediate withdrawal" was a viable option. Kennedy tried to continue the speech, but the "disruptions" went on, only earning the movement a black eye on campus and certainly in the larger community. The point of this is not to criticize the particular individual involved for not having the right answer to Kennedy's rhetorical question. The point is that not enough thought went into our goal that day. Our goal was not merely to "show" our displeasure with the war and make things uncomfortable for leaders until they came around to our side—there were and would be a time and place for that. We needed to reach out to people who were not already convinced. From our vantage point on the near East Side, we knew that in our bones. We didn't think the campus-based radicals really understood it.

In the spring of 1967, we involved ourselves in an aldermanic campaign that preceded the formation (in the fall) of the Wisconsin Alliance. We and others who worked with the alliance (also initially campus-based radicals who lived on the near East Side) believed it was possible to forge an economically based coalition of university antiwar radicals with working-class community residents. Our model ironically was the failed southern Populist movement that had sought to unite black and white members of the same economically oppressed group in the late nineteenth century.[2] We appreciated their attempt and near success. The Wisconsin Alliance's initial pamphlet, printed in April 1968, which argued for such an economically based coalition of cultural opposites, was severely criticized for being "economistic," and in retrospect we did have a rather optimistic view of how easily the economic self-interest of the majority could bridge informational and ideological gaps. We had agreed wholeheartedly with the current argument for an "interracial movement of the poor" that had grown out of the SDS community-organizing projects in both Chester (where Michael had had experience) and Newark. We had actually gone further and sought to argue that farmers and consumers, workers and consumers, blacks and whites, had been divided by "politicians' smokescreens" that obscured the fact that they were economically oppressed by what the pamphlet called the vested interests, identified also as the "monopolies." Even though we now have a greater appreciation of the difficulties involved, we still think that approach has merit. What was good about it was that it got us involved in the community we lived in, and talking to people about local and national issues.

In the fall of 1967, Michael shaved his beard and walked around the neighborhood soliciting signatures for the initiative petition that would put Madison on record in favor of "a cease-fire and the immediate withdrawal from Vietnam so that the Vietnamese people can determine their own destiny." It was an enlightening experience to note the arguments those opposed to the war would make, as well as the ones made by those in favor. Those kinds of discussions were potentially very discouraging. Even those supporting our side had only a rudimentary knowledge of the issues, and those in favor of the war started with both abysmal ignorance and the most chauvinistic instincts. It was no wonder that some leftists gave up on the general population. But true to our intellectual existentialism, we

2. The Wisconsin Alliance's initial pamphlet is entitled *The Wisconsin Alliance, A New Wisconsin Party for the People*. On the failure of the New Left, black nationalism and the counter culture to incorporate women's needs, see Carl Whitman and Casey Hayden, in Mitchell Cohen and Dennis Hale, ed., *The New Student Left* (Boston, 1966), 175–214. Carl Wittman was a friend of Michael's at Swarthmore. As a leader of the Swarthmore Political Action Club, as well as the Marxist Study Group, Carl's positive view of SDS was what caused Michael to join it in 1963.

believed the struggle to change people's minds was worth it, even if we weren't initially successful. Our reason was that we didn't think there was any other *possible* way to succeed.

Jerry's desire to participate in neighborhood activites led him to act in William Lewis's production of Edward Albee's *The Zoo Story* at the Wil-Mar Neighborhood Center, which was right down the street from where he and Adrienne lived. After each performance, the cast and audience would discuss issues raised by the play, including the nature of community and urban life. Michael became a frequent caller and one-time guest on radio talk shows (not as Michael Rosenberg, but as an SDS radical), discussing everything from local taxes to Vietnam.

Another major influence on our lives was Bob Starobin. Bob's uncle, "Lefty," had been a frequent visitor to Michael and his brother during the period of transition from life with their grandmother to their new adoptive family in 1954. In 1957, Lefty took Michael and his nephew, Bob, to a baseball game. Thus we had a "connection" to Bob before we arrived in Madison, and were delighted that he was there. We thought of him as a kindred spirit on the same track professionally but ahead of us. (Though we didn't think of it at the time, he was also a Red diaper baby.) We could look up to him while considering him an equal.[3] He, like Williams, demonstrated that radicals could integrate their scholarship with their politics. Their examples, and those of others, made us feel secure in our role as students and future college teachers. Bob's commitment and his willingness to risk professional disappointment (he was "eased" out of the History Department before receiving tenure) were examples to us that even academics were not immune from the costs of struggle. We hoped we would be as principled as Bob if threatened in similar ways. Later, Bob's tragic suicide led us to recognize that we in the movement needed to do more to take care of one another—the "beloved community" that was so celebrated by early SDS radicals fragmented into too many sects by the late 1960s and 1970s, and Bob's sensitivity and commitment found no home. We still miss him.

3. Bob Starobin was a fine scholar. See his *Industrial Slavery in the Old South* (New York 1969). In 1970, he edited *Denmark Vesey, the Slave Conspiracy of 1822* (Englewood Cliffs, N.J., 1970). He began the book, "When I began to compose this introduction, a white federal judge had just gagged and shackled a black man [Bobby Seale at the Chicago Conspiracy Trial] to prevent him from cross-examining witnesses. . . . Now as I conclude, Chicago police are alleged to have assassinated two more black organizers while they slept in bed [Fred Hampton and Mark Clark of the Illinois Black Panther Party]—another demonstration of the depths of racial oppression in the United States" (p. 1). He dedicated the book to Bobby Seale and in memory of Fred Hampton, and donated his royalties to the Black Panther party and the Southern Conference Education Fund (a 1950s pro-integration organization long accused of being a Communist-Front organization by the U.S. government). That divided donation paid homage to both his Old Left background and his New Left sentiments.

23 *Radical America* and Me

PAUL BUHLE

Paul Buhle remains a paradox, even (or especially) to himself, but not because of any desertion of Madison traditions. He has spent much of his post-Madison time as a radical journalist with historical bent, oral historian of the U.S. Left, and community historian of Rhode Island.

Madison: Old Dreams

As I bent over old newspapers, taking historical notes in the posh marble and oak reading room of the American Antiquarian Society in Worcester, Massachusetts, my mind drifted back over a thousand highway miles and almost twenty years of dreamspace to Madison in the late 1960s. I mull over those Madison years frequently. My friends say it was the time and not the place, and they are no doubt partly right. Yet the visions of liberation I possess return persistently to memories of the spring thaw, when the banners of resistance are first unfurled, to the sticky summer crowded with dope and beer, to the fall offensive and the winter library days. Not that these experiences are any kind of paradigm: They are dead and buried, part of the political geology that the Left builds up, layer by layer, for the footing of succeeding generations. Nevertheless, they remain alive in me. And as I leafed through the *Banner of Light,* a nineteenth-century Spiritualist newspaper, I read about something strangely familiar

> City Hall, Madison, 1869. A little-remembered convention of Spiritualists, then in the most radical phase of that forgotten movement, passed resolutions in favor of sex equality, woman suffrage, progressive education for children, and equal education for women at the College.

> The assembled delegates agreed to the principles of democratic spiri-
> tualism—no guru-leader who directs the unearthly contact by himself,
> but rather a free-floating motion of all those who feel momentarily
> closest to the Other Side. The major resolution passed at the meeting
> underlined the general sentiment: "That we earnestly thank our spirit
> friends for their assistance in breaking dungeon chains and bringing
> forth the captives . . . until free thought encounters nothing more than
> the harmless menace of dogmatism."

One hundred years later, I was walking down the same streets as those convention goers. Was it coincidence that the *Banner of Light,* which must have gone
around hand to hand in Madison, advertised hashish candy as the "Open Sesame
to Dreams" and lavished praise on Victoria Woodhull, president of the American
Spiritualist Association, free-love feminist, and leader of the native-born Americans
in the First International?

Madison has been an outpost of dreamers. I knew some of them well, the
ones who visited my editorial hermitage on Spaight Street, in the old blue-collar
East Side. Others I saw more from a distance, on campus. I watched them sort out
collective visions of the later 1960s. I like to think that I was one of the dreamers
myself.

■ ■

Those who came from Old Left backgrounds to arrive on campus at age seventeen
or eighteen may have matured politically as much as I had, with my Masters in
history, my experience with two SDS chapters, and a fledgling magazine in my
back pocket. I had never, for more than a few political moments, broken the isolation of the village atheist American radical. Madison supplied my first thorough-
going political milieu.

I had grown up in a Big Ten university town lacking nearly all of Madison's
pleasant qualities. Squatted in the prairie, Champaign–Urbana remained foremost
a commercial crossroads and county seat for some of the richest farmland in the
world. Rock-ribbed Republican (the county went Democratic only once in memory, the Roosevelt 1936 landslide), Champaign in particular was just barely
touched by the inherent cosmopolitanism of the campus. College professors could
be found tucked away in private homes not far from my family's. But the town
bore no political or intellectual indication of their presence.

As a teenager, I used to drive back to the blue-collar North End where I spent
my first six years, only a few blocks from the railroad tracks, with the black ghetto
stretching beyond. It was rough, the range extending from "poor but honest" to
kids on the borderline of a criminal life. But memories of my time there occupied
a strange space in my imagination: the foul-smelling Sunbeam Bread factory, ware-
house blank walls covered with circus posters, the dirty little creek ("Bone Ditch,"
we called it) that had crayfish hiding in tin cans for the catching, and the evangel-

ical church with an occasionally visiting "jumping preacher" Bob Richards, who
went from our neighborhood to the Olympics and the Wheaties Sports Federation
and back to the ministry (much later, in 1984, he ran for president on the Populist
party ticket, with midwestern neofascist support). I think that the perception of
class, and a memory of the 1940s culture that had slipped far away by then, left
me wondering. My middle-class neighborhoods to follow were more secure, but
really 1950s dull. Nothing existed but private life and orchestrated sociality.

My political awareness dawned in 1960 with the civil rights movement, stirring local demonstrations that passed quickly but left a lasting impression on me.
I got to walk a picket line, certainly the most exciting thing that had ever happened
in my life. Within a year I saw in Madrid, by pure chance, a political dissident of
some kind chased and beaten, very likely to death (anyway, they pulled the bloody
sheet over him), by Franco's special police. Around that time, my ostensibly conservative mother, a badly underpaid registered nurse, was blacklisted for raising
questions of unionization. I lacked a context to make much sense of these things,
except that they disturbed me.

During my undergraduate days at Illinois, I lived at home until I married at
nineteen, drifting through an apolitical campus life with the help of a bohemian
subculture. Rooted in folk music, drug experimentation, and generalized nihilism,
this little milieu was closely monitored by the university security director, who
doubled as regional FBI chief. For eight months I tried San Francisco, and briefly
attended San Francisco State, where my teacher and model was Vartan Gregorian,
later Director of the New York Public Library and still later, one of the nation's
most distinguished University presidents. I returned to Champaign to be the only
open socialist on a campus of thirty thousand. (Among the secret socialists, it was
rumored, were leaders of the campus Youth Democrats and the editor of the lib-
eral-inclined student newspaper, now a famous film reviewer. Among the bohemians, we counted later *New Yorker* contributor Larry Weiwode.) Widening faculty
and student opposition to the Vietnam war finally brought me into the heretofore
community-oriented SDS chapter. Chairing the first big public forum, marching
at the head of two hundred demonstrators, I felt I had evened my score with Champaign. A friendly professor, who encouraged my study of American radicalism,
pointed me in the direction of Madison.

The professor, Madison graduate, and later prominent immigration historian
Rudolph Vecoli helped me stay a jump ahead of my draft board by sending me to
a former graduate student pal of his, A. William Hoglund, who was teaching at
the University of Connecticut in Storrs. One summer, between semesters, I worked
at the *National Guardian* office in New York, spending an evening every week
arguing with teacher James Weinstein at the Free University of New York. Back
in Storrs, the SDS chapter made some waves but failed to overcome the political
apathy of a weekend commuter campus. SDS nationally progressed to the stage,
however, that a Radical Education Project (REP) took shape. Here my extended
life-by-mail began. Starting as a radical history newsletter and then a crudely pro-

duced magazine, *Radical America* went out to SDS chapters and REP contactees. I couldn't get far alone. Now Madison called, and Hoglund agreed: It was time for my pilgrimage to the spiritual home of radical history.

Over the summer, even before I set foot in Madison, things began falling into place. I wrote my first published piece for the *Guardian,* arguing that American radicalism's legacy had to be recast from Old Left sterotypes and from mainstream condescension. I struck up a conversation with Jim O'Brien, a key intellectual activist already busily engaged in Madison REP work and an eager friend of the new magazine. At the summer national SDS convention in Ann Arbor, I met the tall, raw-boned Madison SDS past chariman, Henry Haslach, sometime printer, Teaching Assistant Association pioneer, mathematician, and Industrial Workers of the World aficionado. *Radical America* had a working group waiting for me.

At the same SDS convention, I ran into some intellectually precocious characters who had been mandated to produce a theoretical supplement to the official SDS weekly newspaper, *New Left Notes.* These New York undergraduates grasped fine points of European theoretical controversies that I read only secondhand in the *New Left Review,* argued with a sophistication and worldliness that made me self-conscious, and understandably considered themselves the coming thinkers of the New Left generation. My best friend among them advised me in a friendly way to give up *Radical America* and throw in with their much-hoped-for project to link European Marxism with U.S. practice. I had already made up my mind to publish, in part from a stubborn feeling that these lucid European minds would never acknowledge a distinct American radical past—let along learn its positive values.

Their *Praxis* lasted two interesting issues. Its moving spirits became Weathermen. One of them, Dave Gilbert, has in recent years been sentenced to life for the Brinks robbery in Nyack, New York. Perhaps they started from too far outside to find their way back to America.

■■

I landed, in September 1967, at the Madison SDS chapter's office (actually, Hank Haslach's living room) just off the railroad switchyard. The most proletarian location on campus, and one of the few surviving remnants of what had not long before been a sizable student private housing ghetto, the place had gapped screens that welcomed in the mosquitoes by night and the flies at daybreak. Still, it had the feel of what I liked in the Midwest, an openness both in landscape and in street affability. Unlike my Midwest, it also had a place for radicals.

The radical history graduate students in Madison were politically ubiquitous, at or near the leadership of insurgent institutions all around the campus. Paul Breines, who had been an associate editor of *Studies on the Left* and would one day take a similar role in *Radical America*—the human link between the two magazines—seemed like an elder statesman of Critical Theory. Avuncular toward me and *Radical America,* as I would be toward the 1970s generation of radical magazines and their editors, he radiated goodwill for my project. So did Bob Gabriner, who had shortly before written a Master's thesis on the Minnesota farmer–labor movement and ascended to the journalistic heights of *Connections,* one of the outstanding underground newspapers in the country. Gabriner worked hard as small-scale popularist of dissenting writers and artists, but he gladly offered the *Connections* office for our layout and printing. Smart, militant, creative types appeared on all sides. I had entered a thick soup of radicalism.

The real scarcity of hard-bitten Old Leftists, which is to say the small-scale role of any sectarian activity on the Left in Madison, now seems to me an indication of the fresh times we had entered. Trotskyists, Maoists, and Communist party regulars attracted by 1967–1968 more personal sympathy than political sympathizers, so lonely did their adherents seem at the literature tables. The war, the draft, educational reform, security against administrative reprisals on active students and teaching assistants, the strikes that took over the campus nearly every semester for three years—these issues and confrontations crowded out the old Stalin versus Trotsky versus Norman Thomas debates entirely. Everyone of New Left vintage believed Russia needed a revolution, the Vietnamese were actively engaged in one, and we ourselves had begun the first phase of preparing a sweeping change at home. Détente conditioned our expectations. So did the liberal campus atmosphere, which seemed violated more by hypocritical university officials defending the ill-gotten gains of financial complicity than by our occasional disruptions.

Meanwhile, America voted in Richard Nixon (a past Madison mayor had run as vice-presidential contender on Lester Maddox's racist American Independent ticket), the erstwhile fighting liberal *Capital Times* joined the hue and cry against student demonstrations, unarmed Black Panthers died before smoking police guns in nearby Chicago, and the war rolled on. We might have believed ourselves, in dark moments, to be enemy aliens wrestling within the bowels of the imperial monster. But we also felt, nearly all of us, that Madison was *our* home, however temporary, its beauty increasingly threatened by development interests; and our just society would save the good earth, the resources and treasures of city and school, from Leviathan corrupters.

For a time, our activity seemed to sustain a LaFollettesque view. Amid public discussions about the university and the war machine, study classes on corporate liberalism provided dense reading and much serious discussion. I recall the intensity of undergraduates challenging both teaching methods and goals; I responded as a radical professor might have, forty years earlier, reading vivid passages from V. L. Parrington's history of democratic thought. In this perspective, we present-day Americans had to work hard to win back the republic, but the university atmosphere could offer its resources even to the dissidents. The friendliness of our favorite professors during the worst of the crises gave us confidence in the strength of ideas.

Even the occasional breakdown in communication could be seen as comical rather than tragic. At the height of the Dow Chemical strike, William Appleman Williams made some ill-advised comments to a *New York Times* reporter about students acting as if they wanted to live in a chimpanzee world. Given the immense proliferation of leafletting on campus, a committee of some kind might have written him a public indignation letter. But something very different happened. Quite spontaneously, a half-dozen students (including myself) bought bananas by the bunch and passed them out one by one as students came in the doors to his lecture class on foreign policy. Calling the class to order, he smiled sheepishly and went on to lecture on the aggressions of American foreign policy. How we loved him on that day.

It was Williams who, only a few weeks later, helped launch the early *Radical America* on a wider scale by recommending a small grant from the Rabinowitz Foundation. (The grant would later be described by a right-wing intelligence-gathering network as Russian-inspired "disinformation funding.") Williams brought the subject of *Studies on the Left* into my first conversation with him. The earlier journal, it may be remembered, had been gone from Madison less than a half-dozen years. In September 1967, its last-phase dominating personality, James Weinstein, dropped by campus for a visit, and I persuaded him to write an obit to *Studies*. Not only in Madison but nationally, we inherited a radical graduate student enthusiasm for history that *Studies* had helped build. The typical boosters (or editorial associates), who kept *Radical America* alive by taking copies into local bookstores and study classes, were of a piece. On the intersecting orbit of student radicalism and historical study, trying to make sense of immediate developments and offer undergraduates a socialist strategy while urging self-defined intellectuals into political action, they rightly saw *Radical America* as an extension of themselves.

The contrast between *Studies* and *Radical America* helped us to define our status and orientation. The *Studies* group generally had seen itself as the nucleus of a theoretically-minded cadre for a New Left that grew all too slowly, and with an unwonted antipathy for theory. *Radical America* grew up in the midst of rebellions which may have lacked an intellectual perspective but decidedly developed their own leadership and their own visionary goals. While some erstwhile *Studies* editors therefore denounced "mindless activism," I wrote enthusiastic *Guardian* reportage and Madison *SDS Bulletin* theoretical notes on "student spontaneity." In my eyes, we SDS-ers had broadcast our slogans but in no sense organized the far-reaching campus response, nor for that matter did the modest growth of the chapter encourage us to think the students interested in some kind of mass-party equivalent. They had acted on their own, it seemed to us, for goals that had come out of their own experiences and desires. Most of us thought that our first responsibility was not to explain socialism to them but to understand their capacity to take charge of demonstrations, of their dorm life, and of various problems attendant on any student strike. Through interaction, we could provide the information and insights they badly needed in order to carry their aspirations through to a successful conclusion.

Differences between the two Madison journals could also be attributed to generational change on the Left. If the *Studies* group had experienced a very intense disillusionment from the proletarian shibboleths of the Old Left, most *Radical America* editors had never met a Communist until they came to Madison. We *Radical America* types looked to Marxism with fresh eyes and some naivete, as a possible way to explain or predict the future links of minorities and workers to radicalized students. A New York Jewish ambience dominated *Studies;* the inner circles of *Radical America* had a preponderance of small-town Protestants whose inherited radicalism (if any) lay generations back.

The two magazines shared a fundamental critique of the imperial juggernaut, and both recalled the Socialist party's pre-1920 educational endeavor as a worthy model. But when the SDS national secretary, Carl Davidson, labeled the contemporary campus movement "student syndicalism," he recalled a distinctly different alternative from that democratic but highly ordered model which *Studies* held up against the Communist party traditions. The Industrial Workers of the World, excoriated by Weinstein as overrated and marginal, seemed to *Radical America* writers and readers a supremely significant example of American radicalism. The Wobblies had abandoned (or absorbed) imitations of European models for the direct action and solidarity that offered a natural economic extension of political democracy. The Wobblies also appealed to the lowly immigrant unskilled workers, counterparts of the 1960s black unionists who challenged the United Auto Workers, counterparts also of the women at the bottom of the workforce and even of the "youth culture"-oriented new industrial workers familiar with the rock music, drugs and Vietnam combat. All these newer forces, when drawn into action, actually seemed to disdain the principle of external leadership and fixed ideology. If, as Weinstein charged, the IWW evoked romanticism, then we hoped to make the most of the romantic impulse.[1]

This romanticism also had definite cultural roots. Both magazines tended to move culture into a relative ghetto, the "back of the book" or the subject of an occasional special issue. Both magazines had editors who considered themselves close to Hans Gerth, Harvey Goldberg, and George Mosse. But while *Studies* emphasized the more formal aspects of a critical theory toward culture, and celebrated theatrical developments like the Happenings or the San Francisco Mime Troupe, *Radical America* placed itself within the surfacing of "underground" culture during the late 1960s. The earlier group continued to live out the avant-garde's link with the intelligentsia, a permanent opposition to the dominant cul-

1. In 1969, 1960s radical Madison and 1950s radical Madison had a small detente. Weinstein had in mind the creation of a socialist political movement by a group of notable intellectuals. In the Chicago studio of historian Jesse Lemisch and feminist psychology pamphleter (and rock musician) Naomi Weisstein, a dozen or so of us met: Warren Susman, Saul Landau, Weinstein, myself, Peter Wiley, and Eugene D. Genovese among others. Political differences remained too great for common action. Weinstein launched the journal *Socialist Revolution,* then went on to *In These Times,* disappointed with the New American Movement in the interim. Genovese, after many years' discussion, went on to found *Marxist Perspectives* (1981–82).

ture. The latter envisioned what Theodor Adorno's translator, Jeremy Shapiro, described as the transcendence of the famous "one-dimensional society," not denial but dialectical negation of a *necessary stage* in the development of postcapitalist humankind. *Radical America's* equivalent to Ronnie Davis—*Studies* ally and Mime Troupe mentor—was thus the Austin, Texas, history graduate student dropout turned full-time cartoonist, Gilbert Shelton, whose Fabulous Furry Freak Brothers epitomized the transformation of popular culture techniques and images into the merry madness of freakdom. I saw the first of the underground comics, *Feds 'n Heads,* personally published by Shelton in Austin, and sent for a bundle, which I personally sold from the SDS literature table. With our grant money from Rabinowitz, Shelton set up one of the first underground comic presses in San Francisco, and published *RA Komiks,* a *Radical America* issue full of his own amazing work. Never before or after did *Radical America* hit a press-run of 15,000 copies—and sell out the issue. According to New York SDS-ers, Secretary of Defense Robert McNamara's nephew was among the most eager distributors.

Which entity, *Studies on the Left* or *Radical America,* was more perceptive in political ideas or cultural insights? The question cannot be answered. All radical expectations fall short, leaving behind an overabundance of people and ideas to blame. Institutions should, in any case, be viewed as part of their larger milieus. *Studies* succeeded in imparting the analytical kernel of "Corporate Liberalism"; *Radical America* succeeded in imparting the importance of working-class, black, and women's history in providing clues to the unique character of American social struggles. Viewed generously, both contributed to the education of political generations and scholarly generations because they conveyed a sense of excitement and relevance about history. Neither penetrated very deeply into the ranks of activists, and neither could avert the catastrophe to come.

■ ■

For the credulous (and I include myself), a link between Madison's near-campus neighborhood "youth culture" revolutionaries and the student rebels in the dormitories seemed obvious. It held a resonance even for many who disdained drugs and retained the staid marriage and scholarship of graduate student life. The one "head shop" on campus sold radical magazines and posters along with underground comics, all flavored slightly with the smell of incense. Excesses were apparent all around, whether worse or just more blatant than radicals drinking and sexually combining in other eras remained to be seen. Some of the more old-fashioned radicals were horrified. But most of us could not help being impressed at the young people's verve, their eagerness to identify themselves with an apparently emerging cooperative order, their struggle against very real slumlords, their evocative if maudlin wall murals denouncing capitalism and embracing universal love. Even an occasional middle-aged anarchist, like Murray Bookchin, came up for visits or moved in for a spell, committed to leading the life of the libertarian youth in motion. Although few of us would be so eager to adapt (Murray broke his leg on a hiking trip with a band of anarcho-hippies), we admired the good intentions.

We had some artistic champions in our midst. Morris Edelson, the misanthropic editor of the literary magazine *Quixote* (he used to staple dirty socks into an occasional issue, to be placed in choice little magazine collections of libraries around the country), was an impressario of magnum proportions, producing Dylan Thomas's *Under Milkwood,* sponsoring poetry readings, and making a nuisance of himself through the Nude Theater (parody of the official New Theater). Broom Street Theater rose like a phoenix from the ashes of the old avant-garde, with productions ranging from *Lysistrata* to adaptations of Kurt Vonnegut. More important to *Radical America* intimates, Cleveland poet d.a. levy, idol of the underground press, came to town in 1968 and stayed a month. He had been arrested for reading his poetry aloud in Cleveland, a *cause célèbre* whose legal case brought in Allen Ginsburg to testify in the defense of levy and poetry. And here he sat, a little guy with a Jewish background and Tantric Buddhist training, a radical who cared nothing for politics but who wrote denunciations of war, police narcotics squads, and the existing civilization. As levy put it in a widely admired poem:

AMERICA WAKE UP!
GOD DOESN'T WANT YOU TO
KILL HIS ANGELS
if you knew the price you will pay
for this
WAR ECONOMY   NATION OF DEATH
STOP THE KARMIC MURDER PIE   NOW

for the innocent & pure of heart
i am raising the flags/a warning of storms
Be Prepared to GO HOME LAMBS

there is no reason to play with death
this is not your country
when i smelled love burning/i cried
& now i smell the Angel of Death

go home lambs

you are trying to build
a temple in a graveyard
YOU/have years to plan, my days are numbered

LAUGH at my fears & ignore my love
yet love & fear are the only wings to move on

when you have visited your own death
every day is the last
　　　　GO HOME LAMBS
let yr children be born in the sun
"this country is insane"
　　　　GO HOME LAMBS
in the world of the spirit one does not
lose what he has gained.[2]

Levy asked me to let him do some clerical work for *Radical America,* and I complied with a mountain of pages to be folded and stapled into issues—enough for a bus ticket back to Cleveland. After a few weeks there, in November 1968, he blew his brains out. I received a postcard shortly before he died, with the message "Thoughts travel like a little bird."

Levy had a continuing spiritual presence in Madison, not least because he had stayed over (and dropped acid) with Dave Wagner, my own poetry mentor and future collaborator. Poetry editor of *Connections* and comparative literature student, Wagner brought Goethe, German opera, Nietzsche, and Tantric Buddhism all to bear on the explosion in ephemeral poetry of those days. Little mimeographed magazines carried hitherto unknown but vitally and utterly nonacademic contributors, "meat poets," who (to quote Wagner's comment on levy) left "the word 'poetry' shuffling around in embarrassment like a disappointed kid who can't go along on a dangerous trip." Not surprisingly, they found their way into *Radical America* back pages, with Wagner's selections and introductions. Along with them came black poets Sonia Sanchez and Etheridge Knight, recruited by Dan Georgakas, a Greek-American activist from Detroit. Also Georgakas's friend, Margaret Randall, co-editor of *El Corno Emplumado* in Mexico City and subsequently a major American propagandist for revolutionary Cuba and Nicaragua (still later, the defendant in a major civil liberties case); and Diane DiPrima, goddess of the beat generation reborn as friend of the student rebellions and a personal ally to *Radical America*. Another rich soup.

One element of the traditional avant-garde, surrealism, also touched *Radical America,* but in a characteristically new way. Marginalized in its French homeland by the middle 1960s, the movement experienced an unlikely revival around Chicago's Lincoln Park where Franklin Rosemont, poet and son of a prominent typographical unionist and of a former local radio personality, gathered enthusiasts. In the 1950s, Chicago seemed closer to Madison because Madisonians so needed the

2. "Rectal Eye Vision #8—part 1," *Stone Sarcophagus,* edited by Paul Buhle and Dave Wagner and published by *Radical America* in Madison, 1970.

big city. By the late 1960s, Madison had become a cultural entity unto itself (perhaps Chicago had also grown a little grimmer). Things moved the other way; the Rosemonts came up now and then to plant a few seeds. Dogmatic and schismatic, but also intellectually far ranging and good-humored, they opened a Chicago Surrealist Show in the exhibition area of the Madison Book Co-op, a center for intellectually curious local radicalism. Soon a group of Goldberg students took an issue of *Connections* in hand, renamed it *Tartuffles,* and stuffed it with surrealist documents. The issue was curiously illustrated: Harvey Goldberg occupied two large pages, waving his arms, a veritable surrealist personification. Rosemont considered this experiment "rather confused." Nevertheless, like the popularity of levy's poems among undergraduates, it showed a cultural yearning.[3]

The Rosemonts had a special contribution to make to *Radical America,* by way of verifying our own historic–cultural experience. Franklin Rosemont apotheosized Donald Duck, the Blues, fantasist Charles Fort, and horrifier H. P. Lovecraft, along with those more distant American precursors of the fantastic, Ambrose Bierce and Charles Brockden Brown, and he preached the surrealist enthusiasm for silent-film comedy. In so doing, he helped set a mental process in motion. Mosse's deeply affecting lectures on the avant-garde origins crystalized the sense (which Mosse, admittedly, shared little) that the gap between militant modernism and varieties of contemporary culture might be crossed. With Rosemont's help, we turned to recuperate childhood joys and, despite Rosemont's pessimism on this point, to find analogies in the campus culture's dreams and ideals.

"Culture," considered in still another way, cross-cut the neo-avant-garde. Through E. P. Thompson's *Making of the English Working Class* (1963), some history graduate students, belaboring their dissertations, began putting forward a cultural vindication of working-class life. This impulse had an eminently practical side to it. If undergraduates could have voted in a binding referendum on the war, peace would have arrived the day after. Beyond teach-ins, demonstrations, educational agitation, and downright riots, what remained? The search for allies stopped with the ghettoes only for those who imagined themselves an advanced column of the unstoppable Third World international revolution.

So, class. Jim O'Brien and a half-dozen other graduate students compiled, through a year or so of study groups, a bulky volume of commentaries on every important historical source for working class studies. This characteristic graduate student effort framed the empirical side of the radical *rapprochement* with blue collar themes. The other side was more philosophic. The mediation could be personified in George Rawick, who had gone on from his Madison days to study with C. Wright Mills and thence to Detroit, where he joined a group oddly prescient of New Left moods. Followers of C. L. R. James—the West Indian-born historian, cricket journalist, and political revolutionary—had translated sections of Marx's

---

3. I am grateful for a letter–manuscript from Franklin Rosemont on the subject of surrealism and Madison.

1884 Economic–Philosophical Manuscripts in the 1940s to expose a hidden core of Marxism wilfully forgotten in East and West. This radical humanism James (following Hegel and the young Marx) described as "self-activity," emancipation not through some privileged leadership but by the masses moving on their own initiatives. When James devotee Rawick helped from Detroit to edit a special issue of *Radical America* on "The Working Class and Culture," he delivered another element of the unique late 1960s synthesis while renewing the bonds of different Madison generations.

James, Rawick, and a handful of co-thinkers anticipated many of the New Left's other particular analyses. Unions had long since turned miserably bureaucratic. The Soviet Union paraded a pseudo-Marxist ideology to justify state despotism. What remained alive from the Marxist heritage could be utilized best to appreciate revolts on both sides of the Iron Curtain—in Hungary, in Paris of '68, in Watts, California, and in the innumerable sites of wildcat strikes, student uprisings, and anti-institutional mobilizations. If previous reformist and revolutionary forms had been swallowed up, turned against their followers by renascent class society, then new socialist institutions would have to be defined *in action*. However romantic such a perspective may seem in retrospect, it had the virtue of avoiding the Mills–Marcuse pessimism about the powers of infinite manipulation, and it helped explain the unique forms assumed by the Parisian worker–student coalition, the League of Revolutionary Black Workers in Detroit, and, for that matter, Madison's *ad hoc* organizing committees forged in moments of high crisis. By refusing to read the bureaucratic present into the past as an inevitable development, by insisting on the discovery of sharp contradictions at every crucial stage of modern social evolution, James and his comrades gave fresh logic to historical study as the discipline of would-be revolutionary activists. We, who had stumbled toward history and often doubted the political value of our work, found here a needed verification.

James himself offered a working model of a subtle cultural history and its generally unperceived significance. As cricket historian, he analyzed the way masses of ordinary people had taken over a gentlemanly game and made it their own, largely through the untutored expression of their playful instincts. His younger followers described an almost similar process in contemporary American factories where discipline had slipped, and assembly-line operatives briefly turned their wage labor into raucous games.[4] These heuristic observations stood near the emerging historical studies that described the symbols immigrants to America had adopted to unify themselves against their oppressors. We grasped the implications more clearly because of the cultural watchwords resonating through the New Left. James had also written a fine book on Herman Melville and essays on West Indian novelists and Calypso musicians. All this made another seemingly simple but in those

---

4. See my biography of James *C.L.R. James: The Artist as Revolutionary* (London, 1988); and James's unforgettable history of cricket, *Beyond a Boundary* (London, 1963).

times really startling point: Marxism could adopt culture without becoming vulgar, like the communist cartoons of the big-muscled worker; or aesthete, like the *Partisan Review*'s modernist defense of high culture. We could make a different choice ourselves.

We certainly tried. The first Madison issue of *Radical America* proclaimed, "Most of all, we believe in shattering forever the walls between the 'activist' and 'intellectual' members of the New Left." The sheer bibliographical character of much activity showed an eager generosity to share sources and raise the common level of discussion—to effect a living culture beyond the old stereotypes. The process of producing *Radical America,* especially in the early days, was an extension of this unpretentious logic. I'd pick up ten or so boxes of paper from a local wholesale paper dealer, haul them in two trips of my Volkswagen to Hank Haslach, who would print the issue at cost (with a few sidelong grumbles about "workers' control"). Then I would have around 50,000 sheets of paper to be collated, folded, and stapled. I'd bring beer to a favorite meeting spot, and we'd hope to get the covers on right by the time we had tippled our way through a few hours. The finished copies went into mailing bags for bulk shipments or manila envelopes for subs, or into my attic (raided by FBI agents a year after my Madison exit) for temporary storage. To produce a magazine in this fashion, bimonthly, for the growing intellectual section of SDS was, in retrospect, slightly ludicrous. (*Studies on the Left* began with enough seed money for commerical typesetting and printing, and graduated to subsidy from an editor–financier—luxuries we never enjoyed.) But the process imparted a certain practicality and philosophy. Later on, a band of anarchists in Detroit printed the issues and gathered the assorted nonsectarians of the local Left to collate the signatures. This seemed to me Madison at one step removed.

We rather expected our notion of culture to be formalized along the way. Study classes on Adorno's just-released *Prisms* ran concurrent with classes on American foreign policy, German visitors leading discussions of the first as older graduate students did the second. Mosse had forced on us the corpus of the pre-Hitler avant-garde, futurism, dadaism, surrealism, *Metropolis,* and *The Cabinet of Dr. Caligari.* Arguments about Marcuse's erotic optimism and historic pessimism floated over the Student Union cafeteria and terrace. Nothing could ever be settled. Perhaps Guy Debord's *Society of the Spectacle,* its first U.S. edition published as a *Radical America* issue in 1970, best reflected our own thinking: Consumerism threatened finally to become such a seamless web that it would implode upon itself.[5] Martin

5. It is amusing to read in Colin MacCabe's "Forward" to Gayatri Chakrovorty Spivak, *In Other Worlds: Essays in Cultural Politics* (London, 1987) that the Situationist project reached the U.S. only in the 1970s, via readings of Derrida by the American academic intelligentsia. *Society of the Spectacle,* the basic text (and *Radical America* issue), was translated in Detroit by the same anarchists, led (although he would never admit to the concept of anarchistic leadership) by Fredy Perlman, who also served as leader of the printshop for *Radical America.* Far from unknown to political activists, Situationist materials were widely studied, debated and sharply criticized by *Radical America* readers and others. They *re-emerged,* it is true, in the depoliticized environment of "theoretical practice." But that's another story.

Sklar, factotum of *Studies on the Left* in past years, spelled out in a *Radical America* issue his optimistic conclusion that the proletarianization of the intellectuals and intellectualization of the proletariat would make this process of what he called "disaccumulation"—creation of false consumer needs and formation of a vast service sector—apparent to all. The "Spectacle" would become plain, and because plain, also vulnerable.

The widening of the Vietnam war and the rebellious student response appeared to foreshadow a vast coming to consciousness, if only because any other possibility seemed to us intolerable. Like the anticipation of a wider working-class response, it was a categorical imperative. Perhaps, I think now, we saw the writing on the wall for our generation. Dave Wagner wrote the introduction to the little collection of d.a. levy's poetry that *Radical America* published, saying in part:

> Right now a lot of people can't understand how . . . the poetry of the future [will] come out of poems which are written far enough back in the mind to criticize the situation of the human being in the universe. . . .
>
> Maybe the future can't arrive without a vision big enough to demand that the entire condition of life be ransacked for information—from the spirit to the belly—to find out how large a criticism the "correct" one must be to destroy what is now hateful and to make room for what will be complete.
>
> If we are in the last place it is possible to go in a dying, strung-out culture, no matter how hard we try to imagine the new one it will be impossible to see until it is won. These are the bones, this is the last look around.

We imagined ourselves on the lip of changes in life and thought more sweeping than anyone had proposed since the surrealists argued that true communism would abolish the distinction between sleeping and waking states. The dreams about a new international community of activists and intellectuals, the expectation of SDS kids being brought, step by step, into a sophisticated worldview, the firm belief that we would fit a missing piece into the class movements and past and future—all these were swept along in an insurgent atmosphere so intoxicating that we hardly understood what had happened until the mood faded. Perhaps, despite the passing years and all the subsequent discussion, we still do not know.

I recall approaching 1970 with fear and determination. National SDS had cracked in Chicago the previous summer, and all but dissolved as a functioning movement. In my exhausting work with *Radical America,* I had stopped attending SDS meetings, but I observed from a distance the same frustration that had led to the debacle elsewhere: the inability to make anything organizationally coherent from the continuing upsurge of student antiwar sentiment; and the racial pattern of political repression that threw the undeniably privileged white middle-class revolutionaries into a paroxysm of guilt. Spontaneity had taken its toll when the necessity for strategic response to protracted crises became apparent. One yearned for a few years of consolidation, reflection, development of new concepts to relate the volatility of students, blacks, Chicanos, or others to the problems of organization and leadership. But yearning did no good. Our race had been run. Subscription renewals fell precipitously in the final months of 1969; printing arrangements in Madison disintegrated; and a trial issue, farmed out to a Buffalo group of youth culture enthusiasts, barely came back in one piece. Things had fallen apart.

Still, we had the determination to send love letters into the future—or, differently put, to create monuments to analysis and sensibility at a time when both seemed to have dissipated entirely. As post–New Left gangs hurled rocks through State Street windows, we were throwing monographs at an intellectually keen audience around the country. Ironically, the full impact of our Madison influences now came to bear.

We also set out on a last, grand, Madisonian gesture. Pulling together a group of determined graduate students around our circles, we produced a summary of where radical history had traveled in the United States and what new directions it had recently taken. From Charles Beard, the shadow over Madisonian history, to the *Students on the Left* historians now emerging in the mainstream, to our own insurgent generation, we stood as an unrecognized tradition in American society. An introduction to this special issue of *Radical America,* drafted by Jim O'Brien, summed up the honest aspirations and self-doubts we felt:

> Our attitude toward the historical profession is one of ambivalence. The most important positive feature we see is that, through imposition of fairly rigorous standards of evidence, the profession has helped to produce a great mass of historical writings which, although they may often ask trivial questions, nevertheless provide data that is [*sic*] generally reliable. . . .
>
> On the negative side, the profession seems to us a bad combination of a gentlemen's clubhouse and a bureaucracy. A gentlemen's clubhouse not simply because there are scarcely any women (not a single female history professor at Wisconsin, for example, among sixty members of the faculty), but also because of its upper-class tone that is carried over from the days when history was written principally by wealthy men of leisure. . . . It is an unhealthy atmosphere.
>
> The profession is also guilty of a certain social irresponsibility. It operates for the most part on two levels: dry monographs, usually accessible only to other historians (although certainly historians have a better record in this regard than do social scientists), on the one hand, and patriotic textbooks, written in a manner that is very careful not to disturb anyone's comfortable notions about the status quo, on the other. The political activism of radical historians is frowned upon, but at the same time the slanting of history in textbooks is accepted as standard practice, necessary in order to get the texts accepted.

> We regard methodology as the key to radical history, a fact that has too often been blurred in discussions of the subject. Radical historians have been no exception to the general rule that the level of historical theory in the U.S. has been extremely low. . . .
>
> We find Marxism the most useful starting point, while recognizing that American Marxist history has not generally been of a high calibre and also that (as our own attempts at research and writing have shown) there are no magic methodological formulas that serve to make the job of writing history an easy one. Marxism seems most useful because it seems capable of absorbing the greatest variety of insights without getting hopelessly mired in complexity.

It would be difficult to find a more generic radical rejection of existing mainstream history, a rejection that did not, however, identify the real goals of historical study as in any way unworthy. Here the Madisonian once again insists on a more rigorous standard than the university has established. On the other hand, Marxism is seen as a means and not an end; the Old Left fixation on alternative accepted truths lies shattered beneath the demands of the scholar. Perhaps our predecessor, Herbert Gutman, put the matter best, that Marxism raised interesting questions even if one no longer had any confidence in absolute answers. We looked to moral commitment and to study, to discovery and fresh interpretation, as the ultimate bottom line.

How could we realize our personal destinies, not merely as radical scholars but as actors in the world? The same introduction admitted to "great uncertainty about our own political functioning as radical historians." A decade or so later, only three of the eight collaborating graduate students remained within academy walls. Union educators, archivists of feminist collections, historic-minded supporters of Latin American and other causes, oral historians—this was the fate of the deinstitutionalized generation. As *Radical America* itself represented a whole straitum of radicalized younger professors, graduates, and undergraduates grappling with methodology while they undertook the struggles of society, so the outward-bound scholar–activists unknowingly stood for a new kind of radical historian in America.

Many pitfalls lay in the path of the further development and ultimate self-consciousness of this historian. The experiences of 1970–1971 in Madison propelled an exodus to parts unknown. The Teaching Assistants Association strike and the ferocity of student resistance against the American invasion of Cambodia nurtured hopes that the rebellion remained at large. Perhaps we might later have taken pride in what Lenin described as the willingness to be the last to call retreat and definitively close the political cycle. Actually, the large disappointments and petty frustrations devastated personalities, broke apart marriages and political institutions that had taken years to build, and left many talented intellectuals with a feeling of utter rootlessness.

Because Madison offered such a richness of learning and camaraderie, it ill prepared its faithful children for an outside chill far worse than the chills of the Wisconsin winter. The graduates of the 1950s and early 1960s had better foreseen their fate and had flowed for the most part automatically into categories society had established for intellectuals. We had to carve out some new status, without the collectivity to share our miseries and our understanding.

We did manage. The underground cartoonist R. Crumb observed in 1977 that if our generation had utterly lost the European sense of craft, we retained the American genius for adaptation. One tribute to Madison's tensile strength must be the survival of *Radical America,* the oldest and one of the few Left journals born in the 1960s carrying on with the same commitments it had in its early days. As the *Village Voice* writer Paul Berman has remarked, the magazine spawned a five-foot shelf of labor and community history. Its former editors joined eagerly in new experiments, from the *Radical History Review* and *Cultural Correspondence* to U.S. versions of the British "History Workshop" efforts. Any compilation of the resulting historical forums, the women's and labor history public presentations, the obscure lectures and booklets created for immediate use, would be futile. One image remains in my mind: a New York radical historians' conference on "Culture" in 1976, bringing together a crowd of perhaps five hundred students and ex-students, professors and ex-professors. I looked around at the sea of faces: a diorama of Madison generations from all the eras covered in this book. However long since they had returned from Madison—or been impelled by Madison life toward New York City—, whatever their particular origins, they shared a fascination with the intersection of history, radicalism, and culture. They were Madisonians, like me.

24 New Left Intellectuals/ New Left Politics

GEORGE MOSSE

While compiling a remarkable record of scholarly productivity and creative influence on historical studies, not in one but several areas—the Reformation, modern European intellectual history, Nazism, the whole field of myth and symbol in modern politics and popular culture, Jewish history, and most recently, the history of sexuality—George Mosse has been one of America's great university teachers. The list of students who have received doctoral degrees under his direction and who have gone on to publish and teach is massive and impressive. Paul Grendler and David Sabean in Renaissance and Reformation studies, and Seymour Drescher, Richard Soloway, Robert Soucy, Albert Kelly, Michael Ledeen, Robert Pois, Beth Lewis, Robert Nye, Paul Breines, Paul Lachance, Tim Keck, Sterling Fishman, David Gross, Anson Rabinbach, and Steven Aschheim in modern Europe, are among the "Mosseans." An instructive sketch of George Mosse's role as a historian, including a survey of some of his major writings, is available in Seymour Drescher, David Sabean, and Allan Sharlin, "George Mosse and Political Symbolism," in *Political Symbolism in Modern Europe,* ed. Drescher, Sabean, and Sharlin (New Brunswick, N.J., 1982), 1–15. See, in the same volume (pp. 275–284), Sterling Fishman's "GLM: An Appreciation," for an account of Mosse the teacher.

It is possible, as far as I have observed, to distinguish three stages of Madison radicalism from the late 1950s to the early 1970s. The way they were formed and the directions they took were perhaps typical for radical American students in this period. The choices were different from those of the European student movement.

The Madison movement first centered on the Wisconsin Socialist Club and the journal *Studies on the Left*. These students were attracted both to the European radical tradition and to the American Populism expressed by William Appleman Williams. The second stage, which began around the time of the 1967 Dow [Chemical] riots, was a time of mindlessly violent activism, and I say "mindless" because it completely lacked a theory of movement-building worthy of the name. This second-phase leadership showed little carryover from the first stage. As the 1960s ended, a third phase began. Its activism was nonviolent. But it, too, continued to break with theory. This third period coincides with the organization of the Teaching Assistants Association (TAA) on the Madison campus.

The first-stage student radicals lacked confidence in the American heritage of radical thought; this is why they had to resort to the European tradition. And this, too, is in part why the European students involvement with theory survived the peak activist years (1967–1968) and carried over for a time into, for example, the Nanterre and Berlin university reforms.

First Stage

Graduate students, mostly in the Department of History, formed *Studies on the Left* in 1959. This period was essentially closed by the protest riots against the Dow recruiters in 1967. The student movement in these years went back and forth between Bill Williams's Populism and the European Left heritage. Williams, born in Iowa, had his strongest effect on the *Studies* group, many of whom where Jewish and from the East Coast. All these students sought a big dose of theory.

But American history apparently proved too arid for most of them. Its method has been positivistic, stuck in detail, with few stimulating syntheses. Those that existed weren't in the radical tradition. But Bill Williams was. This is what drew students to him. He became, for them, the great breakthrough in the field of American history. But he didn't fully satisfy students; although Williams knew European as well as American thought, the students wanted to sample and discuss a variety of theories for social change. That's what brought them to European intellectual history, which grew to have the largest enrollment in the department.

Williams published *The Great Evasion* about the shirking of Marxism in the United States, and yet Williams himself learned not so much from Marx as from American Populism. *The Great Evasion* is a very American book. He wrote it around a seminar we gave together. When, later, I asked students why on earth they were not reading *The Great Evasion* instead of Herbert Marcuse's books, they replied that Williams did not give them the kind of theory into which they so much wanted to fit the American situation.

They had this hunger for theory, and the only theory that answered their needs was European. Williams's democratic vistas should have appealed mightily, but the radical students were in love with the philosophy of history of Marx, and with a sort of Kantian moral imperative that meant to be politically active while harmonizing means and ends. Williams could not satisfy this "Marxism of the heart."

And when the Dow riots era began, he was, I think, turned off by the student movement.

After *Studies* left, and *Radical America* appeared, Paul Buhle tried to resurrect a native American radicalism. A valuable debate over the European versus American orientation was carried on by Buhle and Paul Breines. The American student movement didn't gain much from the study of American history, although it gained from the history of its activism.

It may seem I am biased in favor of the European heritage; I'm really not. I thought, and still think, that Williams is much more applicable to the American situation than was Marcuse, although Marcuse became the "hot name" representing the European radical thought around the mid 1960s. Marcuse, you know, understood very little about the United States. I remember a comparison he once wrote of Lyndon Johnson with [Frederick] Ebert, the first president of the Weimar Republic. When someone does that, it proves he doesn't know what America is about. I felt from the beginning that Marcuse was not applicable. You can't make a revolution based on a foreign tradition.

The first generation of the Madison student movement was not numerous, and Williams's function was to bring the students into the American context, which didn't work very well. In sum, European intellectual theory most strongly contributed to forming this phase of the New Left in Madison—and as quickly contributed to its decline when it didn't "take" well enough to provide confidence and direction during the next stage.

Second Stage

The riots against job recruiters from Dow Chemical marked a sharp turn away from the intellectualism of the first stage. Earlier student leaders were left behind. I also observed this stage of violent confrontations in Paris and Berlin; there, a similar rupture between theory and leadership did not occur. Although Europe, too, became quite violent in these years, the concern for goals and processes was not forgotten by the student leadership. And, oddly enough, in my view, the earlier period's intellectual quality had actually been *higher* in Madison than in Europe. That ended in 1967–1968. The Europeans were at home with their intellectual tradition, and they carried it forward. In contrast, enrollments in American history departments dropped more than 40 percent by the late 1970s.

Why did the first-stage radicals vanish after the Dow riots? If they attended the riots at all, it was as spectators or followers, not as leaders. Let me say it this way. Whatever was read or known by the Dow riot leaders, and however erudite they may have appeared, they simply threw out a spark. It ignited the transition from thinking to mindless activity. Certainly the Dow riots responded to the war, but they were a terrible mistake. I'm not the only one to think so. At that point, many former leaders tried to call the Madison movement back to a foundation in radical theory. If it was not to be back to Populism or Marxism, at least back to

Lenin's principles of organization! But not even that happened. One of the Dow leaders may not have known much of the European radical tradition; he was mainly interested in sports and their history. But another leader did know the European background. I think these people might even agree with the way I have assessed their effect. The riots they created were futile and silly because they couldn't be won. Revolutionary conditions were not at hand. Social institutions were all intact and healthy. Governor Warren Knowles quite correctly said that the students couldn't fight the state of Wisconsin; at least not in that way. Some argued that violence was the necessary and sufficient way to raise revolutionary consciousness. But the later integration of those students into the bourgeois society has disproved the blow-of-a-nightstick pipe dream for consciousness raising. A misunderstood anarchism may have fostered that illusion. It did not derive from Marxism. The Army Math explosion and similar things were not outgrowths of the American Populist tradition or the European radical heritage. In fact, it's intriguing that the most violent of the rioters were very often from small Wisconsin towns. The two brothers who led the Army Math bombing, which killed a research assistant working late and led to the wiping out of the Madison movement, were home-town Madison boys.

The American Populist movement was one of labor and farmer activism, but it either shunned violence or did not depend on it. And when American Populism arrived at violence, it was organized and accountable violence.

Third Stage

Several years after the Dow riots began, some efforts at institution building came along. These included the Teaching Assistants Association (TAA), the food co-ops, and the like. There was a leadership that was not the riot leadership. But these leaders also weren't theoretically inclined.

The TAA can be an example. It followed, and follows, rather clear trade union aims and methods. But this borrowing from American trade union experience also seems to me unmediated by theory; it lacked radicalism even in the Populists' meaning. Concerns that were almost ethical imperatives for the pre-1967 radicals are missing. Such rather conventional goals as featherbedding to keep jobs for union members have been substituted. It focused on special-interest pleading, not the broad democratic values of the earlier movement. And many of the younger teaching assistants are denied chances to get income and experience. But don't mistake me: The TAA sought in part what many of us on the faculty always wanted— smaller classes and an end to exploitation of teaching assistants. But in allying with the trade union heritage, look what they got: the Teamsters as partners. Surely no one thinks the Teamsters are out to change America either by ideals or theory. But then the TAA got more economic power out of its alliance. It didn't have much theory to balance against that economic advantage, and what little theory was there, was muddled. In the absence of any strong support in Populist or Marxist thought, the TAA accepted the available tactics, goals, and power of the Teamsters.

Conclusions

While the European student movement after 1967–1968 developed a strength and continuity that has seen it through, the American student movement did not. It now looks back to the first stage. What became of the first American stage?

The most important Marxist theoretical journal in the English-speaking world today is probably *Telos,* with its contributors heavily salted with former Madisonians. Perhaps you cannot call it Marxist, however. *New German Critique,* long published from Milwaukee and with a Madison contingent, has the breadth of theory of the first stage.

Radical America moved to Boston, but kept a number of Madison people with it, tilting between European theory and Populism. The socialist newspaper *In These Times,* published from Chicago, has old Madison editorship.

Notice, in all these survivals of the European radical tradition in America, that they have taken a social democratic direction. Many of the writers are now professors. Most of them gave up revolution long ago, even in the Marcusean sense. They were not activists even in the beginning. They were Marxist of the heart, Kantianizing Marxists with ethical imperatives. They reject violent tactics as such. They'd like intellectuals to make a revolution bloodlessly, in their own image: with love substituted for hatred, as Staughton Lynd once remarked.

Far be it from me to announce in favor of Lenin's principles of organization as the American answer. Surely not. I talk from the point of view of an observer. But the well-intentioned followers of the European radical heritage did not realize the need for clarity in goals and tactics! Successful revolutions in Europe have been few, in recent centuries; and of those made by intellectuals, only one had a brief moment of power, Munich in 1918. It was put down rather easily. The revolution that succeeds must combine theory and practice. The Jacobins in France and Lenin in Russia had well-defined theories about the countries they wanted to take over and how to gain them. Revolution without that kind of theory is daydreaming.

Why do intellectuals have such a hard time understanding the goals, rituals, and symbols that, when clarified and applied, make social change possible? It is no different today from 1967, or from the time of those French and Russian events. Clear goals, expressed through easily understood symbols and controlled movements of people, and with powerful oratory—this is what changes a crowd into a movement with aims and continuity. Theory may be simplified for popular understanding; much tactical compromise will undoubtedly be necessary. To redeem all these elements from weakening the movement, its theory must be vital and fundamental.

The American intellectuals who teach and put out magazines about social change are basically readers. Often they are not visually oriented enough to appreciate the need of popular, compelling symbols to convey values and information. They may have no grasp of popular images as a clear language to translate Marx or Marcuse or other theory into compelling symbols. In the past, workers' plays, art, and festivals, however simply done, were very important; so too were the First of May demonstrations. Only such clarity of goals and popular forces, combined with discussion and refinement of strategy and theory, can assure continuity among the masses. Thus Ferdinand Lassalle was the person most responsible for building a mass socialist movement in Germany—and no one was more visually oriented than Lassalle. In Italy, Mussolini found such a model in [Gabriele] D'Annunzio; and Hilter, the unsuccessful painter, was also visual in his conceptions of politics.

In Madison, perhaps the visit of the San Francisco Mime Troupe, or the torch-light parade to the Wisconsin capitol, or the mass demonstration against Defense Secretary Melvin Laird were a beginning. But in America it all bogs down in speeches, speeches, and speeches. And then perhaps convulsive violence. From this combination, no sucessful mass movement can be created.

Radical intellectuals have been eager to go on television, but they prove woe-fully ignorant of the potential of that medium. In contrast, the late Abbie Hoffman played the TV medium with astounding success—only further emphasizing the failures of others.

Thus, while the older leadership is still around, it has not recovered from its inability, which appeared when the violence mounted. Does this mean that the influence of the European radical tradition in America was a failure? Many, perhaps most, of the first-stage leaders entered academic life, and to a large extent their success or failure must be judged through the influence they have had as teachers, and on their academic discipline. I have a feeling that their contribution to the realm of theory in their respective disciplines is considerable. From their own point of view it may well be ironic that I have to evaluate their success through academic contributions rather than the change in society they wanted. But it grows out of what I have said about theory and practice among the students, and raises once again the problem of the relationship of intellectuals to revolution.

One final word: The first stage was a terribly exciting period from the point of view of teaching. The students read a great deal, they took their history seriously, and they were eager for intellectual discussion. I have never witnessed their kind of intellectual excitement on campus before or since.

Part Four
Our Teachers

25 Harvey Goldberg

RON McCREA AND DAVE WAGNER

The following essay speaks for itself and its subject too well to be characterized in a few words. Ron McCrea, Madison journalist and editor of the strike paper, *Madison Press Connection,* remains in Madison (uniquely among our contributors), and is politically active, in recent years as an aide to Governor Anthony Earle.

Dave Wagner, founding editor of the underground paper *Madison Kaleidoscope* (1970–1972), long-time reporter at the *Capital Times* and a managing editor at the *Press Connection,* has worked in a management capacity in recent years at *Waukesha Freeman,* among other daily newspapers.

In the middle of the night, in the hospital, Harvey Goldberg asked for water. A friend sitting at his bedside gave him a glass. He took a sip from it. Then he sat up, held the glass to his chest, and said in a clear voice, "and he died ecstatically, with a cup in his hand."

It seemed like the fragment of a lecture. Perhaps it was a waking dream. In any case, the reference seemed obvious. Harvey was thinking about Socrates, the greatest teacher of them all. For thousands of students, and many nonstudents as well, Harvey Goldberg was the greatest teacher in their lives.

■■

By the time he died of liver cancer on May 20, 1988, at age sixty-five, Goldberg had been an institution on the Madison campus for twenty-five years. Although he published comparatively little—his anthology, *American Radicals* (1957), and his in narrative *Life of Jean Jaures* (1962) were his only books—Goldberg engaged in continual, massive research from French archives for use in his courses. He was

241

one of the most popular lecturers on campus, drawing as many as seven hundred students and casual auditors for each performance—a term we use respectfully.

Like his writings, Goldberg's lectures were highly condensed narratives based on meticulously detailed research, but they were above all narratives. In a sense, Goldberg was a storyteller whose scholarship was poured into his genius for the spoken word on the lecture stage. Although his lectures were designed to persuade, they were not polemical, at least not in the material (i.e., in the *history*). He felt so comfortable with the overall validity and comprehensiveness of his basically Marxist approach that he could fearlessly confront any and all contrary interpretations. In short, he was virtually never doctrinaire. Instead, the shape of events in the largest sense, the impulse of the powerless toward freedom, informed his lectures and held generations of students spellbound.

That tradition started early. In 1963, Goldberg began his lecture career at Madison in a comparatively small room that sat fewer than a hundred students. By the second semester of that year, he had been given a large lecture hall. Eventually, his largest audiences had to be accommodated in the vast auditorium of the Agriculture Building on the western fringe of the campus.

Goldberg told one of his earliest graduate students that for a number of years he did not receive a merit pay raise from the university, which in any case always seemed ambivalent toward its star lecturer. Fellow historian Fred Harvey Harrington, president of the university during most of the years of protest against the war in Vietnam, more than once had to intervene to defend Goldberg from the fulminations of State Senator Gordon Roseleip, the most recent in a long tradition of Wisconsin political figures who proved (to their own satisfaction) "Red subversion" in the seat of learning. Meanwhile, Goldberg had become a virtual capital asset to the History Department. Even the conservative section of the department took note that Goldberg employed no less than 50 percent of the teaching assistants and that some 10 percent of all history majors were enrolled in one or another of his courses. As he once understandably boasted, he was responsible for half the History Department's budget!

He also turned out forty-nine Ph.D.s in French social history, personally creating a "Wisconsin School" in that field. Unlike the young scholars around William Appleman Williams or George Mosse, Goldberg's protégés remained fanatically dedicated to empirical research and far reaching in their choice of subjects. If a common moralistic strain could be detected in their studies, it was suffused with a passion for the accumulation of facts, as though facts were the chosen weapon of sincerity. Unlike Marcuseans, who provided elegantly described studies of repressive tolerance, Goldberg would remark more directly on the freedom on choice in, say, the selection of books at the official university bookstore, "I don't call it freedom when you put truth next to lies." If the larger curve of history in his lectures pointed in one direction, the specific task of his graduate students was concrete (although it must be added that he frequently used these students to fight his ideological battles with the French Left and that he did comparatively little to help them advance their scholarship through careers). Goldberg wanted a "step-by-step history of the French Left in its various manifestations from the early twentieth century to the near-present," in the words of a former student, Ed Rice-Maximin.

This is not to say that Goldberg's view of historiography remained static. He kept abreast of current trends in French scholarship, from political studies of the French Left to various aspects of colonial politics; he assigned his graduate students tasks in quantitative history as that discipline emerged, and he encouraged papers in labor history and even local history in the form of working-class, women's, or immigrant studies. Although he never joined a Left party (indeed, he steered clear in particular of the revolutionary Leninist grouplets, Trotskyist or Maoist) or exposed himself to legislative and more remote threats by signing petitions, he was probably closest intellectually to the Movement Social group in Paris. There was a sense throughout his work that he was most interested in selecting historical battles in which he could dramatize a *gauchiste* position, somewhere to the left of the French Communist party; in particular, he looked to individuals who had urged the seizing of revolutionary opportunities that the communists had ignored, repressed, or blundered. His major allies in French history—Jean Chesnaeaux, Madeleine Reberioux, Daniel Hemery, and George Bouderel, among others—had nearly all been members of the French Communist party, highly critical of its colonial policies in particular.

■ ■

As a person, as a stage performer, Goldberg played the role of the famous lecturer and militant *gauchiste* to the very hilt. One sometimes had the sense of Goldberg's perception that a certain posturing in daily life could enhance his political authority and the drama of his delivery in the lecture hall. He could be difficult or devoted in his friendships, attentive, standoffish, or downright cold, depending on mood and circumstances. He was probably never happier than when he could find, at a dinner party, a new audience whose attention he could capture and dominate with his inexhaustible store of precisely turned anecdotes. Physically, he was an unimposing man—small, scrawny to the point of being cadaverous, with a bony face and a shock of hair that never seemed to have permanent arrangement. Up close, Goldberg was all animation, elfish, with a droll smile and a pair of eyebrows that sent out a semaphore of confidential signals when he was amused or appalled.

He was absolutely bohemian, in an old-fashioned sense that almost seemed to vanish into the mass counterculture of the 1960s. Goldberg used to say, "I work in Madison but I live in Paris." And it was in Paris—he maintained an apartment in the *marais*—where he felt he could be more open about his affections, which were quietly but very affirmatively and affectionately gay.

(Although his homosexuality remained very much a private part of his life, especially in Madison, Goldberg did strike one occasion to make a defiant declaration. Rice-Maximin recalls a moment when a court had enjoined a teachers' union from striking somewhere in Wisconsin, on the same day in which a gay film was banned on the Madison campus. Harvey observed in class: "When teachers are not allowed to strike, that's obscene. And as for homosexual films, there's not a movie producer in the world who has either the money or the courage to reproduce my fantasies.")

A rabbi's grandson and a native of Orange, New Jersey, Goldberg did his undergraduate and graduate work at Madison in the early 1940s and began his teaching career at Oberlin College (one of his favorite undergraduate students there had been George Rawick). After three years at Oberlin, he moved to Ohio State University, where he taught until 1963, the year Harrington brought him back to Wisconsin. And that was where his teaching style flowered. An extended tour of Asia and the Middle East in 1962–1963 had, meanwhile, broadened his world perspective greatly and became the basis for his sometimes massively popular Contemporary Societies course.

No one who witnessed his lectures could forget the drama. How he waited in the wings. How he approached the podium and waited for a few beats. How he took off his glasses, looked off to the side of the stage, as if expecting a cue, and then turned to the audience, himself changed, grown larger than life, waving his finger and declaring, "The point is, you know."

The noted musician, music scholar, and former Goldberg student Ben Sidran likened this performance to jazz. "When he was onstage, he was transformed by the process and the information. That's what his relationship with jazz was about, the transformation. He would see jazz musicians become transformed when they played."

Goldberg knew exactly what he was doing. He called it "the authentic artistry of teaching," and he labored at it. One could not visit him for hours before or after a lecture. He prepared as a concert pianist does, "spending long hours weaving each lecture into a coherent tapestry, replete with precise and relevant details but emerging as a lucid, clearly delinated composition," according to notes he wrote shortly before his death.

These notes, an example of the exquisite self-consciousness of the scholar as artist (in this case), were written in the third person and were designed to be incorporated into a newspaper article memorializing his passing, and written of course by someone else. For Goldberg, typically and endearingly, the historical biography that begins with an obituary is to be dramatized from the wings. Nothing is to be left to chance; no interpretation may be entrusted to others on the historical occasion of the passing of the great pedagogue. "Harvey knew why he made that strenuous effort day after day for forty years," he wrote of himself. "Because he had no greater goal than to rouse the historical consciousness of those many students. In Harvey's view, it wasn't historical consciousness without a cause, but rather a contribution of the relevant past to the understanding of the crises of the present, and to forging choices for the future." His fundamental aim, he noted, had been to convey "the sense that history must destroy passivity because the present is so frequently considered to be 'eternal and unchanging.'"

Those were the last remarks for public consumption. Privately, Goldberg wrote in a final letter to a friend:

> I have no last words and never will. I am a dialectician. My analyses, interpretations, passions spring from the horrendous events of the hour, and are a response to them. I have no universals, except the moral criteria which inform all of my views. And in no way do I propose to abstract my moral imperatives. . . . Those who have heard me over the years, and those many others who have been told about what I say, surely understand those moral imperatives which are at the source of so much rage and uncontrolled compassion.
>
> But dammit, prophet, guru? Whenever I have heard such ludicrous words applied to me, I have disintegrated them with a withering look. . . . I have always been a worker in the vineyards, but able frequently to raise my head high and shout to the others: "Resist; this way; neither compromise nor pause."

26 The Mosse Milieu

PAUL BREINES

Paul Breines was chair of the University of Wisconsin Socialist Club in 1962–1963 and a member of the Ad-Hoc Committee for Thinking (ACT) in 1966–1967. He presently teaches modern European intellectual history at Boston College and is working on a book *Without Impact: Ideas Whose Time Never Came.*

You have probably heard the joke that asks how many people from Madison it takes to put in a light bulb, the reply being, five, one to put in the bulb and four to tell what it was like in the 1960s. If not, now you have, and I mention it because, having already written two recollections of my experiences in Madison in the great, crazy decade, I am conscious of being one of the light-blub installers who tells.[1] And I am wary of reifying or simply polluting the memories with yet another retelling. When this volume was in an earlier stage, my contribution took the form of an interview carried out several or more years ago. With an eye to polishing it, at Paul Buhle's prompting, I was immediately embarrassed and irritated to the point of shuddering on reading what struck me as boring, pompous, and unreflective stuff. Needless to add, the challenge of producing something interesting, plain, honest, and reflective is daunting, so I've set my sights on something in between.

---

1. "Germans, Journals, and Jews/Madison, Men, Marxism, and Mosse: A Tale of Jewish-Leftist Identity Confusion in America," in *Germans and Jews Since the Holocaust,* ed. Anson Rabinback and Jack Zipes (New York, 1986), 146–170; "With George Mosse in the 1960s," in *Political Symbolism in Modern Europe,* ed. Seymour Drescher, David Sabean, and Allen Sharlin (New Brunswick, N.J., 1982), 285–299.

Toward this end, I've also, in effect, taken seriously the light-bulb joke in still another way by making the proliferation of retellings part of what I retell here. Specifically, I want to talk about three matters raised in my earlier essays that I've had to think about somewhat differently than I did then because of things some Madison friends have said about what I wrote.

The first matter centers on a small episode involving Martin Sklar, a marvelously creative thinker and, in spite of being a very private person who never sought a following, a Marxist cult figure in the Madison Left in the early 1960s. To underline the unique intellectual ambience of the Madison Left at that time, the excitement about theory and the importance of developing it was, I told in one of my essays, what struck me as a representative story. In the summer following my sophomore year (1961), I had decided to join the Freedom Rides in Mississippi. At a party to wish me well and send me off, I was especially honored by the presence of Marty Sklar—not only because of his renown in our small circle but because one element in this renown was his tendency to shun leftist occasions. The crux of the story, as I recalled and retold it, is that he took me aside at one point to suggest that it might be more worthwhile to remain in Madison to read, study, and engage in intellectual work.

When I happened to meet Marty Sklar in the early 1980s, he had read what I had written and took the opportunity to tell me what the episode of twenty years earlier had meant to him. His point, he observed, had not been to counterpose thought and activism, underlining the former's priority in his—and, as I had wanted to show, in Madison's—scheme of things. He had instead, wanted to communicate the different and, in retrospect, much more interesting point that, as a young participant in the Left, I should consider whether I was being pressured into the Freedom Ride—pressured in the sense of doing it because I thought it was what the comrades or the community wanted; or because I thought I had to prove myself in this way to be a real part of the Left. Sklar had wanted, as he reconstructed it, to give me the space to think about this and, if necessary, to feel all right about not joining the Freedom Rides.

In any case, the now expanded story interests me because if he did indeed make the point he later said he had made, I was completely deaf to it. Had he not spoken clearly enough? Had I so internalized the pressures to which he had referred that I *could not* hear his point, later transforming it into the more superficial one about the Madison Left's intellectual cast? Or was I right about what Marty had said, and did he later reconstruct it in the way that he did?

What now seems to me most interesting is that, while I have no recollection about feeling the sort of pressure to which he referred in *that* instance in 1961, and for all I know I may have said so to him at the time, I could have in principle and surely did experience it, and I know we all did, on numerous occasions throughout the decade. Now, such pressure is not always bad (manipulative, tyranny of the majority, potentially quite dangerous and destructive). It can often be the source of a fruitful, mutually educating sort of tension between an individual and her or his community, through which one really works out what one thinks and wants.

On the other hand, the point that Marty Sklar said he had made, and the role he said he had played, now seem to me the really vital ones. For the space to work out those tensions is rarely, if ever, simply there. On the contrary, political and other sorts of oppositional communities and subcultures tend not to create them—the best of such communities tend to cancel such spaces. It is up to the participants in those subcultures who understand this dilemma to bring it to the attention of the participants who do not.

I don't want to be histrionic here. The psychological dynamics of the Madison Left in the early 1960s bore little resemblance to those portrayed by Dostoyevsky in *The Possessed*. After all, I had chosen to join the Freedom Rides; I'd not been required to murder a comrade as proof of my revolutionary dedication. On the other hand, Marty Sklar's insight looks prescient in the context of the experiences of both mass militance and ultrarevolutionary sects in the late 1960s and early 1970s. Already, in 1966–1967, in the wake of the Madison police riot at the Dow Chemical demonstration at the Commerce Building, the movement was taking on the momentum that made it necessary for one to muster real courage to present anything but the most militant proposal. If, all along the way, no one assumes the position Sklar did, the results, when they are not worse, will without fail be the sort of personal bitterness and disillusionment at having been manipulated that one noticed often by the mid 1970s.

A second and related reconsideration—it concerns the issue I thought I had raised in the Sklar story, namely, the importance of ideas and books in the Madison Left—stems from a recent conversation with two other friends from the Madison early 1960s, Dan Kalb and Freddy Ciporen. (The occasion was a midireunion of roommates from 1961–1962. The fourth, Don Bluestone, was unable to make it.)[2] We talked, of course, about Madison, in particular about the film *The War at Home,* a documentary of the Madison antiwar movement culminating in the bombing of the campus Math Research Center by several movement people in 1971. Freddy appears in the film's early parts.

He was animatedly critical of the film, which, he argued, presents the misleading impression that students in Madison, much like students elsewhere at the time, were radicalized by terrible events and militant responsive actions. Not only does the film privilege activism; it ignores and thus, in effect, suppresses the role

---

2. Danny Kalb, a precocious young Marxist and a stunning blues guitarist, took the Madison Left by storm in the early 1960s. His musical renown was already sufficient to have drawn a then unknown Bob Dylan to town for a couple of weeks of jamming. Danny was the lead singer in the Blues Project later in the decade, and currently lives in Oakland, performing with the Danny Kalb Trio. Fred Ciporen was a forceful critic of dogmatic Leftisms, a genuinely great story teller, and occasional stand-up comedian. He is now the editor of *Library Journal.* Donald Bluestone was the organizer of the Madison chapter of SANE (Committee for a Sane Nuclear Policy), the convener of famed New Year's Eve parties, and later a member of the History Department at SUNY, Old Westbury.

of books, ideas, and teachers within the Madison Left. I found myself agreeing, not least because I had tried to say as much in the articles I had written (in which Freddy also appears), though his remarks brought to my attention the extent to which I had fudged the issue he was raising by writing that Madison had had both activists and theorists and that I was speaking only of the latter. Freddy's point addressed, on the one hand, the tensions and oppositions between them, and on the other, the extent to which today's students have little sense of the New Left as an intellectual phenomenon, effort, and experience.

This got the three of us into discussions of our teachers, particularly George Mosse, who had formed part of a great triumvirate of influences on the student Left consisting of himself, William Appleman Williams, and the late Harvey Goldberg, with Hans Gerth making it into a quartet, though I myself had very little contact with Gerth. Mosse was crucial, Freddy was contending, because, like Gerth, he was not on the Left but cared greatly about it; because, like Williams, he was skeptical of confrontational actions, but was consistently and polemically engaged with students whose moral outrage propelled them into action; and because, like Harvey Goldberg, Mosse was a great performer at the lectern—their courses drawing well over five hundred students in the late 1960s. For Harvey Goldberg's romantic Marxism, George Mosse had little patience, but for the romantic Marxists in Madison he was a constant and critical presence. He warned us, Freddy said; and he was right about everything, which was more a statement of mood than of fact.

But he *seems*, at least to some of us, to have been right about almost everything. Needless to say, Mosse did not influence his students in a vacuum. We were prepared to believe him. Yet even when we disagreed with him most vehemently, he was the one who transmitted the key values, images, and secrets with which we tried to form ourselves as a certain kind of leftist intellectual.

This may not have been Mosse's intention. Active in the reform wing of the Wisconsin Democratic party, Mosse appeared a political liberal, and like many such academics at the time, he possessed the prerequisites for standing fast against radicalism. But it was the specificity of George Mosse's person and career with which he responded, in critical sympathy and rare intellectual engagement, to the emergent student Left of the 1960s. His lectures became, as the decade progressed, part of the dramaturgy of the student movement. His lectures were more often than not directed *against* the Left—which meant that he took us seriously and that he had little patience with the claim that teaching must be neutral, devoid of values.

As a public figure, it could be said that George Mosse, though never *on* the Left, as were his colleagues Goldberg and Williams, was nevertheless linked to us because he was consistently, if polemically, *present for* the Left. He was there, not only to debate and challenge—which he did with gusto—but also to share. To share in what? In camaraderie. George Mosse's deeper, if more narrow, links to the Left developed through his private rather than his public figure; through friendships with leftist colleagues and students. This historian of ideologies, who has unrelentingly stressed their primacy in history, has lived according to the assumption of their weakness in personal life.

It can be said, then, that Mosse, in his own way, contributed greatly to the tradition of "Marxism of the heart" (a phrase popularized by C. Wright Mills in *The Marxists*). He has done so not only as a teacher but through his scholarship: studies of Nazism, racism, the politics of mass dramaturgy, and the challenge of humanistic socialism. His studies point to two vital tasks facing the humanistic socialism to which he has been closer than he reveals: intensive study of the history of popular culture as the soil from which modern mass movements have sprung; and investigation of the symbols, images, and fantasies adequate to a movement for change that is at once massive and humane. As remote as such a quest might appear to be now, I believe it stems directly from George Mosse's historical work, and that if you were to press the point, he would finally admit it.

The third of the reappraisals and retellings of the Madison stories is the most dense and difficult. The central thread in the articles I had written was the Jewish one. As I presented things, the real yeast in the whole scene had been the New York Jewish students in Madison who, for example, had provided me, as a young, suburban, assimilated, and sometimes self-hating Jew, with a new sense of place, belonging, identity. I confess to having taken a certain pleasure in talking openly about this obvious but rarely discussed dimension, though it also seemed to me real and important.

The responses of a number of friends who are not Jews has, however, affected me greatly. As one of them put it poignantly and pointedly several years ago: "After reading your essay, 'I felt left out.'" Since it was obvious, he didn't need to add: like a Jew. I felt hollow. Just as I had been oblivious to the sort of cruel impact my essays could have in this connection, I think my friends don't quite know the extent to which their comments have jostled me from the "little Jewish groove" in which I so cheerfully located myself at the end of one of the essays. And how much it has propelled me back to the real crux and hope of the Madison Left scene: its rootless cosmopolitanism; that is, its conviction regarding the primacy of solidarity and loyalty based on friendship and shared ideals rather than on blood and soil.

My daughter is currently an undergraduate student at the University of Wisconsin. She has created for herself a space that is fruitfully independent of her parents' 1960s New Leftism—she is a Democratic party activist and a sorority member. In 1987, my high school age son and I visited her. On the Saturday night of our stay, my daughter and her roomates took us party-hopping through some half-dozen Greek bashes on Langdon Street—fraternity and sorority row. The combination of many beers, memories, and parental emotions put me in a particularly sentimental state. I managed to keep my overall balance by regaling our little entourage with stories of the old Anti-Military Balls and how fraternities and sororities had virtually vanished from the campus by the early 1970s, supplanted by a mass radicalism. Keenly moved by one particular scene, I took my daughter aside and remarked, gesturing at the curious abundance of tie-dyed T-shirts, peace symbols, sandals, kerchiefs and headbands, boys dancing with boys, girls with girls, and everyone with everyone else in circles, with much Motown, Stones, and Beatles, Rap, and Reggae in the background: "It's amazing, the '60s aren't dead after all. And this is a *fraternity* party. God, Madison is the greatest." I felt tears coming in both eyes.

"Da*aa*d," my daughter moaned, smiling at her mushy old man, "this is a '60s theme party!"

27 The Tragedy of Hans Gerth

ELEANOR HAKIM

Eleanor Hakim, who died in 1981, has been described here as a tragic figure, like that of her friend and philosophical guide Hans Gerth. It is worth spelling out one implication not quite drawn in the previous essays, that by her role in *Studies on the Left,* she became, however uncomfortable she would have been cast in such a role, an outstanding woman intellectual of the New Left. In her discomfort with her contemporary colleagues, and despite her unwillingness to join movements, she was also a pioneer of women's liberation.

If Socrates had accepted Crito's offer and had escaped into exile in Thessaly, would it have been like going into the hinterlands of the American Midwest? Certainly, one cannot carry too far such a Mannheimian analogy between Periclean Athens and the Weimar Republic as to the idealization of intellectual community and its subsequent deterioration. Surely too, what perhaps most characterizes these later days of Western civilization is, precisely, that we survive the bitter cup of hemlock—itself sipped in small doses over the years by which we build up a kind of immunity.

Now, in place of the hemlock cup, the tribute cup, to commemorate, albeit with a pensive sense of irony, the fact that, these days, one survives one's initial exile and perhaps even comes to rest in what might yet prove to be hallowed ground.

My recollections of Hans Gerth during the period that I knew him—the early 1960s in Madison, Wisconsin—are in the nature of witness bearing. To convey the sense of these encounters in exile requires some sketch of the environment we shared and the events of those days: the cracking of the academic hermeticism that had been imposed on, and adopted by, the university system during the McCarthyite 1950s; the first idealistic days of the student civil rights movement; the emergence of a New Left; the independent publication by graduate students of *Studies on the Left (A Journal of Research, Social Theory and Review)*.

Yet my most trenchant perceptions of Gerth were only obliquely in relation to these phenomena. More immediate, and perhaps more telling, are certain remembrances of Gerth practicing the Socratic strategies of daily survival. For our most chance encounters took on the aura of *exempla,* which is to say: One can never really take time out of being an exile. The University of Wisconsin in the late 1950s and early 1960s was hardly a Socratic "marketplace of ideas," despite the motto, proclaimed on a bronze plaque on Bascom Hill, of commitment to the search for truth through "sifting and winnowing" in what was perhaps another "marketplace of ideas." That was indeed what was wrong: a pragmatic, American gold-panning approach to the search for specialized nuggets of cash-convertible truths. It has little in common with Socratic irony and dialectic in quest of illuminating overviews.

What the handful of graduate students I knew there had in common with one another, and with Gerth, was the wryly mocking use of the term "sifting and winnowing" as a code reference to our despair on finding ourselves, darkly spirited Tonio Krogers, mostly from New York City, in an alien land of the dairy-fed "blond and blue-eyed." We realized soon enough that we were the aliens—exiles in an American cultural Siberia, imported under false pretenses to a supposed university oasis.

We had come to the University of Wisconsin in quest of a tradition of American radical thought and stimulating intellectual activity, only to realize that Wisconsin was the state not only of early Progressivism but also of latter-day McCarthyism, and that, even if the university had managed to maintain its formal integrity against these witch-hunt incursions, it had done so at the expense of original and radical inquiry. The civilized fortress had survived its barbaric siege by means of an upright liberal adherence to academic "sifting and winnowing." The radical tradition we had come in search of was not waiting there for us. It was dormant; rather to our surprise, we found that it was we who had brought the quickening spark from afar to that frozen soil at the moment of the post-McCarthy thaw.

We were psychic exiles, spiritual orphans, twice removed; for neither had we felt at home in the environs from which we had come. None of us typically American. The fact that we valued ideas and learning, no less than that we were idealistic enough to believe that it had something to do with the state of our souls, was proof enough of our being displaced persons, aside from the more biographical fact that we were either foreign-born or first-generation American children of minority-group immigrants.

And then there was Gerth. We were aware of being in the presence of a prophet preaching in the wilderness because it was our wilderness. For those of us who knew and revered him, he was more than a teacher; he was a personification of modern sociocultural history—an exile mentor figure with whom we could identify. We did not perhaps fully recognize the extent to which Gerth might have identified with us. For we were somewhat in awe, and strongly aware of the points of difference: He had at least come from somewhere; presumably, then, he had somewhere to which he might return, if only in spirit, some place that might eventually claim him. For him, the return of the wanderer would be sufficient to make hallowed the ground.

He bore the mark of having been directly touched by a mass upheaval in history; we had only received its reverberations from a distance. Still, without having passed through the trial, we bore the verdict of our isolation. Though we had never lived in our Weimar, we nevertheless pertained to the outcasts. The sense of intellectual tradition we carried with us we had somehow salvaged from our intuition, from some sort of psychic cultural memory that had never been grounded in actual experience.

We were still searching for our Weimar, but we sensed that for us there remained only the pale shadow of such an ideal universe and that it was now part and parcel of the banal: The Socratic marketplace had been appropriated in a corporate merger with consumer society. Also, we more than half suspected that this "sifting and winnowing" graduate school wilderness was likely to be the closest we would ever get to our Weimar, and that despite our outrage and our resistance, the academic environment would eventually make gold-panners of most of us in turn.

In contrast, Gerth would ever retain the idealism of youth simply because he could not be otherwise. He had lost his Weimar at the height of youthful engagement in life when one is at the same time proud and humble, expecting all with a stance of believing in nothing, in a universe where every act of the mind is a transcendent unifying gesture and the only sin is compromise with the banal. For this, we identified with him.

Gerth's universe had been vividly fixed in time by a drastic coup of history. Although it had robbed him of everything, it had somehow left him essentially intact. It had become a guarantee of his purity. Gerth could never be caught in the banal; he would ever transform it into a higher signification by means of his fundamentally cohesive ethos—a *weltanschauung* that the upstanding citizens of the state would ever consider dangerously out of joint. For this, we felt a tender protectiveness toward him. But we also had the feeling that he was a living reproach to us. For which of us would dare to risk a similar purity at the price of a similar sacrifice? For this, we felt toward Gerth a sense of shame.

Unlike my friends, who, for the most part, were graduate students in history and sociology, I had never been a student of Hans Gerth. Although I had heard much about him from these friends, I myself, as a graduate student in English literature, was once removed and thus had not sought Gerth out as a counterbalance to the humiliations of the "gray flannel suit" organization-man mentality that characterized graduate school at the time. Yet, even from afar, I felt strongly akin to Gerth.

This sense of kinship deepened all the more as I came to realize that the English Department's favorable reputation was at least twenty years out of date; intellectual passion was at best superfluous and at worst a handicap in the pursuit of narrowly conceived scholarship; the study of English literature was, at that time, specifically removed from sociocultural perspectives; and, for example, teaching assistants of Freshman Composition were under strict orders not to touch on subjects in any way relating to "sex, religion, or politics."

My own approach to literature and to life was interdisciplinary, theoretical, and sociocultural. I was in search of my own methodology, in search of connection with multidimensional reality, in search of that Socratic marketplace of the "poets, philosophers, and creative thinkers" who, as one Milton scholar had told me, significantly, "should not have to be bothered with traditional scholarship," which I had reason to believe also meant that neither ought they to be bothered by expectations of receiving fellowships, teaching assistantships, or degrees admitting them into the hermetically sealed ranks of English literature.

I left graduate school in 1960 and got involved in the civil rights movement at its inception—Madison, Wisconsin, having been the first northern student community to respond to the southern black students' call for solidarity with their sit-ins. These first months of activity were highly communal and spontaneous. Idealistic and high-spirited, students alternated the stuffy, overheated, and overprotected classrooms on Bascom Hill with the freezing, windy, exposed streets around the Capitol Square—sharing gloves, scarves, coffee, and abuse as they astounded the local populace with picket lines in front of Woolworth's, Kresge's, Green's. Thus the line of demarcation between town and campus, the academy and the sociopolitical world, had been breached. The initial reponse of "sifting and winnowing" *in loco parentis* university officials was one of chagrin. Gerth, however, had no hesitation; he was one of the first professors to endorse us publicly.

Participation in these early days of the civil rights movement consisted in harmonious coordination and a remarkable lack of rhetoric. Instead of the usual leading and following or mouthing of received formulations and politcal lines, the emphasis was on taking our cues from the southern black students and acting in supportive concert with them. Thus the tone established in these first early days pertained in spirit to an earlier American tradition of independent ethical radicalism, and even to philosophic anarchism: that is, more to the spirit of Thoreau than to Marxist–Leninism, though each was little read at that time.

Most of the white students who got involved at the outset were undergraduates who were not from urban left-wing or Left-liberal family backgrounds. Those students who were from such backgrounds took a good bit longer to get over the trauma of the 1950s, as did their parents. On the whole these students had inherited little from their parents in the way of specific theory. Indeed, ideological rhetoric was the enemy; instead, they acted to recapture the ideal intent of a double mandate, in rebellion against the bad faith and paralysis of a parental generation that had become comfortably middle class and cautious since their own student activist days in the 1930s.

For those who did come from more traditional, European-oriented left-wing backgrounds of Stalinism and Trotskyism were trying to free themselves of outworn ideologies, were trying to reach out to indigenous alternatives, and thus could be said to have been also going through a period of radicalization as to rediscovering home-grown traditions, perceptions, and solutions. These two strands came together in what became known as the New Left.

Hence, traditional older left-wingers, who had made previous appropriation of the term "radical" so that it applied to little but the factional ideologizing of Stalinism, Trotskyism, or their offshoots, were both confused and indignant, declaring that this new, independent civil rights movement lacked "ideology" and "direction." If this was their diagnosis, they also had a remedy. While genuinely looking to make contact with a home-grown American radical tradition that, paradoxically, their own ideology had earlier helped to smother, and while genuinely admiring the freshness, energy, and idealistic perspective of this new upsurge, they made modest proposal of themselves as heirs to the only theoretical tradition that could provide what they considered to be the necessary ideological shaping and political channeling.

For the most part, the left-wing graduate students who, in 1959, had founded *Studies on the Left* at first dismissed the civil rights movement as "bourgeois"; after all, they reasoned, since the blacks sitting in at Woolworth lunch counters were college students, it meant that they were middle class and not the workers or share croppers of revolutionary prediction. By the same token, my own outlook and commitment were dismissed as "independent" and "existentialist"; it was considered a mark against me that I didn't come from a traditional left-wing family background.

Some months later, these same reasons for exclusion became reasons for inclusion. They had come to realize that the student civil rights movement had to do with something more than cups of coffee, that it represented some sort of upheaval, though they couldn't say what. So now they were inviting me to join the editiorial board of their journal because I was a link to this new radical spirit, because I was "existentialist," "independent," and not of Stalinist background—while they went about New Left-izing themselves.

"Radical" became the self-descriptive term chosen, at that time, by those who did not consider themselves bound by the prescriptions of traditional left-wing ideologies. Indeed, only a few years earlier, independent thinkers who were outraged by social, political, and economic injustices had no such term by which to differentiate themselves and, hence, no space in which to enact their concerns in the political arena without being recruited by the Stalinist or Trotskyist camps (or their splinter groups) that dominated the public sphere of non-main-line politics.

The term "radical" was thus embraced in an entymological sense by those who wanted to get at the root of critical analysis of social and political realities; one short-lived journal of this period was in fact titled *Root & Branch*. The perspective, then, was from a left-wing but nonparochial angle of vision, one that was also concerned with rediscovering an indigenous American radical tradition dating back to John Jay Chapman and Henry David Thoreau, and up through the American anarchist, Progressive, and socialist movements, but with an emphasis on seeking new analyses of contemporary situations. The indigenous American civil rights movement provided such an opportunity for the radicalization of thought, such a wedge for active political engagement.

The term "New Left," in these early days, pertained, then, to two sets of connotations: (1) the new ethical radicalism of an outraged belief in American democratic principles that opened the 1960s with the civil rights movement and then extended itself to other domestic issues and finally to nondomestic issues, particularly those connected with what later came to be known as Third World independence and guerrilla movements—most notably the Castroist revolution in Cuba, which served as a pivot to later involvement in the anti-war-in-Vietnam movement; (2) the somewhat belated regrouping of primarily Stalinist-oriented left-wingers after the Khrushchev revelations and the suppression of the Hungarian revolt, which, in England, produced the merging of the university-oriented *New Reasoner* and *Left Review* into the *New Left Review*.

Thus the terms "radical" and "New Left" gained currency; their variant connotations tending to flow together and intermingle. As such, they were promulgated in *Studies on the Left,* although *Studies* neither specifically grew out of the new student movement nor, unlike its British counterpart the *New Left Review,* out of any previous publications, nor was it connected with any network of New Left clubs, much as some of the editors might have so wished.

The majority of the editors and associates of *Studies on the Left* were graduate students in American history. Although many had taken sociology courses with Gerth, few had what might be considered a European intellectual perspective. That is to say, they were not so passionate about ideas relating to culture and civilization as such as they were about applying ideas to political analysis, tactics, and ideological theorizing. There was a certain lack of overview; *weltanschauung* remained for them a rather nineteenth-century-sounding German word.

In the days prior to and including the initial publication of the journal, the editors had consulted with Gerth, gaining much knowledge and encouragement from him, and strengthening their first two issues in 1959 and early 1960 by publishing his essay "The Relevance of History to the Sociological Ethos" (with Saul Landau), and his translation (with Don Martindale) for the first publication in English of Walter Benjamin's "The Work of Art in the Epoch of Mechanical Reproduction." As time passed, however, except for an *in memoriam* piece on C. Wright Mills in 1962, they came to call on Gerth less and less, as the emphasis of the journal shifted from intellectual radicalism to a pragmatic radicalism for which intellectual analysis became something of an expedient. Put another way, it might be said that the journal shifted focus and readership—particularly from the late 1960 third, "Cuba issue" onward—projecting itself less toward a community of intellectually radical peers than toward a more politically radical readership.

This shift was possible because, from its inception, the journal implicitly embodied three contradictory tendencies: (1) a somewhat defensive attempt to prove that left-wingers could be good scholars from their own left-wing perspectives, and to make such scholarship as academically accreditable as that found in the accepted professional journals (*i.e.,* exemplifying the desire to gain equal standing and acceptance in the dominant society's marketplace of ideas); (2) a desire to analyze primarily American history and politics in the light of current realities and to update and develop left-wing theories that would provide a springboard for rallying direct involvement in politics (*i.e.,* placing radical scholarship at the service of radical politics); (3) a commitment to radical socio-cultural and historical analysis and clarification in and of themselves, in contradistinction to traditional radical politics (*i.e.,* emphasizing the illumination of consciousness as a cultural *politique*).

Despite *Studies'* ambivalence and ultimate lack of success in creating that ideal community of radical scholars, it did make a contribution toward "revisionist" scholarship in both left-wing and academic circles, especially with regard to updating the view of the United States as a corporate society. Also, it participated, for better and for worse, in that revitalizing breakthrough of the 1960s by which scholarship interacted with historical reality and liaison was made between sociopolitical causes of concern among dissident elements in the groves of academe and in society at large, throughout which such concerns became disseminated. On the other hand, it forfeited its claim to reinforcing the remnants of an American intelligentsia; instead, it helped pave the way for the overwhelming of that embattled minority by the newly created wave of a semieducated "intellectual" mass movement. For in reneging on the task of attempting to create a new intellectual and cultural *politique* from which to act, and in succumbing to the easy allurements of the power of political expediency, it failed to stand against that half-formed, *demi*-intellectual's scorn for the intellectual's outsider role and commitment to subtle and complex analyses. Thus did it contribute to the sowing of the seeds of an anti-intellectual nihilism among the student class.

Perhaps the change from privatism, interiority, political frustration, and apathy of the 1950s—with its false academic "objectivity"— to the political activism and social "subjectivity" of the 1960s—with its easy revolutionary poses—was too rapid, transpired in too short a time, to permit radical intellectuals to find their medium of expression and of action in the world *as* intellectuals. Perhaps too, they had little foundation or motivation to do so, preferring instead the neat certainties of nihilism—once the previous neat certainties of old-line left-wing politics and ideology had been discredited.

For the early 1960s had been a period of extremely sudden renewed sociopolitical concern and activity—to which one such as Gerth had responded with a renewed intellectual vigor. Ultimately, however, the promise went unrealized. Neither the times nor *Studies on the Left*'s participation in them foretold a transplanted resurrection of an ideal Weimar. Or perhaps it was closer than we cared to acknowledge to the loss of center of the later days of the Weimar period.

However, there was a telling difference. European intellectuals had come to know the deadliness of the political power game and that what kept one an intellectual rather than a technician in service of power was precisely one's ethical gadfly perspective of ironic distantiation and the ability to hear the laugher of the gods. They also knew that there was no easy solution to the problem of how to be a force of conscience and consciousness and still find a mode of relating to politics and history, while yet not being seduced by the blandishments of power—not even in the form of being driven to politics by the desire to be "on the right side of history"—comes the Day of Reckoning. As for that half-feared, half-longed for urgency of chips-are-down apocalypse—as Gerth, like other World War II German exiles would say: You need not fear the rise of fascism in America; America has Americanism.

But the young American would-be radical intellectuals failed to grasp fully what, for Gerth, was deeply engrained in the European radical stance to which they aspired: To uphold the values of conscience and consciousness requires a measure of isolation and a disavowal of power as such—in contrast to identifying with power, even if it be by way of acting as what C. Wright Mills termed a "countervailing force," all too literally conceived.

This yearning on the part of American would-be radicals to touch and be touched—no matter how—by history, that great Recording Angel, might be said to result from there being so meager a tradition of consequentially taking one's measure against the status quo. To be sure, America has had its expatriates, but rarely its exiles, either internal or external; instead, what the United States of America produces are Prodigal Sons.

Mills was very much a case in point, illustrating this frustrated feeling of disease about being an intellectual—this reaction against the susceptibility toward feeling impotence and loss of faith in the processes of maintaining and promulgating an awareness in relation to a sense of values, this attraction to the pull of the world of actual political applications and public manipulations, this lack of the sense of the gadfly role of an intellectual and of all the entailed risks of isolation, this wishing for acceptance, reward, and even access to power and hero worship for supposedly unpopular ideas, this trying to have things both ways. Socrates perhaps knew better when he made his distinction between the spirit and the letter of the law.

When, in its early days, *Studies on the Left* had solicited endorsement from members of the academic community, Mills—unlike Gerth, who had given his backing and had been a mentor from the outset—was suspicious of the journal's possible "Stalinism" and refused to be listed as a sponsor. Later, after he had published his cajoling, propagandistic *Listen, Yankee* and *Studies* its partisan "Cuba issue" at the close of 1960—which greatly expanded its readership, especially

among undergraduates, at the point when a student movement seemed to be getting under way—Mills, wanting very much then to be "with it," asked to be listed
not simply as a sponsor but as an associate.

In this, Mills perhaps missed a subtle point that had never been lost on Gerth:
the measure to which "Stalinism" is rooted in the intelligentsia's negation of its
role as conscience and as conscious cultural link precisely at moments of upheaval;
that its very identification with revolutionary power helps further polarize society
and create the very power vacuum that permits the rise of dictatorship.

Thus, Mills, who had been in Cuba at a key turning point in its revolutionary
consciousness with regard to the break in U.S.–Cuba relations, contributed little
to an analysis of that sociocultural process by which a population arrives at revolutionary transformations of consciousness; no more of how popular mass movements may be manipulated toward specific political ends, nor of how revolutionary
euphoria may be utilized toward bringing about the atomization of that very population and society, nor of how dictatorship may be reinstated, albeit of the Left
and in the name of "the people." Instead, in *Listen, Yankee*, Mills chose to write
a drugstore pamphlet of political apologia, contriving to merge his voice with a
naive composite first-person voice of the "typical" Cuban, respectfully requesting
a fair understanding from his Uncle Sam.

Infected by the image of the Cuban "intellectual" turned guerrilla, and of
the guerrillas coming to power—no doubt an equivalent of the image, so wryly
amusing to Gerth, of the North American intellectual turned revolutionary cowboy—the educated sons of the would-be revolution were essentially no different
from their fathers; they became hucksters of the revolution, public relations men
rather than analysts. Nor were they, finally, much different in their yearnings for
power from the academic technicians who swore feal service to Kennedy's Camelot.
In short: The Philosopher cannot be King. Socrates understood this: Plato did not.

My first encounter with Gerth occurred when he walked into the new storefront office of *Studies on the Left*, speaking about how disconcerted he was by
Mills's recently published second book of popularization, *The Marxists*. Gerth
spoke more in sorrow than in anger. But I knew, and came to understand even
more poignantly, how deeply ran the sorrow.

Gerth, by this time, after his resuscitating second marriage, seemed to have
largely recovered from the sense of betrayal he'd felt after his split with Mills—
except for one thing: He could never again quite give his trust to entering upon a
collaboration with a promising young graduate student. Thus his own productivity
as to finished work published in English had been severely impaired. He who had
sought the communication of intellectual brotherhood had received instead the
disavowal of the Prodigal Son. Yet what sorrowed him most about Mills now was
that the Prodigal Son was denying the standards of even his own intellectual capacity. It was this that distressed Gerth so deeply.

At first, I thought that Gerth was speaking to me randomly simply because

I happened to be the only person in the *Studies* office. I did not think that he knew who I was—though the clearly visible fact of my being a woman, no longer a graduate student, no less one in sociology, indicated little risk that I might prove to be a Prodigal Son.

Soon enough, he turned his conversation to the essays I had published in *Studies* in 1961 and 1962. In my "Brecht: A World Without Achilles" and "A World Without Achilles Re-Visited," I had taken issue, to some extent polemically, with Eric Bentley's and Martin Esslin's interpretations of Brecht, with regard to what I considered to be their out-of-context appropriation of his work at the expense of a distortion of his complex worldview and the environment in which it had been formulated. My own approach was neither Marxist nor academic nor political in any traditional sense. Instead, it was from the perspective of the sociology of culture merged with an attempt to forge an interdisciplinary methodology that interrelated the intuitive, the creative, and the analytical—a methodology I could nowhere find in the academy and that had had much to do with my leaving that sterile, unhallowed ground.

Somehow, I suppose, in the process of writing about Brecht, I had managed in some degree to resurrect Weimarian sensibility, a philosophic overview akin to Karl Mannheim's, and an impassioned concern about the paradoxes of that balancing act of interrelating aesthetic, ethical and sociopolitical commitments. I had manifested a sensibility corresponding to that of European intellectuals whose consciousness had been marked by events of the 1920s and 1930s, though I myself had only just been born in the mid 1930s, in New York City, of nonintellectual parents whose Jewish Polish peasant and Middle Eastern Sephardic *déclassé* aristocracy backgrounds had more or less canceled each other out, leaving me free to make sense of the world in my own way and to claim nonterritorial universals in piecing together my own heritage. No doubt, such a background of extremes meeting in a collapsing vacuum was in some way analogous to Gerth's Weimar experience.

Gerth's first seeking me out, then, had to do with my being someone who shared his psychic worldview, if not his actual experience, and with my being an editor of *Studies on the Left.* We talked. I listened a great deal. I had much to learn from him. When I visited his home on Sundays, the books neatly arranged on the wall-length, floor-to-ceiling bookshelves in the living room would, during the course of an afternoon's conversation, one by one find their way down to illustrate one point or another, until they were heaped all about the room—covering the sofa, rug, coffee table, chairs, and even the piano. And on that piano, which Gerth took such pleasure in playing, stood the popular sheet music of another era: "Was Ist Denn Nicht Kaputt?"

When, in the course of our conversations, Gerth would propose "think pieces" for the journal, I hadn't the heart to tell him that my co-editors were no longer interested in think pieces or speculative essays; that I and a colleague had

had a variety of our proposals for such think pieces rejected by our fellow editors, most particuarly pieces that Gerth might have undertaken or overseen, and that we had been crowned by thorns into the bargain.

Out of my embarrassment for my colleagues as much as my pain for Gerth at their betrayal, I tried, mistakenly perhaps, to shield Gerth from their private disavowal; from knowing the extent to which he had been mockingly declared *passé* by those whom he had so freely and so generously nurtured just a few years earlier, when they thought that they had need of him. I wished, especially for Gerth's sake, that the seeds of his own brilliant germination might have taken deeper root and brought forth a greater visible yield. But, by this time, the student movement was under way; a stake in leadership having developed, radical intellectual commitment to ideas had devolved to a surface expediency; the seeds of intellectual nihilism and the will to power had been sown instead.

The Prodigal Son, *demi*-intellectual, new American Siegfried were in the saddle. Perhaps Gerth knew full well, even then, from whence it came, and where it might be going. Nevertheless, with his characteristically open generosity of mind and spirit, he went on to lend his suport and energies to the burgeoning new student anti-war-in-Vietnam movement. The nihilistic, confrontational student backlash against Gerth and his generation of intellectuals was yet to come to full manifestation. Had he chosen to remain vulnerable? Vulnerability was not a choice for Gerth, but a manner of being, an aspect—the ever implied risk—of his unswerving commitment to conscience and consciousness.

When, early in 1963, a couple of the more powerful editors of *Studies* decided to move the journal to New York (leaving some of its key editors behind in graduate school while attempting to gain greater access to leadership in the broader movement, not limited by a specific academic environment), I split off from it, going my separate way and to the subsequent confrontations that awaited me. For the duration of the 1960s (in addition to teaching in the City University of New York's SEEK Program, which became explosive by the end of the decade), I taught courses in philosophic literature (mostly European) at the New School for Social Research, to which, decades earlier, so many émigrés of the German sociological tradition had migrated, following the collapse of the Weimar Republic.

I can't help but wonder how different our lives—and Gerth's—might have been, had he, on arriving on these shores, settled in New York, to teach, but also to write for the intellectual journals of that earlier period, instead of having been limited largely to the academy in the Midwest. For he was ever more than an *academe* in the narrow sense; instead, he was an intellectual and a journalist in the broadest Europen sense. No doubt his contribution to our intellectual and cultural history would have been substantial; so too, our understanding of the sociology of culture would have been enhanced by the scope of his learning and the penetration of his observation. And his particular talent and need for engagement in the life of the mind brought to bear on the immediacy of unfolding social history would not have been so isolated and isolating an endeavor.

I realize now that those years in the early 1960s during which I knew Gerth at Madison, Wisconsin, were indeed a crucial turning point in American social and political history. It was a brief moment when the issues and possibilities of a renaissance of indigenous American ethical radicalism were enjoined. But we failed to bring it to fruition. We had—and we lost—the opportunity to create that "Third Force" that Europeans such as [Albert] Camus had been seeking during the 1950s with much less possibility of effecting. It flowered briefly in Europe with the "culture of politics" movement, primarily called forth in the late 1960s by the Prague Spring; rose again with the Polish Workers' Solidarity strike movement in 1980; and remains as a strong undercurrent in Eastern Europe, capable of flowing to the West. And there are indications that the reverse flow from Western Europe will occur again, perhaps, as it reclaims its own outlook more positively and independently of the United States, and as it becomes more than a buffer between the superpowers than it was until the beginning of the 1980s.

But in the United States and in Western Europe in the later 1960s and in the 1970s, the potential for a Third Force deviated into a reaction of nihilism and then collapsed. When and if such a force will regroup itself remains, at this moment in time, a moot point. We, who did not, and perhaps could not, hold the line against the tide of nihilism that continues to be a major threat to civilization in this century nonetheless bear some responsibility for this failure, and for how it affected a mentor figure such as Gerth.

Ever a radical in spirit, though a democratic socialist in political orientation, he gave his all to his students of every succeeding generation, thereby leaving himself incredibly open and vulnerable; he was attacked and denounced by the "Maoists" of the student generation that followed ours—both during his last years in Madison in the late 1960s and during his final years back in Germany in the 1970s. Truly a child of his century, Gerth was born into and paid full witness to its many tragic convolutions.

And so it has become painfully clear to me just how much exile is a question of geography. To be an exile in an arid land is to be twicefold alien. It might be thought, ideally, that certain positive gains could result from a voice crying out in the wilderness—the voice more sharply defines itself as well as the contours of that wilderness, for the mutual achievement of heightened conscience and consciousness. In actuality, however, so great is the disparity that the expense of energy and awareness seems exorbitant, as the voice becomes entangled in a slow martyrdom of daily incommunications; and one is able to do little more than transform those simple encounters into symbolic and, most often, ironic victories of continued survival and occasional moments of transcendence.

28 My Life in Madison

WILLIAM A. WILLIAMS

Little more needs to be added to what has been said about William A. Williams except that his books include *The Tragedy of American Diplomacy* (1959); *The Contours of American History* (1961); *The Great Evasion. An Essay on the Contemporary Relevance of Karl Marx and on the Wisdom of Admitting the Heretic into the Dialogue About America's Future* (1964); *The Roots of the Modern American Empire* (1969); *Empire as a Way of Life: An Essay on the Causes and Character of America's Present Predicament Along with a Few Thoughts About an Alternative* (1978); and the textbook collection of documents, *The Shaping of American Diplomacy 1750–1955* (1956), two volumes. He has recently retired from the University of Oregon and continues to contribute to regional journalism.

I was an active member of the Madison community during two periods: (1) from 1947 to 1950, as a graduate student who worked thirty hours a week to supplement the GI Bill; (2) from 1957 to 1968, as a faculty member. In various respects I gave as much to Madison as Madison gave to me. It was a dialectical relationship, in the root sense of that much abused and maligned concept. My experience and assessment of Madison and other communities and social change is best discussed with some understanding of the several periods in my life.

I was born into, and reared for eighteen years within, a network of interlocking communities. These involved two extended families—a strong civil community based on a political economy of agriculture, manufacturing, and commerce, with regular ties to larger urban centers also in the Midwest; and a primary peer group of approximately thirty children that related to similar groups in play, sports, music, and the local educational environment. All of us became familiar with birth, illness, and death in our own and friends' families. All of us knew firsthand the impact—economic and psychological—of the Great Depression. Most of us also worked at some kind of job as a matter of tradition and necessity.

In general, we were children of parents and relatives who had interests and activities outside of what is now termed the nuclear family. I think it is important here to emphasize that very few of us matured in such a family—all had relatives who were in part of our regular life. In addition, all the children in my neighborhood peer group regularly played, informally and in school sports, with children who were richer and poorer than ourselves. I was very fortunate in that I dealt regularly with blacks, Jews, Italians, and farm children. In addition, during my last fifteen months in high school I spent time with Indians and white southerners, and I spent six weeks in New York City. It is further important to understand that most of our parents shared a value system that expected children to exercise their minds and bodies, engage in many kinds of activity, and participate in the community at large on a reciprocal basis. Most parents were also religious in a small *r* sense, Catholic as well as Protestant, and thus approached community as a moral imperative.

There was prejudice in the community, but it did not become racism. There were classes in the community, but they dealt with one another with respect and a surprising measure of social equality. Poor kids could, for example, play golf at the country club; and the one swimming pool was open to everyone.

Most of us felt, as we matured, a familial and community pressure to do our best as individuals. But there was an equal pressure to be a member of the community. To put it bluntly: I learned how to say "no" to myself in the name of the community. Or, in the contemporary idiom, I learned that doing one's own thing was capitalism's most sophisticated form of cooptation.

This may sound a bit euphoric, and I would not want to give the impression that it was all sweetness and light. Yet, on balance, it was a positive and happy childhood and adolescence. I have often thought in the years after World War II, while raising children of my own, that I was fortunate to have been born when and where I was. We had the benefit of a community structure and community feeling.

The next eight years of my life I spent in a military environment. Two years were at Kemper Military School, three were at the U.S. Naval Academy, two at sea, and then one in various navy hospitals. Most American academics, and in particular Left academics, view such experience as wholly negative—or, at best, as time unnecessarily invested in documenting various obvious evils. There is some truth in that judgment. But the attitude behind it reveals an insensitivity to the nature and importance of the dialectical process that is the essence of life and history.

When radicals content themselves with mocking the camaraderie of the American Legion, for example, they miss the far more significant point that such men found their primary, if not only, sense and experience of community in the military. In a similar way, a simple attack on the military for distorting community blinds one to the process through which that distortion occurs. Likewise, the dangers inherent in any effort to create and sustain a community are ignored or discounted. I view the awareness of that dynamic propensity as one of the important benefits of my years in the military.

In addition—and given the particular nature of my experience at Annapolis and at sea—I reemerged as a civilian, in 1947, with a strong sense of these aspects of life that bear on being a radical intellectual, and on community in general: (1) a high value placed on intellectual excellence; (2) an appreciation of the necessity of walking the mile in the other person's shoes; and (3) a visceral awareness of serious illness, injury, and death—of the interdependence of human beings. I discovered that long hospitalization forces one to consider the human condition (and one's own philosophical condition) in a most serious way. It prompts or incites one to use life as creatively as possible.

My experiences in the South during 1945–1946 also informed my years in Madison. The southern city offered a classic example of the interrelationship between large corporations (industrial, agricultural, and energy), the military, a reactionary religious hierarchy, and local businessmen and politicians—all in the context of class, racial, and sexual confrontations between Chicanos, blacks, and whites.

Along with a handful of other Annapolis graduates, and an equally small number of whites from the city itself, I became a political activist in support of the tiny black movement struggling for economic and social justice. It was unquestionably a major experience in my life. It educated me in the strategy and tactics of radical politics, introduced me to the elementary matters of starting an underground newspaper and ringing doorbells, taught me about the nature of social isolation and routine violence involved in such activity, and gave me valuable lessons in learning from (and working with) the poor and the oppressed. I saw how essential it was to break into the white working and middle class for support to effect structural change as opposed to secondary reform.

■ ■

I arrived, then, in Madison in 1947, a highly motivated twenty-six-year-old with several kinds of experience to draw on. I was terribly excited to be entering what was unquestionably the best on-campus History Department in the country. It was, for that matter, probably the best on-campus liberal arts faculty in the nation. Many exceptional teachers/researchers were on hand—in English, economics, sociology, and political science, and even in the law school.

Equally important, the majority of postwar GIs going to school were knowledgeable in the ways of the world and highly motivated. Though it did not regularly take the form of large public demonstrations, the activism of the GI years was nevertheless consequential. As a group, they were outspoken in the classroom and in seminars. They sustained an active dialogue about intellectual, social, and political affairs (e.g., the election of 1948, McCarthyism, and the Korean war). They campaigned effectively for more adult university policies and regulations concerning campus affairs and housing, dealt effectively with local merchants and landlords—and very nearly destroyed the sorority-fraternity system. In the end, I think most GIs decided the fraternity system was so childish as to be beneath their time and trouble. A mistake, no doubt, but surely understandable.

The combination of excellent faculty and alert veterans created an interplay between students and faculty that has been largely forgotten in all the talk about the silent generation of the 1950s and the activism of the 1960s.

In a more personal idiom, I think that my background enabled me to learn from first-rate conversatives, like Paul Knaplund and Paul Farmer in history and Howard Becker in sociology, as well as from radicals, like Hans Gerth in sociology, and liberals, like Harrington, Curti, and Jensen.[1] I do not want to personalize that capacity in the narrow sense. Many other GIs, particularly in graduate school, were also unblinkered by ideology Right or Left. The essential point is that many, many GIs were able to harvest the unusually bountiful intellectual crops that grew in Madison between 1946 and 1951. I cannot fail to add that it is essential for radicals to sustain a tough, honest, and thoughtful dialogue with first-rate conservatives. The failure to do so is one of the grave weaknesses of the New Left, politically as well as intellectually.

I was particularly fortunate, in 1948, in being awarded a scholarship to attend a special seminar in England on labor government economics. On arriving in England, I was then chosen as a delegate to the last international conference of students that included people from Russia and Eastern Europe. Beyond the obvious social and political education, I benefited from a very tough course in traditional and socialist economics (out of which came my first published essay). And I was confronted with the central problems posed by Left liberals and socialists coming to power as caretakers for a capitalist political economy headed for collapse. That

---

1. Paul Knaplund was an austere, tough intellectual who made his deserved reputation as a historian of the British Empire. He was classically "proper" and wholly honest. He liked a good dialogue with first-rate radicals. He gave Harvey Goldberg As, read all my books, and discussed them with great verve and intelligence. He was kind of Madison's John Quincy Adams.

Paul Farmer was a "sport," a "mutant," in the academic world. Truly brilliant in his field of European history, he was in certain ways the only peer of Harvey Goldberg. A very earthy, slightly cyncial conservative, he was not so cynical as to be flippant. He took the life of the mind very seriously and, like Knaplund, enjoyed tough talk with radicals. Indeed, he took the life of the mind so seriously as to be bored with academic life and therefore resigned and made himself a million in investment banking! He gave me a real sense of how important ideas are in the making of history.

Howard Becker was the reactionary counterpart to Hans Gerth in the Sociology Department. He was not as good a reactionary as Knaplund was a conservative, but he did provide a real challenge to a radical. I remember one day in his class, he got so infernally absurd that I just got up and walked out. One of his teaching assistants knew me and gave my name to Becker. (I was taking my Ph.D. minor with Gerth in social psychology.) Becker made it his business to get hold of me over the phone and ask for an explanation. I told him simply that I got bored to death with the nonsense. Give him credit for saying, "I know some of my lectures are pretty routine. You GIs don't mess around, do you?"

experience surly underscored my experiences during the Great Depression and in the South, and posed, at an early date, the question of how one organizes a social movement to change the structure of society.

■ ■

My various intellectual and social experiences between 1950, when I left Madison, and 1957, when I returned to the History Department, were also influential. I learned that tough intellectual standards were effective and consequential with all kinds of students in all parts of the country. I gained additional knowledge about political activity with people of various classes and ideologies.

To put it simply, I came to understand what I had absorbed from Gerth: *First-rate intellectual performance* is essential to creating class *consciousness*—and class consciousness is essential to *changing the structure of society*.

In a related way, I began to have a feeling for what was necessary to define a *prerevolutionary situation*. I add only that it seems to me that most of the New Left lacked any significant appreciation of either point.

■ ■

When I returned to Madison, I was eager—and reasonably well prepared—to be an intellectual and political activist in the academic and the general community, Madison in 1957 offered a number of positive features:

1. The *Progressive tradition* was alive and well. In many respects, it was the intellectual and ideological foundation over which even the conservatives built their politics. But three further things need to be said. First, the Progressive tradition had always been influenced by the Milwaukee *socialist* tradition—and it had been pushed to the Left during the Depression and the subsequent social changes during World War II. Second, it was a *weltanschauung* shared by nonacademics of all classes (rural as well as urban), as well as academics. And, third, it was a tradition anchored in a *social* conception of society rather than an individualistic ethic, and more so in Wisconsin than in other Progressive states.

2. The university's commitment to *critical intellectual excellence* was a crucial element in the situation. This element was more important, I am inclined to think, than the university's history of involvement in pre–World War I progressivism. I think this was essential in the movement beyond Progressive and New Deal outlooks. Teachers as different as Jensen, Harrington, and Hesseltine all demanded more than one's best, and they hired young radicals without batting an eye. Again, keep in mind that such attitudes went beyond the History Department. Consider only Bob Lampman in economics and his pioneering work on income distribution and poverty programs.

3. In that context, the Korean war, the black civil rights movement, and Madison's own community problems were perceived from a Left liberal and radical perspective.

4. Finally, and by no means least, many non-Wisconsin parents of the Old Left had begun to send their children to the university (and that in turn attracted

other such students). That was a powerful yeast in the Madison brew. In general, they were intelligent, willing to work hard, and proud bearers of an activist tradition.

All in all, it was a special place at a special time.

Not everything in the period was so positive. Madison's response to the "Red Scare" was complicated. We have to start by recognizing that McCarthy was shrewd enough to know that he would be destroyed quickly *at home* if he ever launched a frontal assault on the University of Wisconsin. The most perceptive academic leaders, such as Harrington and Hesseltine, understood that fundamental truth and hence largely said and did what they considered appropriate. That set an example for younger faculty and Left students. On the other hand, many faculty members were either Cold War liberals or conservatives who privately criticized McCarthy's "excesses" while either approving or acquiescing in the attack on the radical Left. This was a useful experience for me in the sense that it impressed on me the importance of radicals maintaining high intellectual standards. To oversimplify a bit, it taught me that the only way a radical can attract and hold a general audience is through being first-rate in his work. Another group, generally more Left, lacked McCarthy's understanding of his weakness in Wisconsin and hence kept quiet for fear of provoking him to attack the university.

Given Harrington's estimate of the situation and the general toughness of the young faculty and the student Left, I never felt any sense of isolation. Quite the contrary. We felt we were the cutting edge of a new radical consciousness that could make a significant contribution to changing American society for the better. And, certainly until 1966–1967 at least, we knew that we had strong, organic ties to the Madison community and, I will add, even to many elements elsewhere in the state and nation.

I will, however, modify that general appraisal in regard to my dreary encounters with the HUAC [House Un-American Activities Committee], FBI, and IRS, beginning in 1960. It was a complicated situation, and it may be useful to review it briefly. Harrington chose to treat the matter as a personal rather than an institutional confrontation. I understood that decision at the time, and I did not feel embittered (nor do I now). I think it was a mistake, even from Harrington's point of view, but he had a case. There is an interesting sidelight to this: C. Wright Mills urged me to play it as a martyr, which on balance struck me as far less meaningful (or consequential), let along honest, than the position taken by Harrington. The point, after all, was to maintain one's ability to communicate with non-Left students and academics, and the reading public. And, as it worked out, I was able to do that, despite the personal difficulties and costs. In general, the Wisconsin faculty pretended that nothing had happened. That was better, of course, than overt opposition. But it was not directly helpful. The people who did provide active help were magnificent, and once again I thank them with deep respect and affection.

Most radical students were inclined to view me as a martyr. That troubled me. It indicated that their radical consciousness, their historical perspective, and their comprehension of what defined even a prerevolutionary situation left a very,

very great deal to be desired—let alone needed. In later years, I looked back on
that episode as a preview of subsequent aberrations of the New Left.

As for the positive in the student movement of that period, while avoiding
detail I will just emphasize two sometimes neglected elements. First, the people
who conceived and sustained *Studies on the Left* played a vital role, nationally as
well as in Madison. Without being falsely modest (or silly) about it all, I want to
pass over my part in that development if only because it was indirect rather than
overt. I prefer to emphasize this point: If there was or is a New Left, as opposed
to the Old Left, then those people were far more central than Tom Hayden or
Mario Savio—or other more famous personalities of the 1960s.

There are many ways to describe their importance. A more recent idiom seems
to involve repeated (and semi-genuflecting) references to Antonio Gramsci. Now I
agree that Gramsci put his exceptional mind to work on some of the crucial problems of Marxism, in particular *class consciousness,* and he offered some extremely
pertinent and consequential answers. But none of the people who created *Studies*
had read Gramsci. Yet they arrived, in the course of their passage through Madison's intellectual environment, at very similar conclusions. It matters little which
professors we credit (and if we began to list them, we would have to include more
than a few conservatives). The vital point is that the *Studies* group recognized the
visceral importance for the Left of *creating a general social consciousness* of the true
nature of advanced capitalism as a necessary preconditon for socialism (read their
first editorial, "The Radicalism of Disclosure").

That outlook, however it was abused or disregarded in later years, involved a
creative break with the Old Left and its reliance on a crudely deterministic equation
between the business cycle and the transition to socialism. The sooner we return to
it, the sooner we will move on toward a prerevolutionary situation.

Then, there were countless students and nonacademics—literally thousands—
involved in the Left-liberal and radical movement in Madison between the Korean
war and the advent in 1967 of random and nonsocial violence. They were the
sustenance of the movement. In later years, the Left has either forgotten them or
castigated them as sunshine radicals. I want to salute them as people who demonstrated the capacity and courage for intellectual change and moral and emotional
commitment. I think it was we who lost them, instead of them abandoning us.

Estimating the Madison "climate" for social change compared with conditions in Berkeley, Eugene, or elsewhere, I'd have to say Madison's was more inclu-
sively social—in the early years at least. There was significant nonacademic support
and involvement. That changed after 1967, for a period, then the old ties began
to be rebuilt. ■ ■

The shift that took place during 1967–1968 hinged on the adoption of a strategy
of creating class consciousness through repeated *secondary* confrontations ("A hit
on the head creates a radical"). This rapidly ruptured the existing bond between

the university and the larger community. I thought then, and still do, that the blacks understood the essential weakness of that approach.

The strategy reached its culmination in the Left attack on the ecology movement. For, in truth, the environmental issue defines and dramatizes the need for a radical social consciousness in a total fashion.

Finally, the fragmentation of the New Left into the attempt to wage semi-guerrilla warfare without a sea for the fish to swim in, and on the other hand the retreat into the laissez-faire of "doing one's own thing," were prefigured in Madison.

Despite their differences, there was too much of the Old Left in the New Left. I say that, not in condemnation of either group, but to make the point that the New Left *tried to impose* its consciousness on the rest of society through what it considered "vanguard" actions in a crisis situation. It did not succeed because it had substituted a moral determinism, as it were, for the economic determinism of the Old Left. As with the depression of the 1930s, therefore, the establishment was able to deal with the crises of race and war within its own framework. In a real sense, it coopted the moral issue, just as it had earlier coopted the economic issue.

In this context, I find it illuminating—and hopeful—that some of the key people of *Studies on the Left* started in 1976 a socialist weekly, *In These Times,* defined by the need to change the social consciousness of the wider community.

To come up with correct answers, one has generally to raise the right questions. The "right questions" seem rather obvious:

1. What is our *working conception* of a socialist community, to be created as the successor to the imperial capitalist marketplace? For as Schumpter said earlier in the century, socialism is by definition a *post*capitalist phenomenon.

2. How do we create—cutting across all classes—a social consciousness of the necessity to create that socialist community before we destroy ourselves and others?

3. What are the appropriate activities, such as the creation of parallel, even extralegal, popular institutions, to focus that social consciousness as an instrument of political power?

I do not think that such social-class consciousness creates, in and of itself, a prerevolutionary situation. But it does seem clear to me that the failures and crises of the capitalist political economy—such as depression, racism, and political corruption—fail to become prerevolutionary situations unless such consciousness exists. A revolution, after all, is a classic instance in which the superstructure determines the base. For, unchallenged by such consciousness, the establishment can sustain its hegemony despite grave weaknesses in the base. Indeed, that is the history of twentieth-century America.

Appendixes

APPENDIX ONE
The Historian's Task

WARREN SUSMAN

This commentary, delivered in 1952 by Warren Susman to a seminar composed of history graduate students at the University of Wisconsin, sums up better than any other document the young scholar's *methodological* objections to the prevailing Cold War temperament. Most of all, he reassesses the Progressive historians' tradition and its utility for today.

I have edited for brevity and clarity. Special thanks go to William Preston, who preserved this document and made it available, and to Bea Susman, who graciously permitted its publication.

American Historians and the Contemporary Crisis

A specter is haunting American intellectuals—the specter of communism. All the powers of the intellectual order have entered into a holy alliance to exorcize this specter: businessman and bureaucrat, [Allan] Nevins and [Reinhold] Niebuhr, unvisited liberals and revisited conservatives.

Where is the widely circulated periodical that has not welcomed the contributions of American historians in the battle of words with communism? Where is the governmental agency that has not sought to bolster its ranks with trained historians?

Two things result from this fact: (1) The historian is acknowledged by important forces in American society to be a vital assistant in our Cold War; (2) it is high time that historians should, in the face of developments within their own nation, examine critically the views, the aims, the tendencies developed or emphasized in the struggle with the specter of communism—high time that historians take stock of the main currents in American historiography that appear central in the period 1945 to 1952.

To this end, this paper is directed to historians and intellectuals of various historical schools or philosophical persuasions in an attempt to define and analyze what I have found to be the main currents and to sketch what I believe to be the consequences of such trends.

■ ■

Ever since the introduction of history as a serious academic study in the seminars of Herbert Baxter Adams at Johns Hopkins, American historians have attempted to stress the utility of their subject. Indeed, the notion of service to the community seems to have been an important correlative of "scientific history" as it was practiced by many leading historians in Germany as well as in the United States. From the seminars of Adams came many historians and social scientists determined to make their researches more "scientific" so that these researches might be more useful. Not content with passing their investigation on to their students or to their colleagues at annual meetings, many of these men attempted an application of their work to the problems facing local governments, the states, and the national government itself. The young men from Adams's seminar who came to the University of Wisconsin to teach exemplify this tradition at full flower by their contributions to the well-known "Wisconsin idea." Moreover, many of these man contributed widely to the periodical press of the nation. It is not beside the point to note that Frederick Jackson Turner was an experienced journalist or that Woodrow Wilson was to become active in American politics.

But if the tradition of service has been persistent in the historical profession, the idea of utility and the nature of the service to be offered have changed in the many decades of professional life since the 1880s. In the midst of the crises of the 1890s, historians like Turner attempted to define the problems that faced America and to investigate their historical origins. Seeking to understand our institution more clearly, they meticulously and carefully examined their origin and development. These historians sought to explain change and to understand the difference between men, institutions, and nations. With the work of Turner, scientific history in America reached its great climax. For Turner, the idea of utility meant even more than it did for some of his colleagues. For he sought, through a study of American history, to explain, to define the crisis in which the American people of the 1890s found themselves. What he contributed was a definition of what he believed to be the reality of the contemporary historical situation; this reality was an America without a physical frontier. Pointing out this reality of the 1890s, Turner then began his investigation of what this physical frontier had meant in American development when it did exist. His definition, then, was to be tested, to be analyzed, and to be used for the study of previous American history itself. But also, since it offered some insight into current affairs, it might be useful as the basis for formulating a program for future action. Turner himself only rarely hinted at what this program might be; that was the task of others in society.

In the period that followed, historians began to look more closely at the problems of the past precisely so that the present might better be able to solve its own problems. The linking of the past and the present was the major aim of what [James Harvey] Robinson called the "New History." Adopting a critical approach the problems of the past, many of these historians were willing to join with others in the community who adopted a critical attitude toward current problems in order to formulate a realistic program of action. In this way, many of these historians became part of what is known as the Progressive movement.

Charles Beard did not write an *Economic Interpretation of the Constitution* so that it might become the "bible" of the Progressives. He wrote his famous monograph—and here is a daring notion—to investigate certain problems related to the establishment of the federal Constitution. That the Progressives quickly adopted this work of cold and often dry scholarship as a document in their cause tells us more about the Progressive movement than it does about the work of Charles Beard. For Beard was not ready to point to any whole view of reality in his America, and only in *The Rise of American Civilization* did he ultimately and slowly come close to such a definition. What Beard provided for the Progressives was an approach to problems, a method and a critical attitude that could be used with equal vigor and success for the investigation of problems of the past and of the present. The idea of the utility of history took on new meaning; instead of using history and its methods to define any whole view of the current reality, history was used more directly to illuminate certain selected problems, and the historian felt justified in attempting to make the past bear directly ont he solution of current problems.

Two world wars elaborated the view of the historian as publicist for a cause, and seriously affected the idea of utility. In the crisis of war, historians rushed to the defense of their country. Mobilized by brilliant government publicists, many of these men entered the service of their country directly. Defining the current reality in terms of the crisis of the war alone, they plunged into the job of defense, sacrificing historical truth when necessary because—given their narrow definition of current reality—without such sacrifices they believed there would be no Allied victory, and without such a victory, nothing left worth having. Their training in critical history was often forgotten.

In one sense at least, the "New History" came to an unanticipated climax with the historians' contribution to the war effort in World War I. In the crisis of peace, many serious historians, carefully analyzing the results of the war and the historians' "New History" venture in support of that war, looked for a redefinition of the role of history and offered a new definition of the reality of their contemporary America. In the period between the wars, a theory of the historical enterprise best known as Relativism, bolstered by the work of such historians as Beard and Becker, the logic of John Dewey, Mannheim's sociology of knowledge, and the writings of Croce, the Italian Hegelian, became the most distinctive American philosophy of history.

Relativism, as I see it, advanced the following propositions: The historian and his work were influenced by a "frame of reference," a view of the world and its problems; that historian was selective in his enterprise and therefore could never define the whole of reality, his results being partial and temporary; each event had many causes, and the historian could reach only a partial truth, for indeed there were many truths; because of all these factors, history was likely to be rewritten by each generation in view of its own problems and "frame of reference."

While this theory was being developed, the New Deal came to power in America and effected important changes in American society. The early New Deal brain trust contained no historians, but the leaders and policymakers of the administration often had an active interest in history, and there is some evidence to suggest that many measures adopted were influenced by this study of American history. But as World War II approached, many historians—who had previously supported many New Deal measures in the periodicals of the nation—became active in the administration itself. The war once again mobilized the historian. By 1945, the war against fascism ended, and in 1946, when the Social Science Research Council issued the report of the Curti Committee—a report committed to the theory and practice of Relativism—this theory found itself on the defensive.

For a new battle (which might now be called the Lukewarm War) had taken the place of the previous open conflict with fascism, and true to the tradition of service, many historians—several of whom had seen government service during World War II—now devoted their efforts to this new struggle. These historians, once again narrowing the definition of realism for our times to this single battle with communism, have seen fit to attack Historical Relativism. This view of history, [Samuel Eliot] Morison and others insist, has limited the historian's effectiveness in mobilizing the youth we teach and the profession we labor in for the titanic struggle that they define as the contemporary crisis. Conyers Read has pointed to the historian's responsibility in this "total war." From positions of high authority in the profession, from posts in some of America's greatest universities, from the pages of a periodical press ever willing to accept their articles, these historians—History's New Men of Power—have flung out the challenge. Since the Lukewarm War is the only reality for America today, history must devote itself in all ways to the problems of that struggle. "Frame of reference" history suggested that we might not be able to discover the Whole Truth and that what is considered Right is only a socially conditioned value judgment, devoid of objective reality. The age demands, however, that we must have the Whole Truth and even more— Truth and Right must be on our side. In adopting this wartime view of service, I believe the historian is doing a great disservice to his profession and his nation.

It is historical justice, perhaps, that this very attack on the Relativist position has resulted in striking evidence to support key propositions advanced by that very view. When Admiral Morison attacks "frame of reference" history and foolish considerations of historical method, he has not actually abandoned Relativism. He praises history devoted to meticulous examination of the facts and re-creation of what actually happened, but surely he does not suppose that the United States Navy is paying for such meticulous and critical scholarship because of a love of facts for their own sake. His own ideas concerning the need of history to prepare youth to face what he believes to be the problems of the present have been shaped by his own selective notion of the present crisis. It is the very problems of the present that lead him to believe that the older relativism has had dangerous results on our thinking, which makes many of us unable to think as he does. Morison's call for a conservatively oriented history of the United States in the interest of "balance" assumes, once again, the writing of "frame of reference" history—substituting, perhaps, just a more appropriate "frame of reference." Thus the attack on Relativism has its "frame of reference," it is selective, it is utilitarian, and it undertakes to rewrite history in view of a particular definition of the contemporary crisis. It is but a new relativism that believes that its conclusions will not be partial and that it will be able to point out the whole truth, the only truth. Here is the basic surface distinction between these two relativisms. While the older relativists have often been forced to retreat to old absolutistic strongholds—expressing transcendent faith in Democracy, Civil Liberties, and Peace—newer relativists have come forth with startling clarity to endorse, by their very practice, much of what they attack in theory.

■ ■

Three . . . historians have been especially singled out for attack: Turner, Beard, and Parrington. With some justification, the particular views advanced by each in his attempt to define reality in America have been critically examined and even discarded. But primarily these men have been singled out for attack by the new historiography because of the support they advanced for the ideal of the liberal national state. Turner, ever the enduring frontiersman, emphasized the unique national development of the American nation and was clearly proud of the achievements he felt were related to this distinctiveness. Beard, ever the enduring federalist, frankly espoused the "Little America" position and was deeply concerned about the adoption of policies in line with the most intelligently conceived national interest. Parrington, ever the enduring Jeffersonian, dreamed of the triumph of Jeffersonian ends through the intelligent use of the national state. All had essentially rejected the forces the new historiography has tended to emphasize.

■ ■

In line with the older liberal creed, which they cannot quite forget, these historians have often insisted that they do not favor the restoration of business to political power [as in the Gilded Age]. But since survival is the key question of the day, we cannot be too squeamish about our documentation of the "free world's" position. Older liberal attitudes toward business must be changed because of our current needs in our current crisis. [Arthur] Schlesinger, Jr., in *The Vital Center*, has perhaps indicated an ideological reason for an alliance: "Liberals have values [that word again! WS] in common with most members of the business community—in particular a belief in a free society."

As a result, there has been an attempt to rehabilitate the businessman and to glorify the achievements made under American capitalism. Very few historians would refuse to acknowledge the tremendous achievements of modern capitalism. Statistics can be brought forward; the percapita number of bathtubs and radios can be demonstrated graphically. Who can deny the material effects of the capitalistic order for some statistical entity known as the American people?

But the rehabilitation of the businessman is directed toward still other conclusions. Allan Nevins, High Priest of Rehabilitation, has suggested that without the achievements of the great capitalists of the post–Civil War period, the United States would not have been able to wage successfully two world wars and now prepare us to wage successfully a third such conflict. If the conservatives are the heroes of our intellectual growth, the businessmen are the "heroes of our material growth." Nevins believes that we have been too apologetic about our material growth, too concerned about minor abuses in the system, too "feminine" in our idealism. Materialism is power, and power is obviously what we need if we are to win out in our battle with the specter of communism.

■ ■

But such a view of American capitalism leads to historical distortion of the most dangerous kind. It limits the critical investigation of the role the businessmen actually played in the history of their own period. It assumes that material achievement can be regarded as an end in itself. It fails to ask the key historical questions: How was such achievement made possible in America? What methods were used to reach such achievements? What were the effects of such methods on the American people and the world? What was the role of the businessman in creating two world wars and possibly a third? What were the effect of the triumph of American capitalism on the political life of the nation and the power structure of its society? What were the spiritual or ethical consequences of the success of American capitalism? Are we willing to stand uncritically on the successes of American capitalism as a platform for the current crisis? If success is somehow equivalent to ethical correctness, what claims could be made for the communist state, also successful by certain standards?

Even more serious than this ethical conclusion is the clamp being slowly placed on those who which to carry on more critical examinations of the role of American capitalism and business leadership in our society. Those who point to flaws in the system, who indicate problems that have not been solved, are called dangerous because they tend to weaken the bulwark against the specter of communism. Thus the current position may strangle historical scholarship. But even more serious is the possibility that if weaknesses cannot be indicated, that if unsolved problems cannot be suggested, we may be unable to correct such weaknesses, solve such problems. This narrow definition of current reality can eventually lead to weakening of the American capitalist system, praised now as so successful

The alliance with conservatism and the business tradition negotiated by the new historiography offers a serious challenge to the ideal of the liberal national state. A more direct attack on liberal nationalism itself has been possible with two of these concepts: the idea of an Atlantic civilization and the idea of a Western civilization. The notion of civilization has become most powerful in recent years; emotively, civilization has come to stand for all that is good, communism has been redefined as all that is evil. Civilization is, conveniently, a very vague term. It serves with excellent effect as a propanganda device in the current conflict, and the specter of civilization has been geared to fight the specter of communism. Historical investigation makes it difficult in the extreme to define with any precision the basic elements and values that constitute a civilization. Such a definition is obviously selective and must compress several centuries of human experience. But how convenient the idea of some vaguely defined Atlantic civilization is as historical or ideological identification that can justify certain diplomatic arrangements like the North Atlantic Treaty Organization! If we are to raise the specter of Western civilization, how do we decide to accept the teaching of the Nazarene who lived out his life in the Near East and to reject the teaching of the German Ph.D. who wrote his monumental work in the British Museum? But perhaps precise definition is really not important. Supported by a series of picture articles in *Life,* bolstered by the constant repetiton of the phrase, the idea of Western civilization makes an excellent, if spectral, bulwark against communism.

These vague notions of civilization have not helped us to more clearly define our position in the world. They have not given us any sharp insights that will enable us to overcome the many problems we a face in dealing with people and nations, East and West. What they have made possible is an attack on nationalism so traditionally related to ideas of liberalism. What they have made possible is the obscuring of America and her internal problems. They have given us a perspective so high above and so far away from our own shores that we can no longer see our important sectional and economic divisions and problems; we can no longer see our nation with people of different races and national origins, different religious views derived from different cultures. By assuming the sameness of men, by refusing to examine the basic differences between cultures, it has allowed us to fall under the spell of Toynbeean mysticism and therefore to believe we—as a part of some vaguely defined civilization—are citing correctly when we "respond" to the "challenge" of communism.

■ ■

In recent years there has been much discussion of a Christian interpretation of history. A recent president of the American Historical Association addressed the profession on this theme. But it remained for Reinhold Neibuhr, a theologian of great brilliance and impressive forecefulness, to advance a Christian interpretation of history and support for the current narrow view of the crisis that well serves the conservative relativists. Ignoring as childish the optimism for the eighteenth-century Enlightenment, attacking the scientific rationalism of the nineteenth century, and dismissing as "pretentious" the work of twentieth-century social studies, Niebuhr's intepretation of history attempts to return man to his proper place in the universe, a creation of history as well as a creator of it. We live in a ironic situation, he maintains, because we have discovered that our ideals and dreams are in conflict with our actual achievement and with the reality of the present. Once again defining reality in terms of the single great conflict with communism, Niebuhr calls the intellectual back to the fold of pessimistic, deterministic Christianity, which offers hope in a future world and no solution in this one, for man can solve no problem worth solving in his own human lifetime. Not only is Man born with the taint of original sin upon him, but nations also are conceived bearing the traces of this sin. While attacking nationalism and defending the conservative tradition, Niebuhr raises an impressive bulwark of Christian pessimism against the specter of communism and in place of traditional history. For history, as we know it, has utilized the optimism, the rationalism, and the pretentious social studies he has discovered to be useless in Man's attempt to answer the problems that face him.

I dwell upon these views because I believe they are definitively related to the conservative relativisim I have been discussing and, indeed, are the intellectual meat on which much of of this new historiography subsists. Morison quotes Niebuhr with agreement, and Peter Viereck, revisiting conservatism, has reminded us that conservativsm is, after all, the "political secularization of the doctrine of original sin." Schlesinger, who so often describes man's fate in Niebuhrian terms, has written this striking passage:

> For history is not a redeemer, promising to solve all human problems in time; nor is man capable of transcending the limitations of his being. Man generally is entangled in insoluble problems; history is a constant tragedy in which we are all involved, whose footnote is anxiety and frustration, not progress and fulfillment.

What Niebuhr and the rest are doing, it seems to me, is destroying the study of history itself. Discarding those forces that gave rise to a modern view of history itself, they attempt to replace history with a variety of Christianity. The Greeks and the Romans wrote brilliant history before the existence of Christianity. We have no great work of history conceived of in Christian interpretation. Although it is true that critical history developed, at least in part, through the work of critical church historians, history as we know it today is primarily the product of the Renaissance and the Enlightenment, modified by the scientific rationalism of the nineteenth century.

What Niebuhr has forgotten is that Christianity itself is a "creature" as well as a "creator" of history, a force moving in history and subject to the same analysis and examination as any other great force. If Niebuhr is too humble in his view of man, he is often too vainglorious in his own view of Christianity. That view of Christianity itself has been shaped by his own narrow definition of the present crisis, and to establish his view he felt called upon to use history itself as his documentation.

The new historiography, then, has failed to consider the consequences inherent in its alliance with conservatism, with business, and with the internationalism of a so-called Atlantic civilization. Accepting many of the views of man advanced by the Niebuhrian Christian interpretation of reality, they have often submitted to views that are in direct contradiction to the very nature of the study of history as we know it.

This new historiography developed because these historians continued to believe in the tradition of service so much a part of the historical profession. But one can doubt that the struggle with the specter of communism presents the only or even the key moral question for our time. We are forgetting to examine the consequences of the present struggle for our own internal development and problems. And all the time the power of the atom and the atomic bomb threatens to make us all the outcasts of Yucca Flats.

What is the answer for the historian who still believes in the tradition of service? Can he return to the older, the liberal relativism? I doubt it. Historians should be greatly indebted to the older relativism for what it taught us about the study of history, but that relativism was too optimistic at the start. Hypothesizing a completely open universe with unlimited possibilities and limitless combinations and permutations, that relativism was unable to give us any working definition of reality. Too often, it was forced to confine itself to isolated problems and unable to relate individual problems to a larger whole. Thus it was not able to assist in the creation of any positive program of action. It failed to consider the changes that were taking place in its own social basis of support, and many adherents of the position have often found themselves "mourners at their own funerals." Since it couldn't solve key problems, since it couldn't seem to provide a whole view of reality that would be widely accepted, it often grew too pessimistic. Its earlier optimism failed it, and under the assault of forces that professed not only to have an acceptable view of reality but a true morality and program to follow (even if that program meant a war), liberal relativism retreated to the sanctity of absolute ideals it could hold against all comers. In the end the older relativism left us, as historians, with little but faith—vitally important, to be sure, but not enough for the meaningful practice of history.

But the newer relativism has begun with too pessimistic a view of the world's affairs and man's ability. It has had its definition of reality in America, but that definition, biased by fear and hate, has been too narrow. Believing that man cannot really solve the many problems that he faces, that the range of choices is extremely limited, the newer relativism has used history as a bulwark for certain vaguely defined values robbed of historical content or meaning, as a support for decisions that have already been made for us by history. Stressing tradition and permanence in times of greatest social change, its pessimism has led to the remarkably optimistic belief that the position is the only correct one. It has often failed to consider the consequences of its own position and has retreated to an absolutistic scheme of morality, to a Christian pessimistic determinism that threatens the existence of the very discipline we usually call history.

What, then is the alternative for the historian concerned about service? . . . It is not facetiously that I suggest our motto be, "Historians of the world unite! You have nothing to lose but your footnotes!" For unless we are able once again to concern ourselves with problems of research, with our methods ore clearly understood and our tools of the best-grade material—bright, shining, sharp—unless we are able to overcome the pitfalls and the pessimism of the current historiography, we shall find ourselves isolated and unread (not because we write poorly but simply because we have nothing of interest or import to say), mumbling to each other, building yet greater stacks of notes, and gaily playing with our footnotes, as the world—too busy for games—passes us by. . . . It is the historians's obligation to improve his craft, to make meaning his scholar's degree; it is the historian's task to do what he can to make all things become more real, to aid man in passing from reality to even more meaningful reality.

APPENDIX TWO
The Boy Scouts in Cuba

LEE BAXANDALL, MARSHALL
BRICKMAN, AND DANNY KALB

The following excerpt captures, in miniature, the spirit of the skit at the 1960
Anti-Military Ball, referred to in the reminiscences of Saul Landau, Lee and Roz
Baxandall, and others.

III. Cuba: Castro and Co. Twist the Lion's Tail

Enter BIG FIDEL, BIG RAUL, BIG CHE, *armed to the teeth, smoking
large cigars*

FIDEL: I tell you, Big Che, I have had enough out of the United States! I have had
patience with them. Endless *paciencia*. But a time comes when patience
must end:

CHE *(consolingly):* I understand, Big Fidel, I understand. They have been pushing
you very hard. But there is no need to worry, Big Fidel. Help is on the
way. Soon we will have factories larger than General Motors! Highways
longer than the Mississippi! Magazines fatter than *Life* magazine! Our time
is coming.

FIDEL *(impatiently):* You speak of factories, Big Che, but all we get from our
friends, the Socialist Nations, is an endless stream of bureaucrats! Ambas-
sadors! Party Members! Heroes of Labor! Commissars! When are the

machines coming, Big Che; can you tell me that? (*Turning to* RAUL *who has been staring the while through a huge pair of binoculars.*) What is it you see, Big Raul? Are the gringos coming yet? Do you see the gringos on the high seas?

RAUL (*responds automatically to the mention of gringos):* Kennedy is an imbecile!— No, nothing yet. I see nothing.

FIDEL and CHE (*with* RAUL): Kennedy is an imbecile!

FIDEL: This makes my heart sad. Our militia stand at their posts. They are ready to cast the harpoon of Cuban freedom into the tough shark of Yankee imperialism—

RAUL: —Kennedy is an imbecile!

FIDEL: —into the hide of Yankee imperialism, as I say, and still there is not sign of the enemy! My heart is extremely sad. Big Che? There you are!

CHE: *Si, Commandante.*

FIDEL: Big Che. I want you to clear all channels of radio and television for tonight. I must tell the Cuban people about the sadness of my heart. I shall have my feelings speak spontaneously to the populace. From eight until two thirty will be satisfactory, Big Che.

CHE: I will see to it at once, Maximum Leader.

FIDEL: *Bueno,* in your breast beats a good soul. (*Exiting.*) Come along, Big Raul. Kennedy will not be coming today.

RAUL: Kennedy is an imbecile. Kennedy is an imbecile! Kennedy is . . . (*His voice trails off in the distance.*)

IV. The Miami Hotel Lobby: Berle Leads the Hike to Guatemala

THE TWO EXILES *sit reading copies of* Revolución. *Both are eating bananas. They converse between mouthfuls*

FIRST EXILE (*almost choking on his banana):* Manuel, Manuel! Look! See the picture! That is *my* estate in Miramar! Just look, there are *people* all over it! (*Disgust spreads across his face.*) It says here the government has made my estate into—a watering spot for *campesinos! Sacre Dios!*

SECOND EXILE: *Los maricones!* Everywhere in Miami, they are saying the discontent grows in Cuba. The *revolución* will not last. Why, when Castro opened the beaches to the workers one week ago, it is said the workers just *threw* themselves into the sea!

FIRST EXILE: They will not last, *amigo.* It is said that Castro evicts the workers and the peasants from their quaint and colorful huts. They are being put into apartment buildings, where they must live *(with revulsion)* in close contact to each other!

SECOND EXILE: Disgusting!

FIRST EXILE: Depraved!

SECOND EXILE: There is no freedom in Cuba . . . the peasants are being made to wear shoes! *(Pause.)* Worst of all, they are being given work to do the year round!

FIRST EXILE: In our time, there was personal freedom!

SECOND EXILE: There was indeed, *querido. (Musing.)* When Castro is out and we get back to Cuba, I shall rebuild all the slums to show my gratitude. *Pobre mio!* When we get back . . .

BERLE *(bursts in):*

> Loyal Cubans, Cubans all,
> Hear my summons, hear my call!
> Your land lies beneath a yoke
> Which we Yankees think no joke!
> Communism rules your land,
> Communists, on every hand!
> Look beneath the banyan trees,
> There you'll see the Red Chinese!
> Search the skies! Do you see jets?
> They come from the Soviets!
> Castro calls it land reform
> But his ways do not conform
> With the way that James Monroe
> Said that Latin life *must* go!

FIRST EXILE: And who are you, *señor?* And what's your name? Your face is not to me familiar. If you have come to help us in our quest At once so sacred and so pressing fair, Then we will give you ear. Your name, good sir!

BERLE: My name you long have known, most surely. My name, *señores,* is Adolf
Berle.

BERLE *sings "The Berle Song":*

> A more patriotic teacher never
> Was in America found,
> To nobody second
> I'm certainly reckoned
> A professor heavenly bound.
> It is my chauvinistic endeavor
> To speak these words to all:
> Each backward nation
> Must yield its ration
> Of profit, however small!
>
> My object all sublime
> I shall achieve in the time
> To have the rest of the world all mine,
> The rest of this world all mine;
> To make each continent stay
> Forever under my sway
> To trade and live in the corporate way,
> But stay in the corporate way!

SECOND EXILE *(as both* EXILES *APPLAUD):* I like your song, I like it well, I do! And
now, *señor,* we wait upon your plans.

BERLE:

> Excellent, my good good neighbors!
> Do not think we do you favors:
> When we lend our helping hand,
> How to chase from out your land
> Castro and his Commie crew,—
> It is in our interest too!
> First then, you need unity.
> Might you be a friend of he?   (THE EXILES *nod.)*
> Will you both be friends of me?   (THE EXILES *nod.)*
> Fine! a state of unity
> Now exists between us three.
> Plans are rolling right along,
> If my judgment be not wrong.

Let me stress this to you men:
We have need of discipline.
Discipline all down the ranks,
Eyes ahead! Defend your flanks!

BERLE *distributes maracas to them, keeps a pair himself.*

BERLE:

Take you these maracas home
Play them loud where'er you roam.
Take them as a sign from me
Of our growing unity!
When you hear maracas' sound
Know you there are Cubans 'round!

Name Index

Aaron, Daniel, 6
Abernathy, Rev. Ralph, 84
Adams, Herbert Baxter, 276
Adorno, Theodor, 1, 111, 198, 204
Agard, William, 139
Allen, William F., 11
Alperovitz, Gar, 22, 103, 108
Altbach, Edith Hoshino, 199
Aptheker, Herbert, 62, 109
Aronowitz, Stanley, 116
Aschheim, Steven, 233

Baldwin, Evelyn, 50–51
Baldwin, Roger, 50, 51
Baran, Paul, 191, 211
Baritz, Loren, 55, 56
Bascom, John, 9, 10, 13
Baxandall, Annie, 145
Baxandall, Judy, 80
Baxandall, Lee, 80, **127–33**, 137, 138, 139, **285–89**
Baxandall, Pamela, 80
Baxandall, Roz, **134–40**
Beale, Howard, 21, 24, 44, 48, 51, 52, 56, 57, 62
Beard, Charles, 19, 23, 43, 44, 203, 211, 231, 277, 279
Beard, Mary, 19, 20, 203
Beauvoir, Simone de, 80, 139, 150, 202
Bebel, August, 64
Beck, Julian, 69
Becker, Howard, 129, 267, 277
Benjamin, Walter, 39
Benston, Margaret, 199
Berger, Victor, 199
Berman, Paul, 2, 4, 5, 232
Bibb, Leon, 79
Birge, Edward, 15
Black, Hugo (Justice), 48

Bluestone, Don, 149, 180, 248
Blumstein, Alan, 108
Bookchin, Murray, 223–24
Bouderel, George, 243
Brecht, Bertold, 69, 80, 81, 132–33, 184, 261
Bree, Germaine, 129, 149–50
Breines, Paul, 33, 139, 149, 151, 233, 235, **246–51**
Breines, Wini, 134
Breitrose, Henry, 107
Brickman, Marshall, 4, 132, 135, **285–89**
Buckley, William F., 91, 92
Buhle, Mari Jo, 33, **197–204**
Buhle, Paul, **216–32**, 235, 246

Carruthers, Bennie, 129–30
Carstensen, Vernon, 55
Castro, Fidel, 83, 119, 124, 132
Chapperon, Matt, 131, 132
Chesnaseaux, Jean, 243
Ciporen, Freddy, 248, 249
Coatsworth, John, 147
Coffin, William Sloane, 190
Cohen, Neil, 137
Commons, John R., 11, 62
Cott, Nancy F., 203
Cranach, Jackie, 71
Cunningham, George, 49
Curti, Merle, 21, 43, 48, 51, 52, 55, 56, 57, 62, 93, 135, 267
Curtin, Philip, 144
Czitrom, Daniel, 33

Davidson, Carl, 222
Davis, Ronnie, 223
De Silva, Howard, 67, 68
Debs, Eugene V., 21
Debuhr, Abby, 182

Delaney, Shelagh, 80
Denning, Michael, 43
Dennis, Gene, 148, 150
Deutch, Carole, 193
Deutscher, Isaac, 129, 191
Dewey, John, 277
Diamond, Dion, 146
DiPrima, Diane, 225
Dobb, Maurice, 211
Dos Passos, John, 91
Douglas, Paul, 103
Drescher, Seymour, 233
DuBois, W. E. B., 208
Dulles, John Foster, 64

Eakins, Anne, 79, 131
Eakins, David, 79, 80, 115, 116, 131
Ebenstein, William, 103
Ebert, Frederick, 235
Edelson, Morris, 224
Einstein, Albert, 167, 172
Eisenberg, Elliot, 149
Eisenhower, Dwight D., 61, 64, 91, 129, 194
Eisler, Gerhart, 24
Ely, Richard T., 12, 13, 14, 62
Ewen, Elizabeth, 134, **148–52,** 178, 180–81
Ewen, Paul, 148
Ewen, Stuart, **178–82**

Faler, Paul, 186
Fanon, Frantz, 191
Farmer, Paul, 22, 43, 267
Fast, Howard, 24
Feinglass, Ruth, 131
Fishman, Sterling, 233
Fleming, Robin, 182
Forcey, Charles, 22, 49, 51
Fraina, Louis, 132
Frank, Glenn, 15, 16, 17
Franklin, John Hope, 48
Fraser, Steve, 180
Freud, Sigmund, 32, 97, 130
Fromm, Erich, 103, 191
Fruchter, Norm, 116

Gabriner, Bob, 182, 219–20
Gabriner, Vicki, 193
Galbraith, John Kenneth, 193
Garson, Barbara, 193
Gates, Paul W., 114
Genovese, Eugene, 26, 122
Georgakas, Dan, 225
Gerth, Hans, 3, 22, 33, 56, 57, 93, 103, 149, 152, 166, 167, 171, 172, 173, 174, 177, 222, 249, **252–63,** 267, 268
Gilbert, Dave, 219
Gilbert, James B., **118–26**
Ginsberg, Allen, 136, 224
Goldberg, Harvey, 22–23, 39, 146, 150, 152, 184, 193, 196, 222, 226, **241–45,** 249
Goldman, Eric, 48
Goodman, Paul, 191
Gordon, Ann D., 200
Gottlieb, Robert, 190
Gramsci, Antonio, 64, 270
Grede, William, 91
Gregorian, Vartan, 218
Grendler, Paul, 233
Gross, David, 233
Guevara, Che, 124, 132
Gutman, Herbert, 22, 27–28, 30–31, 39, 43, **47–49,** 51, 55, 62, 95–96, 97, 202, 231

Hakim, Eleanor, 80, 81–82, 84, 116, 117, 121, 131, 137, **252–63**
Hammadi, Sadoun, 103
Handlin, Oscar, 31
Hanson, Ralph, 175, 176
Harrington, Fred Harvey, 22, 242, 244, 267, 268, 269
Haslach, Henry, 219, 229
Haupt, Georges, 185
Hayden, Tom, 116, 270
Hemery, Daniel, 243
Hermand, Jost, 129
Hesseltine, William, 22, 43, 52, 110, 268, 269
Higham, John, 22
Hill, Christopher, 24

Himmelfarb, Gertrude, 6, 32
Hise, Charles Van, 14
Hobsbawm, Eric, 24
Hoellerer, Walter, 129
Hoffman, Frederic J., 129
Hofstader, Richard, 47, 48
Hoglund, A. William, 218, 219
Hook, Sidney, 104
Hoover, Herbert, 25
Hoover, J. Edgar, 128
Hopkins, Johns, 276
Howe, Irving, 6, 117
Huberman, Leo, 75, 83, 191
Hughes, H. Stuart, 168, 191

Jackson, Doris, 108
Jacoby, Russell, 181
James, C. L. R., 13, 28, 226
Jenkins, Peter, 129
Jensen, Merrill, 21, 48, 51, 52, 62, 110,
    267, 268
Jordan, Pallo, 180, 181
Jordan, Vernon, 49

Kalb, Danny, 132, 148, 248, **285-89**
Kaplow, Jeffry, 49, 57, **58-66**, 108
Katzman, Alan, 181
Keck, Tim, 233
Kelly, Albert, 233
Keniston, Kenneth, 35
Kennedy, Edward (Senator), 213
Kennedy, John F., 145, 151, 168
Kerr, Clark, 167
King, Martin Luther, Jr., 25, 61, 84,
    124
Kingdon, Robert, 184
Kirkendall, Richard, 55
Kissinger, C. Clark, 144, 169
Knaplund, Paul, 267
Knight, Etheridge, 225
Knowles, Warren (Governor), 236
Knudson, Ken, 150, 169
Kolko, Gabriel, 102, 103
Korman, Gerd, 55
Kovenock, Dave, 92
Kramer, Helen, 137

Kristol, Irving, 6
Krooth, Dick, 145

Lachance, Paul, 233
LaFollette, Robert M., 10, 12, 14, 15, 16,
    23, 31, 44, 62, 171
Lampman, Bob, 268
Landau, Beryl, 83, 84
Landau, Gregory, 71ff, 130-31
Landau, Saul, 34, 67ff, **107-12**, 116, 130,
    257
Lattimore, Owen, 24, 91
Ledeen, Michael, 233
Lemische, Jesse, 28
Lenin, V. I., 62, 112, 231, 236, 237
levy, d. a., 224-25, 229
Lewis, Beth, 233
Lewis, John, 145
Leyseiffer, Fred, 89
Lieber, Arnie, 49, 78
Lipsitz, George, 33
Littlewood, Joan, 80
Litwack, Leon, 205, 206
Lively, Robert, 56
Lukacs, George, 111
Luxemburg, Rosa, 56, 79
Lynch, Lincoln, 179
Lynd, Staughton, 116, 237

Maddox, Robert, 31
Magdoff, Harry, 211
Magil, A. B., 109
Main, Jackson Turner, 22
Mann, Michael, 4
Mannheim, Karl, 56, 261
Marcantonio, Vito, 114
Marcuse, Herbert, 3, 178, 181, 197, 227,
    235, 237
Marguilies, Herbert, 15
Markowitz, Adrienne, 210, 212
Markowitz, Gerald, **210-15**
Marshall, George (General), 128
Martindale, Don, 257
Martinson, John, 55
Marx, Karl, 32, 56, 62, 97, 106, 112,
    122, 180, 191

Matthiessen, F. O., 5
McCarthy, Joseph, 24, 43, 44, 55, 61 96,
    105, 107, 108, 128, 142, 178
McCrea, Ron, **241–45**, 253, 269
McClenndon, Austen, 72
McWilliams, Carey, 75
McWilliams, Jim, 84
Meeropol, Ann, 210, 212
Meeropol, Michael, **210–15**
Meikeljohn, Alexander, 15, 51
Merton, Robert K., 171
Mills, C. Wright, 22, 33, 43, 56, 112,
    173, 184, 226, 227, 250, 257, 259–60,
    269
Mitchell, Juliet, 201
Morison, Samuel Eliot, 57, 278–279, 282
Morris, Richard, 47
Moses, Bob, 205
Mosse, George, 32, 36, 110, 123, 135,
    139, 140, 152, 184, 193, 222, 226,
    233–38, 242, **246–51**

Nash, Diane, 143
Nearing, Scott, 15
Nelson, Gaylord (Governor), 82, 107
Nettles, Curtis P., 114
Neumann, Franz, 172
Nevins, Allan, 275, 280
Newby, David, 38
Niebuhr, Reinhold, 20, 272, 281, 282
Noble, David, 19, 20
Norman, Silas, 144, 146
Nye, Robert, 233

O'Brien, Jim, 194, 219, 226
O'Neill, William, 200
Ohrenstein, Manfred, 115
Ollman, Bertell, **101–06**, 108, 110

Parrington, V. L., 220, 279
Parrini, Carol, 108
Perlman, Selig, 49, 103
Petersen, Martha, 137, 140
Petrovitch, Mike, 64
Pois, Robert, 233
Polsky, Milt, 130
Portelli, Alessandro, 38–39

Potter, Paul, 3
Preston, William, 22, 49, **50–53**, 275
Proxmire, William, 107

Quarles, Benjamin, 49

Rabinbach, Anson, 233
Radosh, Ronald, 104, 131, 135
Ragionieri, Ernesto, 184
Rawick, George, 22, 28, 39, **54–57**, 103,
    110, 226, 227
Read, Conyers, 57, 278
Reberioux, Madeleine, 243
Rice-Maximin, Ed, 243
Richards, Paul, **205–09**
Riddick, Rev. Ed, 72, 74
Riefenstahl, Leni, 95
Robinson, James Harvey, 203, 277
Robinson, John, 211
Roosevelt, Franklin D., 20, 125
Roosevelt, Theodore, 23, 52
Roseleip, Gordon (Senator), 242
Rosemont, Franklin, 225–26
Rosenberg, Julius, 114
Rosenberg, Julius and Ethel, 68, 178,
    210–11
Ross, E. A., 14, 62
Rowan, James, 37
Rowthorn, Bob, 211
Rubin, Cora (see Weiss, Cora)
Rubinstein, Annette T., 109
Ryan, William Fitts, 115

Sabean, David, 233
Sachar, Abe, 167
Sanchez, Sonia, 225
Sartre, Jean Paul, 80, 184
Schardt, Arnie, 92
Schecter, Jerry, 89, 92
Scheinberg, Stephen, 131, 132
Schickel, Richard, **85–98**
Schiffrin, Andre, 103
Schlesinger, Arthur, Jr., 7, 20, 52, 279,
    282
Schrom, Nancy, 200
Scott, Joan Wallach, 33
Seeger, Pete, 75–76, 110, 142

Seldes, Gilbert, 85
Serrano, Nina, **67–84,** 107–08, 115, 130–31
Serrett, Harold, 52
Sewell, William, 175
Shannon, David, 22
Shapiro, Gene, 108
Shapiro, Jeremy, 223
Sheehan, Vincent, 90
Shelton, Gilbert, 223
Sidran, Ben, 244
Siks, Geraldine Brain, 74
Silver, Isadore, 103
Simons, Algie M., 18, 19
Sklar, Martin, 49, 57, 108, 109, 115, 116, 121, 122, 131, 132, 149, 150, 247, 248
Smith-Rosenberg, Carroll, 203
Soglin, Paul, 36–38
Soloway, Richard, 233
Soucy, Robert, 233
Spini, Girogio, 184
Stark, Evan, **166–77**
Starobin, Joseph, 109
Starobin, Robert, 209, 215
Steffens, Lincoln, 15, 90
Steidl, Josef, 211
Stein, Maurice, 171
Stickgold, Jo, 193
Susman, Bea, 275
Susman, Warren I., 19, 22, 33, 39, **43–46,** 49, 52, 55, 95–98, 113–14, **275–84**
Sweezy, Paul, 75, 83, 112, 173, 191
Sylvers, Malcolm, **183–89**

Tanzman, Harriet, **141–47**
Taylor, William, 174, 193
Thelen, David, 200
Thomas, Don, 55

Thomas, Norman, 103
Thompson, E. P., 24, 27, 28, 32, 191
Trilling, Lionel, 7
Truman, Harry S., 61, 128, 132
Turner, Frederick Jackson, 11, 13, 18, 19, 21, 23, 43, 44, 45, 276, 279

Veblen, Thorstein, 129
Vecoli, Rudolph, 218
Viereck, Peter, 282

Wagner, Dave, 179, 225, 229, **241–45**
Wallace, Henry, 24, 47
Ward, Richard, 149, 180
Weaver, Marilyn, 72
Weber, Max, 122
Weinstein, James, 46, 83, 111, **113–17,** 121, 122, 187, 218, 221, 222
Weiss, Cora, 70, 75, 107
Wexler, Arnold, 80
Wiley, Peter, **190–96**
Willenson, Kim, 138
Williams, William Appleman, 3, 6, 7, 9, 22, 23, 25, 26, 27, 31, 34, 38, 44, 46, 49, 52, 53, 82, 108, 110, 111, 115, 116, 119–20, 122, 135, 139, 141–43, 150, 152, 170, 174, 187, 191, 193, 196, 211, 215, 220, 221, 234, 242, 249, **264–71**
Winder, Carl, 131
Winspear, Alban, 129
Woelffer, Judith, 132
Wood, Kim, 176
Woodward, C. Vann, 45
Wortis, Henry, 49, 70, 71, 72, 108, 109, 130

Zeidler, Frank, 102
Zeitlin, Maurice, 173
Zuckerman, Stanley, 90, 91, 92